D0898046

This Way Out

John Coyne & Tom Hebert

E. P. Dutton & Co., Inc. New York   1972

THIS WAY OUT

A Guide to Alternatives to
Traditional College Education
in the United States,
Europe and the Third World

378
C8395t

Published simultaneously in Canada by Clarke, Irwin & Company Limited, Toronto
and Vancouver
SBN: 0–525–218009
Library of Congress Catalog Card Number: 70–179838
Designed by The Etheredges

For Elene and Leon Hebert
Mary and Tom Coyne

Contents

A great many people gave us information and assistance on this book. We would especially like to thank Janie Beers, Dr. John Van Brunt, Dorothy Clark, Lee Ann Cafferata, Ginna Frank, Debby Hanrahan, Nancy Timmins, Gerald Schwinn, Pat Zimmer, Neil Boyer. Special thanks to Chandler Brossard for his advice.

JOHN COYNE
TOM HEBERT

I. Independent Study

1. Introduction to Independent Study

You don't need a college to get a higher education anymore. That has changed. If you are on the edge of college, unsure if you want to go, or have already dropped out, consider an independent education, on your own. It may be more valuable to you and to the country.

Many things have changed in the past five years that allow you to break out of the obligatory college education. First, there is the sense that American universities are not working well and that they can't be changed. In addition, experimental colleges have successfully tinkered with every conceivable component of the traditional college. The old limited time place-defined education has been made obsolete by the rush of new technology, the compounding of information, the knowledge that learning must become a lifetime process if we are to participate in a constantly shifting future. As a result, new non-residential college institutions and national examination schemes have been created. Lastly, we feel that a new student has appeared. This student is not concerned with corporate education; is not loyal to any one institution; is not interested in furthering technology. He/she scarcely accepts it. This student must contrive an education in the environment, which has become a learning environment. It is this new kind of education that we call Independent Study.

BREAKDOWN

The *New York Times*, February 26, 1971: "Private College Applications Decrease Sharply." According to the article, Harvard's applications are down 11 percent, Yale's, 18 percent. The principal reason is financial. It is now too expensive to go to many private colleges. But another reason is a "growing disenchantment with college curricula that is prompting some students to question the utility of higher education, and postpone or drop plans to attend college. . . . High school seniors feel no immediate need to go to college.

Time, September 27, 1971, reports that in 1970 6 percent of the graduates of leading prep schools elected not to go to college. This is up from 4.5 percent the previous year.

Nationwide, there were at least 700,000 openings for freshmen or transfer students in 1972. Colleges are closing down, some are beginning to advertise for students, hundreds face bankruptcy in the next decade.

The corporate education: universities are getting larger and most students attend large universities. Thirty-nine universities enroll more than 20,000 students, while twenty-six others have grown to over 30,000 students. That trend is continuing. In 1969 there were 2,525 colleges and universities in America, with a total enrollment of 7,916,991 students. Two-thirds (67 percent) of those students attended universities with 5,000 or more students. A mere 408 schools (16 percent) of the 2,525 total accounted for that 67 percent majority. And there are no substantive differences between the large universities; they are interchangeable.

At the University of Maryland, the modal (average) student knows only *one* teacher on campus. Less than 20 percent of the professors' office hours are used.

Over 50 percent of entering freshmen do not finish college in four years.

Five hundred thousand students will drop out of American colleges in 1972.

> *These findings are consistent with other studies, which indicate that college dropouts tend to be more creative, more complex, more impulsive and more autonomous than their peers who stay.* —ARTHUR W. CHICKERING, "THE BEST COLLEGES HAVE THE LEAST EFFECT," SATURDAY REVIEW, JANUARY 16, 1971.

CANDIDATES FOR INDEPENDENT STUDY

Who are the candidates for Independent Study? Who will be the new Independent Students?

Those young people who can't get into college because of low finances or low grades. The Bureau of Labor Statistics predicts that by 1980 80 percent of the new job openings will be for young people without college degrees. To gain some leverage on the job market, to avoid being a cog in the machine, vocational workers also must learn how to learn.

Students who ten years ago certainly would have gone to college, but now "question the utility" of it. They are on the fence, not anxious to go, but unclear as to the alternatives.

Students in delayed admissions or "interim year" programs. A number of colleges are allowing high school graduates to enroll just after graduation, but postpone actual matriculation for a year, during which time they can work, travel, join a community service group or do independent study. This gives students time to look at themselves and get some seasoning before they attempt college. Many will decide not to return to the college after their "interim year."

The growing number of students with a fairly decent high school education, who feel they can put together a personal learning system that can beat the professional model and probably equal much that goes on in the expensive "experimental colleges" where they would be paying for freedom not to be hassled and the famous name of the place.

BASIS FOR CHANGE

Two-thirds of American universities report that high schools have significantly improved over the past decade. More young people have learned how to learn.

There is a feeling among many students that the "counter-culture," the "radical movement" has failed or at least passed. They know that they are not going to be taken care of, that they must be competent. But they require the opportunity to decide their own education.

The environment is educative. Libraries, work places, clubs, Free Universities, YMCA classes, night schools, community organizations, television, paperbacks, Xerox, newspapers and movies are all educational and can be incorporated into a formal learning system.

Increasingly, employers are interested in employees who are literate, can manage their time, can manage a project and are creative. New technologies need these people. A student who can document himself on these terms can get a job.

People want to teach and learn with one another, on either a tutorial or peer basis. Learning groups, study collectives, Free Universities have been formed in every American city. On August 21, 1971, we ran an advertisement in the *Washington Post* classifieds:

RESEARCH.—IF YOU WOULD BE INTERESTED IN TUTORING AND ADVISING COLLEGE-AGE STUDENTS IN INDEPENDENT STUDY PROGRAMS, CALL 339-9221.

Sixteen talented people answered that ad. For anybody who is interested, there is an unused college faculty out there. You don't need a college to get a "higher education" anymore.

SOME BACKGROUND

The ordinary American college education, as everyone knows, is a *grid* of courses, requirements, hours, tests and professors laid over some of the best years of your life. It is a terrible grid of bureaucratic controls forcing people into cells where more corrosion than learning takes place. You have no responsibility to learn in this grid; only to figure out how to navigate it, and thereby validate it.

If you wonder why some college educated people you know seem to have died some place along the way; if you wonder why you are not jumping at the chance to go to the college of your parents' choice, study this "curriculum guide" we ripped out of a catalog that came our way. Someone thought this school was unusual . . .

THE B.A. IN ENGLISH

1st Semester (Freshman Year)			*2nd Semester (Freshman Year)*		
COURSE			COURSE		
NUMBER	TITLE	Cr.	NUMBER	TITLE	Cr.
Eng 111	English Composition	3	Eng 122	English Composition	3
Hist 111	Western Civilization	3	Hist 122	Western Civilization	3
	Social Science	3		Social Science	3
	Language	3		Language	3
	Science Elective	3		Science Elective	3
PE 111	Physical Education	1	PE 122	Physical Education	1
		16			16

3rd Semester (Sophomore Year)			*4th Semester (Sophomore Year)*		
Eng 213	Introduction to Literature	3	Eng 224	Introduction to Literature	3
	Social Science	3		Social Science	3
	Language	3		Language	3
	Drama Elective	3		Drama Elective	3
	Elective	3		Elective	3
PE 213	Physical Education	1	PE 224	Physical Education	1
		16			16

5th Semester (Junior Year)			*6th Semester (Junior Year)*		
Eng 316	Great English Writers	3	Eng 327	Great English Writers	3
	English Elective	3		English Elective	3
	English Elective	3		Minor Elective	3
	Minor Elective	3		English Elective	3
	English Elective	3		English Elective	3
		15			15

7th Semester (Senior Year)		8th Semester (Senior Year)		
English Elective	3	Eng 500	Senior Seminar	3
English Elective	3		English Elective	3
Minor Elective	3		Minor Elective	3
Minor Elective	3		Elective	3
Elective	3		Elective	3
	15			15

TOTAL CREDIT HOURS: 124

It is doubtful that anyone could survive four such years undamaged. There is a technology behind that grid of requirements. It is the bureaucratic technology that built the Pullman Railroad Car, made Andrew Carnegie a millionaire. A technology of gears, assembly lines, efficiency experts and compartmentalization; eight boxes, 124 credit hours and the system declares you educated and ready to roll.

> The dishonest worker is enriching his own job in a manner that is very satisfactory (for him). This enrichment is costing management, on the average, $1.50 per worker per day. At this rate, management gets a bargain. By permitting a controlled amount of theft, management can avoid reorganizing jobs and raising wages. —LAWRENCE ZEITLIN, "A LITTLE LARCENY CAN DO A LOT FOR EMPLOYEE MORALE," PSYCHOLOGY TODAY, JUNE, 1971.

Max Weber, the German sociologist, originally described the bureaucratic structure in *The Theory of Social and Economic Organization* published in 1922. The features he specified for bureaucracies are helpful in understanding the curriculum shown above:

1) A continuous organization of official functions bound by rules.

2) A specific sphere of competence. This involved (a) a sphere of obligations to perform functions which have been marked off as part of a systematic division of labor; (b) the provision of the incumbent with the necessary authority to carry out these functions; (c) that the necessary means of compulsion are clearly defined and their use is subject to definite conditions.

3) The organization of offices follows the principle of hierarchy; that is, each lower office is under the control and supervision of a higher one.

4) The rules that regulate the conduct of an office may be either *technical* rules or norms. In either case, if their application is to be fully rational, specialized training is necessary. It is thus normally true that only a person who has demonstrated an adequate technical training is qualified to be a member of the administrative staff.

5) It is a matter of principle that the members of the administrative staff should be completely separated from ownership of the means of production or administration.

6) Administrative acts, decisions and rules are formulated and recorded in writing. . . .

That is a fair description of high school and college as most of us have known it. Rules, functions, authority, compulsion, supervision, specialized training and paperwork are needed to keep the delicate mechanism of the bureaucracy in order. Students in slots. The grid curriculum reflects a need of the institution; it is self-serving. It has to organize the henhouse demands of the professors and their contending "ologies." Departments are organized by insecure and hustling academic bureaucrats to gain leverage over the way students learn. Students naturally would go to the teacher who would let them learn. They would wander the streets or the "quads," never thinking they needed a "curriculum guide." But since there are jealous departments and arrogant employers, course grids do give some comprehension to a very complex system that was created to give control to the academic bureaucracy. How do you break out of such a damnable circle? Obviously colleges and universities *do* need students; but do students need them? Obviously, we don't think so.

Education is hanging around until you have caught on.
—ROBERT FROST

INDEPENDENT STUDY

Through Independent Study you can get around going to college. You don't have to go to college to learn, to study, to prepare yourself for some future. One of the elite educations available today is the *non-institutional* education. The message here is that you can organize your own education on your own terms. We're going to present some arguments on your behalf, provide some suggestions for your self-education system and try to give you some confidence to learn on your own.

Independent Study is the philosophy *and* the method.

Independent Study can be defined as an opportunity for students to master an area of knowledge through independent organization and learning. . . . The purpose of Independent Study is to help each student to learn how to take charge of the development of his own learning and to understand that he alone is largely responsible for his education. —DR. FRANK BROWN, EDUCATION BY APPOINTMENT, PARKER PUBLISHING CO.,1968

Independent Study is not a new concept. The movement that Eliot began at Harvard in the 1860's with the elective system which resulted in the curriculum grid was also partly an attempt to give students some independence in what they studied. St. Vincent's (Pennsylvania) in 1870, Princeton in 1905, Reed in 1911 and Rice Institute in 1913 made a concession to natural learning processes by allowing students to design parts of their program. Swarthmore College is given much of the credit for the increase in Independent Study programs in American colleges from 1921 to 1930, by which time over seventy schools had them. Generally these programs were available only to honors students and consisted of individual reading, papers and tutorials. That hasn't changed.

Reading over that paragraph we realize we wrote it to give Independent Study some credibility. Basically, all that can be said of college Independent Study programs is that they demonstrate that the required courses are not necessary.

We are not concerned with college Independent Study. We want to get students out of colleges. Independent Study can do it because it is simple; it is modular; it is linear; it is segmental. It is simple when contrasted to the curriculum grid of four-year egg-crate education. It is modular because in Independent Study you naturally work on only one thing at a time. It is linear because you follow one Independent Study program with another. It is segmental education because there may be time gaps between programs.

Independent Study has these characteristics to recommend it over the grid curriculum:

1) It separates evaluation of learning from an institution. Individuals, and principally the student, evaluate the work done. It will therefore be more precise.

2) Being modular, simple, it requires less hour management than is necessary in a course grid. Racing to a 10:15 lecture followed by an 11:30 . . .

3) Self-pacing. You go at your own speed.

4) You either acquire learning skills or you don't learn. You can't cheat, use "ponies" or hustle anybody but yourself.

5) Independent Study is a creative learning environment.

6) You can go into "advanced areas" whenever you think you are up to it.

7) In Independent Study you are independent. Perhaps for the first time in your life. It will be scary.

8) In Independent Study you must reach your *own* conclusions, give your own opinions.

9) The student becomes a producer of knowledge. Not just a receptacle.

10) Independent Study is self-selecting, self-defining and self-initiating. You won't waste time on the ephemeral, faddish subjects popular at "experimental colleges."

11) The learner takes responsibility for his education; takes that burden off of other people.

12) The student learns his own potential for learning.

13) Successful Independent Study gives the student confidence in his ability to learn.

14) In Independent Study you know what you know.

15) Making and meeting your own goals, you learn how you learn.

16) It is cheaper.

17) Independent Study may be for the "lonely and the brave." An independent education is an *eccentric* education; it does not include many of the supports of a *corporate* education. You'll have to create your own student union.

> *The person educated for flexibility will see the world in a fresh inventive way. He will not be chained to the immediate, the customary, the habitual. He will not be dependent on someone else to plan his route and show him how to get there. He will chart his own course.*
> —EDGAR DALE, THE NEWSLETTER, JANUARY, 1963.

THE CONCENTRATED INDEPENDENT STUDY PROJECT (C.I.S.P.)

The Concentrated Independent Study Project is the method of independent learning central to our argument. Any formal learning needs a structure. Particularly "on your own" learning. The C.I.S.P. is designed around the way we actually learn. It makes use of interest, enthusiasm, excitement and occasionally, "Eureka!"

In the summer of 1968 at the Massachusetts Institute of Technology an experiment in learning occurred. Twenty self-selected students studied one subject full time for *one* month with *one* professor. They learned more; they enjoyed more.

> *Concentrated study represents a basic, but in many ways simple change. It is an educational arrangement that strikes at a basic assumption hallowed by age: namely that study should be distributed. . . . In distributed study there is a fragmentation of time and a dispersion of effort in areas of human activity where they are perhaps least appropriate. Ideally, studying should be characterized by perseverance, involvement with complexity, the growth of insight and understanding, and the cultivation of original ideas. Such*

studying, one suspects, cannot be switched on and off to suit a schedule; indeed our own experience strongly suggests that intellectual activities in which one is deeply involved will not fit neatly into a pre-arranged time-table. —JOHN KING AND MALCOLM PARLETT IN A REPORT ON "CONCENTRATED STUDY," M.I.T., 1969.

In an evaluation of the experiment that followed the month of study, students reported it to have been the most successful learning experience they had ever had. They and the staff felt that they had learned as much as if they had taken an ordinary lengthy course; but intangibles, like increasing enthusiasm, getting to know a professor well or following curiosity freely for once, were the biggest distinctions the students made between ordinary, distributed courses and Concentrated Independent Study. One of the results of the experiment was the establishment of an "inner college" at M.I.T. based upon independent Concentrated Study. We think the program is one of the most interesting at any American university.

> *Montessori schools have proved that the child needs a cycle of work for which he has been mentally prepared; such intelligent work with interest is not fatiguing, and he should not be arbitrarily cut off from it by a call to play. Interest is not immediately born, and if when it has been created the work is withdrawn, it is like depriving a whetted appetite of the food that will satisfy it.* —MARIA MONTESSORI

The twelve- to fifteen-year-old kid is the best learner on the block. The ability to concentrate is never higher than at that age. We wonder if the Boy Scout Merit Badge program isn't a radical education program. Take away the awful aspects like the "Eagle Scout," the dippy badges and all that patriotic role-playing and you have an educational philosophy based on the affirmation that kids can learn like hell when left alone to follow their own heads.

What do you remember from grade school? Perhaps a good or bad teacher or two. And if you were lucky, one of the good teachers let you go deeply into a topic. And that material is still with you. Liechtenstein, the Pyramids, the Aztecs, the honey bee are the great topics. No teacher could "teach" you so much material, keep your excitement so high. All she did was let you concentrate on something that interested you.

A sixteen-year-old fellow, Gary Douglas, of Waterford, New York, is the official Town Historian. We read about his project in the *Journal* of the Smithsonian Institution. He feels that the town is the oldest incorporated town in America and is studying the town's history minutely to prove it. He has been consulted in town meetings on the restoration project in the town. Evidently he is quite a thorough scholar. He is not a genius; he just got turned on to history and is working to his capacity because he wants to.

Nader has teen-age Raiders. And according to one staffer, "They go out and do it!" They have written one book on nursing homes and are assisting on The California Land Use Study, brown-lung (textile worker) disease, aviation safety, auto safety and various other studies Nader has organized at his Center for the Study of Responsive Law. Commenting on his decision to use young volunteers, Nader has said: "I hoped it would show that the very young can do a very creditable job. This country was developed with very young minds and it is important to show what they can do. . . . We look for self-starters. People who can work without having their hands held, who won't be depressed by defeat." The research standards are high. Every allegation has to be substantiated. But as one student volunteer said: "They don't interfere with you. They trust you to do the work right."

The lesson in these cases is that you learn best, one thing at a time, concentrating on it. Get into physics, math or Russian. Write a novel. Go beyond what you have attempted before. In Concentrated Study you can have the time and interest to attack a large project. As an Independent Student you are not supposed to recreate a college curriculum grid. It is so much easier to *concentrate* on one thing after another. Something you believe in, have an interest in and are proud of.

THE PROJECT

Schools are always trying to inculcate a "love of learning." For most teachers, teaching is a trade and they wearily plod through the lunches, syllabi, bells, books and grades squirting facts at cranky kids, only occasionally letting a learner wander away alone into a thicket.

In your Concentrated Independent Study you must have a *project* as a goal. The project gives form and structure to your Independent Study. When someone is said to have a "love of learning," what really is being said is that the person has a love of doing learning projects.

A management theorist, John Stewart, in the fall, 1965, issue of *Business Horizons,* describes a project as a one-time undertaking with a specific end result. Four qualities distinguish it from ordinary undertakings.

1) Scope. A project is larger in scope than the person or organization has attempted before.

2) Unfamiliarity. A project has initial unfamiliarity to those managing it.

3) Complexity. A project is complex. It has many interrelated, interdependent elements, requiring concerted effort.

4) Stake. A project is an undertaking in which the participants have a stake. It is especially important to them.

A project requires *management* to complete. A learning project therefore, requires that you become a manager. The manager of your education.

A learning project is a specific, realizable, complete-unto-itself *work* that must contain all of these elements:

- The Quest
- Formulation
- Planning
- Scheduling
- Investigation
- Analysis
- Presentation
- Critique

THE QUEST. The quest is the search for your project. The deciding of what you want to study. You say, "Hell, I don't know what I want to study; that's the problem." Go to the library and note which book titles, particularly in the "new books" display, interest you. You are not there to read them, just to find general areas of interest. What things interest you in *Time* magazine, for example. What in your recent experience didn't you completely understand? Vietnam. Do you know the history of U.S.–Vietnamese relations during 1946? "We started the war in 1946." What, if anything, is true in that statement?

The quest for a question, task or problem should be a definite stage. It is like looking for agates on the beach. Finding out the "stuff" of what you want to know. Ask yourself, "What do I want to know more about? Where don't I know enough? What did Alexander the Great do, really? Why are there pinball machines in my city? How did the Greek government work?" Be free with yourself at this point. Just range about in the "green fields of knowledge."

FORMULATION. Chop out the problem. Define the issue into manageable terms. Our first notions of what we want to learn are often unrealistic. When formulating the project, be specific. Don't nail yourself on "How the Greeks Governed Themselves." "The Form of Athenian Government in 500 B.C." is narrowing it down. But "The Function of Athen's Agora" is going to open up more interesting books, keep you out of the generalist literature and create more useful knowledge for you. Once you understand the Agora, you'll appreciate why there is no decent municipal government in the United States, for example.

PLANNING. "Predetermining a course of action." Louis Allan in *The Management Profession* (McGraw-Hill, 1964) says that planning involves:

1) *Establishing objectives* to determine the end results to be accomplished.

2) *Programming* to establish a sequence and priority of steps to be followed in reaching objectives.

3) Establishing *procedures* of standardized methods of performing specified work.

4) Developing *policies* that apply to repetitive decisions, questions and problems.

SCHEDULING. Scheduling is not to be confused with planning. Scheduling has to do with time, and it is a separate step. Projects should have a time-frame. You do not want your ideas and effort wandering all over the calendar. It produces anxiety.

Determine when you will have the project complete, *before* you begin. That, basically, is all that modern technology is about. Sophisticated forecasting. A decision is made to reach the moon by the end of the 1960's; the rest is just filling in the spaces with time, chemistry, physics and men. A project's time-line can be changed easily. That's no problem. But the requirement that one complete a master's degree in six years from the time of enrolling in the program causes many people to never get it done. Six years is too much time to fill up. A month spent studying the Greek Agora would be a stimulating month, delving into Greek governance, architecture and city planning, urban life.

INVESTIGATION. The processes of your learning. The library research. Interviews with knowledgeable people. Taking notes. Wandering around bookstores, looking at Tables of Content. Phone calls. Getting bibliographies. Observing at public meetings, trying to get invited to non-public meetings because you are a student and you want to know how the outfit makes decisions. Figuring out where the information is.

ANALYSIS. Select and weigh your information. Determine how a particular note can be used. Sometimes you will have to decide that a piece of information just doesn't belong. Perhaps the most difficult thing to obtain is the ability to withhold judgment.

PRESENTATION. The form your project will take. It should be worked out in the beginning. Are you going to write and print a small book? Are you going to see if the newspaper will print your story? Maybe you will make a super 8mm film. Quite probably you will give a talk at the high school on your study. If it is an ecology issue you have researched, your project might be to persuade local TV to do a story/exposé of the killing off of the coyotes, which you have researched. Whatever you are learning, there should be some form of presentation of that learning. Presentation of your project makes you a producer.

- There will then exist a record of the learning accomplished.
- The record will be validation of that learning.
- We all need recognition. Basic.
- There will be something substantial to evaluate prior to the following project.
- By doing a learning project with a presentation of it you gain experience in project management.
- Presentation can help give you *intellectual style.* In an Age of Information, style, which is quality, will be as necessary, and in as short supply, as ever.

The worst project presentation we can think of is a term paper.

CRITIQUE. Feedback on what you have done. The form the evaluation will take should be determined at the outset. Who will do it for you. What will be the standards you and they will use. Build into your Concentrated Independent Study Project a critique. You need both peer and "older authority" criticism. Good critiques or evaluations are very hard to come by in this world. Yet it is difficult to learn and grow without them. Good critics of your work are as necessary as your objects of study. Line them up. Old teachers, your tutor, an audience, students, readers of a newspaper.

You can see that Independent Study is not "dropping out." We are not saying it is easier. You have to create your own administration. Even your own paperwork. An independent education is a matter of production; not just going along with the crowd.

As an independent student, you are not alone, isolated. You need tutors, advisors and listeners. We shall now discuss the creation of your own personal faculty and Board of Trustees.

2. People in Your Education

The first thing: create a Board of Trustees for your education. People who are willing to help you plan it, suggest faculty to you, advise you, help you find employment to support your studies; generally to follow your progress and give a damn.

In your community whom do you respect? A family lawyer, your high school principal, a local newspaper editor or writer, a librarian, a corporation executive known to your family, a civil rights worker, a minister, a college professor or administrator. As a student asking for assistance, you can approach rather influential, interesting people. Everyone likes to advise the young. A parent should be asked to serve on the board. Perhaps one of yours.

After you have identified four or five people whom you would like to get to know better and think you might trust, make contact. A parent can make the first approach in some cases; that would be quite useful all round. Have somebody sound out the person you seek. If the individual is interested have that person say that you will be contacting them *formally* soon. Then you arrange a meeting either by phone or letter to explain who you are, why you are an independent student, what your goals are and some of the rough plans for your education. Suggest how that person fits into them. They won't have many responsibilities. Perhaps a meeting with you every now and then to work through problems and an annual dinner, if you feel you should get them all together at some point. Say that you are convinced that there is an education in the community environment and you want to try it out. Be specific why you are not going to college. Your board will try to convince you to drop out of your education and into a college, so you must squelch that in the beginning. You must try to get them really interested about the possibilities of self-education and their role in yours.

Alternately you may want to go slow. (Any college president would tell you not to let a board think it is powerful.) Also you may not know the person at all. So a short meeting to sound him/her out and to let him/her get a sense of you may be appropriate. Friendships take time, and that is what you are looking for in your board—friendships.

As you *assemble, orient* and *utilize* your board you will be learning how to manage the basics of your education. Once you have a board you have to determine your relationship with each person. They must be kept informed. You will probably be checking in with them monthly or bimonthly. They will be shooting you books, topics, friends and maybe jobs. If they are valuable to you, remember that you are valuable to them. It may be a new experience for them to be near a healthy human process such as learning.

FACULTY/TUTORS

If you have a strong Board of Trustees, you will have leads for tutors. They will be suggesting and arranging contacts with people they believe to have potential as tutors in an Independent Study Program. If you let the word out in your circle of family friends that you are looking for tutors in a private educational scheme, you may be swamped with suggestions.

Your high school principal or counselor may be of assistance. They undoubtedly know of some professional who would tutor you or a small group of students. Once they begin to think about it.

Run an ad for a tutor in the weekend edition of the classifieds. Also run it in the classified section of the neighborhood newspaper, if you have one. During the phone calls keep notes on the conversation. Explain your ad. Ask questions about the person's background and what his interests are. Be friendly and courteous. It is probably the first time that these callers have ever offered to be a teacher to anyone over the phone. They may be a bit uptight. If it sounds like you have compatible interests, gear up.

We earnestly recommend that you advertise for faculty tutors. From experience we know that it works.

Some of the people who called us to talk about Independent Study:

A young scientist with the government's Environmental Protection Agency. His special field of interest is water pollution. He has taught single students in college-level chemistry and ecology. He would enjoy tutoring in physics. He has charged seven dollars per hour in the past, but he would prefer to work with a group of students studying chemistry. He suggested that a great group project would be an investigation of an industrial polluter, some corporation that is pouring wastes into a navigable river. He cited the Refuse Act of 1899 which allows citizens to bring class actions (law suits) against offenders. The plaintiffs in any action under the Refuse Act of 1899 receive ten percent of the fines. This would cover the costs of hiring this scientist to tutor a couple of students or teach a course to a group of independents.

A young woman getting her Ph.D. in Community Psychology. She has been a housewife for a year since her baby's birth. She could be a qualified program advisor in Child Development as well as psychology. We talked a bit about day care. She said that she could get an independent student employment in a day-care center where the student could pursue an Independent Study program under her supervision while working in the center. She would only need enough money to pay for a baby-sitter.

A retired reference-research librarian of the Library of Congress. Two M.A.s—one in Economics and another in Business Management. Spent his career researching material for the Library of Congress. Thought he could help independent students learn research techniques, how to fully exploit a library. For a very nominal fee he could develop a private course in efficient library use if asked. The *Whole Earth Catalog* would call this man an "access to tools."

A retired Air Force colonel. Logistics and data processing. Degrees from the University of Chicago. Taught at the Air Force Academy. Now teaches an English course at George Washington University. But he wants some independent students "to keep him occupied." He could put together Independent Studies in English (his degree field) or Computer Science. We thought there would be some fascinating projects in logistics (how projects and activities are supported). Money is no object.

A Peace Corps volunteer recently returned from India. She now works at the Urban Coalition in Washington. She is an Urban Affairs specialist in housing. Has done research on new towns. Could develop a survey program on India: culture, politics and people. She would be interested in Independent Study projects in Urban Affairs. Returned volunteers, who are everywhere, may be good resources for Independent Studies.

A retired professor of Philosophy who has taught at Black Mountain College, Sarah Lawrence, Jamestown and other colleges. We talked for an hour about Independent Study. He enjoyed the idea immensely. "No grades, no guidance counselors, no spoonfeeding! Modern universities are like delicatessens. How can you focus on anything in a delicatessen?" He said he would enjoy "learning together" with an independent student.

A linguist with a Ph.D. from Georgetown University. Thirty-five years old. Founder and president of a corporation. Sees an opportunity for a student working in his corporation that designs and makes products for the blind. There are many possible projects in their research labs. And he was interested in the possibilities of a student studying their corporate management. We thought that many corporations have such educative work environments. Some might respond positively to a student out to get an education on his/her own. He agreed. He said he would also like to help someone studying linguistics; and the blind culture.

Another ABD (All But Dissertation). Teaches in a local community college, while writing his Ph.D. dissertation. His B.A. is in Math, his M.A. in Psychology. He lives in Rockville, a suburb of Washington, D.C. His academic field is population statistics. He teaches a course in "Micro- and Macro-Population Patterns." A Micro-Population is the neighborhood. He sees many projects involving research at that level. Says there is not much being done in neighborhood studies. One project title he suggested: "What makes Rockville a dull place for teen-agers."

Two meetings a week for twenty weeks at five dollars a tutorial would be two hundred dollars. It sounded like one of the best educational deals we have heard about.

So break out! Run an ad:

INDEPENDENT COLLEGE STUDENT NEEDS A TUTOR/PROGRAM ADVISOR FOR INDEPENDENT STUDY IN (AREA OF INTEREST). IF YOU WOULD BE INTERESTED, PLEASE CONTACT (NAME) AT (PHONE).

Of course you can make direct approaches to organizations that work in areas that interest you and determine if there are people with the expertise you want willing to tutor you. And there are also good teachers in the colleges.

Go to a nearby college and talk to students. They know who the good ones are. Find the department that offers courses in areas where you have interest. There will be students in and around the department offices. Tell them what you are about and that you want recommendations as to who would be a tutor, who might need the extra cash, etc.

Try the student government offices. Perhaps they have had a teacher evaluation recently. Ask the people in that office for leads. The student newspaper might also suggest prospects.

Back at the departmental office you might talk to the secretary and see if she thinks seeing the chairman is a worthwhile idea. Maybe he would be helpful in recommending one of his faculty to you. In looking into this possibility we have talked to numerous professors. Almost all liked the idea and believed that a student would get advice from faculty people. Incidentally, it is an unwritten rule that a tenured professor can have one day a week for outside work, like tutoring. Many professors multiply their salaries with industrial and governmental consulting.

Put a notice on a bulletin board at the college. You might do best to get a graduate student or upperclassman. Often they are the best teachers anyhow. They need the cash and the *opportunity to teach.* They know that teaching is learning, if it is well done.

> FREE COLLEGE. *If you want to go to college free send away for the schedule of courses at the college of your choice. Pick your courses and walk into the designated classrooms. In some smaller classes this might be a problem but in larger classes, there is no problem. If you need books for the course, write to the publisher telling him you are a lecturer at some school and are considering using the book in your course.* —"FREE," WHO IS, PERHAPS, ABBIE HOFFMAN, REVOLUTION FOR THE HELL OF IT, DIAL PRESS, 1968.

We were talking with Dick Graham who was Director of the U.S. Teacher Corps under Presidents Johnson and Nixon. He told us of some brain-storming he had done with a friend some time back that related directly to our propositions for self-education. Compilers that we are, we asked him if he would go back into his files and write a draft of the ideas that he had been kicking around. We liked the letter he wrote us and decided to print it as is.

> *Dear John and Tom:*
>
> *You asked that I write you a letter about ideas for getting a "patchwork transcript." I find that I've got to do more work on this than I have time to do now, but I'll take the first crack at it, if it's not too late, rewrite it when I get back.*
>
> *Getting a college degree and getting an education are not the same. You may not need a college degree, but you do need a* record *that will help you get the job you want. You can make it an interesting one.*
>
> *The best indicator of future performance is past performance. If you've been editor of the* Law Review *at Harvard, you can get just about any law job you want, but your chances of doing that are slim. As a substitute, here are some ideas for making a record which will have something of the same effect:*
>
> *1. Take a semester or summer session at one of the prestigious institutions. Take only one course if you want and get a job if you need to, but go to Harvard or to Stanford or to Berkeley.*
>
> *2. Once you're sure you know how to study on your own, take a semester or a year abroad, or a year of Independent Study here at home.*

3. Apprentice yourself to a leading professor for a semester or preferably a year. Publish something. Here's why.

1. Harvard—it looks good on the record, but it's more than that. Most schools deserve their reputation, and even the summer session will expose you to new standards, new ideas, people and a new life.

2. Independent Study here or abroad—You must be sure that you're up to it. It's harder by far than just showing up for class. But if you can handle it, it lends prestige to your record. But more than that, it's apt to open up new vistas, develop new interests and perspectives.

3. Apprentice yourself to a leading professor—In good colleges, some of the world's leading authorities are without typists, researchers, administrative assistants or baby-sitters. Take anything that you can get provided that you are in frequent contact with your leading professor. Make a proposition. Work two full hours a day and get as much academic credit for it as you can. Agree to take whatever exams that are expected and don't ask for pay, but do ask to be mentioned in the next thing he or she writes, as coauthor if you're up to it and your professor is willing. There is no better way to get launched in your field. You'll probably have to learn how to type and proofread and operate a machine. That couldn't be a better investment. Write something in collaboration with one of your professors or on your own, if need be. Propose a study or a special project for which you receive a semester's credit. Outline the objective and the criteria by which you can demonstrate that you've learned what you set out to learn. There's no field in which you won't ultimately have to know *how to write if you're going to reach any kind of prominence. And nothing will do more to set you apart from those who have "merely gotten through college."*

Dick Graham

P.S.

I wanted to talk about: greater use of the College Level Examination Program, taking French and Spanish at the YMCA or other low-cost places and receiving credit for it either by the CLEP examination or others given by a college; attending the city universities where credit is as low as $2.00 a credit hour; more about getting credit through summer school and extension programs and then transferring them.

The general idea is to get credit, to learn how to learn in the process and how to do it at least cost. But I've got to catch the plane. See you when I get back.

Dick.

THE TUTORIAL RELATIONSHIP. In America there is a problem with the word *tutor*. The word suggests that someone is in trouble and that a worried parent has taken action. Ninety percent of the students using professional tutoring services are in academic trouble. For ten dollars an hour someone tries to get them out of it. And they do. Tutors we have talked with say that students who do not learn in classrooms generally start doing better work and get confidence in themselves working with tutors. Yet one-to-one learning has a bad name in America. But that is changing.

In our survey of experimental colleges and programs we found numerous uses of the word *tutor*. Often it sounded like a small seminar with coffee, which isn't a tutorial. But clearly the word *tutor* is gaining academic prestige, as more and more colleges promise something in tutorials. A tutorial education has always been an elite one.

The essentials of a tutorial education: one, sometimes two students meeting regularly (once a week or at least every two weeks) for an hour or more with a person deeply informed about an area of knowledge or field of experience. A tutorial should last at least six months. And it should revolve around a project, we believe.

> *Tutorials provide an opportunity to experience an exciting and relevant education. In tutorials, interaction between professors and students is close. Education becomes a dynamic experience. You read original works and draw ideas from them. You learn to discuss your thoughts, accurately putting your concepts into words. Writing assignments become opportunities to express your thinking concerning art, science, and philosophy, and no longer what you have been told. You begin to think about the relevance of your learning to life, to your role in society.* —THE SAN JOSÉ STATE HONORS PROGRAM

Tutorials have four purposes:

1) To give the student mastery over some material;
2) To allow the student to be creative;
3) To permit a close relationship to develop between a teacher and a student;
4) To build literacy in the student.

Earlier we mentioned that the tutorial system was an Oxford-Cambridge one. It seems useful now to quote at length from *Handbook to the University of Oxford* on the subject of tutorial education. Few people in this country know how it operates.

THE OXFORD TUTORIAL

As lectures become more formal and audiences increased, there was a change in the functions of the college tutor. By the end of the nineteenth century it became usual for pupils to come singly or in small groups to their tutors' rooms for guidance in their work and to bring essays or exercises for his criticism. At the same time the range of subjects which could be offered for examinations increased, and colleges tried to meet the demand by appointing tutors to teach them. In this way the tutorial system was created as it exists today.

Throughout his academic career, the undergraduate is under the care of the tutor in charge of the subject which he is reading, and for the greater part of his time he will be taught inside his own college. . . . Each undergraduate has at least one tutorial a week, usually by himself or in a pair. The exact form of the tutorial naturally varies with the subject, although the basis is always the submission of work written or prepared by the undergraduates since the last tutorial. In subjects such as mathematics or classics the undergraduate will have been set a particular exercise which the tutor will criticize, suggesting improvements in method or phraseology. In subjects such as history, philosophy or literature the undergraduate will bring an essay which he reads out to his tutor. After the essay has been read (or before, if he cannot resist the temptation to interrupt) the tutor will make criticism and comments, both on the substance and the manner of presentation. If the tutorial is attended by more than one undergraduate generally only one essay is read; the others are left for the tutor to read, and are given back the following week with his comments. The preparation of an essay that has to be read to an expert and critical audience is an important part of the system, but the discussion that follows the reading is equally important.

If two or more undergraduates are present the tutor will encourage them to argue among themselves—indeed some tutors reckon the success of a tutorial to be in inverse proportion to the amount they have found it necessary to say themselves (others rate it in terms of the difficulty of the questions the undergraduates ask them) . In all cases the atmosphere is essentially informal. . . . The end of the tutorial is taken up with a brief discussion of the work to be done in the ensuing week, for which the tutor will suggest a subject and give a list of books and articles which the undergraduate will find it useful to consult. Work done in this way is not confined to preparation for examinations. If an undergraduate is especially interested in a particular aspect of his subject the tutor will try to give him time to pursue it, even if he is not to be examined in it at all; conversely, every tutor is likely to have some especial field of interest and his enthusiasm will communicate itself to his pupils. . . .

The main outward stress of the modern tutorial system at Oxford thus falls on the educational side: it is recognized that the primary function of the tutor is to instruct. But it must not be supposed that the other side, which played so large a part in the relations of tutor and pupil in earlier days, has been lost sight of in modern Oxford. In some colleges an undergraduate is assigned for all his time to a 'morals tutor', who is often not the tutor to whom he is going for his reading, but one who undertakes to keep in touch with him during his career and to help and advise him generally in his life. . . . It is far less easy to define or even to describe this 'moral' relationship of tutor and pupil than the educational side. . . . The principle today is that the undergraduate is responsible for the organization of his own life within the general bounds of college and university discipline. Certain others of the functions which a tutor used to exercise have been formalized and taken over by the university. . . . Despite all this, there continues to exist a very personal relationship between an undergraduate and his tutor, which may often develop into a lasting friendship. A tutor feels responsible for more than the academic development of his pupils, and is always ready to give advice, as far as he can, with personal problems. No formal 'Student Counselling Service' exists in Oxford because the tutorial system makes it unnecessary. . . .

Here closeness of the relationship between undergraduate and Fellow, with its social and psychological as well as educational significance, is something that other universities feel the lack of. A man or woman knows and is known by, his tutor by the time he has graduated with an intimacy and understanding impossible where the method of instruction is in lectures and large classes. It is therefore surprising that some Oxford undergraduates, and even dons, call the tutorial system in question. Of course it is extravagant. A tutor will not often have more than twenty pupils, more likely he will have about fifteen, whom he will see separately every week. If the system were abolished, he could give classes to scores and lectures to hundreds. But the tutorial is the essence of the Oxford way. Without it the college system has very much less to recommend it, save its pleasantness for the individuals. . . . it is Oxford's most original and valuable contribution to educational practice, and at its best the form of instruction more closely related to individual needs and attainments than any other. —CYRIL BAILEY, "THE TUTORIAL SYSTEM," [REVISED BY J. B. BAMBOROUGH]. HANDBOOK TO THE UNIVERSITY OF OXFORD, 1967. REPRINTED BY PERMISSION OF THE CLARENDON PRESS, OXFORD.

Last thoughts:

You don't have to have a specific learning plan in mind when you first begin to work with a tutor. Let him assist you in your quest. Your ideas may still be "floating," which is fine. He will know his way around a bibliography, and can draw you out in early conversations to find why a particular area interests you.

Do unto your tutor as you would have him/her do unto you. The tutor should have enthusiasm for the subject. If the tutor isn't excited to some degree by it, dig around to find where the tutor's interests really are. We found in our many conversations with tutors, that they all had some area that they were just itching to get into with someone. That's where the real learning for both of you may take place. It works both ways.

Fees. We think you should generally pay tutors. We didn't talk to any that had firm ideas about it. Figures ranged from two dollars and fifty cents per hour to seven dollars per hour, open to negotiation. Some retired persons would tutor for little or nothing, just to keep their hand in. Retired people are a wonderful resource for a student. But for anyone who doesn't have a guaranteed income, you get what you pay for.

Write lots of short papers. Long papers kill tutors and students alike.

Write lots of short papers. It will teach you to write and that, as we will demonstrate later, is essential.

The "Buddy System" was recommended by a number of tutors that we talked to. Is there someone else who might be interested in a breakout?

Tutorials and Independent Study are different. In tutorials you learn through study and the process of meeting regularly with one person. Independent Study is casting loose from much supervision. But they are on the same continuum. They are both personal learning. The distinctions between them are often impossible to find, once a student has reached his "take-off point." We suggest that you don't worry about which system you are in. The Concentrated Independent Study Project (C.I.S.P.) which we proposed in the first chapter spans both.

3. External Degree Programs, CLEP and Correspondence Study

Projects and tutorials can be related to these three programs, particularly if you must work toward a degree. External degree programs are new, snowballing in importance; the College-level Examination Program (CLEP) has been available since 1965 but used very little; correspondence study is the oldest form of non-institutional higher education in America, going back one hundred years.

For the independent student they are "enabling devices," ways to learn, get credit and earn degrees. Each student with his/her tutor can work with a combination of these possibilities.

EXTERNAL DEGREE PROGRAMS

There are now more than sixty programs or proposals floating around the country. The non-residential or external degree will be the most talked-about phenomena in U.S. higher education in this decade. In four or five years everyone will know about these programs and be enrolled in one. The federal government is planning to make more funds available for these programs as a result of proposals made by the Department of Health, Education and Welfare's special Task Force on Higher Education which called for national degree-equivalency examinations to any interested person, regardless of how their knowledge was acquired.

There are two varieties of external degree. The first one happens when, as a reform measure, a college begins to give credit for a substantial amount of off-campus learning. The second kind depends upon external examinations like the College-level Examination Program

(CLEP) to assess achievement. The Goddard Adult Degree Program is an example of the first; Empire State is an example of the second.

The Educational Testing Service, which is becoming heavily involved in external degrees, keeps track of their proliferation. They prepared this list of existing programs in March, 1971.

DEGREE PROGRAM	INSTITUTION
Bachelor of Independent Studies	Division of Continuing Education, Brigham Young University
Bachelor of Arts	School of General Studies, Brooklyn College
Bachelor of Arts in Liberal Studies	Office of Continuing Education, State University College at Brockport
Bachelor of Science in General Studies	Evening College, University of Cincinnati
Bachelor of Science	School of General Studies, Columbia University
Bachelor of Science in General Studies	College of General Studies, George Washington University
Bachelor of Arts	Adult Degree Program Office, Goddard College
Master of Arts	Graduate Program, Goddard College
Bachelor of Arts in Extension Studies	Division of University Extension, Harvard University
Master of Arts	The Evening College, Johns Hopkins University
Bachelor of Arts in General Studies	University College, University of Maryland
Bachelor of Arts	Division of Continuing Education, Mundelein College
Bachelor of Science in Industrial Technology	New York Institute of Technology
Associate of Arts	School of Continuing Education and Extension Services, New York University
Bachelor of Liberal Studies	College of Continuing Education, University of Oklahoma
Master of Liberal Studies	College of Continuing Education, University of Oklahoma
Bachelor of Arts	School of General Studies, Queens College (N.Y.)
Bachelor of General Studies	Division of Continuing Education, Roosevelt University

Doctor of Science of Theology   San Francisco Theological Seminary
Bachelor of Independent Studies   Center for Continuing Education,
                                              University of South Florida

Bachelor of Arts in Liberal Studies   University College,
                                              Syracuse University

Proposals that have hardened into some reality:

> *Campus-Free College (Mass.) 1971*
> *Empire State College (N.Y.) 1971*
> *Union Graduate School, Union for Experimenting Colleges, Antioch College 1970*
> *University of the Commonwealth (Mass.) 1971*
> *University of Maine 1971*
> *National College, Inc. (Fla.) 1972*
> *National Urban Studies, Dept. of H.U.D.*
> *New York Regent's Degree 1972*
> *University Without Walls, Antioch College 1971*
> *Westbrook College (Maine) 1971*

Proposals in the works:

> *California State College Plan (Dumke proposal)*
> *College of Independent Learning (Conn.)*
> *The National University [CEEB-ETS] (New York)*
> *New Jersey Open University*
> *University of California, The Extended University*
> *University of North America (Mass.)*
> *University of Wisconsin, College of Extended Studies*
> *The International University of Independent Studies, New York*
> *   (in connection with College of Independent Learning and Future*
> *   Resources Development, Inc.)*

These and other programs are going to be opening like supermarkets over the next few years. Michael Marien, a Research Fellow at the Educational Policy Research Center at Syracuse University, has speculated that by 1978 four million college-age students and adults may be enrolled in external degree programs or as he calls them "Space-Free/Time-Free" programs. Four million students would amount to 30 percent of the total college enrollment in America. Those are consequential figures. They could turn American higher education inside out.

These programs are going to happen for important reasons:

• Financial. School systems are broke. Many universities are operating on their endowment funds now. They cannot expand. One-half of the country's private colleges will be eligible for bankruptcy in ten years. The government has not been anxious to directly subsidize higher education. External degree programs are estimated to cost only 10 percent of the cost of conventional universities. Count finance as the principal impulse behind external degrees.

• Political. With external degrees the lower classes will feel that important barriers between them and the educated classes are falling; the sense of upward mobility will be reinforced among blue-collar and ethnic groups; "under-represented minorities" will see them as new opportunities for success. Giving voters an egalitarian, bargain-priced opportunity for higher education is attractive to any administration.

• Educational. The experts believe that external degree programs will educate people. The evidence supports them. As they won't affect existing institutions (no college will close because of them), educators will support them. Students will surely support them. The programs are an effective answer to "student unrest" and the demand for "student control." The problem of the dropout will diminish. Many students who find residential colleges a bore, will cling to some academic status in external degree programs. Finally, educators will look upon them as the first steps in the direction of "life-long learning" that they have been dreaming about for years. Alumni who swore off education long ago, will find easy entry into these programs.

What's wrong with external degree programs?

• They may become "computerized monstrosities."

• They are not based upon any sound knowledge about the way people learn.

• They are still based upon *academic* skills, and traditional values. There is a great need for interdisciplinary degrees that reflect "new things about people" and the changing needs of society. The national testing agencies like the College Board are slow to change. As one official at H.E.W. said, "Nothing is more glacial than changing a society's credentialing processes."

In balance, we feel that the external degree programs we have looked at support the aim of this book: to give students a measure of control over their education.

Elsewhere we discuss three external degree programs: Campus-Free College, Empire State College and University Without Walls.

THE COLLEGE-LEVEL EXAMINATION PROGRAM (CLEP)

The College-level Examination Program (CLEP) makes it possible for anyone to earn up to two years of college credit through a series of weekend tests. Over one thousand colleges and universities recognize the examinations and give credit for it. After a slow start, 240,000 exams will be administered in 1972–73.

There are two types: General and Subject. The General Examination is in English Composition, Mathematics, Natural Science, Social Sciences-History and Humanities. All are multiple-choice and take about seventy-five minutes each. The Subject Examinations are in thirty-four different fields, are multiple-choice and take ninety minutes each.

The examinations are given in sixty CLEP centers during the third week of each month. The General Examination fee is fifteen dollars and each one of the Subject Examinations is fifteen dollars.

The CLEP examinations are based, according to the College Entrance Examination Boards who offer the program, "on the assumption that many Americans know more than their academic credentials would suggest. This is because most people do not stop learning simply because they have stopped going to school. Many people are avid readers; many receive training on the job; many watch educational programs on television or take noncredit courses in adult education programs offered by their high schools, community colleges, churches, or clubs. In fact, most people learn on their own in more ways than can be counted."

Although the CLEP people did not originally design the program for students going to college, or of college age, it is an excellent opportunity to complete two years of college soon after high school. The tests are hard and CLEP does not give a passing grade, just an evaluation of how well you have done on the material. Each college or university establishes its own passing mark. Of the one thousand schools who say they will give credit, less than half are explicit about it. It is necessary to shop around to get full credit for your exam results. Schools with liberal policies: Texas, San Francisco State, The California State College System, most Florida schools, University of Chicago, Indiana, Iowa.

CLEP is an accurate measuring instrument. The rising cost of undergraduate education guarantees its acceptance. It allows schools to trim the faculty, reduce the number of classes. After business and industry accept it as a credential, it will be a degree unto itself.

To obtain a description of the exams, a list of the schools using the program and information on test centers, write:

College-Level Examination Program
Box 592
Princeton, New Jersey 08540

Here is a sample of the College Entrance Examination Board's General Examination in Humanities, which is fully described in their booklet on the exams. Reprinted with permission of the College Entrance

Examination Board, from *College Level Examination Program: A Description of the General Examinations,* College Entrance Examination Board, New York, 1971. The sample questions are reprinted with permission of Educational Testing Service, the copyright owner.

HUMANITIES

The Humanities examination measures what you know about literature, art, music and philosophy. The examination is broad in its coverage; you will find questions on all periods from classical to contemporary and in many different fields: literature, archaelogy, painting, sculpture, architecture, films, the mass media, jazz, dance and opera. No specific course or reading list can prepare you for the test, but a lively interest in the arts— going to museums and concerts, attending the theatre and seeing motion pictures, reading widely—constitutes an excellent preparation. The test is a way to measure your cultural interests and your familiarity with the basic subject matter of the humanities.

There are about 100 questions in the test, which is 75 minutes long. Approximately half the questions deal with literature and one-third with art. Many ask for factual information. . . . Other questions call into play your skill as an observer, your ability to understand and to deal with an unfamiliar passage from literature or a reproduction of a work of art.

SAMPLE QUESTIONS

Directions: Each of the questions or incomplete statements below is followed by five suggested answers or completions. Select the one which is best in each case.

1. Pablo Casals and Gregor Piatigorsky are both

    (A) flutists   (B) cellists   (C) Wagnerian tenors
       (D) composers of electronic music
          (E) innovators in twelve-tone music

2. Which of the following would use a technical vocabulary including the words *cupola, cornice, portico, rotunda,* and *finial?*

    (A) A poet   (B) A dancer   (C) A sculptor
       (D) A musician   (E) An architect

3. The ethical theory which holds that each man ought to act in whatever way will maximize pleasure and minimize pain for the greatest number of persons, irrespective of who they are, is known as

    (A) utilitarianism   (B) egoism   (C) pantheism
       (D) existentialism   (E) subjective idealism

4. All of the following accurately describe Greek drama EXCEPT:

    (A) The actors wore masks.
    (B) The dramatists competed for prizes.

(C) The plays were performed in sacred temples by priests.

(D) The plays were performed as part of religious festivals.

(E) Scenes of violence were usually performed offstage.

5. The figure above is

   (A) an Etruscan warrior   (B) an Aztec deity
     (C) an Egyptian tomb figure   (D) a Hindu Siva
      (E) a Sumerian portrait bust

Questions 6–7

        Nature and Nature's laws lay hid in night;
        God said, *Let Newton be!* and all was light.

6. The lines above were written by

   (A) Geoffrey Chaucer   (B) Alexander Pope
     (C) William Blake   (D) Robert Frost
      (E) T. S. Eliot

7. Which of the following describes the lines above?

   (A) Blank verse   (B) Free verse   (C) A triolet
     (D) A couplet   (E) A quatrain

8. Which of the following Roman deities is NOT correctly identified?

  (A) Pluto . . god of the underworld
  (B) Mars . . god of war
  (C) Mercury . . messenger of the gods
  (D) Diana . . goddess of the hearth
  (E) Minerva . . goddess of wisdom

Questions 9–10

> I tell you, hopeless grief is passionless;
> That only men incredulous of despair,
> Half-taught in anguish, through the midnight air
> Beat upward to God's throne in loud access
> Of shrieking and reproach.

9. In the context of the lines quoted above, "passionless" (line 1) means

  (A) reasonable   (B) practical and efficient
    (C) numb and still   (D) devoid of agony
      (E) able to find release

10. "Half-taught in anguish" (line 3) describes

  (A) those men who have not experienced total desolation
  (B) those men who have experienced only the extremes of sadness and joy
  (C) those men whose feelings do not change
  (D) that despair which cannot be distinguished from anguish
  (E) that despair which only partially prepares one for anguish

ANSWER KEY TO SAMPLE QUESTIONS
(HUMANITIES)

1. B	3. A	5. B	7. D	9. C
2. E	4. C	6. B	8. D	10. A

CORRESPONDENCE STUDY

On all those matchbook covers: "Which big-pay career do you want?"; "Turn your life around!"; "Choose from twelve ways to bigger pay. Mail this coupon."

You might close the cover before striking, but correspondence study works. At one time in the late nineteenth and early twentieth century it was going to give the Common Man a "share in the intellectual and spiritual pleasure and the material benefits of the accumulated knowledge and wisdom of the race." It never did that. After a thorough survey of American correspondence study it is plain that it hasn't been the force for popular higher education it should have been. Today there are less than five million people enrolled in home study courses. Take away the federal/military enrollment and there is less than two million. Only 175,000 students are in college credit programs. Pitiful figures. (Sweden enrolls 10 percent of its population in home study courses.)

Yet the achievement levels for correspondence and classroom courses are equal, with some evidence that correspondence students learn slightly *more* than residential students. Correspondence students do get better grades. A recent study at the University of Oregon reported that 72 percent of the students in the sample would enroll in another correspondence course and 89 percent said they would recommend correspondence study to others.

THE METHOD OF CORRESPONDENCE STUDY. In correspondence study you exchange prescribed lessons by mail with an instructor who grades your work, comments upon your progress and returns them to you. It is possible to develop a real tutorial relationship with your instructor. In fact, it is said that you stand a better chance of getting to know a teacher well in correspondence instruction than in conventional classes. In the good schools an effort is made to do this. You are encouraged to write the instructor regularly as well as complete the lessons. Some schools have "telephone hours" during which home study students can call their tutors: others encourage the students to visit them. Videotapes, audio-tapes and records, films and film strips and telephone lectures are coming into use. Instructors will often dictate detailed letters in response to the work of a student. All this is done, because Independent Study by correspondence is a lonely affair.

THE DISADVANTAGES. It takes "initiative and resourcefulness" to complete a correspondence course. You don't get the immediate correction, approval/disapproval of the classroom. Unless you are in a study circle, you are alone out there, relying on your own commitment, discipline and motivation.

As the schools have few admission requirements, you have to know when you are prepared to take a given course. The university schools will often have prerequisites on a course, but it is possible to ignore them or fake it. To little purpose, however, because it is a truism in correspondence study that it is harder to hustle an instructor in a correspondence setting than in the classroom. In correspondence study you write, write and write, and that you can't fake.

It is difficult to get an overview of the course. By definition, correspondence study comes in pieces and by the time the course is completed you may or may not know where you have been.

It is frustrating to wait a week for a response to some important work.

We think that both public and private correspondence study schools are improving, but you will occasionally encounter out-of-date materials, poorly packaged. You should remember that your tutor didn't create the course that he is working on. He may have doubts himself.

The student is rarely asked to give his own opinions, feelings or reactions about the readings. Very objective stuff. Of course, if the relationship with the tutor becomes what it should, then more subjective and personal elements will come in to the course. The creative and intuitive often have a difficult time in correspondence study.

THE ADVANTAGES. Selection. There are 15,000 courses you can take by correspondence. Between the private schools with their skills orientation and the university schools there is a course in anything that can be taught. The gamut: Archaeology, Architecture, Art, Drama, Journalism, Languages, Literature, Motel Operations, Paper Making, Pipefitting, Real Estate and Upholstery.

Pace. You proceed at your own pace. University courses have a twelve-month time limit, but extensions are available. You can concentrate on a course and finish the lessons in a month of heavy study or you can spread them out and do them on weekends. The private schools set no time limit. There seems to be no relationship between achievement and the length of time spent on a particular course.

Concentration. Normally you only take one course at a time. As we said in the first chapter, this is less distracting and more to the point.

Credits. The university correspondence courses give *full* credit, usually three hours for each course. The amount of Independent Study credit which may be applied toward a degree varies from school to school. Generally no more than thirty hours (ten courses) may be applied, although some schools do allow up to two years' credit.

Grades. Pass/fail is coming into correspondence study.

Costs. As we said—modest. The university courses average about fourteen dollars per credit hour, less than fifty dollars per course plus books. Naturally the private schools cost more. Anywhere from fifty to five hundred dollars, depending on the length and complexity of the course. Some of their professional courses require three years of study.

Starting. You can begin a correspondence course at *any* time of the year.

Libraries. All state university libraries are available to you.

HOW THEY WORK. The university courses contain twenty-four assignments or lessons on the average. When you enroll you order the required textbook from the university bookstore C.O.D. or buy them locally. There is always a syllabus with the course outline, directions, special readings, self-tests and theme assignments. There will be twenty-four writing assignments with perhaps seven or eight themes of five to seven hundred words, the rest being essay questions. As you finish them, you send them in. They come back within a week, marked, corrected and graded if all goes well. Spend the extra three dollars for air mail. When you need help you can write or call the instructor or simply talk to friends.

The University of Kansas at Lawrence has one of the more innovative correspondence study programs in the country. Their composition and literature course, English 3C, is entitled "Modes of the Hero." In it you read *Prometheus Bound, Marat/Sade, Faust, Wiseblood* (Flannery O'Connor), *Great Expectations, Steppenwolf, Don Quixote.* Obviously that is not a three-hour easy course. It looks solid. The third and fourth lessons were devoted to *Marat/Sade.* The learning objectives for the third lesson:

> *The student should exhibit an awareness of the dramatic tradition that produced* Marat/Sade. *He must be able to discuss the historical background of the play and to show how the author relates the French revolution to broader thematic concerns. The student should also be able to abstract and synthesize the major topics of the intellectual debate between Sade and Marat, a central aspect of the play.*
>
> *Reading Assignment: Peter Weiss,* Marat/Sade, *the entire play and Historical Note, pp. 145–150.*
>
> *Good encyclopedia entries on the following topics: French revolution, Jean Paul Marat, Marquis de Sade, Charlotte Corday.*

There are two long essay questions to answer.

You can either wait until your writing assignments and themes are returned or begin the next lesson immediately. Before the last lesson, you send in an examination form, stating when and where you want to take the final exam. If you can't take it at the university campus, you can arrange to have it given by a local college administrator or high school principal. The grades and credits are then transferable to any college or university.

To find out more about university courses write for the

> *"Guide to Independent Study Through Correspondence Instruction"*
> *The National University Extension Association*
> *Suite 360*
> *One Dupont Circle*
> *Washington, D.C. 20036*

They cost fifty cents each and are worth it; the guide lists the sixty-two universities, their addresses and the hundreds of courses they offer.

These are the best schools:

Independent Study
University of California
Berkeley, California 94720

Correspondence Study
Owen Hall
Indiana University
Bloomington, Indiana 47401

Independent Study
University of Kansas
Lawrence, Kansas 66044

University Extension
University of Kentucky
Lexington, Kentucky 40506

Independent Study
University Extension Division
University of Nebraska
Lincoln, Nebraska 68508

Independent Study
Office for Continuing Education
State University of New York
30 Russell Road
Albany, New York 12206

College of Continuing Education
University of Oklahoma
Norman, Oklahoma 73069

Correspondence Study
3 Shields Building
Pennsylvania State University
University Park, Pennsylvania 16802

Independent Study
227 Extension Building
University of Wisconsin
Madison, Wisconsin 53706

The private schools, the matchbook universities, are the best. Some of them like International Correspondence Schools (ICS) and LaSalle have been around for generations. They know how to work up a course and they have the money to do it. It can cost hundreds of thousands of dollars to develop new materials and package them. The average university correspondence course has sixty students enrolled. The private schools will enroll thousands in one. They make profit from students who pay the enrolling fee and then don't complete the course; and most don't. The private schools offer something of everything, but concentrate on the technical skills. The people enrolling want to "upgrade" themselves at the office or factory. They may want a new profession. They also have work and family commitments that make it difficult to study independently. They drop out in large numbers. But the 15-20 percent who complete their courses get one of the best educational bargains in the country. Many of the courses are superior to those offered in resident universities.

Unfortunately, at the present time, only a handful of the private schools are offering college level courses. The managements aren't aware of the new external degree programs and don't relate to the younger students who are dissatisfied with campuses but not with learning. The private schools are competent but staid. Long ago they realized that workers and businessmen needed a leg up to get job security and correspondence schools could provide it. International Correspondence Schools has had over eight million students in the last eighty years.

The private schools operate in similar fashion to the public schools. No time limit. The school provides the lesson materials. They don't send all the lessons at once, but keep the student supplied with three or four ahead. The reputable schools want you to complete the course and give the student's work personal attention.

How do you find the reputable schools? They have a government-recognized accrediting organization, the National Home Study Council. Each accredited school (there are 152) meets the following standards:

- It has a competent faculty.
- It offers educationally sound and up-to-date courses.
- It carefully screens students for admission.
- It provides satisfactory educational services.
- It has demonstrated ample student success and satisfaction.
- Its tuition charges are reasonable.
- It advertises its courses truthfully.
- It is financially able to deliver high quality educational service.

The council will send a free "Directory of Accredited Private Home Study Schools" which includes a list of the subjects taught by the schools. Write:

National Home Study Council
1601 Eighteenth Street
Washington, D.C. 20009

Two schools which offer college level courses useful for the CLEP examinations:

American School
Drexel Avenue at 58th Street
Chicago, Illinois 60637

Future Resources and Development Inc.
49 John Street
Southport, Connecticut 06490
(a division of Famous Artists Schools)

Dr. Homer Kempfer of the Virginia Polytechnic Institute is a recognized authority on correspondence study. He has also taken twenty-one of them. He gives this advice to prospective students:

- Do you want credit or not? Decide.
- Know exactly why you are taking the course. Understand your motivation from the beginning. Is it just an impulse?
- Get guidance.
- Be careful. Don't get in over your head. The schools will generally let you take anything you can pay for.
- Set aside a time to work regularly on the courses.
- Take the courses as fast as you can.
- It is possible to do two lessons per day or four over a weekend. Most people can do a single lesson in two evenings.
- Telephone or visit your instructor occasionally.
- *Finish the first lesson.*

STUDY GROUPS

We suggest you form a study group or circle. One person enrolls for the course, but shares the material with the group. Study circles based upon correspondence courses are common in Europe. In Norway there are five or six thousand with perhaps forty thousand participants. In Sweden any group of people forming a study circle is entitled to government subsidies for the cost of materials.

Our government is not yet ready to do that, but the Higher Education Act of 1965 entitles correspondence students to participate in the Guaranteed Student Loan Program. Loans of up to fifteen hundred dollars per eighteen-month period are allowed. The school loans the student the amount of the course, the government guarantees it and pays any interest over 7 percent. The student must begin to repay his loans within a year after he either completes the course or ceases to submit lessons regularly enough to be considered at least a half-time student. It is a good deal. Write the National Home Study Council for the Directory of Accredited Private Home Study Schools and more information on the student loan program.

It would appear that half a dozen enterprising students could form a mini-college, take out loans with the American School in Chicago or Future Resources and Development in Southport and put together one hell of a learning program, cheap and of their own design.

We have heard that some financially hard-pressed colleges are offering to give academic credit for home college study. Conceivably a small group of students could propose a cut-rate degree program to a local college based upon correspondence instruction done with a commercial institution.

The external degree programs that are coming along will be awarding credit for independent correspondence study in the very near future.

4. Literate You Got to Be

- If you can write English clearly, you'll never go hungry.
- Don't confuse good spelling with good writing.
- If your mother can understand it, it's probably well written.

An independent student has to be literate. Well-rounded? No. You can be trapezoidal, polygonal, screwy as hell. The nuttier the better. (Eccentrics produce new things, go new ways and are scarce.) But without a degree, to make any difference at all in this world, you must read easily and write well.

As an advanced technology takes over more of the physical tasks of our maintenance, the demand for the "knowledge worker" is increasing. The nature of our existence has changed. It is now predicated and dependent upon the flow of information and the people who manage it.

> . . . we are now in the process of moving from the industrial age into a cybernated era and this involves changing the basis of our society from a production-transportation net to an information net.
> —ROBERT THEOBALD, AMERICAN II, SWALLOW PRESS, 1970.

Flowers in your hair? Fine, but learn the pleasures of the simple, subject-predicate sentence. Maybe you think you can read and write well enough now to get by. Researching the chapter on "How to Get Things Done," we talked with a vice president of Booz Allen and Hamilton, one of the largest management consulting firms in the country. He didn't have any advice on how to do things, but he did have complaints about the college graduates that come to work for Booz Allen. The majority

1) can't write;
2) can't do simple math;
3) can't manage time.

In that order. He said those skills were more important to him than degrees. If you have ever read any consultant's reports, you know that they can't write. Like most college graduates.

> *I got into my bones the essential structure of the ordinary British sentence—which is a noble thing.*—WINSTON CHURCHILL, SPEAKING OF HIS DAYS AS A STUDENT AT HARROW.

English teachers for years have been diagramming sentences with negligible success. College teachers condemn term papers as occupational hazards, the writing is so bad. We know from our own teaching experience that the hardest thing to get students to write is a simple declarative sentence.

READING

Your writing will only be as strong as your reading. (Our tradition in oratory died with the Chautauqua Assemblies and William Jennings Bryan.) The following writers can be read to discover the "essential structure of the ordinary British sentence."

SHAKESPEARE, *Julius Caesar* (funeral orations)
T. S. ELIOT, *Four Quartets*
DYLAN THOMAS, *Adventures in the Skin Trade*
JAMES JOYCE, *Portrait of the Artist as a Young Man*
WINSTON CHURCHILL, *Speeches*
W. H. AUDEN, *Collected Poems*
HENRY DAVID THOREAU, *Walden*
ERNEST HEMINGWAY, *The Sun Also Rises* (fishing sequence)
JOSEPH HELLER, *Catch 22* (The Man in the White Suit)
KURT VONNEGUT, *Short Stories*
RICHARD BRAUTIGAN, *The Abortion* (the abortion chapter)
NORMAN MAILER, *The Time of Her Time*
JERZY KOSINSKI, *Steps*

Investigate some lines or paragraphs of these writers. Say them out loud. Orate them. Hear the rhythms. Notice the economy of words. Many short sentences. Generally one idea to a sentence. Gertrude Stein to Hemingway: "Cut out all your adverbs and adjectives."

Graham Greene's *The Power and the Glory* (Penguin Books, 1962) begins with this paragraph:

> *Mr. Tench went out to look for his ether cylinder, into the blazing Mexican sun and the bleaching dust. A few vultures looked down from the roof with shabby indifference: he wasn't carrion yet. A faint feeling of rebellion stirred in Mr. Tench's heart, and he wrenched up a piece of the road with splintering fingernails and tossed it feebly towards them. One rose and flapped across the town over the tiny plaza, over the bust of an ex-president, ex-general, ex-human being, over the two stalls which sold mineral water, towards the river and the sea. It wouldn't find anything there: the sharks looked after the carrion on that side. Mr. Tench went on across the plaza.*

In one exquisite paragraph Green has set the scene, introduced a character in some depth, created tension and a sense of sure doom, starting the irresistible run of the story. And the words! "Tench," "flapping," "bleaching," "wrenched," "splintering," "Mr. Tench went . . ."

Intensive reading of one author at a time lets his style sift into yours. Such reading is simply putting tools into your toolbox.

WRITING

KEEPING A JOURNAL. This is an excellent way to take your daily dose of writing. A journal is a ledger in which you make daily entries of your activities and encounters, errant thoughts and observations. Buy a book of blank pages, in a size comfortable to you. The average diary with its little lock is too small. Commit yourself to its daily maintenance. Keeping a journal is an important act. Its purpose here is to start you writing in the belief that you'll get so bored with your own writing that you'll improve. Of course the journal has functions of keeping track of your intellectual developments and providing a bin into which you will toss ideas for later retrieval. One page a day in your journal is a minimum requirement. More tools.

> *I put down my ideas as they present themselves pell mell to my mind, fanciful, extravagant, sentimental, bawdy, irreverent, irrelevant, they are all welcome. . . . I consider the greatest difficulty to be overcome by immature, untrained writers is lack of confidence. They are too self-conscious. When once the pen is in the hand it is important to forget about the opinion of others and to write away after your own fashion with careless, proud indifference.* —LLEWELYN POWYS, THE CREATIVE PROCESS, MENTOR, 1955.

WEEKLY REQUIREMENTS. In addition to your daily journal you must produce 1,000 to 2,000 words a week in reviews, short papers for your tutor and in serious correspondence. By "serious" we mean letters that exchange ideas in your best writing.

FELT NEEDS. Paulo Freire, the Brazilian educator, has shown that illiterate peasants can learn to read and write in thirty hours if the material used relates to their actual political condition. The tenanted peasant cannot be concerned with whether the rabbit runs; "land reform," "primary schools," "malaria" are terms that he is anxious to read and write down. The peasant understands that if he can read and write those words, he has power to change his condition. Paulo Freire is in political exile.

The principle that works for the Brazilian peasants is universal: you write best about your concerns, your real interests, something you know about. Be modest in what you write about; extravagant with the effort you put into it. Writing that has vitality can overcome every other problem. We can only write with vitality about things we know about.

POETRY. Write poetry to learn about language. Writing poetry will eventually teach economy in language, compression. One page defines a battlefield where obscurity, ambiguity and verbosity are at war with emotional precision, simplicity, form and the right words.

CRITIQUE. After you have written, show it around for reactions. Know someone who understands good English and will help you.

> A real writer is always reacting to the sentence he wrote before. That's what good writing is. The beginning of bad writing is when a writer forgets what he's just written. That's what I'd tell kids if I ever had a writing class. I'd bang that home. —NORMAN MAILER, WASHINGTON POST, JULY 11, 1971.

RESPONSIBILITY. There is a connection between clarity, simplicity in writing and responsibility. Responsible writing is clear writing. We Americans have terrorized the English language for our official purposes:

OPTION C. *Progressive squeeze-and-talk. Present policies plus an orchestration of communications with Hanoi and a crescendo of additional military moves against infiltration targets. . . . The scenario would be designed to give the U.S. an option at any point to. . . .* —FROM A PENTAGON MEMORANDUM.

That is language that cannot reveal consequences. It can barely give directions. It cannot be held accountable.

Identify yourself with what you write. Stand behind your words. In "OPTION C," the words have been pushed out in front of the men, to do the dirty work. If you try to write responsibly to yourself and others, you will try to write clearly.

That is why I started to write. To save myself. I realized that no one could save me but myself. . . . I had to seek out the truth and unravel the snarled web of my motivations. —ELDRIDGE CLEAVER, SOUL ON ICE, DELL, 1970.

THE LITTLE BOOK. There is a little book you should buy, read and carry with you. It is called *The Elements of Style* by William Strunk and E. B. White. It is seventy-one pages; it is published by Macmillan Paperbacks and costs ninety-five cents. Get hold of the book. The first section is the shortest, clearest explanation available to the rules of usage and the principles of English composition. It was written by Mr. Strunk who brooks no nonsense. E. B. White, who had been a student of Mr. Strunk, wrote the second section, "An Approach to Style." He offers twenty-one hints and suggests to anyone who would write in English. "Be clear," number 16. "Make sure the reader knows who is speaking," number 13.

We have both had the book for over ten years. When we refer back to it, we sit up straight.

I have gained a deep respect for the demonic power of the word. Words are not idle. They have consequences. —NORMAN O. BROWN.

5. Learning Skills

CONVERSATION. Good talk is an absolute in education. Study is a solitary action. But study is only a part of education. Research indicates that the "informal learning" in a college environment (the halls, the dorms, between classes over coffee) is where most of the learning takes place. The best teacher around is a smart student explaining to some friends what the last class was all about. Someone who is describing a book he/she thinks is interesting, automatically summarizes it for you and generally interests you in reading it. Friendly taverns and studious coffee houses are wonderful places to learn. We mourn their passing. There are some things that are so difficult to understand that in order to be comprehended, they must be discussed among good-talking friends in a crowded corner. Be around people who like to talk about what they are reading.

READING. This is the big one. If you don't like to read, you'll have to stay in college. A college's faculty presumes that students don't read without threats of failure, expulsion, Christmas assignments. But if you like to read, if your natural desire to read wasn't thwarted in grade school, your education will take place, despite everything.

It may give you some confidence to know that most of us don't read books from start to finish. People who like to read often start in the middle of a book, read around until they want some connecting material, and only then, if they have been seduced into it, do they start at the beginning of the book. If a book is a bit imposing, look over the Table of Contents to get a sense of what it is about, then just muck through a few chapters, warring on the book, so to speak. Some books you just have to get control of. The most difficult book we have ever encountered is Mortimer Adler's *How to Read a Book*. We couldn't dent it until we had read almost every chapter out of sequence, torn out one totally incomprehensible chapter and waited for three months before going a second round with it. Now we can recommend it to you:

How to Read a Book
(The Art of Getting a Liberal Education)
A Clarion Book
Simon and Schuster
1940; 1967

Price: $1.95

With a tough book, read it over a period of time, in five- or six-page chunks, gnawing at it.

Don't try to read textbooks. They cannot be well-written; they are dated in five years; they are pap printed for the unwilling.

> *Current textbooks in special subject matters do not belong to the classics; they are the best examples we can find of books that are detached from the liberal tradition and therefore doomed to an early death.* —SCOTT BUCHANAN, 1937–38 CATALOG OF ST. JOHN'S.

Straight reading doesn't work. If you simply pick up a book, read a chapter, in three weeks you will have forgotten almost all of the information. You'd flunk any test on the material. There is no one way to plug that drain, but there are some techniques you can use, in combination, to "set" what you have read.

• Note the significant passages with vertical lines in the margin, underlining only the important words in topic sentences and a few supporting facts. Nothing more.

• Be aware of the author's chapter structure. Make a note, circle the chapter number when the author lists objectives, gives a ranking of items or makes some major points.

• Give yourself a self-test *immediately* after reading a section of the book. Ask a question out of the material you just read. Recite the answer from memory, then return to the text to check your answer. Immediate self-testing "sets" the material in your memory. It requires discipline; it is required.

Looking at the few books we know we have read well, we find that we did a number of things: we underlined consistently; we ticked the best chapters on the Table of Contents; we wrote comments in the margins throughout; we listed the best pages on the inside cover of the book; and finally and most importantly, ladies and gentlemen, we wrote a *summary* in the blank pages at the back of the book along with our opinions and new ideas.

Carl Sandburg didn't like underlining much. When he read an idea that needed saving, if the book was his, he just ripped the whole page out, filed it away. We've done that for this book. With paperbacks it seems a form of therapy. Up to a point, ideas that are literally ripped from their context, are likely to be easily retrieved.

That's why it is mandatory to own the important books: their contents can be easily retrieved; they can contain a record of where your head was at.

NOTES. Make a decision now for life, just how you are going to keep your lecture and reading notes. We wish we had done this earlier so that we could have saved them. We're always in situations where we take notes. Watching a TV discussion, public lectures, conversations. We have finally settled on 4- by 6-inch scratch pads, and yellow legal pads for interviews and long lectures. There must be better systems. One friend takes notes (any size), quotes and interesting miscellaneous Xeroxes, staples them to 5- by 8-inch cards which he labels and keeps in a card file.

Never, in all the world, take notes on both sides of a sheet of paper. If you do that means you can't cut them up to put them in a writing order. So now you won't do that any more. The last word on notes: if a friend is taking an interesting class somewhere, ask to borrow his notes. You can recreate a lecture you didn't attend from good notes.

WRITING. You have to write, so write well. To write well, write a great deal. At least 1,000 words a week; go for 2,000. Four to ten pages. If you do that as a student, you'll never have to go hungry later. We may even say that again.

When on a long writing assignment, don't finish the section you are working on at bedtime; come back to it in the morning. You'll be happy that you don't have to start from scratch. The first paragraph is the obstacle. Get over that and you are on your way. Every writer has the "starting problem." Some of us stare at the typewriter for hours. We write the title, tear it out of the machine, crumple it up just like the playwrights in the movies. Hebert puts a chair in the doorway to keep himself out of the kitchen.

To find out what you want to write about, put aside your notes and just talk out your subject with a friend, a mirror or a tape recorder. This is good advice folks. Talk out what you are going to write about. After you have thoroughly explained it out loud, an order will emerge. Write down that order. It is your outline. Your writing will be fresher, in a personal style and more communicative.

> *Cutting had always been the most difficult and distasteful part of writing to me; my tendency had always been to write rather than cut. Moreover, whatever critical faculty I may have had concerning my own work had been seriously impaired, for the time being at least, by the frenzied labor of the past four years. When a man's work has poured from him for almost five years like burning lava from a volcano; when all of it, however superfluous, has been given fire and passion by the white heat of his own creative energy, it is very difficult suddenly to become cold surgical, ruthlessly detached. . . .*
>
> *My spirit quivered at the blood execution. My soul recoiled before the carnage of so many lovely things cut out upon which my heart was set. But it had to be done, and we did it.* —THOMAS WOLFE, THE STORY OF A NOVEL, CHARLES SCRIBNER'S SONS, 1936.

DICTIONARIES.

The American Heritage Dictionary of the English Language
American Heritage and
Houghton Mifflin
1969

This is a beautiful dictionary. We can't get over the fact that somebody has made a beautiful dictionary. It cost four million dollars and five years of work. There are 155,000 entries. It weighs a bit over five pounds. There are wide margins, a readable typeface and hundreds and hundreds of fine photographs. It is a feast of a dictionary.

The reason somebody spent four million dollars plus one million dollars in advertising and promotion on a single book, is that three million college dictionaries are bought each year. There is a huge market and this dictionary will probably get most of it. How much do students use dictionaries? That's the question. It's ridiculous to say again that words are important. Here are some ideas about dictionaries and vocabulary.

• Keep the dictionary where you study.

• Leave it open at the reference last consulted to save wear and tear on the binding. Left open it will get used more.

• Always read the derivations.

• After you have read the word, noted the definition, circle the word with a pen. That provides reinforcement when you happen upon that page again.

• As you read and come upon words you are unsure of, unless it is necessary for the meaning, *don't* look them up immediately. Only note the word in the flyleaf or on a "New Words" list. Later, look the word up and write down the definition. Grade school teachers make a mistake when they have kids stop their reading and look up words. It is a negative practice. Keep those word lists and go over them occasionally.

• Once a week, post a list of ten new words and their definitions in the bathroom.

• Do not buy a pocket-size dictionary of any variety. Without exception they are awful. They have never had the word. For traveling, the best small dictionary is the *Concise Oxford Dictionary,* published by Oxford University Press. It is a proper second dictionary.

• Take those little word quizzes in the *Readers' Digest.*

• *Atlases.* Let's hope there is an atlas in the house. If there isn't, two excellent atlases are:

Cosmopolitan World Atlas
Rand McNally

Price: $14.95

National Geographic Atlas
National Geographic Society
P.O. Box 2806
Washington, D.C. 20036

Price: $18.75 (standard)

They also have a fine selection of sheet maps available. Write for the price list.

ENCYCLOPEDIAS. Use them whenever you can. You may have had ignorant teachers who frowned on the encyclopedia because they wanted you to work hard. That was their problem. On most learning projects you can start with the encyclopedia. The best one is the *Encyclopaedia Britannica,* without a doubt. It has 24 volumes, 28,711 pages, 35,000 articles and 10,335 expert contributors. As the *Britannica* is heavily cross-referenced, it is best to start your investigation with the index. There are sixty-three pages on "Africa" for example. You might not want to read all that, but in our experience one eventually reads all of the articles. They have sound scholarship and generally are well written.

If you are living at home, perhaps you can talk someone into buying a set. Don't buy a new one. They cost around five hundred dollars. Check the Yellow Pages or the classifieds. We found a 1971 set at a used bookstore for two hundred and fifty dollars. Any edition less than ten years old is valuable. Bargain.

The best one-volume encyclopedia in English is the *Columbia Encyclopedia* published by Columbia University Press. It costs around fifty dollars. We'd like to have one.

> *The encyclopedia offers a summary of the knowledge most signifi-cant to mankind. The good encyclopedia does this more authorita-tively and with more illustrative and bibliographic support than are found in any single format in the entire collection that is the true university.* —LOUIS SHORES, "THE LIBRARY-UNIVERSITY," SCHOOL AND SOCIETY, MARCH, 1971.

TESTS. Tests are life. Rites of passage. They can be good, they can be bad. They should be learning devices. Take as many tests as you can. Take the CLEP tests. Have your tutor give you tests. (Experimental colleges are rather gutless places. They are afraid of everything. They have a fear of tests. Consequently few people at experimental colleges have any sense of what they can do.) Tests train you to operate under stress; to stop, think, read before you act or say something. Someone told us that they read a study which showed that up to 40 percent of a student's learning time can profitably be spent taking tests. We haven't seen the study, but we believe it. If you are not taking the tests for grades, are only competing with yourself or a friend or two, tests are fun, educational and revealing of what you do and don't know.

There are skills to taking tests.

- Know what the exam is going to cover.
- Know what kind of an exam it is going to be: objective, essay or a combination of both.
- Review methodically and ahead of time.
- Study the terminology of the subject.
- Review the hardest (or worst) things first. Get them out of the way.
- Cram just before. Good cramming is just good reviewing.
- Read the first and last paragraphs of the chapters to be covered in the exam. In the first paragraph the writer tells you what the chapter is going to cover and in the last paragraph he tells you what you have read. To review a whole book, read the first twelve pages of the book and the last twenty pages. On a page or two in those parts of the book, the author says all he has to say.
- When you get to the exam, glance over the whole examination first. This relaxes you and keeps you from answering something twice.
- Study the directions. Often they are confused. They are rarely clear. Understand the rules before you start.
- Allocate your time according to the point-value of the questions.
- Answer the questions in any order that is comfortable.

- Make sure you understand the question.
- Make sure you understand what you have been asked to do with the question: compare, discuss, define, explain, etc.
- If the question is vague, make your interpretation clear before attempting to answer it.
- For an essay question, make notes; outline it first.
- Change your answers if you have a hunch that your first one was wrong. Studies have shown that students change from wrong to right about twice as often as they change from right to wrong.
- On most objective tests, guess.

SET DEADLINES. Decide how many hours a piece of work is going to take you. Or say, "I am going to write five pages before I go to bed"—or before noon or whatever. Break up your work into accomplishable chunks.

SPACE. You need your own place to work (territory). We treat learning space in detail in Chapter 10. Here we remind you to have a long work table, a good chair, files and a book rack. And the sense to create for yourself a proper place to learn.

HANDWRITING. If you are interested in improving your handwriting, buy a decent fountain pen. Felt tips are okay, but they wear out in a week. In fact we're tired of them and have gone back to pencils. Ballpoints are to fountain pens as margarine is to butter. Handwriting experts all agree that a fountain pen is the best thing for writing. And since your handwriting is you . . .

TYPING. Typing is so important that we had unconsciously thought that it would require half a chapter to fully explain our feelings about it. Now we find we don't have much to say except "learn how to type." Only about 30 percent of college students type. Here is a quote from McLuhan's *Understanding Media* (McGraw-Hill, 1964).

> *The poet or novelist now composes on the typewriter. The typewriter fuses composition and publication, causing an entirely new attitude to the written and printed word. Composing on the typewriter has altered the forms of language and of literature.*

John Holt says someplace that children love to type and that he doesn't understand why teachers don't have typewriters in classrooms so that children can type when they want to. It seems such a natural thing to have typewriters around children. One wonders.

Some stray notes about typing:

The invention and distribution of typewriters increased the sale of dictionaries, thus suggesting a relationship between typing and literacy.

Use twenty-pound, heavy-weight, 25 percent cotton content erasable paper. The erasable paper gives you freedom to *compose* on the machine.

To teach yourself how to type there is a decent little book:

Personal Typing in 24 Hours
Philip Pepe
McGraw-Hill
1965

Price: $3.95

We discuss typewriters in the chapter on "Worldliness."

MOVIE-GOING. Be a movie person. Belong to a movie people. Cinema is good; film is better; a movie a week is best for your soul.

We go to movies for three things:

1) Entertainment
2) Relaxation
3) Enlightenment

Pauline Kael, one of our fine movie critics, rasped a meeting of professors of Film Arts with the following: "We go to movies because we want to. . . . The greatest advantage movies had for us and still have, the great advantage of film over the other arts, is that it has *not* been forced on us. It has been ours like Jazz and popular music—something we wanted, not something fed to us!"

So forget film courses. It hasn't been demonstrated that they are worth a damn, except insofar as they present interesting movies.

Movies do two things for your independent education: 1) create a personal aesthetic; 2) give the freedom to react.

Over a period of time a student of movies can acquire a taste for better things for him/herself. The development of an aesthetic. This should start with indiscriminate movie-going. A movie a week with good company if possible. Aesthetic judgment is a self-taught thing. The human mind left to itself can sort out the genuine from the specious if it is trusted to do it.

The second educational value to movie-going is that it gives one the opportunity to react freely. Admittedly movie-going is spectatorish. Having decided to part with the admission price, a movie-goer has lost the freedom to do anything but laugh, cry, look, listen, believe, not believe, stay or huff out. To the charge that movie-going is a mere passive thing, we can say that one can *act* in the world only to the extent that one can *react*. To react is not to withdraw. Reacting to a movie should be a "springy," elastic sort of involvement. Sometimes you only have to listen and watch a story, sometimes you have to fence.

Remember the last time you had a hilarious laugh at a movie. When was the last time you cried or almost cried? The last time you cheered a villain. The last time you applauded a film? (Applause is for the audience as well as the show and performers. In most parts of the world today, the actors join in the applause to the astonishment of Americans.) Applaud a good movie.

By the time the average student breaks out of high school, her/his ability to respond to such things as movies has been severely threatened. This student has been prefaced, textbooked and commentaried to the point that his/her own opinions are not trusted nor easily expressed. Perhaps movies is one arena that will allow the student to learn to trust personal reactions. Thus the student can start developing ideas, opinions and theories that really belong to the student; not to us.

SOME POINTERS TO MOVIE-GOING.

• See one a week.

• Survey your town or city to know where the movies are. There may be film societies; out-of-the-way movie houses. Of course, follow the entertainment pages.

• For a relaxation-entertainment movie, sit with the audience, house center. A good audience can *make* a dopey film.

• For a serious film, sit where the French cinema people sit, down front.

• If it is good, see it again. Sit in a different section of the house, the second time.

• Don't just follow the action and the lead actors. Watch the background, the minor characters. See what they are doing and why.

• The locale-scenery. How does the director tell you where the action is?

• See foreign films; subtitles don't make any difference.

• In your journal, review the films you see. Put down your impressions, evaluations and things you didn't understand.

• Always use the student I.D. if there are student prices. Borrow one if you are not a student.

• Read

James Agee On Film, Volume 1
Grosset's Universal Library
1969

Price: $2.95

This is a highly thought-of collection of reviews and essays about the movies. It is also the best.

• Watch for TV Film Festivals, revivals of old movies. They may be on the increase as a type of programming for TV. Viewers of some of the programs will be able to get packets of program notes monthly, early reviews, etc. And there is a book!

The New York Times Guide to Movies on TV
H. Thompson (ed.)
Quadrangle Books
c/o The New York Times
P.O. Box 590
Yonkers, New York 10702

Price: $1.95 postpaid

• Movie prices have probably hit their ceiling. Some chains are experimenting with dollar evenings. Seek out the cut-rate theaters.

• Movie buffs eventually start going to movies by themselves. It is natural. Not to worry.

So you can go to movies to learn about you, your society, your time. If anyone asks you what you're doing, seeing a movie a week, running off at 11:20 P.M. by yourself, tell them you're in an independent learning program, learning off the land, building your aesthetic and finding freedom to react; learning about yourself.

XEROXING
"Where you going?"
"Xeroxing."
"What you Xeroxing?"
"Some stuff."
"Be back in time for lunch."
"Yeah."

Everybody is going to Xerox. Get the habit. Get near a machine. Make a book. Flip, flip, flip. Don't pay more than five cents a copy. Find a copy shop that is open Saturdays. There will be photocopy machines in apartment houses soon; next to the washing machines.

Keep a file "To Xerox." Borrow magazines and Xerox the articles you need. Don't let an important article get away from you. Xerox it quick. Make Xerox copies of important personal papers, letters of reference, etc. Xerox transcripts, résumés, the works. Budget a dollar a week for Xeroxing.

The best home copier for students is the COPY-MATE, Model 400. It costs only $29.95, weighs seven pounds. Buy 3M-Type 727 copy paper, 100 sets to a $7.50 box. That works out at 7½ cents per copy. These little copiers are a bit slow, but they do work. If you don't have access to a Xerox or copy center, you might buy one of these.

More and more copy shops have photo-offset presses. Photo-offset presses are amazing creatures. You put an original in the front end and in a few seconds copies start pouring out the back end. For a small book they are ideal. They are completely automatic, thus cheaper than the ordinary offset operation. If you bargain at a small shop you can have fifty copies of a twenty-page booklet printed for around $45. Writing term papers is drudgery and not particularly useful to anyone. But making your own book is heavenly.

"And, Daniel Ellsberg, don't stop to play with those roughnecks!"
"Yes, mother."

TERM PAPERS. We clipped an article from *The New York Times,* July 10, 1971— "Market in Term Papers Is Booming." Apparently now you can buy new and used term papers. Term Papers, Unlimited, Inc., a student-owned firm in Boston has sold ten thousand term papers at $3.50 a page for a paper written from scratch; $2.00 a page for a copy of one in the files.

It is possible to have ambiguous feelings about buying term papers but we tend to agree with the academic vice president of Northeastern University (which is located across the street from Termpapers, Unlimited, Inc.) when he says, "There may be favorable aspects because teachers might be forced to review the nature of their courses." We don't know the address of Term Papers, Unlimited, Inc., or their Zip Code, for that matter. Their latest phone number is (617) 267-3000. But that wouldn't interest the independent student. A scabrous practice like buying a term paper is only for those who have not *broken out* of college.

From a Speech to Students, 1957

The world is yours, as well as ours, but in the last analysis, it is yours. You young people, full of vigor and vitality, are in the bloom of life, like the sun at eight or nine in the morning. —QUOTATIONS FROM CHAIRMAN MAO TSE-TUNG, FOREIGN LANGUAGE PRESS, PEKING, 1966.

6. How to Get Things Done

Here is a cram course in getting things done. It starts with the small and necessary, moving into executive practice, systems theory and management techniques. It is material you can work over for your own needs. The world needs competent people. Competence is learned.

> *Discipline is considered a method of regulating the customary, in order to set free the creative faculties.* —SOCIETY OF FRIENDS, IN THE PENDLE HILL CATALOG.

BASIC TOOLS

FILING. First, filing makes you *evaluate* the storm of paper you live in. Second, it allows you to *retrieve* information needed for your expression, your education, your work, your survival. It is serious business to the independent.

> *The objective of paper management is to keep it alive, limited and tangible.* —ROBERT PROBST, THE OFFICE, THE BUSINESS PRESS, 1968.

Buy a box of files; we prefer the heavy blue cloth, hinged files made by Oxford. Ask for the "one-fifth cut." That means the tabs will be staggered, not one behind the other. Now determine your classifications. Your first ones will be in terms of things past. File your personal correspondence according to years: 1963, 1964, 1965, etc. Read through everything. Purge the unimportant, but use your imagination. If you enjoyed reading through it, if it had pungent memories for you, file it. If the schoolwork is coherent, file it. Save report cards, diplomas, pictures—chronologically. In your files try to recreate as much of yourself as you can.

Label some files from your current interests. We'll talk more about clipping articles later, but you might have a "Possible Future Projects" file, a "Political" file, a "Local Ecology" file—perhaps an "Africa" file. We have "Résumé" files, keeping all flattering material together. This book didn't get started until we had a filing system worked out.

PAPERCLIPS. Putting information together. Paperclips *collate* material and *combine* ideas. Batches of facts, hunches—unrelated until you connect them with a paperclip. Buy two boxes of clips. A box of large ones; a box of small ones. Have them handy in a shallow tray or dish. One of the nice things about paperclips is that they allow you to change your mind.

STAPLES AND STAPLERS. When papers have to stick together. When you've done all you can do, your mind is made up, there is no doubt that the documents jibe: *staple*. Stay away from the big desk models; they don't transport easily and they are generally ugly. Keep a stapler with you. Keep control of your paper.

ENVELOPES. Envelopes must be thrown away. This is very important to getting things done. Never save an envelope unless it is a special size that you can recycle. Some people staple the envelope to the letter to save the address. We find it is much simpler and keeps the files neater if you note down in your address book the address, write it at the top of the correspondence, then discard the envelope.

SCRATCH PADS. Get a supply of 4- by 6-inch pads. Carry them with you. Go to a print shop where you can get them cheap. They use scrap paper and often sell them for a dollar a pound. Scratch pads are wonderful things to think with. An idea to a page. You can throw it away without worrying about the trees.

For typing out useful quotes, use the 4- by 6-inch cards. When you are into some writing, the yellow legal notepads are very helpful. Something about their size and color brings out your best. For a buck and a half you can buy a heavy vinyl cover for them, with pockets to hold loose pages. Useful on the second-class deck of the ferry that runs between Oron and Calabar, Nigeria. You won't miss a thing.

When you have many ideas, sources, a shapeless mass of intake that is beating you down, get a *large* tablet of newsprint. The ideal size is 14 by 17 inches. Then just randomly space out your main subjects, points, on the large sheets. Seeing all of them in one glance helps you visualize your paper or project. An order will come.

DESK. Keep it clear of *old* things. Decide at what point it is too messy, then clear it at that point. Station a box nearby for material that has to be filed. When it fills, empty the papers into your files. You can't think clearly with a collection of old *unevaluated* material on your desk. We talk more about desks in Chapter 10, "A Personal Learning Space." President Johnson used to walk through the White House offices at night leaving admonishing notes on the cluttered desks. He obviously was worried that he wasn't getting enough labor from those persons. He was probably right. A person who can't organize the top of a desk won't be trusted with much. The old theory was that you had to "clear your desk" every night. That's nonsense. But a desk is like a gun; if the working parts of it aren't cleaned regularly, it ain't gonna fire.

A CALENDAR. A large calendar is needed near your working space. An office supply store will have them. It should measure at least 18 by 20 inches. That size will give you a clear picture of a month. In the day-boxes there is room to write appointments, parties, concerts, lectures, classes, meetings, etc. A calendar isn't really useful unless it pictures what is happening when.

Office supply stores, incidentally, are where you outfit your work space. They are the equivalent to the "country store." All sorts of little devices to help you organize your work.

"THINGS TO DO." Make lists of "Things to Do." Do you do it? This is an essential habit. Make a list of about *five* things to do each day. The secret is to stay right with each item until you can't do any more on it. Pursue the items. When you have completed the task, check it off. The checks give you a "status report" and a sense of getting things done. Take this form we devised down to a local printer (phone around to get a good price, *i.e.* ten dollars for twenty pads). You could also Xerox it cheaply, two to a page.

SOME MANAGEMENT THEORY

This is your education we are talking about. It is not going to start somewhere soon. This is it. Ordinarily, as a student, you are not expected to learn, just to stay out of the job market; there isn't room for every able body. When in your middle or late twenties you are allowed to actually work, you will be taught what you need to do a job. But the important *people skills* you can start to learn now. Those are the skills of *people support, interaction, planning, leadership*. In our experience on college

NO._____

THINGS TO DO

Date_____

	Project	Started	Completed
1.			
2.			
3.			
4.			
5.			
6.			
7.			

NOTES

staffs, we have seen very few people who could skillfully work with others.

In the following section, picture yourself as having accepted some responsibility, such as heading a local voter registration drive, working on a block party committee or finding housing for a disaster relief project. Pick anything you might be interested in, to model in your mind while you read this.

HABITS OF MIND. Peter Drucker in *The Effective Executive,* Harper & Row, 1966, suggests five "Habits of Mind" that he believes competent people must develop.

1) You must learn to *manage* and *consolidate* your available time.

2) You must focus on your possible *contribution;* on the *results* you want. Not on how much work you have to do.

3) You must build on the *strengths* in yourself; those around you in the possibilities of the project at hand. Don't deal with the weaknesses. Can't change those.

4) *Concentrate* on those few major areas where you can make a difference.

5) Competent people make few decisions, but they make the effective decisions. They know how their decisions interrelate. They make *fundamental decisions,* knowing that other decisions will proceed easily from those.

COMMITMENT. Don't do anything unless you are committed to it. Half-assed jobs are the result of someone not being committed. If you do good work on projects you're not committed to, you hurt yourself. *Commitment* is to work as *enthusiasm* is to learning. Without them something bad happens in the soul.

MANAGING. As an independent student you are a manager; you manage time, your resources and your relationships with others. In classic management theory, there are *five* major functions in managing. We have added a badly needed sixth. This is a rather old-fashioned way to look at management. But it is useful as a checklist.

1) Planning—establishing goals and a way to attain them.

2) Organizing—developing a coherent use of your resources.

3) Staffing—finding the right people and utilizing their talents to the fullest.

4) Directing—developing decisions that are understood (communicated) , can be accepted and that motivate people to implement them.

5) Controlling—assessing and regulating the work in progress until completed.

6) Documenting and self-study—objective written analysis and discussion of the activity in relation to the original goals and their usefulness.

If you are heading up a project, memorize these functions.

PEOPLE. Decisions about people must be studied, and restudied. Take your time on people decisions. Test a decision in your mind for a time, model it there before you try it on reality. Good managers know that they spend most of their time on people issues. When a college president devotes his energies to raising money, the faculty and student body go to pot.

CRISIS MANAGEMENT. Crisis management is for those without a policy tied to a need to feel important. Presidential politics are characterized by crisis management. The modern executive is unlike old U. S. Grant. U. S. Grant, according to General Sherman, was the greatest Civil War general, because he didn't worry about what the enemy was doing on the other side of the mountain. He knew what had to be done, did all that *he* could do, then drank a little sour mash. If you're always in a crisis of some sort, you are poorly managing your affairs. Your personal organization is faulty.

DILLYDALLYING. Make a list of the usual things you do when you are avoiding work that needs to be done. For example:

1) Walk around the room
2) Take a rest break
3) Sharpen pencils
4) Go to a movie
5) Call long distance
6) Go downstairs and talk
7) Go out for a beer
8) Pick at beard

Make your own list:

1)
2)
3)
4)
5)

Tack a list near your work space. It will make you aware of your own processes.

SOURCEBOOKS. Here are ten books that will help you get things done:

Changing Organizations, WARREN BENNIS
Critical Path Method (PERT), A. T. ARMSTRONG
The Effective Executive, PETER DRUCKER
Finding Community, W. RON JONES
The Human Side of Enterprise, DOUGLAS MACGREGOR
The Human Use of Human Beings, NORBERT WIENER
Modern Organizations, AMITAI ETZIONI
The Peter Principle, LAWRENCE PETER and RAYMOND HULL
Systems Thinking, F. D. EMERY (ed.)
Up the Organization, ROBERT TOWNSEND

That alphabetical listing would also be an orderly way to read them.

CREATIVITY. Creative behavior is characterized by
- New use of materials
- Dissatisfaction with the usual expectations
- An expansion into new areas of expression
- High energy at the point of application

Most of us are creative if we are allowed to be. Psychological researchers say that creativity is mostly related to the environment we are raised in. If you see yourself as a creative person or as a person with creative potential, then be unwilling to do an ordinary piece of work. If it is "scut work," try to improve the system it is in: rearrange the materials when doing a bulk-mailing. People do repetitive tasks best, working from left to right, so stop and figure out the best room layout for eight people collating, folding, stuffing, sealing and stamping. Determining a favorable layout for such work is creative.

We can't tell you how to be creative; it is something you have to demand of yourself. Then you must find means and people to support your creative habit.

LEADERSHIP. There are two kinds of leadership: (1) the leadership that is conferred by suggesting to people what they have almost decided to do. Here the leader is generally charismatic and regarded as "one of the people." (2) The other form of leadership results from an action. As Stewart Brand, founder of the *Whole Earth Catalog* says: "Get there first, if it is worthy, the others will come." Here the leader is an original person, not necessarily likable, a pioneer. Four things that leaders have to *learn* how to do.

1) Carry water. Carry water to those that are helping you. Support those that are following your leadership in any activity. Robert Townsend in *Up the Organization* declares that this is the main function of the executive. The wise person spends most of his time making it possible for others to work up to their potential. Carry water.

2) Deal honestly. Deal honestly with people and you can expect much from them. In our experience "people become what you expect of them." It is a line of Camus'. Encourage someone to do something that he/she has not been asked to do before. Give them support if needed. Then step back. (Difficult to do if you have Power Hangups.) If you can do this, you can get things done with people.

3) Delegate. If you are ever in a position to delegate work, realize that you must therefore relinquish control over it. If you delegate responsibility, you must delegate *authority*. That is a hard lesson to learn. Once someone starts something for you, you can't fiddle with it. It is their baby. Again, step back. Delegation is not easy for most people.

4) Learn. There are four ways to learn: reading, listening, talking it out, doing it.

GROUPS. Develop group skills. These are going to be very necessary skills. In the future you will be in political groups, learning groups, civic action and work groups, you might travel in a group at some point. One of the lessons of the Venceremos Brigade that went to Cuba was that Americans didn't have the ability to work easily in groups.

> The key word will be "temporary." There will be adaptive, rapidly changing temporary systems. These will be task forces organized around problems-to-be-solved by groups of relative strangers with diverse professional skills. . . . Adaptive, problem-solving temporary systems of diverse specialists, linked together by coordinating and task-evaluating executive specialists in an organic flux—this is the organization form that will gradually replace bureaucracy as we know it. —WARREN BENNIS, "THE COMING DEATH OF BUREAUCRACY" IN BEHAVIOR IN ORGANIZATIONS, ATHOS AND COFFEY (eds.), PRENTICE-HALL, 1968.

Skills that you will have to develop to work in groups:

- Listening to others
- Disagreeing with others in groups
- Giving and accepting criticism
- Expressing feelings
- Being careful not to dominate
- Watching group processes
- Knowing when to let the group dissolve, as all good groups should

ENDS AND MEANS. These should be chosen at the same time. When you consider an objective, an end, a goal, test it out against the method you might use to reach it. Once you decide on "Free Non-Communist Governments in Southeast Asia," there is no alternative but to beat the shit out of the Southeast Asians, destroying yourself in the process. Once you decide on a "War Against Poverty," the poor, obviously, become your enemies, which is what happened.

If you want to see the country, don't fly. Means are as important as ends.

> *The existence of the Maginot Line along the French-German border failed to call forth a corresponding effort along the Belgian frontier to guard against the possibility of a German strategy aimed at circumventing the Line. This example illustrates an important point: A "System" or economy is never quite finished. Today's system or economy-in-balance is likely to turn into tomorrow's subsystem or economy-out-of-balance.* —A. O. HIRSCHMAN AND C. E. LINDBLOM IN SYSTEMS THINKING, F. O. EMERY (ED.), PENGUIN BOOKS, 1969.

DISORDER. Disorder is not new; it shouldn't threaten. Indeed, many are beginning to see its value. Total law and order serves the status quo. Change in the schools, civil rights, women's rights, the urban environment wouldn't have occurred if "business-as-usual" hadn't been disrupted in the 1960's. If someone's order is imposed on everything, natural patterns will be lost. If all farms are farmed the same way because it is initially more efficient, soon there are dustbowls, unacceptable pesticide levels and displaced farmers, victims of the gang plow, looking for work in the cities. One person's "order" is generally achieved with a *limited* supply of knowledge. Without disorder there would be no creation. Learn to see that disorder may be another person's freedom.

> *Modern man has a genius for contriving efficient, productive institutions. But inevitably institutions betray him. . . . When institutions fail, there is disorder, discontent and a sense of grievance that leads to large-scale moralizing. This moralizing triggers positive action.* —THEODORE J. LOWI, THE POLITICS OF DISORDER, BASIC BOOKS, 1971.

THE ECCENTRIC. Go ahead with the eccentric, the out of order, the unbalanced, the fragmented. These projects may point out the problems, show the way in other activities. Your own hunches may have as much validity as would result from a massive search for information and understanding. Master plans, because they are incomplete (they rarely include the truly human), soon become the masters. Their makers have too much invested to change or drop them.

> *A friend of ours in Monterey, California is helping to organize an Ecology Center there. It began as a recycling center but the organization is now capable of larger projects. Their first project will be to put a roof on the*

bus stop the city recently constructed in the center of town. They selected this as a project because they were capable of it, it wouldn't make unnecessary enemies and because the shelter would make a specific improvement in the ecology of Monterey.

This may be considered an eccentric *point in which to enter an ecological system. It will have unforeseen effects. Who can say what will happen after you have quietly yet directly humanized the work of a city bureaucracy?*

SYSTEMS THEORY

Our parents have been shocked by our indictments of America. The ease with which we describe it as

- racist
- imperialist
- middle class
- materialist
- ecologically threatening
- sexist
- etcetera

has dismayed them. As frightening as our words has been the growing sense that we think differently than they. We have a different conceptual framework: we have an *instinct for systems.* We have perceived America as a system: "an organized or complex whole; an assemblage or combination of things or parts forming a complex or unitary whole." We see virtually everything as part of a system.

We were taught systems in grade school. Once we have it in our heads that

warm winds   meeting   cold winds   over the Rockies
causes snow to fall

and that snowfall can cause floods or high crop yields throughout the Mississippi River Valley, we *cannot be kept* from understanding that

automobiles   air pollution   respiratory disease   oil spills
a Nigerian Civil War (oil fields)   investments in Houston
investments in Detroit   the State Department

are elements of a system also.

And so we talk of "attacking the system." Both our parents and we think we are talking about "attacking" when in fact we are talking about "systems." The "Radical Left" has been more educational than revolutionary to most of us. It taught us *systems*.

You find systems by asking "generic questions": what are the underlying causes? How does this relate to the original mission? Are there larger questions that we aren't asking? What are the spin-off effects? Who else is affected by this decision? Ultimately, who is responsible? Where is the money really coming from? What are their real reasons in giving it? What other problems could be causing such behavior? What business should we be in? Are we in it? What is the function of the Police Review Board to the Mayor? If we dig more wells, what happens to the water table, and what effects on topsoil does a lowered water table have, and if the topsoil begins to shift, is the thigh bone connected to the leg bone?

WRITING UP A PROJECT DESCRIPTION

It may be that you will need to do a "long form" for someone, such as a relative who is funding a particular study project. Adapt this form to your situation.

In the actual writing of the project description (1) get your story across early, (2) be yourself, (3) be specific, (4) use simple, active language, (5) make the organization of the paper obvious.

QUESTIONS TO DEAL WITH

• Describe the project. List the objectives of the project in order of their importance. How did you happen to select it? What was the original impulse? Describe your search for a project.

• What do you anticipate will be major problems in your project? Where are the foul-ups likely to be? What will you do then?

• What form is the project going to take? How will you present it? Will the presentation be useful to someone besides yourself?

• What people are going to help you on this project? Is it a group? Who will do what? Has it been clearly agreed? How will the group make decisions?

• Who is your tutor/advisor? What role will he/she play? How much interest do they have?

• Include a budget listing transportation costs, materials, books, equipment bought or rented, lecture fees, tutorial fees, etc. Also include an estimate of your income for the period of your project.

• List the books you think will be helpful. What library or libraries are you going to use?

• Who will you interview?

• When will your project be completed and presented? When will it be half-finished?

• What other interests, projects or jobs will you have ongoing at the same time? How much time per week or day can you give to the project?

- List *four* dates for conferences with your principal tutor/advisor.
- Is there a possibility of your teaching or tutoring someone in this study field after you have finished your project? Are there younger students who might like to work on the project?
- How will this project be valuable to you? How does it fit into your educational plans?
- Are you going to do the typing?
- Who will critique your project? Your tutor; perhaps a newspaper editor, other students, an audience, etc.

7. Book Lists and Bibliographies

Book lists and bibliographies are forms of exchange, of currency. We have included in this book kit a number of them on the premise that among friends, one trades them around.

There is a difference between book lists and bibliographies. Book lists are horizontal. They encompass knowledge by ranging over human activity, bumping into themes. Good lists can outfit you with knowledge and experience, equipping you to traverse difficult passages with a sense of what you are about. The great lists are sacred.

Bibliographies are vertical organizations of information. They are educational in themselves. Whereas a book list tells you what *can* be known, bibliographies tell you what *is* known. A good bibliography, compiled around an idea or project you're into, is a hell of a thing to come across.

THE HARVARD CLASSICS
(ELIOT'S FIVE-FOOT BOOKSHELF)

The Harvard Classics were selected by Charles Eliot, President of Harvard from 1869–1909. There was a reading scheme that went along with it. Fifteen minutes a day, reading little snippets of great and some of the not-so-great books on the list. Of course that doesn't work. Mortimer Adler warns us that the Harvard Classics give one "intellectual St. Vitus's dance."

If you can get hold of an old set of Harvard Classics in a used book

store, do it and keep quiet about it. Start reading anywhere. Be accountable to no one.

Darwin (*Voyage of the Beagle*)
Bacon, Milton Brown
Bunyan, Isaak Walton
Emerson
Famous Prefaces
Plutarch
Tennyson to Whitman
Thackeray, Newman, Ruskin, Huxley, Thoreau and others
American Historical Documents
Plato, Epictetus, Marcus Aurelius
Aesop, Grimm, Anderson
Virgil
Addison, Steele, Swift, Defoe, Johnson and others
Edmund Burke
Dana
Cervantes
Marlowe and Shakespeare
Homer
Franklin, Woolman and Penn
The Thousand and One Nights
Dante
Collins to Fitzgerald
Chaucer to Gray
Index

Thirty-one and a half inches.

THE ST. JOHN'S COLLEGE LIST OF GREAT BOOKS

Scott Buchanan (1895–1968) created the monumental Great Books
program at St. John's College, Annapolis, Maryland. Before we present
the list we want to quote from the 1937–38 Catalog of St. John's College,
written largely by Scott Buchanan to establish the new program.

> The "classics" which liberal education made use of until recent decades
> were Greek, Latin, and mathematics. But it made increasingly bad use of
> them. It made, indeed, such bad use of them, that it eventually forgot why it
> had chosen them. In the circumstances, it began quite naturally to drop them
> out of the college curriculum. Unfortunately, it has never since succeeded
> in finding adequate substitutes, and its wild efforts to find such substitutes
> have resulted only in cluttering the college curriculum with tidbit courses

in ill-related subject matters. So conspicuous has this failure been that the college student long ago turned from his scheduled courses to athletics and other extra-curricular activities to find the discipline which the classroom no longer supplied. Curiously enough, at this point the college, recognizing that the courses it offered were educationally less successful than student activities, turned some of the activities into courses, in a vain effort to re-capture control of the educational process. This is the unconscious origin of courses in journalism, public speaking, athletic coaching, current events, which characterize liberal colleges today.

Buchanan went on to state the standards by which one may judge a book to be a classic.

1) A great book is one that has been read by the largest number of readers.

2) A great book has the largest number of possible interpretations.

3) A great book should raise the persistent unanswerable questions about the great themes in European thought.

4) A great book must be a work of fine art; it must have an immediate intelligibility and style which will excite and discipline the ordinary mind by its form alone.

5) A great book must be a masterpiece of the liberal arts. Its author must be a master of the arts of thought and imagination whose work has been faithful to the ends of these arts, the understanding and exposition of the truth.

The list has been revised numerous times. This is the list in current use at St. John's. There, it is a four-year program of reading. Most of these books are available in paperback.

HOMER, *Iliad; Odyssey*
HERODOTUS, *History*
AESCHYLUS, *Agamemnon; Prometheus Bound*
SOPHOCLES, *Oedipus Rex; Oedipus at Colonus; Antigone*
EURIPIDES, *Hippolytus; Medea*
ARISTOPHANES, *Clouds; Birds*
PLATO, *Meno; Republic; Sophist*
THUCYDIDES, *History of the Peloponnesian Wars*
ARISTOTLE, *Organon; Poetics*
EUCLID, *Elements*
APOLLONIUS, *Conics*
LUCRETIUS, *On the Nature of Things*
VIRGIL, *Aeneid*
The Bible
TACITUS, *Annals*
PLUTARCH, *Lives*

GALEN, *On the Natural Facilities*
PLOTINUS, *Fifth Ennead*
AUGUSTINE, *Confessions*
ANSELM, *Proslogium*
THOMAS AQUINAS, *Summa Theologica*
Song of Roland
Volsunga Saga
DANTE, *The Divine Comedy*
CHAUCER, *The Canterbury Tales*
LEONARDO, *Note-books*
RABELAIS, *Gargantua and Pantagruel*
MACHIAVELLI, *The Prince*
GALILEO, *Two New Sciences*
MONTAIGNE, *Essays*
BACON, *Novum Organum*
KEPLER, *Epitome of Copernican Astronomy IV, V*
DONNE, *Poems*
CALVIN, *Institutes*
LUTHER, *Commentary on the Epistle to the Galatians*
SHAKESPEARE, *Plays; Sonnets*
CERVANTES, *Don Quixote*
CORNEILLE, *Le Cid*
DESCARTES, *Discourse on Method*
HOBBES, *Leviathan*
RACINE, *Phedre*
MOLIÉRE, *Tartuffe*
SPINOZA, *Ethics*
MILTON, *Paradise Lost; Samson Agonistes*
PASCAL, *Pensées*
LA FONTAINE, *Fables*
NEWTON, *Principia*
LAVOISIER, *Elements of Chemistry*
MONTESQUIEU, *The Spirit of Laws*
SWIFT, *Gulliver's Travels*
LOCKE, *Essays Concerning Human Understanding*
VOLTAIRE, *Candide*
FIELDING, *Tom Jones*
HUME, *Enquiry Concerning Human Understanding; Second Essay on Civil Government*
BERKELEY, *Principles of Human Knowledge*
GIBBON, *Decline and Fall of the Roman Empire*
Constitution of the United States
Federalist Papers
KANT, *Critique of Pure Reason; Critique of Practical Reason*
GOETHE, *Faust*
HEGEL, *Science of Logic*
SCHOPENHAUER, *The World as Will and Idea*

DE TOCQUEVILLE, *Democracy in America* (abridged)

KIERKEGAARD, *Philosophical Fragments*

BALZAC, *Père Goriot*

THACKERAY, *Henry Esmond*

DICKENS, *David Copperfield*

FLAUBERT, *Madame Bovary*

DOSTOEVSKI, *Crime and Punishment*

MARX, *Capital; Communist Manifesto; Preface to Critique of Political Economy*

TOLSTOI, *War and Peace*

NIETZSCHE, *Birth of Tragedy; Beyond Good and Evil*

ZOLA, *Experimental Novel*

IBSEN, *The Doll's House*

DARWIN, *Origin of the Species*

BERNARD, *Introduction to Experimental Medicine*

BAUDELAIRE, *Poems*

WILLIAM JAMES, *Psychology-Briefer Course*

FREUD, *A General Introduction to Psychoanalysis*

WHITEHEAD, *Modes of Thought*

PEIRCE, *Philosophical Papers*

VALÈRY, *Poems*

EINSTEIN, *Relativity: The Special and General Theory*

A BIBLIOGRAPHY OF EDUCATIONAL CHANGE

Books about education are usually written by and for adults, so that they can better "deal" with students and their "schooling." Students aren't encouraged to understand what is happening to them. Here is a fine list of books on education compiled by New Schools Exchange, which is "the only central resource and clearing house for all people involved in alternatives to education." If you are a student you should be reading these books.

ASHTON-WARNER, S. *Teacher*. Simon & Schuster, New York, 1963.

BETTELHEIM, B. *Children of the Dream*. Macmillan, New York, 1969.

DENNISON, GEORGE. *The Lives of Children: The Story of the First Street School*. Random House, Inc., New York, 1969.

DEWEY, JOHN. *Interest and Effort in Education*. Houghton, Boston, 1913.

———. *Experience and Education*. Collier-Macmillan, 1963.

———. *Schools of Tomorrow*. Dutton, New York, 1962.

ERIKSON, E. H. *Identity: Youth and Crisis*. Norton, New York, 1968.

ERIKSON, E. H. (ed.). *Challenge of Youth*. Doubleday-Anchor, New York.

FADER, D. N. and MCNEIL, E. B. *Hooked on Books*. Berkeley Publishing, New York, 1968.

FREIRE, PAOLO. *The Pedagogy of the Oppressed*. Herder and Herder, Inc., New York, 1970.

FRIEDENBERG, EDGAR Z. *Coming of Age in America.* New York: Vintage-Random House, 1965.

————. *The Dignity of Youth and Other Atavisms.* Boston: Beacon Press, 1965.

GLASSER, WILLIAM. *Reality Therapy.* New York: Harper & Row, 1965.

GOODMAN, PAUL. *Growing Up Absurd.* New York: Vintage-Random House, 1960.

————. *Compulsory Mis-Education.* New York: Vintage Books, 1962.

————. *The Community of Scholars.* New York: Random House. 1962.

HOLT, JOHN. *How Children Fail.* New York: Dell Publishing Co., 1964.

————. *How Children Learn.* New York: Pitman Publishing Corp., 1967.

HOLT, GOODMAN, KOHN, and OTHERS. *Radical School Reform.* Simon & Schuster.

ILLICH, IVAN. *Deschooling Society.* New York: Harper & Row, 1971.

JEROME, JUDSON. *Culture Out of Anarchy.* Herder & Herder, 1970.

KOHL, HERBERT. *The Open Classroom.* New York: New American Library, Vintage Books, 1969.

————. *36 Children.* New York: New American Library, 1967.

KOZOL, JONATHAN. *Death at an Early Age.* Boston: Houghton Mifflin, 1967.

LAING, R. D. *The Politics of Experience.* New York, Ballantine, 1957.

————. *Knots.* New York: Pantheon, 1970.

MCLUHAN, MARSHALL. *Understanding Media: The Extensions of Man.* New York: New American Library (Signet Book), 1964.

MONTESSORI, M. *Dr. Montessori's Own Handbook.* New York: Schocken Books, 1965.

NEILL, A. S. *Summerhill: A Radical Approach to Child Rearing.* New York: Hart Publishing Co., 1960.

POSTMAN, NEILL, and WEINGARTNER, CHARLES. *Teaching as a Subversive Activity.* New York: Delacorte Press, 1969.

REPO, SATU (ed.) .*This Book Is About Schools.* Pantheon, 1970.

RIESMAN, D. *Individualism Reconsidered.* New York: Free Press, 1954.

SANFORD, N. (ed.) . *The American College: A Psychological and Social Interpretation of Higher Learning.* New York: Wiley, 1962.

SILBERMAN, CHARLES E. *Crisis in the Classroom.* New York: Random House, 1970.

TAYLOR, HAROLD. *How to Change Colleges.* New York: Holt, Rinehart and Winston, 1971.

VEBLEN, THORSTEIN. *On the Higher Learning in America.* Kelley, 1918.

New Schools Exchange,
301 East Canon Perdido Street,
Santa Barbara, California 93101

TWO READING LISTS FROM ANTIOCH

One of the programs that came and went during the two years that Antioch had a college at Columbia, Maryland, was the Program of Personal and Organization Development, or P-Pod. It was directed by Dr. Barbara Raines. This list reflects the changing conceptions of the person and organization that may make formal colleges obsolete.

FOCUS ON INDIVIDUAL DEVELOPMENT
ROGERS, CARL   *On Becoming a Person* and two others at least
BUGENTAL, J. F. T.   *The Search for Authenticity*
CLEAVER, ELDRIDGE   *Soul on Ice*
ELLISON, RALPH   *The Invisible Man*
FRIEDENBERG, E. Z.   *The Vanishing Adolescent and others*
LAING, R. D.   *The Divided Self*
MASLOW, A. H.   *Toward a Psychology of Being*
ERIKSON, ERIK   *Childhood and Society*
JOURARD, SIDNEY   *The Transparent Self*
WATTS, ALAN   *The Book*

FOCUS ON SMALL GROUP BEHAVIOR
LUFT, JOSEPH   *Group Processes* and two others
HARE, CATWRIGHT and ZANDER   books of readings on small group research
MILES, MATTHEW   *Learning to Work with Groups*
NTL Reading Series and Lab Reading Books
SATIR, VIRGINIA   *Conjoint Family Therapy*

FOCUS ON COMMUNITY DEVELOPMENT
ALINSKY, SAUL   *Reveille for Radicals,* et al.
GOFFMAN, ERVING   *Stigma, Asylums*
KLEIN, DONALD   *Community Dynamics and Mental Health*
KOTLER, MILTON   *Neighborhood Government*
WOLFE, TOM   *The Electric Kool-Aid Acid Test*

MISCELLANEOUS
BUBER, MARTIN   *I and Thou*
MORRIS, VAN CLEVE   *Existentialism in Education*
PUTNEY and PUTNEY   *The Adjusted American*
ROGERS, CARL   *Freedom to Learn*
LYND, HELEN MERRILL   *On Shame and the Search for Identity*

A graduate student at Antioch-Columbia, Brian Corlew, taught an interesting course there in the winter of 1971. It tried to define the myths under which Americans live, like the myth which suggests that technology is going to give us a better life. Here is the reading list used in that course:

THE LIVED MYTH: SEARCH FOR A PERSONAL LIFE STYLE
HESSE, HERMAN   *Siddartha; Journey to the East; Demian; Narcissus and Goldmund*
AXLINE, VIRGINIA   *Dibs in Search of Self*
MORRIS, CHARLES   *Paths of Life; Varieties of Human Value*
BARTH, JOHN   *The End of the Road; Giles Goat Boy*
HEINLEIN, ROBERT   *Stranger in a Strange Land*

HERRIGEL, EUGENE   *Zen*
BUBER, MARTIN   *Between Man and Man; I and Thou*
WIENER, NORBERT   *The Human Use of Human Beings*
WATTS, ALAN   *The Book*
KESEY, KEN   *One Flew Over the Cuckoo's Nest*
WOLFE, TOM   *The Electric Kool-Aid Acid Test*
LAING, R. D.   *The Divided Self*
ERIKSON, ERIK   *Childhood and Society*
SCHUTZ, WILLIAM   *Joy*
BUGENTAL, J. F. T.   *The Search for Authenticity*
PUTNEY and PUTNEY   *The Adjusted American*
WHEELIS, ALAN   *The Quest for Identity*
LYND, HELEN MERRILL   *On Shame and the Search for Identity*
CAMPBELL, JOSEPH   *The Hero with a Thousand Faces*
BLAKE, WILLIAM   *The Marriage of Heaven and Hell; There is No Religion*
DYLAN, BOB   '65 poems, Woodstock tapes and others
DOSTOEVSKI, FYODOR   "Pro and Contra" (from *Brothers Karamazov*)
ROSZNACK, THEODORE   *The Making of a Counter-Culture*
ELIOT, T. S.   "The Wasteland," "The Four Quartets" and others
JOYCE, JAMES   passages from *Portrait of the Artist as a Young Man*
YEATS, W. B.   later poems on Art
GINSBERG, ALLEN   "Howl" and other poems
FULLER, BUCKMINSTER   *I Seem to be a Verb*
VONNEGUT, KURT   *Cat's Cradle*

GOOD READING

Good Reading is a ninety-five cent paperback containing the "concise assessments of about 2,000 books and authors." It is published by The New American Library (A Mentor Book). It first appeared in 1933. The last revised, updated edition was 1969. *Good Reading* has sold five million copies. It has annotated lists of books under twenty-eight major headings, each preceded by a short essay. It is well indexed. You should go out and buy it.

BOOKS FROM *THE WHOLE EARTH CATALOG*

The Whole Earth Catalog is subtitled "Access to Tools." And the great majority of the tools listed in the catalog are books. For sure, there are windmills, axes, glues that hold bridges together, but it is interesting that most of the items listed are books. That's the way it still is. Reading.

We are as gods and might as well get good at it. . . . a realm of personal power is developing—power of the individual to conduct his own education, find his own inspiration, shape his own environment, and share his adventure with whoever is interested. Tools that aid this process are sought and promoted by The Whole Earth Catalog.

The message is *competence*. How and what to read in order to gain competence in the internal and external world in order to have power over your life in the face of all those "ocracies" and "isms" that are putting you up against some wall or other.

It's work completed, *The Whole Earth Catalog* has ceased publication. But you can still buy the books and back issues from them. Write:

Whole Earth Catalog and Truck Store
558 Santa Cruz
Menlo Park, California 94205

This is a list of books we have read or would like to read. We collected it from the inch-thick final issue of the catalog. The catalog is an important document and we are grateful that it happened.

Village Planning in the Primitive World
Douglas Fraser
1968; 128 pp.

From:
George Braziller
One Park Avenue
New York, New York 10016
$2.95 postpaid

Culture Breakers, Alternatives and Other Numbers
Ken Isaacs
(a square little book with no page numbers or copyright)

From:
MSS Educational Publishing Co., Inc.
19 East 48th Street
New York, New York 10017
$5.00 postpaid

Domebook Two
1971; 128 pp.

From:
Pacific Domes
General Delivery
Bolinas, California 94924
$4.20 postpaid

The Way Things Work
1967; 590 pp.

From:
Simon and Schuster
630 Fifth Avenue
New York, New York 10020
$9.95 postpaid

The RSVP Cycles: Creative Process in the Human Environment
Lawrence Halprin
1969; 207 pp.

From:
George Braziller, Inc.
One Park Avenue
New York, New York 10016
$15.00 postpaid

Capitalism & Freedom: A New Radical's Guide to Economic Reality
Milton Friedman
1962; 202 pp.

From:
University of Chicago Press
5801 Ellis Avenue
Chicago, Illinois 60637
$1.50 postpaid

The Natural Way to Draw
Kimon Nocolaides
1941; 221 pp.

From:
Houghton Mifflin Company
Wayside Road
Burlington, Massachusetts 01803
$6.00 postpaid

Nature and the Art of Workmanship
David Pye
1968; 101 pp.

From:
Cambridge University Press
32 East 57 Street
New York, New York 10022
$4.95 postpaid

This is the bibliography Ralph Nader sends out in response to people who write him, wanting to know if they can help change things.

BIBLIOGRAPHY OF MATERIALS ON THE ENVIRONMENT

General Readings: Books and articles covering a variety of environmental issues. An overview of the subject.

CARNOW, DR. BERTRAM W. "Pollution Invites Disease." *Saturday Review,* July 4, 1970.

COMMONER, BARRY. *Science and Survival.* New York: Viking Press, 1967.

DEBELL, GARRETT (ed.). *Environmental Handbook.* New York: Ballantine/ Friends of the Earth, 1969.

———. *Voters' Guide to Environmental Politics.* New York: Ballantine, 1970.

Environmental Action. *Earth Tool Kit.* New York: Pocket Books, April, 1971.

KORMONDY, E. *Concepts of Ecology.* Englewood Cliffs, N.J.: Prentice-Hall, 1969.

MC HARG, IAN. *Design with Nature.* New York: Natural History Press, 1969.

MITCHELL, JOHN G. *Ecotactics.* New York: Pocket Books, 1970.

National Academy of Sciences, National Research Council. *Resources and Man.* San Francisco: W. H. Freeman and Co., 1969.

National Wildlife Federation. *Conservation Directory.* 1412–16th Street, N.W., Washington, D.C. 20036.

RIENOW, ROBERT, and RIENOW, LEONA. *Moment in the Sun.* New York: Sierra Club/Ballantine, 1969.

SAX, JOSEPH L. *Defending the Environment.* New York: Alfred Knopf, 1971.

SINGER, S. F. *Global Effects of Environmental Pollution.* New York: Springer-Verlag, Inc., 1970.

STORER, J. *Man in the Web of Life.* New York: Signet Books, 1968.

SWATEK, PAUL. *The Users' Guide to Protection of the Environment.* New York: Ballantine, 1970.

Air Pollution:

Air Pollution Control Association. *Air Pollution Experiments for Junior and Senior High School Science Classes.* 4400–5th Avenue, Pittsburgh, Pennsylvania 15213.

ESPOSITO, JOHN. *Vanishing Air.* New York: Grossman, 1970.

National TB and Respiratory Disease Association. *Air Pollution Primer.* 1969.

Scientists Institute for Public Information. *Air Pollution.* 30 East 68th Street, New York, N.Y. 10021.

Scientists Institute for Public Information. *Air Pollution Workbook.* 30 East 68th Street, New York, N.Y. 10021.

Water Pollution:

BRENNER, THEO. "Biodegradable Detergents and Water Pollution." *Advances in Environmental Science.* Vol. 1. New York: Wiley-Interscience, 1969.

Izaak Walton League of America. *Clean Water.* Glenview: February, 1970.

MARX, W. *The Frail Ocean.* New York: Ballantine, 1969.

MERRIMAN, DANIEL. "The Calefaction of a River." *Scientific American,* July, 1970.

"NTA." *Environment.* September, 1970.

"Qui Tam Actions and the 1899 Refuse Act: Citizen Lawsuits Against Polluters of the Nation's Waterways." Pamphlet available from the Subcommittee on Conservation and Natural Resources of the House Committee on Government Operations.

Scientists Institute for Public Information. "Water Pollution." 30 East 68th Street, New York, N.Y. 10021. 1970.

The Water Lords. Nader Task Force Report on the Savannah River. New York: Grossman, 1971.

Population:

EHRLICH, PAUL. *The Population Bomb.* New York: Ballantine, 1970.

EHRLICH, PAUL, and EHRLICH, ANN. *Population, Resources and Environment.* San Francisco: W. H. Freeman and Co., 1971.

Planned Parenthood—World Population. *Bibliography: Family Planning, Population and Related Subjects.* 516 Madison Avenue, New York, N.Y.

Zero Population Growth Reporter. Zero Population Growth, Inc., Los Altos, California.

Pesticides:

CARSON, RACHEL. *Silent Spring.* New York: Crest, 1967.

Department of Health, Education and Welfare. *Mark Commission Report on Pesticides.* 1969.

PEAKALL, DAVID B. "Pesticides and the Reproduction of Birds." *Scientific American,* April, 1970.

RUDD, ROBERT L. *Pesticides and the Living Landscape.* Madison: University of Wisconsin Press, 1964.

Scientists Institute for Public Information. *Pesticides.* 30 East 68th Street, New York, N.Y. 10021. 1970.

Wellford, Harrison. *Sowing the Wind:* Nader Task Force Report on the U.S.D.A. New York: Grossman, 1971.

Mercury:

"The Effects of Mercury on Man and the Environment." Parts 1 & 2. Hearings before the Subcommittee on Energy, Natural Resources and the Environment of the Senate Commerce Committee, 1970.

MONTAGUE, PETER, and MONTAGUE, KATHERINE. "Mercury: How Much Are We Eating?" *Saturday Review,* February 6, 1971.

Wilderness:

MUIR, JOHN, and KAUFFMAN, R. *Gentle Wilderness.* New York: Sierra Club/Ballantine, 1968.

North Star Chapter of the Sierra Club. "A Wilderness in Crisis—The Boundary Waters Canoe Area." North Star Chapter of the Sierra Club, Box 933, Minneapolis, Minnesota 55440.

SCHWARTZ, WILLIAM (ed.). *Voices for the Wilderness—The Sierra Club Wilderness Conference.* New York: Ballantine, 1969.

WILDERNESS SOCIETY. *Handbook on the Wilderness Act.* 729–15th Street, N.W., Washington, D.C. 20005. January, 1970.

WHYTE, WILLIAM. *Lost Landscape.* New York: Doubleday, 1968.

Miscellaneous:

LANDSBERG, HANS. *Natural Resources for U.S. Growth: A Look Ahead to the Year 2000.* Baltimore: Johns Hopkins Press, 1967.

Proceedings of the 24th Annual Purdue Industrial Waste Conference. Purdue University, Lafayette, Indiana. 1969.

Scientists Institute for Public Information. "The Environmental Cost of Electric Power." 30 East 68th Street, New York, N.Y. 10021. 1970.

Others: See publications of the Sierra Club, Wilderness Society Environmental Action. See also *The Whole Earth Catalog* and books by the great naturalists Loren Eiseley and Joseph Wood Krutch.

> *Public Interest Research Group*
> *1025–15th Street, N.W.*
> *Washington, D.C. 20005*

THE PERIODICAL LIST

There are fifteen thousand journals published regularly in the world, containing at least one million significant papers annually. That's what we meant by the knowledge explosion. Better move in close to it. We have compiled a list of forty-six magazines and journals that we believe can at least maintain you in the information flow. As a student you should be reading at least ten of these a month.

Two ways to read them. Go to the Periodical Room of your library. Pass by *Time* and *Life*. Introduce yourself to some serious magazines. Carve out a list of magazines that you understand as to editorial policy, type of readership and regular contributors. Then expand your list.

The second method is to subscribe to them, reading them as they arrive. As a student you have subscribing privileges that can cut the cost of subscriptions by as much as 50 percent. At prevailing student rates you can receive *Newsweek, Psychology Today, Esquire, The Village Voice* (weekly), *Harper's, New York Review of Books* (biweekly), *The New Republic* (forty-eight issues) for $38.58. That is cheap, folks. Go to a *college* bookstore and ask if they have any Student Rate Subscription Forms. Generally you can order all the magazines you want on one form.

Then just fill in the name of the college nearest the bookstore. Give yourself sophomore standing. You can also find the forms thumbtacked to college bulletin boards.

In the information flow, you either sink or swim.

MAGAZINES

American Heritage	Harpers
Architectural Forum	Harvard Business Review
Architectural Record	Horizon
The Atlantic Monthly	Modern Fiction Studies
Atlas	Monthly Review
Bulletin of the Atomic Scientists	The Nation
Car and Driver	National Review
Challenge	The Negro History Bulletin
Changing Times	The New Republic
Chicago Journalism Review	New York Review of Books
Commentary	The New Yorker
Commonweal	Popular Science
Consumer Reports	Psychology Today
Current	Ramparts
Ebony	Saturday Review
Esquire	Scientific American
Film Quarterly	Sports Illustrated
Forbes	"This Magazine is About Schools"
Foreign Affairs	The Washington Monthly
Fortune	

FOREIGN PERIODICALS

Economist (British)	Manchester Guardian (British)
Ekistics (Greek)	Le Monde (English edition)
New Statesman (British)	Paris Match

Belonging up there in the M's:

Mother Earth News
P.O. Box 38
Madison, Ohio 44057

Rates: One year (6 issues) / $5.00

And among the E's:

Edcentric   A Journal of Educational Change
Center for Educational Reform
2115 S. Street N.W.
Washington, D.C. 20008

Rates: One year/ $5.00

8. The Local Library

The library will be open on Wednesday between the hours of one and two P.M. and Saturday, one half hour before prayers, and at no other times. —OBERLIN COLLEGE RULES, 1867

Any criticism of libraries short of looting and burning is acceptable to most of us. Somehow they are antithetical to how we want to learn today. In the system of learning presented in this book, you'll rarely have to do an "assignment," but you'll have to use libraries, and we're sorry, but the library you need rarely exists.

In an independent education you are going to have to have access to books. More than you can buy. A study at Cornell a few years ago showed that the average student there checked out about eighty-five books per year, fifteen feet of them. It is probably edging toward one hundred books now.

In this chapter we are going to talk about a lot of things: some background on American libraries; what's wrong with them; some suggestions on ways to improve them and then advice on how the independent student can best utilize a library. We present all these opinions and thoughts because the American Library is one of the most passive institutions we have. You need information about it so that you can make it work for you.

We chat on and on about libraries because we figure that your first introduction to them went something like this:

A word about librarians and the library atmosphere. Librarians know and like books. They like reading and handling them. They like students, too. They like serving them and helping them. Don't hesitate to approach them with your problems. You will find a warm, helpful welcome. The well-run library is quiet. That's the way it should be—a place to read, to study, to do research, to be alone with your thoughts in the specially hospitable setting that only the library provides. Cherish and respect those who create and maintain this haven for you. (ABRAHAM LEE AND EUGENE S. WILSON, THE COLLEGE STUDENT'S HANDBOOK, THE DAVID WHITE COMPANY, 1965.)

And we don't think that was helpful at all. . . .

PROTECTION, STORAGE AND RETRIEVAL

Our first libraries were in the "great and ancient" tradition of the medieval universities. Very possessive places. They were depositories/repositories. In 1667 the overseers of Harvard ruled that "No scholar in the Colledge, under a Senior Sophister shall borrow a book out of the library." Books were scarce and for the elect. Haunting the sleep of librarians was the Viking or Vandal about to sack the Western Tradition. So collections were protected from readers.

But by the nineteenth century, books were no longer rare and expensive. The logistics of storage became the principal concern of libraries. A French architect, Henri Labrouste, designed the first storage library, the Bibliothèque Nationale, Paris, 1857. On the outside it was a great, domed, high-ceilinged pile of marble. On the inside he built a small skyscraper of steel beams and cast-iron columns, a gigantic rack for 900,000 books. You have seen the descendants of this cage on most campuses or in the large city libraries. The "stacks" are where you aren't supposed to go, not because you might steal, but because you will confuse the order that is maintained among the books.

Most large university libraries are in this tradition; they don't work very well. They are too big for anything but research and prestige. Once a library gets beyond a certain size the librarian has problems keeping track of the material, the average user can't get to it and the personal contacts with the staff that are necessary to a student are decreased. The changes that are needed in libraries have to do with changing those conditions in a wholesale manner.

Some things are changing. Gothic librarians are being pursued by the new demons: computers. Now the rush is into Information Retrieval Systems, book miniaturization and photocopy. This doesn't mean, let us hasten to add, that libraries are going to get better. It just means that some people are going to get more information faster. Let us listen to a

Mr. Sol Cornberg. Sol Cornberg was head of his own firm of "designers in the communication arts" when he designed one of the most "up-to-date audio-visual centers" in the country at Grand Valley State College in Michigan.

The library now being built here will contain 256 carrels each with a microphone, two loud-speakers, an eight-inch TV picture tube, and a telephone dial. Any information stored in a "use attitude" will be available to the student. There will be up to 310 audiotapes—that is, 310 talking books. These will be programmed for self-learning. In a typical day the student would go to his class or laboratory. That is, he would participate in a group learning activity. After his lesson he goes to his carrel for individual learning. There, by simply dialing a code number, he will be able to get a repeat of the lecture, excerpts as they apply to his assigned lesson, a list of problems. He will use the microphone to record his answers on tape, erase and correct them, if necessary, then dial his instructor. He then plays the tape for the instructor.

The campus library is doomed. Books are inefficient. It's not that we don't like them—my wife is a novelist, as a matter of fact—but they just aren't the best way to transmit information anymore. We don't like the laborious problems of finding information in them. Furthermore to serve a thousand students you need multiple copies. You need storage space for them. In a cabinet the size of my desk or a bit higher we can store 20,000 volumes on microfilm. Nobody can tear a page out of them. They don't smell of old vellum or glue, but you can browse through them and sit there and read them. Today's student learns more easily from a television screen than from a book. My advice is: plan no more buildings for library use. The library space is a concession to the past. (ALVIN TOFFLER, "LIBRARIES," BRICKS AND MORTARBOARDS, EDUCATIONAL FACILITIES LABORATORIES, INC., 1966.)

And there are people out ahead of him trying to find systems to codify information, put it directly onto tape so that the computer can scan itself for information stored under a list of categories.

Obviously we are dealing with someone else's need, besides the student. The C.I.A. and F.B.I. have funded much of the retrieval development. Files on everybody is a lot of files. One librarian filled with dread remarked that libraries might "grind to a halt" under the incredible input of information. Our suggestion is that if that should occur, slip in the side door, find a kindly looking librarian, ask for a stack pass and lose yourself up in the humanities mezzanine. We doubt that the machine with its current managers is going to make life better for the student. All it will do is make us more and more "informationally insecure," and subject to those with more information.

IDEAS THE LIBRARIES MIGHT TRY

To be open twenty-four hours a day. It has been tried and it has worked. Some people just function better in the wee hours.

All libraries should have "open stacks." We have to browse! (Theft is not a big problem in libraries: 5 percent).

A librarian, Bob Haro, has these suggestions for colleges: (1) students on library advisory committees; (2) library support of experimental college programs and their libraries; (3) student control of browsing collections, which might be anywhere on the campus.

Libraries should give away books. If you wonder why, quick, get this book:

Hooked on Books
Daniel Fader
Berkeley Publishing Company
1968; 244 pages

Price: $1.00 postpaid

This is an amazing book. One reformatory we know reports that about the only thing the young kids take with them when they go over the wall is the pocket books that they have been given. If the library was to give away a wide assortment of reading material, kids and adults would have a chance to get "hooked on books."

• Smoking rooms. With books in them this time. Music.

• Few libraries understand that paperbacks are not sinful and have a rightful place with their stiffer brothers. Paperbacks allow a library to have more copies and not to be so worried about rip-off and ruination. And a library should never spoil a good paperback cover with that green buckram binding. Small paperback libraries, run on the exchange principle whereby you get a book when you turn one in, could be tucked all over the campus, the town or city. We heard of one library system that had boxes of paperbacks in beauty parlors and taverns. Terrific!

Bookmobiles are a good thing. They carry up to four thousand books and periodicals and they probably do more things but that corner of the newspaper clipping is gone, so we don't know.

There should be a "reading floor." A carpeted, slightly inclined space, a soft sound system, cushions and book and magazine racks on the circumference or suspended from the ceiling. Students who prefer to lie down while studying average the same grades as those that sit at their desks, by God.

There should be outdoor reading courts with refreshments adjacent.

For the winter months, there should be some sort of pleasant snack bar. A coffee house boggles the mind. . . . Put books in it too.

In the 1920's The Carnegie Corporation funded a program that was to create subject guides and bibliographies. It was never finished. This would be a helpful thing for Independent Study students. These were to have been distributed free in the libraries.

In colleges and universities, keep Freshman classes from beginning for about ten days after registration. The freshmen should be in the library daily during this period, to learn it and do some reading in things that interest them.

A suggestion to keep the libraries from getting too big: for each book acquired by the library, one should be thrown away, discarded. An academic friend once said that throwing away books was a positive educational device.

Install some stand-up desks. Hemingway, Churchill, Wolfe. . . .

Bring birth control, draft, occult, commune, war resistance, abortion information into the library.

Each library should get itself studied, researched by a team of outside librarians, behavioral scientists and students. This team could give a profile of the clientele, the type of service offered, its quality, how the library communicates with its clientele and with itself and then the team could present a list of recommended changes and alternatives for the management to consider. There should be a press component on the team as well, I suppose, to put some muscle into the report.

• Until a new generation of teacher-librarians is created, which will be a long time, libraries should encourage any academic interests their staff people have. Then these interests, skills in particular bibliographies, should be transmitted to the clientele.

Every library should have an Independent Study Office to advise and consult with independent students. This office would act as the clearing-house for the network of independent students suggested by Ivan Illich. The office would match people according to their current interest, whether a project, book, film or record. This office would allow the library to fulfill its real function: to enable education to take place. Even the best libraries today only collect and hold information, then parcel it out to the aggressive.

HOW TO USE A LIBRARY

Now that we have looked at how libraries were, are, should be, some practical advice on how to make do.

As an independent student you have the advantage of finding a library that suits you. If there is more than one in your town, you must visit them individually. Even though you are a "non-matriculant," most college and university libraries will issue cards to town residents if they can show real need and present good references. A personal approach to the head librarian is needed, along with a written explanation of your situation as an independent student and a list of your references. The librarian should be encouraged to contact these references to hear good things said about you. Using an academic library is better than using the local public library because you can have access to better materials and the atmosphere is more supportive. You might also get invited to classes by students you meet.

Once you have found the library you will use, find your librarian. Make contact with the staff. Having a friend there is terribly important. Nose around to identify the staff people who will be able to give support. Let them know you are a serious student trying to get an education on your own through the library.

Wander all over the library. Get a student or the friendly staff person to show you around. Get acquainted with all the collections, all the rooms. Then select your space.

Browse. We can't emphasize too much the good things that happen when you browse. Just walk up and down the aisles looking at titles and covers; when one looks interesting, look through it, checking the Table of Contents, looking at the illustrations. You may be drawn into the book. It is amazing how much information you can take in this way, and somehow without the pressure to remember, you remember. Those titles will come back to you months and years later. The creative process works this way. At least 30 percent of us learn best from unorganized, uncataloged materials. The process is called "associative recall." Teachers and machines cannot match it. Browsing brings out the best in the human mind—an incredible computer.

If you have a project and don't really know where to start, ask the librarian if he/she knows where you can get a bibliography. Sometimes they can make a call to a teacher in that subject field.

Near the front entrance you will see a monster. This is the old card catalog. Alvin Toffler says that the catalog is to the library what the memory is to the mind. And you have got to get acquainted with this benevolent monster. Books are catalogued alphabetically, three different ways: by author, by title and by subject. And it is cross-referenced. You probably understand the catalog, so further information is tedious. One thing: each card has the book's Table of Contents; very helpful.

In the Reference Section you will find the trusty encyclopedias, the Reader's Guide to Periodical Literature (which, by the way, doesn't use a very comprehensive list of books, a better list is the International Index of Periodicals). Wander up and down the aisles in this section to get some sense of the material it contains.

Unless you have some urgent work to do, stop in the periodical setion each time you are in the library. Browse through the journals and magazines you wouldn't generally get to.

Most of the older libraries have large reading rooms with huge (often wonderful) tables and chairs stretched across them. Robert Sommer in his book *Personal Space* describes the territoriality of library users. We include this quote so that you may understand some of the human processes at work in the institution where you will be spending so much time:

> *Library readers protect their privacy in several ways, sometimes through offensive displays and other times through defensive measures. . . . If a reader can hold the high ground, he should be able to dominate the area effectively. To sit in the middle of a long table will protect the entire table against timid invaders who will shrink away rather than risk the occupant's displeasure, yet aggressive intruders will be able to surround the occupant on all sides, something that would place him in an extremely uncomfortable position. Against an aggressive invader, a remote position in a corner or alcove will make it physically impossible for the enemy to come close or surround the defender.*
>
> *We investigated the effectiveness of territorial markers during periods of high room density. . . . Each of the markers delayed occupation, although some were more potent than others. A sport jacket and a notebook-text-pen combination reserved the chair for the entire two hour period. Magazines piled neatly in front reserved the chair for 77 minutes, whereas the same magazines randomly scattered kept it for 32 minutes. . . . There was an interesting sidelight on the role of the person adjacent to the marked space. In all five trials with the scattered magazines, the weakest marker of the five, the potential invader questioned the "person beside" as to whether the space were vacant. As a neighbor he is held responsible for knowing the status of the adjacent space.* (ROBERT SOMMER, PERSONAL SPACE; THE BE-HAVORIAL BASIS OF DESIGN, © 1969, PRENTICE-HALL, INC., ENGLEWOOD CLIFFS, NEW JERSEY. USED BY PERMISSION.)

Work in a library. Like bartending it is something everybody should do. For the independent student it is especially useful.

Concluding thoughts about libraries:

• Once you lose your fear of libraries, the large ones can be made to serve you well. The richness and depth of some of our large libraries suggests that the barbarians have not yet swept through.

• We recommend a new guide to library use:

Who-What-When-Where-How-Why Made Easy
Mona McCormick
1971 Quadrangle Books

This is a compact, readable explanation of all the reference books you will be using. It tells what reference books are available on the subject you're concerned with, how and where to get a hold of them and how to use them. It discusses 323 reference sources; libraries and how to exploit them; dictionaries, magazines; *The New York Times* Index and encyclopedias. The middle section lists the reference books available in twenty subject areas. The book may be coming out in paperback, in which case it should be taken along on each trip to the library.

• Suggested information source for the independent student in addition to public and college libraries.

1) Newspaper libraries
2) Government Printing Office. Subscribe to the biweekly "Selected U.S. Government Publications." It's Free.

c/o Superintendent of Documents
Government Printing Office
Washington, D.C. 20402

3) Local industrial libraries and film loan offices.
4) Union libraries
5) Private research corporation libraries
6) Government agency libraries (Labor, Interior)
7) Embassies and consulate libraries and film loan services
8) Government depositories in various public libraries.
9) Law firm libraries
10) Museum libraries
11) Association libraries

Most of these sources would welcome an independent student.

• Bookstores. Throughout this book we suggest other books to get hold of. Your local bookstore will order them for you. If you become a regular visitor to a bookstore, you become known; often bookstores, particularly in small towns, will go to a great deal of effort to get a book.

TO DO

• FIND YOUR LIBRARY
• FIND YOUR LIBRARIAN
• FIND A GOOD BOOKSTORE
• READ INTO ONE HUNDRED SERIOUS BOOKS A YEAR

WITH FELLOW INDEPENDENT STUDENTS, FORM LEARNING GROUPS THAT MEET IN THE LIBRARY. ASK YOUR LIBRARIAN TO HELP YOU ORGANIZE THEM.

9. Clipping the Paper

Just like the unemployed, the independent student has time to read *and* clip the daily newspaper. A boon! Enjoy your paper because you're going to be reading one daily, to dig out leads, facts, ideas for your learning projects. An hour a day, perhaps.

The paper is full of raw, unorganized, slanted material, but there it is. With careful reading and clipping of the paper you can beat the high cost of information. Read, clip and file the articles/stories relevant to your studies and future projects; this way you can cheaply put sophisticated information into your education. Newspapers are invaluable to your independent education. Some of the papers may even be getting better.

The technique of clipping the paper:

Find and subscribe to a strong daily and Sunday paper such as

The New York Times
Washington Post
Los Angeles Times
San Francisco Chronicle
Boston Globe
Chicago Tribune
Atlanta Constitution
Christian Science Monitor
St. Louis Post Dispatch
Dallas Times-Herald
Houston Chronicle
New Orleans Times Picayune

Wall Street Journal
Portland Oregonian
Seattle Post Intelligence

Work it into your daily schedule.

First, read the front page headlines to see what the editors believe is important. The front page is a "show case" to get you to buy and read the paper; there isn't too much information in it. Spend a minute or so running through the lead articles. If you are in a hurry, run your finger down the center of the column, forcing your eye to scan. The eye will pick up "minimal cues" to enable you to get an idea of the material. *The New York Times* plays its leading news story in the last column to the right, in column eight. Other papers have their own editorial customs, which you will learn. In many papers, an interesting "by-line" article will begin in the center columns on the bottom of the front page, then be continued in the back pages of the paper. The size of a headline indicates the weight the editors attach to a particular story.

Some papers have a News Summary on the second page.

Go through the news section page by page glancing at the headlines, looking at the pictures, having a good time.

We generally have at least one or two subject areas that we are clipping in, so we circle the headlines of articles that are to be clipped later.

After you have finished surveying the news sections, particularly the local news, go into the special sections where you have interests. The Women's Pages are evolving into readable sections. In the 1960's they held the "arts" columns with their powerful critics, who believed culture was going to save us. Today, more and more politics are coming onto the Women's Pages; Women's Liberation is being given some play. It is fascinating to watch a newspaper respond to the "changing role of women in our society" in the pages of what used to be the worst section of any paper. It may be significant that the only left-leaning columnist in the *Washington Post,* Nicholas von Hoffman, is on the front page of the style section.

Once you have gone through the whole paper, go back through those sections that need more reading. When you come to an article that has been circled, read it carefully this time.

After you have finished reading the paper for the day, go through it, *tearing out* the pages that have articles that you want to clip and save. Put these full pages on a "save" pile. *Discard the rest.*

Once a week go through the pages you have saved and reread the articles, *underlining* as you read. Then clip the article from the page and put it into a file that you keep for that month's clippings. As you clip, write the date and newspaper near the headline.

Once a month, paste all the clippings on sheets of paper; in this process reread the articles again. This is an important step. To make clippings work, they must be pasted flat onto sheets of paper. Use rubber cement.

Then file those month's clippings under the file headings that you are currently clipping for. If an article is worth keeping, but is not now in any subject area you're interested in, file it according to the month it appeared.

The annual purge. Once a year, go through your clipping files, rereading them, throwing away the outdated.

We pointed out in the chapter on "Learning Skills" that we forget most of what we read. This clipping system reinforces your memory by having you read important articles at least *four* times:

1) The first reading
2) The weekly clipping session
3) The monthly paste-up and filing
4) The annual purge

Wherever you are, you should subscribe to the daily and Sunday *New York Times*. This will cost $95.00 a year, airmailed. *The Times* is a newspaper of record—it prints the precise words of important pronouncements. Its news staff is about the best available. Even the government in Washington learns what it itself is doing by reading *The Times*. The Pentagon Papers didn't come as a surprise to careful readers of *The Times*. It was all there through the years, tucked into the last paragraphs of the daily articles on Vietnam. The headlines were always about "body counts," while the final paragraphs contained the bits of the mosaic that eventually caught the government. We have a lawyer friend who worked at the Justice Department. He says that *The Times* is a major source of information about the department for its employees.

Most newspapers do not report much of anything in depth. Once a year they turn a couple of reporters loose for a series or an exposé. *The Times* covers more things in depth than any other paper. Their international news section in a year will report on almost every country in the world, usually with competence.

Libraries receive *The New York Times* Index twice a month. Every article is indexed there along with a capsule report of it. Most libraries now contain *The New York Times* on microfilm. If you can't afford the daily and Sunday *Times* or if you have a suitable local paper, subscribe to the Sunday edition of *The Times*. It contains the "News of the Week in Review," *The Times* Magazine Section and the Book Review Section. The "News of the Week" offers analyses and interpretive articles by correspondents. Excellent.

Forget about their editorial pages, as you can forget any editorial page. It is, as someone said, the process of the publisher's accommodating themselves to an outrage. Read the "Op Ed Page." *The Times* brings to reading a newspaper richness. There are about 1,800 newspapers left in this country. Read *The New York Times*. And tear it apart.

10. A Personal Learning Space

The independent student needs a private learning space of some sort: a den, office or study. A space to organize and manage; a turf, a place to be alone, to concentrate without distraction. A flexible space with visual and acoustical privacy, various work stations, conversational and reading areas can be created easily in a basement, garage, attic or rented space.

Make some space available. If you are living at home, discuss with your parents the possibilities there of a private learning space. We feel that the typical bedroom with the little desk in the corner is not going to give students the freedom to come and go, work when they want to, establish their own habits. Dr. Christopher Alexander, Professor of Architecture at the University of California, Berkeley, writing in *Ekistics* magazine notes some changes he foresees for our living environments as a result of new social and psychological demands:

> 13. *The teenage room/cottage/studio. Teenage a period of exploration and identity seeking—new in industrial society, since choice of adult life not automatic. Require possibility of exploration while at home. (Silverstein)*
>
> HYPOTHESES
> a. *Relation between parents and teenage children better if children have place of their own, private access. (Clinical subjective reports)*
> b. *Where room close to parents children report constrained feeling.*
> c. *Incidence of run-aways higher in homes where this relation does not exist; lower in homes where it does.*

We feel that a student who has decided not to go to college has the same need to be "away from home" as the college student who has a dormitory room or an off-campus apartment. For reasons of sociability or economy it may prove feasible to live at home, but a private space is a requirement. Look around town for some cheap office space. Ask a friend to rent their garage. An apartment is not needed, only a ventilated temperature-controlled space; windows aren't needed.

Move everything out; survey the space you have secured. Don't move anything into it for a day or two. Get acquainted with the form of the room. Let it assert itself. Stand in the middle of the empty space; extend your arms. Stand there a few moments. Walk around the edge of the space, against the wall. These exercises will help you to organize the space; they also will keep you from filling it up with unnecessary furniture. Keep it simple. Perhaps there are partitions that should come down, doors that can be taken off their hinges to open spaces.

Decide upon the basic areas: desk (both sit-down and stand-up types), reading and conversation. If you have one large space you will want to enclose part of it. This is easily done. At a used-lumber or house wrecking yard buy two or three sheets of one-half-inch plywood in the standard four-by-eight-foot size. Used plywood is cheap. Buy some two-by-fours while you're there. Don't build yet.

The desk. You need a long, clear space. The hollow-core door is still the best. They are 6 feet 6 inches long, although you can get smaller closet doors that are useful. A damaged or "factory second" door costs two dollars to four dollars at a used-lumber yard.

There are a number of ways to support the door. The standard desk height is 29 inches. Building blocks will work. Hardware stores carry wrought-iron and wooden legs for doors, but these are flimsy. Two methods that work: obtain two metal and corrugated cardboard file cabinets for about sixteen dollars. Large office supply houses carry them. They come unassembled. With the metal base they raise the door to a normal height. The heavy cardboard is strengthened by the metal frame. The files will support five hundred pounds. The door and filing cabinets make a simple, easily movable desk. The second method is to buy four metal sawhorse brackets at Sears and Roebuck, cut two 30-inch pieces of two-by-four for the top rails and eight 25-inch lengths for the legs, which are inserted in the brackets. Now you have two carpenter sawhorses. Lay the door on them and you have a desk. It instantly dissasembles for moving. It looks good. At an office supply store buy some plastic trays for paper and writing materials.

Place the desk facing a wall. No one can concentrate looking out a window.

The chair. Get a comfortable swivel chair; for fifteen dollars at a used-furniture store you can get an adjustable office chair that probably cost seventy-five dollars new.

Visual display. Buy a package of corkboard. It comes four 12-inch panels to a package, with adhesive backing. Four panels arranged around your desk hold the right amount of paper. Too much tackboard and the eye wearies. The eye is attracted to horizontal movement (lateral scan). The tackboard holds the paper so that it can signal the eye, demand action.

Storage. For file storage get a secondhand two-drawer file cabinet or use the door file cabinet system described above. Don't get the tall four-drawer model. The top of the two-drawer provides a second work-space. Position this at right angles to the desk. Put the phone on it.

For books and other objects go to the shelving department at Sears or a hardware store. Either buy the steel rack shelving which comes unassembled in two-foot, four-foot and six-foot sections, or buy the "standard and bracket" shelving which is attached to the wall. It is useful to have two shelves right above your desk for files and reference books.

A second work station. Many people like to have a second work station, a stand-up one. A secondhand drafting table is possible or construct one out of the plywood and two-by-fours. The leading edge should be about 43 inches high with a gentle upward slope. The dictionary can go on this table.

Space definition. Returning to the problem of the large open room. Now that you have a sense of the space, start experimenting with the plywood. What size office feels most comfortable? Where are visual screens needed? With these screens you don't need doors. To make them, cut the plywood in the lengths required to partially enclose the space. The screens are to be 60 inches tall; the plywood which is in 48-inch widths must be raised one foot. Cut two-by-fours into 3-foot lengths and nail them onto the plywood, two to a section to make legs 12 inches long. Join the sections with large hinges so that they can be shifted. Now paint them.

In college dorms, women's rooms average 112 square feet of floor-space; men's average 106 square feet.

Acoustics. If the space is large or there is an outside noise source, put a rug on the floor; hang drapes of some sort; keep mood music going on the hi-fi; put up ceiling tile. Put a rug down in any case.

Lighting. An adjustable crane lamp, clamped to your desk is the best. Two will light most study spaces. Avoid "hot-spots" (unshaded lights), and fluorescents (they make everyone look awful).

THE BEST LEARNING SPACE WE'VE HEARD ABOUT

"One" in San Francisco. "One" occupies a large, abandoned chocolate factory/warehouse at 1380 Howard Street. "One" is a communal working, living, learning organization founded in 1970 by a mixed group of architects, "street people," lawyers, community organizers, men, women, children, artists. They rented the old building and reworked it into various studios and offices that are rented to members who pay some rent, apparently not much. Some people live there as well, singly and in families. The administration is by long meetings and consensus. The professionals do not dominate. "One" is an example of a city rejuvenating itself through finding new uses for old buildings. Jane Jacobs described the process in *The Death and Life of Great American Cities* (Random House, 1961).

It is more than that. It is a grand model for new learning communities. Every town and city has old buildings at reasonable rents. Student collectives could be organized around the acquisition and remodeling of buildings like the chocolate factory. Paul Goodman has reminded us that the medieval practice of protesting students and tutors seceding from universities and moving to new places is still viable.

A few students and tutors could pool their resources, rent a loft, build screens as we suggested and move their learning activities into it. A learning collective, based in a single building that had been organized to encourage communication as well as privacy, would stand a fair chance of surviving. It should be tried.

For more information about new communities designed by the people who live in them, contact:

Sym-Bas Inc.
c/o "One"
1380 Howard Street
San Francisco, California 94103

11. Woman as Student

It is probable that the first student to break out of *institutional* higher education will be that already overprivileged person, The White American Male. He will be joined by some women, but they will be few in number.

For those women who, for one reason or another, have to stay in school we wrote the following in hopes that they can change the nature of their education and the nature of the institution that is giving it. But understand that we urge women to quit college also.

Women's Liberation came cracking into the college halls in 1968–69. But got stalled somewhere in the student union long before it reached classes, faculty lounges and administration offices.

Although women went into real leadership positions in radical campus organizations, male chauvinism was and is the norm in the student movement, where one would think things would be different. What then is the outlook for women students?

Women, best listen to a couple of old trained chauvinists when they warn you that in the immediate years ahead it will be difficult to acquire an education that will

1) leave your creative abilities intact;
2) leave any enthusiasm for learning;
3) leave you with a positive sense of your worth;
4) leave you with the knowledge that you will make equal contributions to any activity on the basis of your education, abilities/talents or who you are as a person.

Colleges and universities are having no real problems admitting women to classes and degrees, but understand clearly that higher education in America is for men. You should understand the nature of your dilemma. Independent Study may be for you.

The differences between women and men in America are made quite early; but little girls are not made in heaven: they are made when mother denies them the rough and tumble because it is not passive (ladylike). Little boys are encouraged to be aggressive (manly little fellows). Girl babies receive much more attention, fondling, than little boys. Boys are encouraged from this early age to be self-reliant, independent. They are learning the skills of the dominant sex. Girls are learning the supposed connection between achievement, tomboyishness and old maids.

The man-child, aware of similarities between himself and his father and of differences between himself and his mother, aware and also envious of his father's strength and power, identifies with his father and strives in various way to be like him. As Tyler has pointed out, the variety of male roles in our society, associated with the variety and prominence of occupations in men's lives, channels the boy's identifications importantly, although not solely, along occupational lines. The father, uncle, older brother, neighborhood men, all go to work, come home from work, talk about work (as well as baseball and politics, which are also male dominated), reinforcing the boy's impression that maleness and occupation are more or less synonymous. Men come to the house or apartment in connection with work which the boy has a chance to observe: meter readers, bill collectors, milkmen, mailmen, plumbers and others. The boy, whose father was at first his only male object of identification, finds that he can resemble a number of other males and assume a variety of masculine roles, can choose his identification on the basis of what appeals to him most. This is less true of the girl-child whose adult counterparts more often work at home, or, if they go to work, tend to talk about it less than the man and seem less involved in their occupations.

Tyler (1951) has shown that in line with these observations small boys' interests are more likely to agree with their measured aptitudes than those of little girls. —DONALD E. SUPER, CAREER DEVELOPMENT: SELF-CONCEPT THEORY, COLLEGE ENTRANCE EXAMINATION BOARD, NEW YORK, 1963.

As if that weren't enough, just read this clipping from the *Baltimore Sun,* March 9, 1971.

London (AP) —Boys develop larger vocabularies than girls because they have more freedom than girls, says a British schoolteacher.

Girls read more than boys, but boys learn more words because of the wider variety of experience their freedom gives them, he says.

Rothwell Bishop, who teaches at Slough, near London, wrote in the journal, "Educational Research," of a 12-year-old boy who made a 400-mile round trip in a day for "train spotting"—watching railroad locomotives.

A girl would not have been allowed to make such a trip, he said.

Rothwell found that children learn as many, if not more, new words during vacations as during schooltime, because the experience of being out and about is the important thing.

By the high school years we have created a young woman conditioned to accept a less effectual role in society and someone who probably has not been "out and about" in as many positive, open-ended learning situations as the boys around her.

In high school girls do get better grades than boys. Indeed at all levels of U.S. education the women will get the better grades. From our high school days (1950's) we remember that girls were getting better grades than us. No problem. We quite accurately sensed that the girls were simply playing more of the games that comprised high school than we were. With all that "studying" it would be difficult to learn. Girls did assignments on time, did extra problems, read more, had better handwriting, didn't horse around, paid attention and didn't do as well on tests. High school was a perfect place for girls to get grades. And it wasn't their fault.

The channeling into female roles has continued. A 1970 nationwide study of interests in high school subjects reported by the Educational Testing Service gave this ranking:

BOYS' INTERESTS	GIRLS' INTERESTS
1) *Industrial Arts*	1) *Home Economics*
2) *Physical Sciences*	2) *Secretarial*
3) *Business*	3) *Foreign Languages*
4) *Biology*	4) *Art*
5) *Social Sciences*	5) *English*
6) *Mathematics*	6) *Business*
7) *Secretarial*	7) *Social Studies*
8) *Foreign Languages*	8) *Music*
9) *Art*	9) *Biology*
10) *English*	10) *Mathematics*
11) *Music*	11) *Physical Sciences*
12) *Home Economics*	12) *Industrial Arts*

By 1970 Women's Liberation had not reached into the American high school. Ironically the female fiefdoms of Home Economics and Secretarial "Arts" are still competing for the girls. Giving them smashing opportunities to cook creamed chicken and Brussels sprouts for Marine sergeants recruiting the guys on Armed Forces Day and then of course letting the bright girls type for the principal.

The college years. A few facts and figures randomly arranged from some good research we got hold of (American Association of Higher Education, Report number 5, "The Undergraduate Woman," by Patricia Cross).

• Twenty years ago 70 percent of college students were men.

• Today women are about 41 percent of the college population.

• The number of women in the labor force has increased at the same rate (5 percent each decade) to the same percentage: 42 percent of workers are women.

• Nine out of ten girls graduating from high school today will work at a paid job sometime in their lives. There is about twenty-five years of employment outside the home ahead of the average high school female graduate.

• Only 25 percent of female college freshmen want their future occupation to center around the home.

• In national tests, at the senior level, men score higher in social and natural sciences, women score higher in the humanities.

• In the spring of 1970, for example, 46 percent of the freshmen women at Berkeley made averages of B or better, compared with 39 percent of the men.

• Women with high academic ability have high aspirations, and when asked to indicate what jobs they would like to have, would enjoy, show a great deal of enthusiasm for professional positions. But when they are asked to be "realistic," the only job that is likely to be realized is that of high school teacher.

• Median income for all women with B.A.s employed in 1969 was $7,396; for all men with B.A.s, $12,960. After four years of college, therefore, women earn only 57.1 percent as much as men.

• A bright, but poor male has a much better chance of going to college than has his equally able sister.

• Women have much lower confidence in their academic ability than men. Despite their higher grades.

• But it appears that women are shucking the old roles, at least in their minds. One college questioned its freshmen women in 1968 about "full freedom from domestic responsibilities in order to work on an equal footing with men at all occupational levels." Only 19 percent of the women advocated this equality. By 1971 53 percent of the women, now seniors, endorsed the statement.

Another study of women college dropouts revealed these things:

• College dropout rate is about equal for men and women.

• Women who do drop out are less likely to return.

• Women generally do not leave college for strictly academic reasons.

• Men who drop out are, to a high degree, non-conformists, perhaps highly original, antiauthoritarian. The ones the colleges need.

• Female dropouts tend to be depressed about themselves; they do not feel a part of the college. Dropping out for women is not the positive step that it often is for men.

> *The feminist movement is the first to combine effectively the "personal" with the "political." It is developing a new way of relating, a new political style, one that will eventually reconcile the personal— always the feminist prerogative—with the public, with the "world outside" to restore that world to its emotions, and, literally, to its senses.* —SHULAMITH, FIRESTONE, DIALECTIC OF SEX, WILLIAM MORROW & CO., INC., 1970.

SOME ISSUES AND ACTIONS

Feminist groups on various campuses have organized in the past around these conditions:

• The lack of gynecological services on campus, *i.e.,* abortion counseling, birth control information and pills.

• Unequal wages and salaries for female members of the college community, from professors to kitchen staff.

• Lack of child care centers to enable mothers to attend class.

• The low ratio of women professors to men. This condition hurts both men and women students.

• Housing regulations that limit women's enrollment to the number of dormitory spaces available. The success of open dorms on many campuses is a good argument against the housing quotas.

• Parietal rules that unfairly discriminate against women, such as dorm sign outs, hours, campusing for infractions, etc. We just heard of a situation that had the library open all night during exam week for everybody but the women who had to be in their dorms by 1:00 A.M.

• Channeling of women into nursing, teaching, home ec, and away from science and math. Counselors rarely encourage a girl to follow the path she really wants to.

• The absence in the curriculum of courses on **Women**.

Patricia Cross, mentioned above, suggests to administrations these actions:

• Improved career counseling.

• Dissemination of information about changing patterns in women's lives.

• Campus visits by outstanding women.

FOR THE INDIVIDUAL WOMAN STUDENT

This is going to be an attempt at advice. Some educated hunches that may help a woman student through the morass of maleness in our colleges.

Decide that you don't want to be a teacher. Don't take any of those ridiculous education courses. Remember that the market for teachers is drying up, there is not a good future there and further, most teachers are not good for young people anyway. If later you find that you *want* to teach, getting a license is not a big problem and the *best* schools won't require them anyway. So take the courses you want.

Ask advice of other female students when registering for particular professors. If a professor, male or female, expects better work from men, it's probably best to stay out of that class. Prejudice can be a subtle thing.

Women tend to participate less than men. One class will demonstrate that to you. It goes back to early childhood training. Fight any tendency you have to withdraw, unless the class is demonstrably bullshit and you can't bear to attend to it. Ask questions. Defend your positions.

If you are having problems with a particular course relating to lack of confidence and hesitation to get more involved, see if there are some other girls in that position. Form a women's cell to support one another.

You might need such a cell to "raise the consciousness" of a male student or teacher who is oppressing you as a woman. If someone keeps putting you down, design a little action to orient the men to your rights to equal learning. If you are convinced of an injustice, disrupt a class. Or at least talk to it.

Sororities. Doubt it. Perhaps there is a sorority that is seriously academic and not filled with that type of "overachiever" sister who is at college fulfilling parental expectations and who ultimately becomes an authoritarian, conservative suburban housewife and mother. The type really exists. If you are considering a sorority, be careful.

A sad irony is that the technology of the late twentieth century is going to accomplish what the nineteenth century should have: the liberation of men and of women from cultural roles. Sexual differentiation is not necessary or useful to the machine. A man and woman checking each other out when the cards need sorting is counterproductive for the machine. So we are afraid of an alliance between Women's Liberation and an unhuman technology.

But in balance we support the full rights of the silent women we have seen at many experimental colleges and their more stylish, but equally silent sisters at the straight schools. And remember that chauvinism on college campuses has long hair and beards, is barefoot. Many young men have absorbed the news and views of the women's movement with the ease that comes with successfully having let their hair grow, survived dope and the Beatles' breakup. These men assume that you are liberated and that they have done it.

We suggest that you take any course available on Women or Women's Liberation. Two hundred were offered in more than one hundred colleges in September of 1971. And if your college doesn't have any such courses. . . .

Or drop out, and join the independent students.

12. Worldliness

Go through this world simply, lightly, without much of anything. "Simplify, simplify, simplify," commanded Thoreau. "Simplicate and add lightness," added Buckminster Fuller, who also said, "Property is obsolete."

Most Americans are threatened by obsolete property they haven't discarded. Property gathers more property without decisions being made. Quickly we are working to support our property and to add to it. Soon we have so much property and unnecessary addictions to candlesticks, skis and drapes that we can't move without a big truck and a damn good reason.

Ruth Benedict in *Patterns of Culture* describes property-limiting customs of the Indians of the Canadian northwest coast. Annually they placed all of their household goods onto a fire, thus ridding their longhouses of evil spirits and the year's broken pots. The tradition of the "potlatch" ceremony in which boasting, competing men gave away or destroyed their wealth, also served to limit the power of material goods in a well-off Indian society. Americans have few such customs. The "spring cleaning" restores only the floors and removes only some clutter to the basement or attic. The worst of it may make its way to the Goodwill or St. Vincent de Paul. No dance, no ceremony.

It is true that many young Americans are getting control of property. They are trying to create a "scarcity culture" or as Margaret Mead calls it, a "non-cumulative" society. But it is also true that most youth communes are cluttered with broken sofas and chairs, piles of newspapers, old TV and hi-fi sets and rotting suitcases. They are not yet good places to live. Communal societies learn to discipline property or they collapse.

The Amish and Shaker societies learned this long ago. Their requirement of simplicity goes far beyond abstinence, mere doing without. It is a conscious decision to hold only those things for which there is an absolute need, that are of a compatible style, are beautiful without excessive adornment and are of quality construction.

There are skills to dealing with personal property—learned skills that become pleasures. The best teacher of these skills is Thoreau. In the clearest English he lays out his system of living at Walden and why he chose to live there. Everything is of a piece. He wanted to leave many things behind, but he wanted to live well. He enjoyed the lovely stone which served as a paperweight, but it required too much dusting. All his possessions were selected with precision. Thoreau was among the first to realize that industrial technology created a large, new problem of abundance. He was trying to deal with it. Read at least the first chapters of *Walden*.

The military life, on the other hand, is not recommended, but the army footlocker is. It's a way to organize your material possessions. You know where everything is, that it has a place. The footlocker is clean, orderly and as it doesn't expand, you don't accumulate. A footlocker can simplify your life. Live out of a footlocker for a year and read *Walden* three times. It will leave you intolerant of clutter and selective of what you own.

Do this: place all your personal property on the floor. Your clothes, bags, cameras, boxes of papers, golf clubs, twirling batons, furniture. Get it all out and evaluate each piece for its utility, value, beauty and emotional attachments. Have a box ready for Goodwill and another for unfixables. Cut down your possessions ruthlessly. Estimate how many footlockers of gear you have collected. Would it be easy to move across country? Would you go over the 150-pound luggage limit of the buses? Keep yourself transportable. A single person with kitchen utensils, furniture, clothes, bed and bike should be able to go into a rented Econoline van.

When you must make purchases out of need or because you are rewarding yourself for succeeding in a major economy, like taking the bus rather than a car, go to the library and read what the consumer testers report on the available products. Three magazines are especially good: *Consumer Reports, Consumer Bulletin* and the Kiplinger magazine, *Change*. Read the annual editions, which will allow you to quickly assemble informed opinions.

WORLDLY POSSESSIONS

Keep them few and simple.
Regularly inventory and occasionally purge them.
Keep your possessions light and transportable.
Have some beautiful things.
Buy only what you need.
Investigate alternative products carefully.
Generally buy the best you can afford.
Have few possessions that you cannot afford to lose.
Consider future storage and shipping when buying a new possession.

A BUYING GUIDE

TYPEWRITERS. Typewriters can last for decades; buy a good one. Buy a portable; don't get stuck with a heavy office-size machine, even though they type better. Buy a manual portable because they are lighter (9–17 pounds) than electric ones (25 pounds), less likely to break down and are not dependent upon the proper current.

The basic typewriter is the Olivetti Lettera 32. Its cast-aluminum frame will absorb much punishment. The Lettera 32 weighs only 11½ pounds and is less than four inches high. It is small enough to go nicely into a suitcase without its case, saving another bag to carry. Strictly a utilitarian typewriter, it does not have the "feel" of the better machines, but is perfectly adequate for the duffer. The Lettera 32 costs anywhere from sixty to seventy dollars.

The better manuals are the Olympia SF Delux (12 pounds), the Facit, and the Hermes 3000, which is probably the best all-around manual typewriter. It weighs 17 pounds, costs around $125. A beautiful machine.

If you want to buy an electric portable go to Sears and Roebuck. The Sears Celebrity Electric costs about $150 and weighs 25½ pounds. Smith-Corona makes it for Sears. The same machine at a Smith-Corona outlet may cost $35 dollars more. All the Sears models are acceptable.

The ultimate electric portable is the Smith-Corona Cordless Electric, a combination battery and AC/DC model. The State Department and White House have bought it for overseas assignments. It will run ten hours straight before it needs recharging. It runs on any electricity in the world, 110/220 volts, 50–60 cycles. If you can afford $220 and are going to study overseas, look into this one. Keep it under the bed.

Two things before you buy any typewriter: first, shop around. Prices vary on typewriters. You may be able to get an electric portable for one hundred dollars, on sale. Second, "store-check" the typewriter before taking it home. If it doesn't feel right, try another.

RADIOS. The best portable radios are the Grundig TR-301, AM-FM, $60; the Sony Delux 4-Band FM-AM, SW$_1$-SW$_2$, $70, the Tanberg and the Panasonic RF-759.

CAMERAS. Yashicas, Minoltas, Nikon, Canon, etc. But perhaps all you need is a Kodak Instamatic camera. The old Argus C-3, if you can find one secondhand, is the most batterproof camera we know of. Start with a simple camera, work up to what is needed. Many people own cameras that are smarter than they.

TELEVISION. *Consumer Reports* says that the Wards Airline, 9-inch diagonal is the best small TV, if you want a TV; $99. Or buy a reconditioned TV.

CASSETTE TAPE RECORDER. The Norelco 175 at $80; the Ampex or any of the Sonys.

STEREO. The GE Trimline 500 at $100 is cheap and has a "pleasant sound." Hi-fi experts we talked to recommended the Zenith portables.

SLEEPING BAGS. Spend a bit of money. Anywhere from $60 to $80 for a "rip-stop nylon, downfilled, baffle-seamed, differentially-cut, mummy-style, good for 20 degrees." Don't skimp on a sleeping bag. Check *The Whole Earth* catalogs for sources or just go to Sears at sale time. When you travel, take a bag so hosts don't have to round up sheets and blankets.

A BACKPACK. We prefer "hand or shoulder-carry" bags, but you may be hitching and camping. Spend about $25 for a rip-stop, nylon packsack with aluminum frame.

13. Moving Out

The university as we know it was created by foreign students seeking a sort of temporary citizenship from the hardships of being an alien in a medieval town. In the late twelfth and early thirteenth century, concentrations of scholars (masters and students) at Paris, Palermo and Bologna caused thousands of young men to travel to these towns from all over Europe. The traveling student is a stock character in medieval literature and theater. Almost by definition a university student is someone who has moved out and is on his own.

In our original outline for this section we spent a lot of words on VW buses and why you needed one or access to one to be a student. It was a cheap mode (as such modes go), had a flexible internal space that allowed trucking, camping, sleeping and could go long distances if asked. And VW seemed to be a Model A for the times. A basic tool. *The Whole Earth Catalog*, who we rarely argue with, treated it to competence. And finally, Californians called it "Good."

Don't buy into wheels. As a student you can't afford it. A car is going to cost at least one thousand dollars a year, probably closer to two thousand, just to operate. It takes two or three months of someone's labor for such funding. Irv Taylor's article in *The Mother Earth News*, May, 1970, goes into good detail on the economic and emotional costs of car owning. He also describes a system that will wean you away from your car over a thirty-day period if you are already infected. Start by leaving it at home, taking the bus, walking, then with the money you save, buy a ten-speed bike as a reward.

VOLKSWAGENS. How long can the 1930's keep going? The Beetle was designed in the early thirties and everything about it is German and pre-war, much like our space program. We're not purists, the thing seems to be getting better looking, stockier. But one of the great questions of our times is whether the quality is going down year by year. We have heard that the best VW is made in France. Undoubtedly a pagan story.

Some things about the Volkswagen:

1) Maintain it yourself. That's the point. Buy the book *How To Keep Your Volkswagen Alive* by John Muir. It is 242 pages long. It costs $5.50 from John Muir Productions, Box 613, Santa Fe, New Mexico 87501. It is chummily written, takes one through all the parts and processes from holding a wrench to repairing the differential. There is also a section on buying a secondhand VW. Good.

2) VWs do wear out; sometimes soon. And they can nickle and dime you to death.

3) They tend to topple over, particularly in wind and rain and in corners. They steer themselves. New York State and New Jersey have done statistical studies of accidents, what kind of vehicle, types of casualties, frequencies, who was at fault, etc. Volkswagen was shown to be the least safe car to be in. They are not agile, they lose the big arguments.

4) They are poorly built up front. No front end protection. No iron engine, only the flimsy tin.

5) Despite the literature, VWs are not meant to run fast all day. Keep them around 60 mph and they last.

6) Women VW drivers are excellent.

7) The VW van is underpowered, underbraked and is especially prone to fall over. But you feel a he-person driving it. Sort of a rig.

8) Especially in California, vans are a culture, fixing them up, coloring them, living in them. It's because the van approaches Art. Sheer rickety.

THE CAMPER. That's the pickup under the mobile home. Don't do it either. They are as unsafe as they look. *Consumer Reports* did one of their typical in-depth eight-month studies. The houses fall off the pickups easily, the pickups do not have enough springing for the weight, not one of the models tested (Chevy, Ford, International) had adequate brakes. They too fall over. *CR* did recommend those tent-trailer deals, if anybody is interested.

THE VAN. Our buddy and research assistant, Pat Zimmer, said that "the van, you dumb guys, is the thing." The American van. And we looked around the campuses and the road and she was right. Hadn't noticed that the folks had turned to vans. Econolines, Step-vans, Chevys,

Dodges. Been seeing some well set-up ones. The American vans are probably going to be safer than the VW. Better handling and brakes. Possibly easier maintenance too. The Step-van delivery truck is a great space. A commune was living in one in Mexico. We asked and they said they were happy. Seen some jolly old U.S. Post Office trucks too. Some of them have character. (See *Mother Earth News,* No. 8.)

THE BIKE. The bike thing looks big. We can only hope. Foldables, tandems and five- and ten-speed bikes. Going to sell more bikes than cars in 1972. In some places like New York City and Portland, Oregon, bikes and the right to ride them safely are becoming political issues. Bikes strike fear into highway lobbyists. Students, rather strangely, don't seem to be riding the bikes. And you rarely see a freak on a bike. The big emphasis now is on the ten-speed bike. Over a hundred dollars. That is fine, but not city-saving. A sure-fire People's Bike, like the good-for-twenty-years model they are making in China to the amazement of some recent American visitors, that's what is needed.

Anybody's Bike Book
Tom Cuthbertson
1971

From:
Ten Speed Press
2510 Bancroft Street
Berkeley, California 94704

$3.00, postpaid

HITCHHIKING. The streets and highways of America must be filled with young people on the road, hitchhiking. Do it, they're your roads as well as the automobile/oil industry's.

A fairly decent little book is available, useful for the person new to long-distance hitchhiking. *The Hitchhiker's Handbook* by Tom Grimm, 1970. It is published by Vagabond Press, Ltd., P.O. Box 83, Laguna Beach, California 92652. Cost: $1.95. Sort of book one can show to one's parents as well, to let them learn of processes like hitchhiking. It discusses the need to:

1) Stand on the shoulder.
2) Travel light, a backpack for the correct image.
3) Carry a sign.
4) Check out the driver.
5) Look as straight as possible.
6) Smile.

We are seriously urging students to hitchhike as a decent, honorable, cheap, educational way to travel. We think it is fairly safe. At this point in time, women should probably not travel alone. A young man and woman have no problems getting rides and there is little possibility of anything untoward occurring to a couple.

Phil Jones, once a student at Antioch, spent the summer of 1971 on the road. He wandered in the other day returning some books. He told us some grand hitchhiking stories.

Phil says that toward San Francisco there are so many hitchhikers that they must line up at the approaches to freeways. He said it was like waiting for the bumper cars at a carnival when he was a kid. Except for Washington State, which he had to diagonal across because of its foul antihitchhiking law, there is much more "warmth" in the West toward hitchhikers than in the East. One problem is trying to keep a clear head. Folks in cars and merry vans offered him tastes and tokes all the way. From Wisconsin to the West Coast, he was in a cycle of friendships and encounters. A real community grew on Route 90. About a dozen people were hitchhiking in his cycle. They would travel independently during the day and more or less by accident arrive in the same park for the night. Lots of U.S. Department of Agriculture food from welfare vagabonds fed them well. And in the evenings they told stories of "Big Foot," northern California's mountain man-ape and the old "Trike Man" who peddles a large trike across the Trans-Canada. Gathered that the Wife of Bath would have enjoyed this company.

Phil says to carry a good down bag, a nylon mountain tent, a large piece of plastic and Woolite.

"The road provides."

AIRPLANE. Youth fares. It is *not* a student fare. It is for anybody under twenty-two. Independent students note. All the major carriers have them. They generally run one-quarter to one-third off. All of them require that you purchase a Youth Fare Card; shouldn't cost more than three dollars. You'll need a good legal document that will show you are under twenty-two (birth certificate or driver's license). Any card is good for any airline. And the card is a good I.D.

You travel "space-available." There are no reservations. When you know your plans, phone the reservations desk and ask about the probability of a youth fare getting on board for the particular flight you are interested in. The reservationist will try to give you an informed opinion. Flying Student Fare you get a seat *after* regular, full-fare standbys and military standbys. Generally youth fares get on board. It is first come, first served. Get there early to be high on the waiting list. On weekends and holidays of course, you might end up waiting through a couple or more flights.

Flying jet is efficient, once in the air. But, more basically, flying is *waiting*. The skilled air traveler is one who knows how to wait. Now to say a few obvious things about waiting.

• As soon as you have settled the ticket and departure business, investigate the terminal facility. Wander through it, noting the services, impulse-to-buy shops, eating and drinking alternatives, observation areas and good places to sit.

• Take along a good book, but one that you will realistically want to read. Don't depend upon the newsstands/terminal bookstore. Some of them are large, but they are weighted toward Harold Robbins and Vance Packard. Pack some reading and writing material on the top of your carry-on.

• A well-equipped terminal will have a "Computer I.Q. Quiz Machine." Fifty cents into one will help you blow twenty minutes. Highly recommended.

• Study your fellow waiting passengers. From details of clothing and behavior try to figure out who they are and what they are doing in the terminal. Then ask the question of yourself. Then think about the unrelieved poverty of the 1970's airline experience. And wonder why it couldn't be better.

> *A behavioral scientist with "The Environmental Design Group," an architectural consulting company in San Francisco, wrote an interesting paper for the Seattle-Tacoma Airport Authority. It is about the phenomena of Waiting. "Waiting and Design." He said that airports are uniform at the expense of the individual, people are not accessible to one another, people cannot act themselves, passengers either lose status automatically in them or they have to work hard to maintain it, the quality of the waiting experience does not express gratitude to the passenger for flying. Some suggestions were to create more specialized spaces like the V.I.P. rooms, breaking down barriers between the gate lobbies to open up the spaces which now act like corrals; carrels or booths for real privacy, a library-like quiet room, more private seating arrangements with chairs one can move. Travelers should be able to find settings representative of their self-image. And finally, the ticketing and baggage functions should be isolated from the concourse area, which should be designed as a total environment that makes the waiting experience positive.*

And of course the plane cabins are among the worst travel environments ever created. They are micro-environments that bring the act of living to the meanest proportions. Too bad the 747 has become just another "suburb."

Sit toward the rear of the plane; you get fed last, but in a crisis, the tail hits the ground last.

SKY LIFTING. Corporate jets and private little airplanes may be going where you want to go. Hitch out to the local airport, head for the operations area, *smile* and start asking around if there is anybody going in your direction. *Time* magazine, sleuthing around the "youth scene," turned up this thumbs-up technique. *Time* gives these rules-of-the-road:

1) Forget deadlines; you'll never make them.
2) Girls will always get rides more easily than boys—but not in jeans; wear a skirt.
3) Never leave the operations area for a minute, because the moment you depart a ride always seems to turn up.
4) Make friends with everyone—the ground crewmen always know where a ride might be found.
5) Bring cotton or earplugs.
6) When asking for a ride, be direct but lighthearted, and don't push if the answer is negative.
7) Carry lots of books for long waits.

BUSES. After hitchhiking the bus is the most educational mode of travel. Bus passengers tend to talk among themselves. On some long trips, we've seen real clans form. Because of the interstate highways, they are getting faster. Not much cheaper than airline Youth Fares over long distances. No discounts on either Greyhound or Trailways. For the small extra-service charge, take the Trailways "Golden Eagle Service" if you can. A hostess is aboard, snacks, toilets and more comfort. We gather from talking with bus line officials that they are upgrading their images and terminals. They are trying to become airlinelike, which is not all that good a model. You can carry a lot of baggage, up to 150 pounds. Cross-country is about two and a half days now for $93.65. At night take a mild sleeping pill and you might sleep through Salt Lake City.

FREE CARS. We think Abbie Hoffman wrote the following. We can't improve upon the writing; as students we did the driving four or five times across country and really recommend it.

If you want to travel a long distance the auto transportation agencies are a great deal. Look in the Yellow Pages under Automobile Transportation and Trucking. You must be over 21 and have a valid driver's license. Call them up and tell them where you want to go and they will tell you if they have a car. They will give you the car and a tank of gas free. You pay the rest. Go to pick up the car alone, then get some people who also want to go *to help with expenses. You can make it go to San Francisco for about $80 in tolls and gas in four days without pushing. Usually you have the car for longer and can make a whole thing out of it. You must look "straight" when you go to the agency.*

TRAINS. We're lucky. We remember the last of the good days of train travel. Once, on the Northern Pacific outside of Boise, heading toward Texas, the chief of the dining car came through the lounge car. He was in morning coat and pin-stripe gray trousers. He had thirty-one pencils in his lapel pocket. He announced a roast squab dinner. So we sat down to heavy silver, a white tablecloth and a rose in a slender vial. Have never forgotten that meal. Ten years later and we have seen the almost total collapse of decent train travel. For this paragraph, we interviewed an official of AmTrac, the new government train agency that was created May 1, 1971, to see if there was any hope for improvement. He said the government is committed to reviving the passenger train. It will be some months yet before they know if innovative ideas they have will get approved. We asked if there was anything brewing for students. They would like some student fares; are going to request them. Another of their ideas is patterned on the European Couchette. This is a sleeping car that has people bunked six to a room, twelve rooms to a car, totaling seventy-two sleepers. He thought this would be terrific for students. We suggest you write your senator and congressman and demand this couchette car from AmTrac. Until then, however, if you can travel and have the money, take the train once. Sleeping in a berth is glorious.

Of course it is possible to "ride the rails." Our reading of this activity suggests that it is as dangerous as ever; not to be lightly entered into. Wait till the times get worse.

A COLLEGE ON WHEELS. "Road Hog" has been put out to pasture on a rural commune in northern Maryland. "Road Hog" was the mobile hallucination, the lead bus in the Hog Farm commune's caravan of six buses. "Road Hog" is one of the significant vehicles of our times. "Road Hog's" story is one of great cross-country boodles, the festivals, child births, hallelujahs, busts and freedom. She was the Woodstock of buses.

Such school buses, collectively owned and rebuilt are being used throughout America and Canada as moving stores, workshops, music caravans and churches. They are the ultimate traveling environment, when filled with people playing, working, living and, for the purposes here, learning. A learning collective traveling and studying together is a legitimate involvement with gasoline vehicles. And an exciting alternative to campus.

"Road Hog" slept and boarded fourteen people with room for an office in the back. She had a toilet, kitchen, stove and bunks. A rather decent mobile home.

An itinerant company of learners would need at least three buses, one of which could be the study center–library. With a mobile phone it could be a communications center also.

Some things to deal with:

- Identifying enough people (25?) who are able to spend at least a year on the road as students and members of a community.
- Enough money from the participants to buy and outfit three buses. Someone with a financial and accounting sense is needed from the outset.
- A study program designed around an itinerary compatible to the group. Academic people should be asked to join the project as partners, members of the collective. Plan to hire faculty consultants, seminar leaders from colleges on your route. The network should be established before departure.
- Academic credit is possible, obviously.
- Things to think about:

  1) legal problems in bus living
  2) required equipment for licenses
  3) parking in cities
  4) propane heating systems
  5) water systems
  6) cooking systems
  7) bed arrangements
  8) work space
  9) storage space
  10) furniture
  11) maintenance of equipment

We're back now where we began this section: traveling students establishing their own learning community. (One such school is a *studium generale;* two or more is a university.) We think this is feasible; we know from our work around experimental colleges that such a scheme would find student and faculty support, perhaps even financial. But the best part of it is that students pooling their resources could do it on their own, contracting for what they couldn't provide for themselves.

Colleges of learners wandering over America. . . .

14. Bread, Résumés and Interviews

In the absense of a new world, government tuition vouchers and government Independent Study loans, independent students will have to work their way through their education. Call it "work/study" like they do at the fancy experimental schools and be prepared to work at least six months a year. Think "work/study" so that your work experience becomes a learning one as well.

We make these assumptions about the work world you are entering:

• The nature of the U.S. population is changing. The "center of gravity" of the population is shifting from the eighteen-year-olds to the twenty-one-year-olds. Soon there will be more people in their middle twenties than in any other age group. In other words the "youth culture" will not be the center ring of America as it was in the sixties. The seventies and eighties are going to be concerned with marriage, jobs, security and leisure, as well as personal mobility, freedom, cleaner environments. Surely the nature of home and family, interpersonal relationships, work and sex roles has changed in the past decade, but it appears that the next decade will be as much concerned with "competence" as "confrontation."

• It seems that the "movement," the counter-culture, has passed. It is difficult to see that many of the institutions of the counter-culture will prevail in the forms that we had expected. The communes, collectives, Free Universities, underground papers, counter-groceries and free clinics are not getting new people, younger people into them. Each generation wants to do its own thing. And further . . .

Fourthly, in the era of monopoly capitalism, no small businesses are permitted to survive for very long. And the counter-culture farm or candle shop is essentially a small business. . . . Fifthly, the ruling class has innumerable written and unwritten laws that enable it to close down, co-opt, and opportunistically use any counter-culture experiment in any way that suits their needs and interests. —LYNN O'CONNOR IN "THE WOMEN'S PAGE," REPRINTED IN "THE RADICAL THERAPIST."

The time of instant collectives is over. In this book we have suggested learning collectives of various sorts. They must survive on their own merits, the quality of their organization and management. They will not close down the universities. The next decades will be lonelier for the young.

The universities are not getting smaller, as we pointed out in the first chapter. They are kept filled with people who wouldn't have gone to college a generation ago: the poor, the blacks, "ethnics," people who want to move up in the world. The technology of this period, which is more and more supplanting the formal government as the primary controlling instrument of America, needs our universities to create the willing workers of the change-based technology of tomorrow. Schools for the electronic hardhats, more powerful because they are not threatened by change. Indeed, the universities will create people who will thrive on regular adjustments. To compete with these people for jobs requires the ability to learn quickly, think originally, manage projects and get along with people, bringing out the best in yourself and them. These skills are not learned at a university.

According to the U.S. Census Bureau, today's average worker changes jobs every five years. People have eight careers in a forty-year work life. Presumably that five years on a job will shrink. You can expect to go from work team to work project to independent research quite regularly in the future. You will thus have many mini-careers in a lifetime. Until work-force management is completely computerized, everyone will undergo periodic unemployment. We will all need survival skills, itinerant trades like carpentry, offset printing, bartending, clerk-typist. Those things can be learned in high school and should be. Anyone can learn to operate an offset press and shrewd students will learn now.

Most people will work in government or large corporations. It will be difficult to live outside the maternal corporate life, which will provide cheaper medical insurance, recreation, a guaranteed retirement, security of all kinds. The Japanese corporation is the model of the future. For better or for worse, it will be difficult to get fired in the large corporations.

By the eighties most jobs will be white-collar. Most won't require a college education. Various technical positions like systems analyst, medical technician, electronics designer, office specialist and pilot will be important.

For those that are locked into corporate life, leisure will be more important than work. But workers are not going to work less. Many heads of family will moonlight to buy the second homes, skimobiles, swimming pools that everyone will want. It is difficult to see how industrialized leisure is better than a "job well done," but the advertisements are going to convince us that it is.

Perhaps we will see the emergence of the "poor intellectual" that Paul Goodman has called for. Intellectuals have been overpaid in this century. Perhaps a few will opt out in the manner of the 1960's, deny the sirens of leisure, the pursuit of security, the dreams of success and think independently. We believe it necessary.

All signs point to the four-day work week. It has been suggested that the "fifth day" be devoted to learning, to continuing education. That makes sense. It will be a requirement in some fast-changing technologies. Steady, ongoing learning is better than periodic retraining, a return to graduate school, etc.

We feel that 10 percent of one's personal income should be reinvested in education of some sort: books, classes, magazines and journals. At that rate of investment, one can "take off" educationally, can move from one career to another on one's own terms.

THE JOB SEARCH. To find out why it is always easier to work than to find work, we talked to experts in the field of executive placement at Frederick Chusid and Associates in Washington, D.C., and Management Recruiters in Baltimore, Maryland. It is their experience that the jobs are always available to the person who knows what he wants to do, what he can do and then goes after it. Frederick Chusid puts the problem of job hunting this way: (1) identity—to know both what you want and what you are most capable of performing, (2) location—to find the companies that have the job you want, (3) selling yourself—obtaining the best rewards for your efforts, and (4) preserving your self-esteem and dignity by not allowing job hunting to become a degrading experience.

We were told that 95 percent of job seekers go about the job search in a manner almost guaranteed to make it degrading and frustrating. It was stressed that the job search must be organized and methodical. What we learned about executive placement is applicable to student work/ study jobs. The problems are similar: a person is without income and position and must still function effectively.

The first step is a thorough *self-appraisal*. Make a list of everything you like to do. Maybe fifty items: sew, sell, swim, talk to people, make honey, chemistry, cook, write, make candles, etc. Write this list out; make it as long as possible.

Take the top three items, *i.e.*, talk, work with people and write. Perhaps a research assistant at a psychiatric hospital. What combinations do you come up with: reporter, news writer, copy writer. As a student it may be difficult to get those particular jobs, but they are suggestions where you might start to look for jobs, in environments that you will find interesting, educational.

In this self-appraisal stage, talk to your Board of Trustees, your tutors, other close friends. Ask them what are your strengths and weaknesses in relation to your job search. Get a picture of the kinds of things you could do at this stage of your vocational development. What do you want to do, what can you do?

The second step is to set some *personal goals* for your work experience. This is most important. What do you want out of your work? Can you relate a job to an Independent Study project? Do you need to establish work habits? Do you want to learn skills or information?

The last step is the *patient* job search itself. This should be a full-time activity. Stop everything else while you look for work. It is tedious, persnickety work and it requires full-time attention. To give you more specific help, we recommend three books.

How to Beat the Establishment and Get that Job
Normal File and Bernard Howroyd
Apple One Publishers
1971

Price: $2.95

The Moonlighter's Manual
Jerry LeBlanc
Nash Publishing Corp
1969

Price: $4.95

Résumés That Get Jobs
Résumé Service
Arco Publishers
1963

Price: $2.00

Here are ten bucks of books that can keep you in work. The first one has good chapters on agencies, interviewing, résumés, taking tests, want ads, etc.

Jerry LeBlanc's book has ideas for three hundred jobs. Everything from reweaving to engraving to notary public to raising small animals to setting up a clipping service. It is a fine book. *Résumés That Get Jobs* is the standard reference book on résumés. All you need to know.

POSSIBLE JOBS. The number of occupations doubles every ten years or so. Here is a list of jobs common to students.

library assistant	*radio and TV repair*
bartending/waitress	*process server*
orderly, hospital and nursing home	*sales*
aide	*day care aide*
aide in psychiatric hospital	*gardener*
museum guide	*construction worker*
maintenance man	*VISTA Volunteer*
security force	*caddy*
cab driver	*usher*
clerical work	*life guard*
delivering phone books	*forestry*

- Pick up an "itinerant skill" in high school.
- True work/study jobs are learning experiences. Your Board of Trustees can arrange a job opening where you can learn the most. It might be possible to apprentice yourself to a professor or executive.
- If you want just a survival job, need the cash, work the graveyard shift and pick up an extra dollar an hour.

WHERE TO LOOK FOR JOBS

- Board of Trustees, family friends.
- Personal research in state agencies, libraries.
- Knocking on doors.
- Help-wanted ads (buy first edition).
- Hanging around places you would like to work: "Can I observe?" Sometimes if you work voluntarily, it can work into a job.

RÉSUMÉS. Before you go out job hunting, prepare a good résumé. The best advice is to keep it neat and short, one page. Have it professionally typed. The purpose of the résumé is to secure an interview. It doesn't land the job. It should make the person reading it want to talk to you in person.

Skeleton Resume To Show Basic Form
SYNOPSIS PART OF RESUME

Synopsis of Resume of   Street, City, State
John Doe   Phone

JOB OBJECTIVE

	EMPLOYMENT
Dates (start-end) Present or last company	Name of Company, Address of Company. Company line Job title
Dates (start-end)	Name of Company, Address of Company. Company line Job title
Dates (start-end)	Name of Company, Address of Company. Company line Job title

MISCELLANEOUS EMPLOYMENT
Grouping of part-time and/or minor employments

EDUCATION

Dates (start-finish)	High School — type of diploma (academic, etc.) Note: unnecessary if college is shown.

Dates
  (start-finish)
	College name—location
	    Degree: Major: Minor:
	    Class standing:
	    Honors:
	    [Expenses: percentage earned] *
	    [Activities: extracurricular]

Miscellaneous Education	Company courses. Correspondence courses. Seminars. Home study.

PERSONAL

Age:	Day, month, year of birth. [Place of birth.]
Appearance:	Height. Weight.
Married:	[Year. Wife's maiden name and education beyond high school.]
Children:	Number. [Ages.]
Health:	State of—any physical limitations.
Residence:	[Own, rent, live with parents. Will or will not relocate.]
[Hobbies:	Optional.]
Affiliations:	Optional unless specifically related to occupation.
Service:	Dates of entry and discharge. Branch of service. Rank. Type of discharge. Reserve status, if any.

(FOR AMPLIFICATION SEE FOLLOWING)

*Items in brackets are optional, depending on position applied for.

AMPLIFICATION PART OF PROGRAM

Resume of
John Doe

EMPLOYMENT

Date of starting to present
FULL NAME OF LAST OR PRESENT COMPANY

>   Responsibilities:

>   Results:

>   Reason for leaving:

Date of starting to date of leaving
FULL NAME OF COMPANY

>   Responsibilities: (less detailed)

>   Results: (less detailed)

>   Reason for leaving:

Date of starting to date of leaving
FULL NAME OF COMPANY

>   Responsibilities:
>   Results:
>   Reason for leaving:

(Note: If resume is in proper sequence, this and ensuing employments will usually be of less importance and correspondingly less detailed)

MISCELLANEOUS EMPLOYMENTS
(Dates can be approximate, but should indicate
length of period involved. Example: 1952-1960)

>   Here, group your minor employments, stating in general the type of work and for which companies. Also your part-time work during school periods.

REFERENCES

DISTRIBUTION OF RÉSUMÉS. By this time, you should have an idea of the jobs you want. Do not send out résumés like scattershot. Ten carefully sent résumés will do more than one hundred mailed like Christmas cards. Be methodical. Go to the library and look at the Dun and Bradstreet *Million Dollar Book,* which contains the pertinent facts of all large companies in America. Use the Yellow Pages. The Chamber of Commerce will have information. Do some legwork.

Send the résumé to the person that will be responsible for hiring you. As a general rule, do not send résumés to the Personnel Office. They don't hire anybody but the ill-used and ill-fated. Finding the right person to send the résumé to is half of the work.

COVER LETTER. Always include a cover letter to the résumé. Eight out of ten résumés go into the wastepaper basket. Only a good cover letter can spare a résumé that fate. It can get you the interview. Write in a more personal style. Say how you happened to write the person and that particular company, why you have an interest in working for it, how your past history relates to the work you think you can do. "I had a summer job last year that got me interested in electronics. My supervisor had once worked for you . . ."

At the end of the cover letter, say that you will be phoning later in the week after he/she has had a chance to read the résumé. This must be done. Do not let the résumé lie on the desk. It is your opening, and you must follow it up quickly with a call. This is when you need discipline, method.

NOTES AND CALLS. Résumés and cover letters rarely get anyone jobs. They are easy to ignore. It is necessary to reinforce them. In fact, employment agencies do not use them much. They rely on phonecalls for the initial contact. The advice call is a worthwhile technique. Anyone responds to these eight words, particularly from a student: "I have a problem. I need some help." With those eight words it is often possible to get through to a corporation executive. We all like to give advice. Advice calls create a situation in which no one is under any obligation. Describe who you are and what you are studying and why you need a job. Ask for advice on things you could do to improve your chances of getting a job. Ask the person if they have any suggestions on people you should call for interviews or more advice. Sometimes the person you are calling has a job opening that your call brings to mind.

But the advice call is just one of many calls that you make.

Always Follow Letters Up with Calls.

Follow Calls or Interviews Up with Letters.

Write your thank-you notes the same day you called or had the interview.

If you have an acceptable telephone manner, work up a list of twenty organizations to call, with good ideas on who you need to talk to. Then sit down and make the calls in a single day, trying to find people who want to see your résumé.

One of the secrets to keeping up your morale in the job search is to lay on as many interviews as possible, so that you don't get too anxious about any one interview, which could lead you to blow it.

INTERVIEWS. "I don't know what I want exactly; I don't want shit work; I don't know exactly what I can do." That's the typical student opener. It never gets a job. If you are granted an interview, you have a good chance for the job if the interview is successful.

Be prepared for the interview. If you haven't done your homework, you won't get the job. Find out all you can about the company, the organization and the possible jobs. Find out what the company does, its future, its policies. Call the firm's Public Relations department and in your student role ask all sorts of questions about the company.

Interviews are usually straight; but sometimes they are purposefully stressful. Beware of the chair that is four inches shorter than the interviewer's or the interviewer who stops talking to see how you handle an awkward silence. Sometimes the phone keeps ringing.

You want the interview to be a balanced dialogue between you and the interviewer. You want to know about the job and the company. If the interviewer asks you to "Tell me about yourself," modestly and succinctly describe your background, interests and goals and then turn the question back to the interviewer and let him talk about himself.

Here are some pointers on the interview:

- Eat breakfast.
- Dress in a suit or quiet dress. You almost always have to appear straight.
- Be on time or a few minutes early.
- Fill out the forms neatly, precisely.
- Have a firm handshake. Shake a woman's hand. Practice entrances and handshakes at home.
- Don't smoke.
- If you are a man with beard or long hair, joke about it in passing.
- Answer questions succinctly, but do explain.
- Don't talk money at first interview. If it comes up, know what you think is fair.
- Say what you can offer to the organization.
- Be honest; don't jeopardize future references.

- As a student emphasize that you learn quickly. Say you are going to relate the work to a learning project.
- Explain your goals, why you want the job.
- Look for signals that indicate the ending of the interview.

And there are five points that you must make before the end of the interview:

1) That you can do the job.
2) That you want the job.
3) That you are available immediately or at a specific date.
4) That you will hear from the interviewer by a certain date.
5) That you appreciate the interview.

If you are interested in the job, after the interview, write a follow-up note to that person saying that you enjoyed the interview, that you liked the organization, that you want to work there, that you can do the job, that you will study for it, that you are available, yours truly.

You do have some advantages in the interview: he/she doesn't know much about you except what you choose to tell; many interviewers are looking for straight people with stock answers, so you can easily think up the things they want to hear. After the first few interviews you get the hang of it and it becomes a game. Interviews are obviously not an accurate way to hire people, but they are used relentlessly, so get proficient at them.

A BOUND PORTFOLIO. Actors and artists have always had to show bills, reviews, pictures, examples of their work. They put a great deal of time and money into their portfolios. We recommend this practice to independent students. Assemble a portfolio containing:

- "patch-work" course transcripts
- letters of reference
- résumé
- project descriptions from your learning projects
- articles that you have written
- pages from your journal
- short biography
- some pictures

In a phone call mention that you have such a portfolio that could be left at his office for a couple of days for a reading. This portfolio would give a more complete and interesting picture of you than the résumé. You might get a more interesting job, a "work/study" job that lets you learn.

15. A Primer for Parents on the Problems of College

A short compendium of readings for parents involved in the education of a daughter or son. This list is a starter, to give parents a sense of where they and their family are going to be taken, educationally, in the next few years.

The first article, by Dr. Malcolm Knowles, we happily stumbled upon during our research on correspondence and adult education. It is from Dr. Knowles's Ph.D. dissertation at the University of Chicago, which was later published in 1962.

For further reading, we have included a bibliography in Chapter 7. Parents should read the books by Paul Goodman and Ivan Illich.

CONTENTS

SOME REQUIRED NEW ASSUMPTIONS ABOUT
EDUCATION FOR CHILDREN AND YOUTH

The introduction of this new force into our culture--the compressing of the time-span of major social change into less than a single lifetime—requires a whole new set of assumptions about the education of both youth and adults. It is necessary to examine those regarding children and youth first, since they largely determine the requirements for the education of adults.

1) The purpose of education for the young must shift from focusing primarily on the transmission of knowledge to the development of the capacity to learn. Traditionally, the central purpose of education has been to transmit culture from one generation to the next. And always before this purpose has served society well, since our ancestors were born into a world that they could rely on to be essentially the same when they died. What they learned from their fathers about how to think, what to think, how to make a living, and how to relate to other people proved to be adequate throughout their own lifetimes and they had to add very little to these learnings to equip their sons and daughters to live adequately throughout their lifetimes.

But in the modern era much of what we learned in our youth becomes at best inadequate and at worst obsolete and even untrue by the time we have to apply it in adult life. This phenomenon is highly visible in regard to science education; it is widely accepted now that a scientific education is good for about seven years. The phenomenon is also highly visible in regard to vocational education; automation and technological advances render thousands of workers obsolete almost daily. The phenomenon is less visible, and perhaps therefore more insidious, in regard to other human competencies. Ways of thinking about art, music, literature, and drama that we of the current generation of adults learned in our youth ill equipped us to keep up with the sequence of intellectual revolutions that have occurred in the last quarter century. Attitudes that we learned at a time when world power was controlled by Caucasian peoples are no longer functional in a world in which world power is shifting to colored peoples. In fact, the very bases of understanding ourselves as human beings shift like ocean sands as the researchers of psychology, sociology, anthropology, medicine, and other human sciences uncover new facts and insights about us.

If it is true that the time-span of cultural revolution is now less than the lifetime of a human being, the needs of society and the needs of individuals can no longer be served by education that merely transmits knowledge. The new world then requires a new purpose for education: *the development of the capacity in each individual to learn, to change, to create a new culture* throughout the span of his life. Certainly knowledge must continue to be transmitted, but no longer as an end in itself—only as a means to the end of mastering the ability to learn. The central mission of elementary, secondary, and higher education must become, then, not teaching youth what they need to know, but teaching them how to learn what is not yet known. The substance of youth education, therefore, becomes process—the process of learning; and accordingly the substance of adult education becomes content—the content of man's continually expanding knowledge.

2) The curriculum of education for the young must shift from subject-mastery basis of organization to a learning skill basis of organization. If youth are to be taught *how* to learn over *what* to learn, then learning activities will have to be organized as ever broadening and deepening sequences of inquiries in which the students find the answers to their own questions. The curriculum will be organized around problem areas or questions rather than around fragmented subject areas. Fortunately, excellent starts have already been made in organizing certain sequences in this way, especially in mathematics and some sciences. But a school curriculum that has changed only in degree and not in kind from the medieval trivium and quadrivium still has a major revolution ahead of it before it can meet the requirements of the modern world.

3) The role of the teacher must be redefined from "one who primarily transmits knowledge" to "one who primarily helps students to inquire." This shift will, in turn, require a new kind of training for teachers, in which relatively less emphasis is placed on the acquisition of huge volumes of subject content to greater emphasis on understanding the processes of learning and on gaining skill in guiding (and serving as a resource to) students in conducting self-inquiries.

4) A new set of criteria must be applied to determine the readiness of youth to leave full-time schooling. If knowledge is doomed to obsolescence every few years, then it is no longer valid to test the readiness of a student to graduate by testing how much information he has acquired. Rather, it would seem that three radically different criteria are required.

First, has the student mastered the tools of learning? To measure a student against this criterion will require instruments that will provide data that would answer such questions as these: Can he read up to his capacity? (It is estimated that the average high school and college graduates today can read only at half their trainable capacities—yet reading is the primary tool of continuing learning.) Can he think symbolically? Can he ask questions that get at the heart of the matter and that can be answered through inquiry? Does he know how to collect and analyze various kinds of data? Does he understand the basic concepts and can he use the basic methods of the various intellectual disciplines? Can he communicate effectively with populations that are relevant to his welfare? Is he familiar with and able to use the important sources of knowledge?

Second, has the student developed an insatiable appetite for learning? If he is leaving formal schooling feeling that he has finished a full meal at the table of knowledge, then he is not ready to graduate; he needs more education. But if he is leaving with an overwhelming sense of dissatisfaction with his inadequacies and a burning desire to overcome them, he is prepared for the adult world.

Third, does he have a definite, but flexible, plan for continuing his learning? Certainly before his final year is completed every student should have skilled guidance in (1) diagnosing his individual needs for continuing learning, (2) identifying the resources available to him in the community for satisfying these needs, and (3) building a personal program of further learning that will possess continuity, sequence, and integration. It would help to symbolize the concept of learning as a lifelong process if every institution for the education of youth would convert its graduation ritual into an exchange between the student, who would hand the president a scroll detailing his plan for continuing learning, and the head of the institution, who would hand the student a certificate stating that the institution has taught the student all it now knows about how to learn, but will continue to make its resources available to him for further inquiry. —MALCOLM S. KNOWLES, THE ADULT EDUCATION MOVEMENT IN THE UNITED STATES (NEW YORK: HOLT, RINEHART AND WINSTON, INC., 1962). *Copyright © 1962 by Holt, Rinehart and Winston, Inc. Reprinted by permission of Holt, Rinehart and Winston, Inc.*

ON STUDENT RESPONSIBILITY

Every student should take an increasing responsibility for his education. Student responsibility should be greater than is now usual; in addition, student responsibility should grow as the student grows, until as an adult he can assume his full role. And there is the catch. Many of our students, like many adults, want to be led around in every way. Most students want complete lectures, complete textbooks, complete specifications of what to learn. They want examinations and tests set by professors. They want to play "follow-the-leader" even when they are adult scholars and productive intellectuals. So much of the science and technology of this country is determined by a few people who lead the pack and set the course.

No intellectual system will produce one hundred percent self-starters, but we should be trying to swing the distribution over into that direction. —JERROLD R. ZACHARIAS, DIRECTOR, EDUCATIONAL RESEARCH CENTER, M.I.T.

"SHEEPSKIN NO LONGER PROTECTIVE COVERING"

No longer is it certain that a young person will obtain a cushy post at a neat salary if only he secures a bachelor's degree. Indeed, it's not sure that he will obtain any white-collar job.

The argument that a college education will guarantee affluence always was fallacious, though widely disseminated by empire-building educationists. Until recently, many college boosters were declaring that the average college graduate would earn some $200,000 more in his lifetime than would the average citizen.

On this subject, Dr. Roger Freeman, of the Hoover Institution, recently made some perceptive remarks during an address in California. (Dr. Freeman was an important White House advisor during the first two years of the Nixon administration.) . . .

"There probably exists a positive causal relationship between school attendance and income level—with important exceptions," Dr. Freeman says. "For example, a plumber is now paid $355 for a 40-hour week in San Mateo county, which is more than the average teacher there gets.

"But to attribute all of the higher income of persons who have stayed in school for more years to the fact of their longer attendance is naive or misleading. Extended school attendance, as well as economic successes in later life, are causally related to the same personality traits, more than to each other: higher intelligence, ambition, motivation to work hard, to plan ahead, to forgo immediate gratification for future advancement, and so on. In other words, a man earns a higher income for the same reason for which he attends school for more years: brains and tenacity." —RUSSELL KIRK, BALTIMORE SUN, FEBRUARY 17, 1971. *Copyright General Features Corporation. Reprinted with permission.*

HOW TO CHANGE COLLEGES

What is wrong with the university as a teaching institution is precisely this: It has no philosophy of education, no unifying principle around which reforms can be made, either to meet the problems of student unrest or to engage the students in their own learning.

It has instead a system of administrative conveniences. The whole apparatus of departments, divisions, institutes, lectures, research, grades, examinations, academic credits, classes and faculty appointments is based on an administrative plan for dealing with students and academic subject matter, not on a philosophy. . . .

Yet it goes on and on, sanctified by custom and convenience. The system is what it is, not by imaginative educational thinking and the continual search for alternatives, but by the gradual accretion over the years of such practices as seemed administratively useful at the time they were installed. . . .

. . . when students and other contemporary critics condemn the system they are not arguing philosophical or psychological principles. They are saying that it is a bad education and that its practical effect is to dull their interest in learning and frustrate their efforts to become educated. If you look at the system as it now works it is not very hard to see why, nor is it hard to see what the changes are that must be made once the university is redefined as a place for students to learn what they need to know in order to be fully human. . . .

The educational problem is not with the minority of protesters and activists who are raising the basic questions and insisting on basic changes. It is with the eighty to ninety percent of those who accept the system as they find it, and, in the absence of teaching which can arouse their intellectual and moral commitments, remain in a state of mental and social acquiescence. —HAROLD TAYLOR, HOW TO CHANGE COLLEGES, HOLT, RINEHART AND WINSTON, 1971. *Copyright © 1971 by Holt, Rinehart and Winston, Inc. Reprinted by permission of Holt, Rinehart and Winston, Inc.*

"RISE IN UNIFORMITY FOUND AMONG NATION'S COLLEGES"

A study conducted for the Carnegie Commission on Higher Education has found that colleges and universities are becoming increasingly uniform and are creating a "monolithic status system" prizing academic specialization. . . .

Clark Kerr, chairman of the Carnegie Commission, described the new analysis as the "most comprehensive study ever made of change" in the country's private, public and sectarian colleges and universities. . . .

Among the general conclusions of the report, which offered no recommendations, were the following:

There is a widespread movement for institutions to offer ever more advanced degrees with students and faculty being rewarded according to the extent of their specialized interests and competence.

Despite a "commonly held assumption" to the contrary, there are not "major differences in educational institutions in different sections of the country."

The "homogenization" of higher education is affecting public, private and church-related institutions, although public institutions contribute a "vocational, pragmatic and utilitarian complexion" that is not fully matched in other sectors. —THE NEW YORK TIMES, JULY 19, 1970. © *by The New York Times Company. Reprinted by permission.*

THE AMERICAN CAMPUS IN THE 1980's

. . . what will it be like to be on the campus in 1980? Will a distinctly new student character dominate the new generation? Will the ways in which students learn and professors teach have changed radically under the impact of social forces and emerging technology of instruction? Will courses of study be different in response to the influx of students with a wider range of abilities and interests? . . .

The young demonstrators of today will, many of them, be the assistant and associate professors of tomorrow. They will probably support and arouse the students that follow them, and thus even further involve American students in their own government and in the major issues of society. The sources of student unrest—war, poverty, racism—will still be with us in 1980. Far from being a mere cyclical phenomenon, the present activism of college students is possibly the beginning of continuing development. . . .

The college generation of the 1950's was the last quiet one we will see in a long time. To match these varied and more socially committed students, the undergraduate instructional program will have to become more relevant, flexible, and enterprising. The typical academic career of tomorrow's student, according to Professor Lewis Mayhew of Stanford, will range from independent study of religion or other subjects to Peace Corps work in a South American village, from work study activity as an electronics technician to anthropological field work. In the course of his undergraduate work this typical student may drop out for a year, come back to the campus, undertake some independent work, all without any disruption of his scholastic record or learning experience. Moreover, the time spent on the campus will be differently organized for effective learning. No longer will students merely pile up credit hours through fragmented specialized courses. Rather, each student and his teachers will define the specific goals to be achieved, and then the means to those goals will be devised to meet the particular student's needs. He may attend class regularly or learn by reading in a library. He may master his field by watching televised lectures or by apprenticing himself to a recognized scholar. Only the end results—the criteria the student must satisfy to earn his degree—will be fixed. —ALVIN EURICH, "THE AMERICAN CAMPUS IN THE 1980's," THE FUTURIST, DECEMBER, 1969. *Used by permission of World Future Society, Washington, D.C.*

FROM ALBERT EINSTEIN

One had to cram all this stuff into one's mind, whether one liked it or not. This coercion had such a deterring effect that, after I had passed the final examination, I found the consideration of any scientific problems distasteful to me for an entire year. . . . It is in fact nothing short of a miracle that the modern methods of instruction have not yet entirely strangled the holy curiosity of inquiry; for this delicate little plant, aside from stimulation, stands mainly in need of freedom; without this it goes to wrack and ruin without fail. It is a very grave mistake to think that the enjoyment of seeing and searching can be promoted by means of coercion and a sense of duty. To the contrary, I believe that it would be possible to rob even a healthy beast of prey of its voraciousness, if it were possible, with the aid of a whip, to force the beast to devour continuously, even when not hungry—especially if the food, handed out under such coercion, were to be selected accordingly. —ALBERT EINSTEIN (QUOTED IN COMPULSORY MIS-EDUCATION AND THE COMMUNITY OF SCHOLARS BY PAUL GOODMAN) .

DOPE

American Colleges and Universities are immunizing a generation of leaders. —JOHN GARDNER.

II. Experimental Colleges

1. CHOOSING AN EXPERIMENTAL COLLEGE

2. WELL-KNOWN EXPERIMENTAL SCHOOLS
   Bensalem • College of the Potomac
   Franconia College
   Friends World College • Goddard College
   Hampshire College
   The University of the New World

3. NEW AND EXPERIMENTING SCHOOLS
   California Institute of the Arts, Calif.
   College of the Atlantic, Maine
   The Evergreen State College, Wash.
   Mount Angel College, Ore.
   New College, Fla. • Prescott College, Ariz.
   Purchase College, State University of N.Y.
   Ramapo College, N.J.
   Redlands' Johnson College, Calif.
   Royalton College, Vt.
   Stockton State College, N.J.
   Thomas Jefferson College, Allendale, Mich.
   University of California, Santa Cruz, Calif.
   University of Green Bay, Green Bay, Wis.
   Washington International College,
   Washington, D.C.

4. SMALL AND INNOVATIVE COLLEGES

Alternative One Keene State College, N.H.

Antioch College, Ohio • Aquarian University, Md.

Bard College, N.Y. • Beloit College, Wis.

Berea College, Ky. • Berry College, Ga.

Blake College, Oreg. • Bowdoin College, Maine

California College of Arts and Crafts, Calif.

Campus-Free College, N.H. • Carleton College, Minn.

Coe College, Iowa • Colby College, Maine

College of the Person, Washington, D.C.

College at Old Westbury, N.Y.

College of the Virgin Islands, V.I.

Colleges-within-the-College,
University of Kansas, Kan.

Colorado College, Colo. • Deep Springs College, Nev.

Earlham College, Ind.

Elbert Covell College,
University of the Pacific, Calif.

Empire State College, N.Y.

Experimental Program, University of Montana, Mont.

Experimental Program, University of Vermont, Vt.

Fairhaven College, Western Washington State, Wash.

Franklin Pierce College, N.H. • Goucher College, Md.

Hutchins School, Sonoma State, Calif.

Inner College, The University of Connecticut, Conn.

Inter American University, P.R.

International Community College, Calif.

Justin Morrill College, Michigan State University, Mich.

Lawrence University, Wis.

Life Studies Program, University of New Hampshire, N.H.

Linfield College, Ore.

Lyman Briggs College, Michigan State University, Mich.

Mark Hopkins College, Vt.

Monteith College, Wayne State University, Mich.

New College, Hofstra University, N.Y.

New College, Oakland University, Mich.

New College, University of Alabama, Ala.

New College, University of Hawaii, Hawaii

Oberlin College, Ohio

Off-Campus College, SUNY at Binghamton, N.Y.
Ottawa University, Kan. • *Pacific Oaks College, Calif.*
Pendle Hill, Pa. • *Pomona College, Calif.*
Project Ten, University of Massachusetts, Mass.
Raymond College, University of the Pacific, Calif.
Reed College, Ore. • *Ripon College, Wis.*
Rochdale College, Canada
Roger Williams College, R.I.
Shimer College, Ill. • *Sierra Nevada College, Nev.*
Simon's Rock College, Mass. • *St. John's College, Md.*
St. Olaf College, Minn.
Student Center College, Calif.
Experimental College, Fresno State College, Calif.
Experimental College, Tufts University, Mass.
Western College, Ohio
Unified Science Study Program, M.I.T., Mass.
United States International University, Calif.
University of Alaska, Alaska
University of Guam, Guam
University of Puget Sound, Wash.
University Without Walls, Antioch College, Ohio
Washington-Baltimore Campus, Antioch College,
Washington, D.C.
Whitman College, Wash.
William James College, Grand Valley State, Mich.
Windham College, Vt.
World Campus Afloat, Chapman College, Calif.
Yankton College, S.D.

5. SPECIAL PROGRAMS
School for International Training of
the Experiment in International Living
University Year for ACTION

1. Choosing an Experimental College

Colleges are trying to be relevant, developing shiny programs to attract students. This usually takes the form of a school within a school, *i.e.,* Livingston at Rutgers, the experimental program at Boston University or Redlands in California. You can read all about them in their catalogs.

College catalogs are careful productions which when studied tell a lot about a school. Those slick-paper, high-gloss editions, heavy and crammed with course titles, mean the college is big, state-supported and impersonal.

If it's an urban school, there won't be external photos, just another picture of the library from yet another angle, or a shot of the city's art museum. And if the place is in the country, you'll have wide-angle views of lakes and woods and mountains. No classrooms, no students.

Private schools, or schools that want to give the impression of serious institutions, come on with quality paper catalogs which are more somber, have few pictures and are always done in browns and grays.

Tucked into the center of these two types of catalogs is the section on the experimental school. Usually the paper cover is different—a brighter scale to attract attention and to show that *here's* something different.

The problem with these places—experimental schools within a college—is independence. Bensalem was wide open at Catholic Fordham until it began getting publicity. Read these catalogs all the way through. See who makes decisions for the experimental school and who reports to whom. Find out about budgets—are the purse strings controlled? Is the place significantly different? Students at Hofstra's New College say they don't even realize they're in an experimental branch. Find out the criteria for selections. Is it only the students with four-point averages? Does the experimental college have its own community? Its own uniqueness? A sense of togetherness? Ask before you go.

If the college itself is experimental, then you'll have another kind of catalog. It will have most, if not all, of the following:

1) Mimeographed pages stapled together.

2) A profound statement of what the college will be, listing various sins of higher education and declaring that at *this* school, students will always be first and foremost.

3) Artists' renditions of the campus' new buildings, because they haven't been built yet. The buildings where you'll be attending school for most of your four years—temporary structures—won't be shown.

4) A partial list of the faculty and staff, mostly staff, giving a brief account of what they've done, not what they're going to do.

5) No list of courses—that hasn't been decided yet.

6) An elaborate application sheet, asking such questions: Who, living or dead, would you want to teach at this college, and why?

Anyway, you read these catalogs, and they may have something to offer you. A program in Urban Studies, independent studies here and overseas, mini-courses, intensive courses, special seminars. Today almost all of them have an ecology-flavored course like Life Sciences and the Current Human Crises, or Urban Ecology.

Be leery of places that sound too good, too loose, too free. You're investing time in these places, even if it is just to fill out their lengthy applications. Choose with care. There are a few ways of telling what an experimental college is all about. Points to check:

If the college has been in operation for more than ten years, it's not likely to be very open. The first "experimental" schools like Reed, Sarah Lawrence and Bennington have become set and established. In February, students at Reed were upset at the new conservative controls and walked out. They formed their own "College in Exile" and put a picture of Reed's president on a billboard with the message: "Would you buy a used college from this man?" Experimental branches of established schools— places like Livingston College of New Jersey, Johnson College of the University of Redlands and Bensalem of Fordham—were established in the late sixties and are legitimately experimental. The State University of New York's College at Old Westbury started as experimental but turned itself into a community college under a second president and new faculty. Therefore, first things to note: how old is the place and how is it operating now?

Strangely enough, church related and state supported schools have produced some of the more experimental colleges, including Friends

World (Quaker) ; Bensalem (Catholic) ; Livingston (state supported).
Don't dismiss a school if it comes from a religious or state system. One
great advantage of attending a state school is that it's cheaper than a
private institution.

The disposition of a president means a lot at experimental schools.
These colleges are always small, and his/her presence often is felt. Find
out what you can about the person, especially from speeches. They'll tell
you a lot about his/her idea for a school.

What kind of background does he have? Is he just another fifties'
liberal? Has he been in the academic world all his life, working his way
up? Is he from government? How a person thinks is usually set in his late
twenties. He will make certain assumptions about people, education,
behavior, and these attitudes will dictate his responses to situations on
campus. For example, if a president has moved around a lot, done a
variety of jobs, and been close to young people, he'll have a sense of what
you're about and what you want from a school.

Be careful, however, of too much *in* talk, too much of a desire by the
president to be with it, relevant. If he's trying too hard, chances are he's a
phony, and you'll find that out the first time there's a confrontation.

Don't get excited about a pass/fail grading system—it doesn't mean
anything. Pass/fail was first tried in Michigan in 1851, and almost all
schools are turning in that direction. And now modifications are being
added—there's high pass and low pass and eventually it will be just
another ABC system. If the catalog doesn't refer to grades or accumula-
tion of credit at all, then you've found a truly experimental place.

Be careful of artists' drawings in catalogs. They mean the buildings
aren't finished and that you'll have to make do with something else.
College buildings are never completed on schedule. The Parthenon, built
in 438 B.C., was completed in four years—about as long as it takes con-
tractors today to build a dormitory. And that's how long it takes to get a
degree. So unless you see the actual buildings, don't believe you'll live
and study in them.

If the catalog tells you that the social behavior of students is something the students handle themselves, then you know it's a free place.
Campuses on the whole, even stately places like Bryn Mawr and Princeton, let students run their personal lives. Still there are other traps. Do
you have to live on campus? Do you have to take the food plan? Can you
have pets? What about cars? Students sometimes select a school just
because freshmen are allowed to have cars on campus.

But if a school still has hours for women, or visitation days and no
coed experimentation, forget it. The place isn't innovative; it's worried
about *its* reputation, not yours.

Don't fill it out in one sitting. Take your time, move slowly on each question, think about yourself. Be yourself. Don't give "answers" you think they want to hear. Try very hard to write, in clear and simple English, what you think and feel. Don't fake it. Don't lie. Talk about yourself honestly; no one expects you to have all the answers.

Interviews are usually required for acceptance at an experimental college. They'll want to look you over and see if you're right for them. Studies show interviews are the least dependable means of measurement. (The Peace Corps found that references from volunteers' mothers gave the most accurate appraisals of the volunteers' strengths and weaknesses.) Nevertheless, everyone figures he can sell himself better in person than on paper.

Perhaps.

A few points. Don't try to sell yourself in an interview. Anyone who has been at all involved with admissions can spot a hustle, and it turns him/her off. These colleges aren't looking for stereotypes. They want diversity. They want more diversity than they can get, so if you think you're off the norm a bit, fine. That's in your favor.

Now if you've done something unusual lately, like been to Cuba, don't hit the interviewer over the head with the fact. Mention it in passing, letting it slip out casually, saying, "One thing I learned cutting cane is the value of a day's work," and keep talking. Make the admissions person ask you where you cut cane.

Another thing. There aren't any right answers. An articulate answer, wrong or otherwise, shows you're thinking. That's all experimental schools want: people who want to think and learn on their own.

Interviews are good for another thing. They give you a reason for visiting the campus, which is certainly something you need to do. One day on a campus can tell you more than any catalog. Here's what to look for:

How do the students spend their time outside of class? See where they live. Cruise the library—see if it's crowded, talk to the work-study students, ask if anyone reads there. They may be great readers, but like someplace else instead. The library might not be warm and friendly, so see if there is a place to study.

If there's something you're into, like writing, photography, crafts, see what the school offers and what equipment they have. Most experimental places are slim on equipment, especially when they're new. Don't go to a place where you can't work on your hobbies or interests. Look for the students on campus who have interests like yours and see what they think of the place. Talk to at least four students. Trust their evaluation but decide for yourself whether what hassles them will hassle you.

What happens in the cafeteria? What's the food like? How's the atmosphere? You can tell a lot about a school from what happens in the dining hall. It's the real news center of a college; it tells the lifestyle of the school.

The experimental college of your choice—if it wants to work—should have at least the following:

1) A nice place to live and work, not worn-down buildings or even an old estate. A place that's in touch with what's happening.

2) A good library where one can sit and read books. A comfortable place. A place that's nice to go to.

3) In-house food service. Food service that brings folks together.

4) A coffee shop, not machines. An after-hours place run by students with a good music system.

5) A student-faculty lounge where it is easy for everyone to gather and where they'd want to gather.

6) An organized poster and notice board, not a swarm of information fly-papered to a wall.

7) Faculty not only interested in their subject, but also fascinated by it.

8) A set of goals shared by the majority. A curiosity in learning, not in ego-tripping, power or position.

Don't expect experimental colleges to be happy campuses or little paradises tucked away in the woods. They're not. They are tough places in which to live and study. You need a great deal of reliance, knowledge of who you are and an idea of what you want to study.

They are not easy. Academically and emotionally, a lot is demanded of students. Students are involved extensively and intensely with planning of programs, hiring of teachers and community living. It takes a lot out of you, and gives a lot to students who go there.

If you can give positive replies to most of the following questions, the chances are you'll be able to adjust and learn at an experimental college:

• Have you completed projects in high school or extracurricularly that you also designed?

• Has anyone you respect said that you can handle a free-flowing environment?

• Do you like small seminar classes with lots of personal attention?

• You're not looking for some Utopia full of happy free spirits and love for everyone?

• Have you been a good high school student? Have you mastered the basic skills of English, math and science?

• Do you want to study independently, following your own interests and studies?

- Can you travel on your own, overseas and at home, and not be hassled?
- Do languages come easily to you?
- You're not concerned about getting quickly through college, establishing a career and settling down?

Once at an experimental college—or any small liberal arts place—be aware of the *mama-mind*. This is a term we first heard Judson Jerome use in his book, *Culture Out of Anarchy*. Generally it means the atmosphere of a college. A mama-mind college envelops a student. It anticipates concern and anxiety, hurries to intervene. By this method, the mama-mind college keeps a student young and dependent.

It also identifies those faculty and administrators—particularly deans of students—who live off the emotions of students, usually young women. Mama-minds are always "doing things" for students, loaning their cars, having students to their homes day and night, rushing out themselves after midnight to lend emotional support to distraught students. They are *emotional usurers* and the payment collected is the dependency of the students. Mama-minds don't want students to stand alone, free. They live off the students' need for them.

At nearly every small college we've visited, we've seen this parasite and his band of students. Watch out. Don't be misled by this kind of kindness. It isn't kindness at all.

Don't let us frighten you away from experimental schools. We recommend them—not to everybody—but to those students who are together and who know the kind of education they want—free and loose, open and friendly, and of one's own making.

We recently came across another gauge for selecting a college. It was done by Susan Crain of Manhasset Public Schools on Long Island, New York. Her system works this way:

- The tweedier the admissions officer's suit, the higher the cost of the college (*Law of Sartorial Front*).
- The less the need for students, the more forthright the admissions personnel about the college's weaknesses (*Law of Truth Deplored*).
- The newer the school, the fewer the girls (*Law of Prudence*).
- The greater the number of cars, the fewer the rules (*Law of Horizontal Mobility*).
- The faster the cars, the slower the learning (*Law of Perennial Non-Bloomer*).
- The larger the campus acreage, the fewer the buildings (*Law of Under-Expansion*).
- The more bizarre the students' appearance, the greater emphasis on self-realization (*Law of Inner Chaos*).

- The more expansive the plan for the future, the greater the school is in the red (*Law of Color Blindness*).
- The poorer the school, the less emphasis on accreditation (*Law of Irrelevant Standards*).
- The poorer the living facilities, the more important the student's potentiality (*Law of Inevitable Growth*).
- The more difficult the college to locate, the more possibility of outdoor sports (*Law of Adolescent Sporting*).

The following colleges and universities have experimental, innovative or interesting programs worth considering. We have divided the schools into three sections. The first seven colleges are *well-known experimental schools*. We have visited them, talked with students, faculty and administrators. We have tried to give you an understanding of what the academic programs and campuses are like at these schools.

Fifteen colleges and universities are listed under *new and experimenting schools*. These new colleges have all begun within the last ten years and offer imaginative academic programs, designed to give students the freedom and opportunity to develop their own programs.

The last section has seventy-eight *small colleges* in the United States and its territories that are not well known, but are worth considering. Many are located in rural locations and all offer a personal kind of education. In total, one hundred schools where you might attend. The selection is yours.

Tuitions and fees change almost monthly at colleges today. We have tried to obtain the most recent information, but due to time required in publishing the book, we know the costs are not absolutely accurate.

2. Well-Known Experimental Schools

BENSALEM, THE SUMP OF EXPERIMENTAL COLLEGES

Bensalem takes its name from Francis Bacon's *New Atlantis*. The island where a new society and a new world began. This island began in the Bronx in 1967 as the experimental college of Fordham University. Its creator and first dean, Elizabeth Sewell, had a romantic dream of a community of scholars, living and studying together. She left after less than two years, overwhelmed and shaken by the college. She was followed by Hamid Kizilbash who came and went quickly, "never talking," as one student put it, "to the women." Kenneth Freeman, the third dean, quit in the spring of 1971 calling Bensalem "the most hostile place I've ever been in my life."

Bensalem really is the sump of experimental colleges. Housed in a five-story, dark and smelly, run-down apartment outside the massive gates of the Rose Hill campus of Fordham, the college has deteriorated from Elizabeth Sewell's dreams of love and learning.

The entrance door to the dormitory/college was locked—not uncommon in New York—and we indiscriminately pressed a buzzer. The door buzzed open after a moment and we got inside, into a tight damp hallway. A voice shouted down the stairwell, wanted to know who we were.

We explained we were doing research for a book on experimental colleges and wanted to talk to students.

"I don't talk to any fuckin' people," the voice called back and then an apartment door slammed.

The stout, harassed Italian who worked as secretary and receptionist for the college told us to wander around. "They're upstairs, someplace." She waved us away.

Two flights up we found a teacher, shirtless, barefoot, with the door opened to his three-room apartment. A couple of mattresses were tossed on the floor and the place smelled of grass.

"I don't want to talk about Bensalem, if you don't mind. The place is a zoo, you understand. A real zoo. I'm leaving." He offered us a cigarette, lit one, meditating a moment, collecting his thoughts. Then he blew out a puff and began. "They oughta shut the place down, really. It's only ruining lives. People come here and go crazy. We end up not talking to people, hiding out. But the kids, of course, won't let us. They come in all hours. My wife and I will be making love and some student would walk in to bum a cigarette. Weird, I tell you. We're getting out, you understand."

We asked if he could tell us where it all went wrong?

He shrugged his shoulders. "Who knows. No one trusts anyone. I don't trust anyone under thirty and I'm under thirty. It's too much. Too many people have gotten hurt." He brushed his long hair away from his eyes, then stretched out on a mattress, moving an ashtray within reach. "You guys want any grass?" he asked, as an afterthought. We shook our heads and he continued. "They got sixty kids and their girlfriends, boyfriends, all the dogs and cats. Christ this place smells like the Bronx zoo!

"We got five faculty members and the idea is the students come for three years and at the end of that time one of us signs a slip, says they've been at Bensalem for three years and get a Fordham degree. Simple as that. No questions asked. A student could have done shit for three years and still get a degree."

But hadn't the 1970 graduates done well? Three Woodrow Wilson scholarships, one Danforth. And others recommended for Watson and Rhodes?

He kept nodding. "Yeah, but they were Sewell's students. Those classic freaks, into Greek and Latin. Students now aren't into heavy stuff. Oh, you understand, there's the odd person. One woman did a brilliant piece, I hear, on Czechoslovakia, lots of footnotes, that sort of jazz, but she's the exception. Believe me!

"No, most of these kids are screw-offs. They hang around because the rent is cheap, fifty bucks a month; the tuition is something like a thousand dollars a semester, three hundred dollars for the summer session, but most everyone splits for the summer. There's a few good students, I have some in my classes. And they take advantage of Big Fordham, go to classes across the street. It's not the lack of academics which bugs me. It's this living, insane living. Rock music blasting all night, no consideration for anyone. Students think teachers are at their disposal all the time, like we were public telephones. Then the place smells; it's an open sewer."

We left him and went up another flight, heard dogs barking and knocked on a dark door. It opened a few inches and a woman asked what we wanted. It was twelve o'clock, noon, and she yawned as we told her our reasons for being at Bensalem.

"I'm not a student, but you can talk to my husband, I guess." She widened the entrance and two black pups dashed out between her legs. She cursed and slammed the door, leaving them on the stairwell.

It was another apartment without furniture. A mattress was on the floor, wrapped in a giant American flag. There was a black trunk to sit on and a sling chair. The apartment had two bedrooms, a kitchen and down a long hall, a john. There were also two more dogs and a small kitten, which she scooped into her arms and cuddled close. The woman looked as if she hadn't been in the sun for a long time.

She began to talk. "Everyone wants to know about Bensalem. They come around in droves. There was an article in *Look* or *Life* two years ago and the school got three thousand applications." She yawned. "Say, do you have a cigarette?" We shook our heads and she scrounged around among books and records piled on the floor.

The bedroom door on the left opened and another woman appeared, dark hair, dark eyes and incredibly tiny. She was wearing white, lacy panties and nothing else. She watched us for a moment, testing whether our gaze would flinch, then the two women silently embraced. Down the hall the toilet flushed with a clang of metal and the husband appeared, buckling his jeans and nodding hello.

"They're writing a book on Bensalem," his wife explained us.

"I don't talk about Bensalem." He sank into the sling chair. The tiny woman went down the hall to the john and one of the dogs followed, licking at her heels. "You guys got a cigarette?" the husband asked. His eyes lit up.

"I've already asked," his wife explained.

You're leaving soon, we said, making conversation.

"As soon as we can get the hell out. Going to Maine, going to live in the woods, away from this asshole of a city."

Coming back next fall?

"I'm finished. Graduated. Three years of this rip-off." He shook his head in disbelief.

What did you study?

What might have been a smile or a sneer slipped across his face. He was not looking at us, at anything, but gazed off through the room, his sight not centered on a thing.

"Shit, man, you don't study at Bensalem. It's a fuckin' joke." He kept shaking his head. "I'm into photography, film. This place didn't help me a bit. A couple of us pooled our bread, bought equipment. Anyway, you don't learn to be an artist from someone. You're your own genius. Your own teacher." He gestured at a dozen 9-by-10 photos pinned about the room. "That's my stuff." The prints were foggy and faded.

Are you picking up a diploma? We heard a graduate last year wouldn't take one, said it was a sellout.

"Well, that guy had his own kind of sellout. Frankly, I don't give a double shit for that piece of paper, but I'm no jackass. They want the degree out there." He pointed toward the windows.

Did you learn anything at Bensalem?

He sighed. "Sure I've learned. I learn every day of the week. I'm alive, man. But this place didn't teach me anything."

What about the other students?

"Assholes, the whole lot."

"Not everyone," his wife interrupted. "There're some cool people." She looked at us, trying to be convincing.

"Yeah, sure, a few of our friends. But the rest . . . assholes."

"We see as little as possible of everyone. Just stay here, lock the door. It's supposed to be a community, you know," the wife was explaining, "but it's nothing like that. No one trusts anyone. You knock at their doors and you can see them inside looking out through the peephole, but they don't answer. That's what kind of people they are."

"It's all these little cohorts," the husband continued. "We have these community meetings. What a joke! Downstairs in that dinky room. You seen it?" We nodded. "That's the only place we can get together; Fordham won't give us a fuckin' thing. But it doesn't make any difference, no one agrees on anything. Freeman's leaving, that bastard, but there's no one to run this place. No one is acceptable. It's the same way with admissions. We tried to get our friends in so we'd have someone to talk to. We had to go around hustling votes, but no one would help. The blacks fixed us. They got together, see, so twenty of the new students next year are black. That's half the freshman class."

How many black students are there?

"Maybe ten. I don't know. You never see them. They live in a building down the street and don't talk to whites."

You won't recommend Bensalem?

"If a guy wants to fuck off for a year or two, do his own thing, get an easy degree, sure."

"Are you going to tell them how shitting this place is?" his wife asked.

"It's going to change anyway next year. Fordham just did this super-evaluation of the place. It's going to get uptight. They're even putting a Big Daddy in the building, a resident hall director or something. Students will have to get their academic programs okayed every year. They got a whole list of new regulations. It's going to turn into another crummy college. I'm glad I'm getting out. Try to get a copy of that report. It's confidential and everything, but the secretary downstairs has a copy."

We got up to leave, said our thanks. The toilet flushed with another clang and the tiny woman appeared. She had found a shirt and as we angled by her in the narrow hallway, she asked if we had any cigarettes.

Downstairs the Italian secretary banged her fist on the desk and shouted. "Those students have no right telling you about that report. It's confidential. What were their names? Who were they?" She came storming around the desk, but we were out the locked door, into the sunlight and the street, and had fled Bensalem.

Later, sitting on the new green grass of Big Fordham's campus, watching students preparing for final examinations and enjoying the strange, heavy beauty of all the Gothic buildings, we asked a "straight" student who was studying Latin verb endings if he had heard of Bensalem. The student was young, red-haired, Irish-looking, and on the warm day was wearing a coat and tie. Yes, he had heard of Bensalem, he said smiling, friendly.

"It's right across the street, sir, on a hundred ninety-first. It's an honors college, I believe. You got to be smart to go there. I didn't even try." He shook his head in wonderment and went back to his verbs.

LESSONS OF BENSALEM. Bensalem was created by one of those quick Jesuitic decisions. The president of Fordham, Father Leo McLaughlin, bought Elizabeth Sewell's collective living and learning experiment. Now McLaughlin and Sewell are gone and Bensalem lives on like an embarrassment.

The dreams and the dreamers are gone. The idea of the learning community, as simple as it was pure, could not stand the pressures of human failings and faults. Lovers find romance in beautiful settings, perhaps what Bensalem needed was that island in the Atlantic. The dreary environment on 191 Street in the Bronx does not provide the imagination, the charm or the escapes required for such ventures.

RECOMMENDATION. We can't recommend this college. The next year or so we see it going through dramatic changes and developments. We think it will close. If Fordham moves Bensalem from that apartment, gives it leadership, financial and human support, then it might make it as an experimental college. Or whatever.

Bensalem College
558 East 191 Street
Bronx, New York 10458

COLLEGE OF THE POTOMAC

College of the Potomac has no president, no campus, no full-time faculty, no curriculum, no requirements, no money. It does have a Development Building in Washington, D.C., seventy students, nine part-time faculty members, three administrators, nine trustees, and a twenty-two-year-old provost.

The college opened in 1969, established by James Russell who by May, 1971 had quarreled with the trustees and left, leaving behind a scattered idea of a college, an assortment of students and faculty, survival questions and Arthur Webster, the Development Officer, teacher of economics and migrant experimental college buff who has moved with the semesters from one academic watering hole to the next, settling now on the banks of the Potomac.

Webster is important at Potomac because, as the only experienced educator and administrator around, he dominates the scene. Jim Arend, the twenty-two-year-old provost, is likable, earnest and aware, but clearly the progeny of Webster. It was Webster and seven others who put together the six-page memorandum to the Board of Trustees that reorganized the college in June, 1971. This memo, later incorporated into the school's first catalog, pulled what was left together for a second try at being a college.

Russell did not leave much legacy. Just those same elusive dreams shared by folk who rendezvous at experimental schools: "involve the learner," "create a context for completely self-directed learning," "learning without fear," "freedom to fail," "follow the questions where they lead." Webster has, however, his own private vision of experimental colleges. He doesn't think Potomac needs a president. "It's a luxury" they can't afford. He wants administrative costs to be kept to a minimum and Potomac is not prepared, able or willing to provide "a campus" for the students or all those social and academic paraphernalia usually associated with college. But the college is promising itself an interesting twenty-acre campus in Virginia, buildings made of ferro-concrete. These are structures that go up in a few days, but last forever.

What Potomac does best (and only) is facilitate and legitimatize a student's life. And a student's life at Potomac is very much his own world. The catalog says: "The College of the Potomac is designed to serve the educational needs of students who have found that their most profitable learning experiences occur in response to their own inner promptings rather than to supervised, graded course assignments."

Students get assistance from one of the core faculty advisors who plan a year's work with a student. One woman we spoke with had spent a year studying Vietnam, that's all. Her course material was from the Library of Congress, Brookings Institute, the Congressional Record, classes audited at George Washington and Georgetown Universities and the daily newspapers. At the end of the year she did not take an examination or present a paper, though she said she wouldn't have minded doing either. "Vietnam," she said, "I knew!"

Students and faculty take a multi-discipline seminar which meets "at stated frequency." The seminar gives the students exposure to other fields of study and brings the college into something of a community. It's about the only community that there is. Students live throughout the city, finding apartments where they can, but usually locating near DuPont Circle, the youth subculture center of Washington, D.C.

When they're "at school," they are gathered in a wooden brownstone, an arm's length from an expressway artery. It's not much of a building, rickety and worn, bits and pieces of furniture, two telephones and a few bulletin boards. Surprisingly, the walls are free of graffiti, either from respect for their school or total disinterest, non-involvement.

The College of the Potomac does not exist in any place, for it must be more than that one building to survive. It does not reside in anyone (though we suspect the heartbeat of the place is Arthur Webster). The college drifts, like the Potomac itself, among consenting minds. The role of the student "is voluntarily assumed." They come to Potomac for four reasons:

1) the perfecting of learning techniques;
2) the development of new skills;
3) participation in the operation of the college;
4) the development and expansion of areas of awareness.

The faculty is there to:

1) foster the learning experiences of the students;
2) practice in his areas of competency.

Nothing less for either and not much more.

Students wanted by Potomac are those who "are sufficiently motivated, self-reliant, perceptive and creative to take advantage of this form of individualized program." They also must know how to write. This is actually the only admissions requirement. Students submit transcripts, other documentation of previous educational or creative work and essays describing themselves. All applicants are interviewed. In the past almost anyone has been able to get into Potomac, but the school talks about being tougher on admissions. We'll see. So far, there has been much interest and talk about the college, but not many students have applied. It is expensive.

LESSONS OF COLLEGE OF THE POTOMAC. Potomac has been a vague place, difficult to "see." Students were always away and faculty came and went, seldom casting more than a shadow on the school. James Russell was the school. His departure allowed the college the opportunity to move away from a one-man dynasty, to see if there is an idea, a rationale beyond one man's personality and several people's money.

In a way, the people who founded the place, those street people of academics, pausing this time at the Potomac, giving higher education one last chance before dropping out, have been killed off by the new breed of students we've been seeing filling classrooms: students seeking competence.

These students want more structure, or at least *some* structure, in an environment that's non-threatening. They have arranged a new program at Potomac that responds to these needs and they'll spend the next two years seeing if their guess is right.

RECOMMENDATION. How do you recommend an idea? For that's what they're selling. An idea, a notion, a hope that people are inclined to learn and a college need only knock on a few doors, give out I.D. cards and show them where to catch the bus.

The city's the campus! Unfortunately true. It's hard to feel close to the Library of Congress, the White House. In Washington, everyone is a tourist, no one unpacks a suitcase, the whole damn town's a dormitory!

Potomac doesn't separate the student from life, no ivory tower this place. Not even a classroom. Students on the street living to learn. No retreats, no library of one's own. Books can be read anywhere. It's the closest college we've seen where a student can get a degree without going to school; therefore, we recommend it. If you can live with total flexibility, try Virginia's College of the Potomac.

College of the Potomac
2534 K Street N.W.
Washington, D.C. 20008

FRANCONIA COLLEGE

Franconia College looks domineering from a distance, coming toward it from Vermont on Route 117 we saw it high in the round green mountains of New Hampshire, like a white sheet stretched in the trees. It once was a winter resort—this massive building—the Forest Hills Hotel that went bankrupt. Now the wood structure that rambles, floor after floor, dark hall after dark hall, houses student rooms, faculty offices, classrooms, a library and bookstore, the cafeteria. The college is set on a mount with clear views of the Cannon and Lafayette Mountains, the White Mountain Range.

Besides the hotel, the college owns a dormitory in the village of Franconia. The dorm is called Frost Hall after Robert Frost, one-time president of the local Dow Academy. They also own a small secondhand store in the village and we stopped there to ask directions. The young woman in a granny dress storekeeping told us she was a junior at Franconia and was going to Spain for her Out Reach Program. We asked what she planned to do.

"Oh, dance in the streets. Sing."

Franconia started all this in 1963, beginning modestly as a junior college. The community sponsored the place. In 1965 it added a bachelor's degree. Students have to pass two admissions, applying a second time for the upper division. To be admitted for the B.A., students design their own program, present it and obtain faculty who will support their studies. Students usually spend one year in an Out Reach venture during this time. And all students produce a thesis to graduate.

Neil McLaughlin, Dean of Students at Franconia, wrote us about Franconia.

Franconia right now is a good place to be. It is growing together again. We are wrestling constantly with what higher education ought to look like and what our limited resources will allow us to do. The place is going to stay small enough so that an idea will not be lost in the inertia of a bureaucracy. We intend to keep an open admissions policy in an attempt to avoid the inherent stagnation of too homogeneous a student body. We are an expensive school, however, and are trying to get more and more financial aid.

The notion of a social commune/college is disappearing. In its place is a more serious attempt to understand each other's reasons for coming to this place. I came in on the tail end of the commune thing and look back on it as an escapist, fantasy ideal. The people pushing for it saw it as the answer, an immediate solution to all our problems. It wasn't.

The rest of this letter ought to be free associations to your questions.

What a student needs to make it here? He has to be involved in something. An energy level which allows him to get outside of himself and into some quest. We do a lot better with transfer students, who are older and have experienced an alternative educational setup. The student who can make it here is the one who can leave, who can go and do something somewhere else.

Life style? I have heard people refer to us as Freaks, Druggies. . . . I am amazed at the differences in the people who teach and study here. Some of the straightest people I have known exist here. Also some of the craziest. The lack of prevailing attitude such as "we have made it, we are in . . ." is one of the healthiest things about the place. There is a lot of questioning and self-doubt, sometimes it is a drag, but it keeps us honest.

One major turning point for Franconia was the appointment of twenty-four-year-old Leon Botstein. Botstein came to the college by accident. He was visiting the place with friends while the Board of Trustees, faculty and students were searching for a new president during the winter of 1969. He found himself, after several long discussions with students, being considered for the job. Botstein, who has history and music degrees from the University of Chicago and Harvard, and who teaches courses at Franconia like Greek Civilization from Homer to Aristotle and The American College and University in Historical Perspective also runs the college choir. He sees himself as someone who handles "the shit" and he has been handling it quite well.

But he has been lucky. The violence of the drug culture has passed. Students either have experienced this phenomenon in high school or passed it by altogether to become involved with the Jesus Movement or something like Ashtanga Yoga. These activities do not have the built-in destructiveness of hard drugs. These movements depend on contact, on sharing and giving. A neo-idealism is free on the college campuses. Students are becoming *happy* again. And Franconia, one of the few eastern barometer colleges, is attracting the vanguard of the youth movement, new people who have seen older brothers and sisters dropping out and disappearing, "missing everything" as one student put it. These freshmen need to believe and the depression of the campus is over. If anything, they feel greater freedom, a love for peace and the simple things of life. They are not frantic.

Botstein has had the advantage of catching these kinds of people, but more than that, he is honest, efficient and reasonably ambitious. He is able to respond to the relatively simple needs and wants of 350 students. At weekly community meetings he is harassed and badgered by students who are seldom artful or diplomatic in criticism, but he has their good will, and with some humor this place, attacked repeatedly by local conservative papers and its own inhabitants, has weathered the storms, not an easy task in winter where the climate most months is criminal.

Franconia, perhaps more by accident than design, has its own fail-safe device, the two-year flush of the A.A. degree. Only two out of five students continue to the upper division. Admission for the B.A. depends on the quality of the student's proposed program, evidence that he is able to work seriously and independently, and the willingness and competence of a faculty member to advise him. Once in the upper division, the student is still on trial and his progress is evaluated and tested. This method gives Franconia the opportunity to clean the campus of students who are obviously unprepared or unwilling to handle the freedom of advanced work.

Students doing upper division work can spend a year away from Franconia on the Out Reach Program doing research on their Senior Thesis. Many of the topics and Out Reach programs are impressive.

THESIS	OUT REACH
History and Dynamics of Bureau of Indian Affairs Policy in Indian Affairs: The Case of the Navajo	1965–66 VISTA Volunteer, Navajo Indian Reservation, Thoreau, New Mexico
Psychosocial Analysis of Two Lives	Fall, 1966, Halbrook Hospital, Westport, Connecticut, Psychiatric Aide
	Winter, 1966–67, Quakerbridge Home, Ossining, N.Y., resident aide in home for emotionally disturbed
	Spring, 1967, Same
The Cooperative: An Effective Tool for Rural Development	Winter, 1968, Kibbutz Sasa Israel; participatory observation, independent study
The Hand in Education	Fall, Winter, Spring, 1967–68, Antioch College Academic courses
The Importance of Goals in Music Therapy	Fall, Winter, 1968, Overbrook Hospital, Cedar Grove, N.J., clinical training as musical therapist
Education and Its Effects on Perceptual Development in Ghanian Children	Spring, 1968, Ghana Independent Study
	Summer, 1968, Interdisciplinary seminar, University of Ghana
	Fall, 1968, lectures, Institute of African Studies; research with school children

Others went off on Out Reach years and failed to finish the B.A. One student became the youngest clown in the country and worked for Barnum and Bailey circus. He dropped out of Franconia to work full-time as a clown. Another student joined VISTA and lived for one year in Alaska where he wrote several lengthy and outstanding papers.

On-campus students have limited, but eccentric courses:

SUPER SEMINAR — *Glen Marcus*

A seminar course on the comic book as Contemporary Literature and a 20th-century phenomenon. Our aim is to understand why and how the comic book is relevant to our present society as an art form. We will discuss the medium's historical background ranging from scrawls on caves, to the pulp magazines to R. Crumb. Artists' techniques will be surveyed in order to appreciate the work of Ditko, Adams, Kubert, etc. Current trends in the industry will be explored. To earn credit each member of the class will be required to take full part in discussions and read the texts.

Texts employed will include: *The Great Comic Book Super Heroes; The History of the Comic Book;* All in *Color for a Dime.* Seminar will be held twice a week, two hours a session.   *2 credits*

THE PHLEGMATIC FIFTIES? — *Michael Wallace*

An examination of the 1950's, with some consideration of the immediate post-war period. Three critical areas: 1) American imperialism and the rise of the cold war; 2) Domestic politics of the Eisenhower era with some emphasis on McCarthyism and civil rights movement; 3) The culture of the fifties; movies, rock music, theater, comic books, etc.

A presentation will be required: all students will become experts in an area of their choice, will write a paper on that area, and will be responsible (in the second half of the course) for directing a class discussion on the subject of their expertise.

4 credits

GOOD BOOKS, FAIR COFFEE AND TALK — *Richard Hindley*

This evening seminar is intended for students interested in reading certain works of literature in depth. They will present for consideration their critical positions on major works to a group of students who care about books and wish to develop their own ability to articulate what they have read.

Students not interested in earning credit may attend the meetings if they wish.

*Credit variable depending on
involvement and pre-arrangement.*

The college has been doing more lately to connect the school with the village at the bottom of the hill. Two attempts have been the Franconia North Country Players and the Cooperative Nursery School. The theater is outstanding and Franconia is worth going to just for that, but the college offers little more in the way of a defined program. The catalog is whimsical, a collection of items, but no focus in the curriculum, no development of theme. A potpourri. The college bends with the moods of students, with what the current faculty can teach and wants to teach.

Students, faculty and trustees share in the decision-making at Franconia, serving on three major committees. Botstein takes orders from them, but is a voting member of them all. Therefore, he is involved with all aspects. But still, at small Franconia, students have a way of disappearing altogether into private worlds and aren't touched by him.

We talked with a woman in her room in New Dorm, a building designed and built by students and faculty in 1968. She had never spoken to the president.

Why, we asked.

She thought a moment, answered, "Well, I never had anything to say to him."

Like most students at the school, she was from an urban area (Long Island), had transferred from a state school, wanted "snow, the countryside, a little peace." She raved about the white birches which grew thick at the windows of this imaginative and homey dormitory.

Well, how do you like it, we wanted to know.

She nodded rather absentmindedly. "They leave you alone, you know. I mean, no one bothers."

Are you learning anything?

"Sure. I'm alive, aren't I?"

Learning at Franconia costs over forty-five hundred dollars for all experiences. And students going to Franconia are monied and usually from the eastern states, but lately the college is becoming known and applications are coming in from all over. Students are applying to Franconia, according to Skip Lau in the admissions office, because of the rural setting, close to the land. Students are also buying land, settling into the state, far from the cities.

The remoteness of Franconia is its greatest attraction, but it can be, during those long months, a desolate location. Lovely to look at, but hard to live with, even though students ski outside their dormitory rooms. The college has over two hundred acres of woods and fields, including an old golf course. Students do take off, often for weeks, and the Out Reach Program takes everyone away for a year or more, but on campus there is little to entertain. The college runs a speakers' program, and there are movies. The library is small—reminds us of a used bookstore—and the whole place resembles a resort slum. A couple of years ago they didn't even have enough money for clay in the pottery classes. Things are that tight. But the bookstore is a jewel.

LESSONS OF FRANCONIA. Franconia, which went bankrupt once, is proving the hard way that it can work. It has been able to bounce back, to change, to adjust, to respond from within, to handle bitter in-fighting and revolt. Now with a governance policy that is spread through all parts of the school—among students, faculty and trustees—Botstein need only be an administrator, but a good one. He appears to be that. This new governance and full partnership has worked at Franconia where it hasn't worked elsewhere, perhaps because of Botstein's attitude and age.

Besides this, Franconia has Out Reach responding to the desire of students today who want to travel, be involved off campus, earn credit for learning on their own.

RECOMMENDATION. This is a game place with a terrible track record. Its faculty is limited in size and scope, but it is, as Neil McLaughlin has written, "wrestling constantly with what higher education ought to look like." It's trying to shape a program which gives students full range, and the stages—the progression through two degrees—helps the students to handle the intoxicating freedom of the place. Strangely, Franconia works in that funny hotel.

Franconia College
Franconia,
New Hampshire 03580

FRIENDS WORLD COLLEGE

Friends World College opened in 1965 and now has three hundred students spread thinly throughout the world. It's a private school chartered by New York State, and expensive. Tuition is $2,000 a year (another $700 to $1,800 is needed for room, board and travel). Admissions is based on a formal application, references, transcripts and personal interviews. The college is looking for students who have had some cross-cultural experience—at home or overseas—and want to study while traveling, want to live closely and extensively in other cultures, want to learn several languages, and who are able to manage independently far from the United States.

Students spend six semesters around the world, studying at or near one of the regional centers in Cuernavaca, Mexico; Kaptagat, Kenya; Cambridge, England; Bangalore, India; Kyoto, Japan; Los Angeles, California, and Long Island, New York, getting what the college calls an education "experimental in nature, transitional in scope, and Quaker in spirit." (Though only 10 percent of the students are Quaker.)

Students going to Friends World are concerned about problems of the world, but are not heavy into academics or careers. Their lifestyle at the North American Center is free; a bit tighter and more restricted at the other centers. The administration lets students handle their own lives. The college's position on sex indicates the openness of the place.

While the college recognizes the right of each of its members to make his own judgments in the area of sexual relations, it emphasizes the importance in all interpersonal relationships of a constructive attitude based on respect for the sensibilities of third parties. Recognizing different customs of different areas, the reputation of the college itself must be considered. In order to make the judgments free from direct or subtle pressure in the sexual revolution, individuals who wish to resist this pressure will be supported by the college. The privacy of one's own room will be respected by the college community.

The academic program also lets a student build his own curriculum. It works like this: within the first month of each semester—and almost every semester is in a different country—the student, with a faculty member or resource person, works out a field of study and a location. This study is usually connected with a community school, social organization or some professional in arts, science or humanities. One advantage of Friends World, and the key element in the education program, is the college Resource Data Bank. This is a collection of people throughout the world doing innovative work. These resource people and organizations work with students in developing projects and evaluating their progress.

Besides this project, which sometimes means a job with a minimal salary, the student continues tutorial work through correspondence with his home campus. At the end of the semester—and each semester is six months long—the student comes back to the center and presents his project, giving his own evaluation of it and his achievements or failings. There are no grades. Some of the projects students at the North American Center have done are:

Studying health and healing, including "the nature premise, the chiropractic principle, and the astrological realm" with a nurse in Virginia

Participating in a wilderness experience and working on a farm in rural New Brunswick; also reading in psychology and philosophy

Working for a commission of farm workers in the South

Living on an Indian reservation in northern Quebec

Studying archeological techniques in a West Coast university to be followed by digging on a newly-discovered site formerly inhabited by Indians

Doing a photographic documentary with an author on poverty in the United States

Working in a legal services office in New York City; considering welfare problems, housing problems, family problems

Teaching art in a free school

One requirement students have is to keep a journal. It's an open journal kept at the student's home campus, and is the cumulative record of a student's work and progress. Sanno Keeler in the first class explains what her journal is about:

> *I plan to make it far more than just a record of experience; I plan to record my philosophies, ideals, thoughts, struggles. . . . I will record my experiences in foreign countries and will also include my creative writing and reports on world problems and interesting books.*
>
> *Perhaps I should mention that the school is problem-oriented. Instead of studying specific "subjects" as in other schools, we take definite problems and study them and try to arrive at solutions. We travel a great deal in order to live with the problems and experience them and understand them as far as possible. Our discussions are framed in silence, a silence for meditation. We live as a close community. Students and staff are searching together for answers. There is no need of arbitrary rules or policies to govern us; any problems concerning our community are settled in a Quaker business meeting using the method of consensus rather than voting. I hope this gives a general impression of the school. This is the first year and we are, of course, very experimental.*

Fifty percent of Friends World students don't finish at the college. This high attrition is not seen as a failing. The majority of those who drop out continue college elsewhere, indicating to Friends World that the student has found, through the exposure of experimental learning, an area or subject to study in detail.

Those who stay with Friends World travel. They go from one center to the next in all sorts of ways, by plane, bus, Land Rover, lorry, VW camper, traveling alone or in twos and threes. Freshman students, going to Mexico from Long Island for second semester in February, 1971, went there by way of Canada, following the border to the West Coast, then south. Four other students in 1970 traveled overland from England to India.

After the initial semester at the North American Center, the majority go to the Latin American program, starting at the Center in Cuernavaca, Mexico. Everyone receives four to five weeks of Latin American orientation and Spanish in Mexico. This is tough language study, at least five hours a day. Then students move further south into Latin America, studying such things as regional planning, economic, political or social innovations, population control, distribution of wealth. In 1969 one group of six students with faculty member spent five months doing a survey of conditions in twelve countries in Central and South America. They traveled by VW bus, separated in each area for individual assignments, then reunited and traveled to the next area, sharing their findings on the journey.

The next semester (or an alternate semester) is in England. Using Cambridge as a base, the resources of London, students study Europe, traveling as far east as Moscow. The Friends World Center at Cambridge has four faculty members and offices in a rented building. Students make their own living arrangements—as they do at most centers—with the help of the faculty.

Students going to Africa or India usually wait until the second year. In Africa, Friends World has a twenty-six-acre campus in the Rift Valley. The resident faculty in Kenya is African and the curriculum concerns Africa, all aspects of it. From the center at Kaptagat, students travel on field trips to game parks, Mount Kenya and Mount Kilimanjaro, along the East African coast and into Central Africa. Students have gone overland from Kenya to the Congo. Other students went by Land Rover from Kenya to India.

India, usually the next stop, has its Friends World Center in Bangalore, the seventh city of the country, and situated high on a southern plateau. The orientation lasts six weeks and emphasis is on social systems, the village, family, caste relationships and religion. Then students go off on their own. Recent studies were: yoga exercises; making batik; lessons in Indian music—sitar, veena and tabla; classical Indian dances; Indian languages—Kannada, Tamil and Malayalam.

Students arriving in Japan go first to Hiroshima, then to Kyoto and live in a Zen Buddhist temple for lectures, discussions and language. They also visit an intentional community near Mount Fuji, travel to South Korea for two weeks, and return to Hiroshima for instruction in brush painting and calligraphy, dance and Koto music, language and more lecture and discussion in Japanese history, literature, economics and politics.

The faculty of Friends World is involved with their students and come to Friends World for a variety of reasons, but money isn't one of them. Salaries are very low, as low as four thousand dollars a year, though living quarters are usually provided. The names and interests of a few teachers at the North American Center are:

BARRINGTON DUNBAR—*Development of an Afro-American Study Center which provides the atmosphere to facilitate dialogue, discussion and depth inquiry about the problem of race. The Center, known as the Malcolm X Center, serves as a reference library with books, periodicals and artifacts pertaining to the history, culture and lifestyles of black people in Western Civilization, and social programs. The Center will also stimulate and sponsor programs, depicting the cultural expressions of black people.*

THOMAS W. FINDLEY—*Environmental sciences: interaction of man with his physical environment (water, air and soil pollution). Local applications of science and technology (i.e., soap-making).*

DAVID ROOMY—*Study in depth psychology and religion directed toward inner concerns and relationships between people of different cultures.*

C. KISH SAINT—*Education and living; critique of the existing systems and their historical and theoretical supports; educational systems as modes of institutional legitimization; search for alternatives in modes of living—Illich, Reimer, Freire, Gandhi.*

P. VEERAVAGU—*Mass Media and Human Events: A study of the reporting of controversial national and international events. East and West: the philosophical quest of man in various times and cultures. A study of universities and student activism in world perspective.*
Science and Society.

And writes the co-director from Japan:

"I am just Nicola Geiger, with no added letters, who learned whatever she may know from a miscellany of teachers, from life, from attempted practice of its lessons, and, I hope, from study of my own failures and shortcomings."

Friends World College is still evolving, establishing and modifying its philosophy. Education at the college is not a static set of knowledge, facts and figures, not a particular course to be mastered.

Pat Barr, a student in 1969, writes about this in her orientation:

I have not really gained a great deal of factual knowledge. I have gained something just as important and much more basic—I have changed my previously restricted and narrow concept of world problems and issues to a more humanistic concept which is unlimited in depth of understanding. My growth is not only measured by becoming aware of my conditioned responses but also by my beginning to really think with a mind that is much more open, aware, and sensitive to ideas that come from a completely different background (than my quote, upper-middle-white-American-up-bringing).

As I look back on the orientation period, I see the following stages that I went through:

1) relating the issues to my own life—becoming overwhelmed at the immenseness of the problems—seeing only the faults without thinking about positive solutions.

2) *concentrating more on solutions—becoming impatient with discussing such urgent needs for social change without taking any action.*

3) *realizing how much there is to be done—feeling frustrated with the fact that as one person I can only accomplish a comparatively small stride in social change.*

4) *tiring of repeating discussions of ideals—feeling like I am dealing only in the abstract—wondering what I can do.*

5) *deciding to get my feet on the ground—planning work in a real-life situation.*

The orientation period has been very successful for me. I don't believe it was planned to give the students a wealth of knowledge. I have tasted the wines and now I am ready to get drunk!

Thank you for your patience! And also for the tip on worrying too much. You're great advisors—I can't get away with any bullshit when I talk with you.

LESSONS OF FRIENDS WORLD. This kind of education really has no semester beginning or ending, but is continuous. This wandering from country to country, from one culture to the next is purposeful. The wandering itself is educational, the vehicle of learning. Three new cultures in four years makes for a tough education.

The college really is a series of experiences, intense and demanding, that make a student deal with himself, other students, a community and new cultures. Realizing success and failure and testing oneself by one's hard evaluation is what education is about. It is what Friends World is all about.

RECOMMENDATION. Much of what you've just read sounds, we're sure, exactly what you want in a college education. Friends World has a brilliant idea: learning by travel and experience. But like almost everything else, it sounds better than it actually is.

Organization problems have always plagued the college, very little continual contact is maintained with students, and the scattered centers have had trouble keeping faculty. Also, there's not a lot of money at Friends World and equipment and facilities are limited.

The freedom of living on your own and planning your own academic career is not easy. We recommend Friends World College with the warning that it will provide you great opportunities for learning, but not much personal support or academic direction.

Friends World College
North American Campus
Mitchell Gardens
Westbury, New York 11590

I GOT IT AT GODDARD

We went to Goddard, Vermont, in the first warm weeks of May and at the beginning of a new trimester. The campus was a happy place; couples strolled hand in hand and smiled at strangers. What had been a hard winter, ten feet of snow, bitter campus politics, was past. Students sat on the small green patches of lawn outside of the dining hall, smoking dope and selling vases, bottles and pots, leather pouches made in their craft classes. And they were reading—an uncommon phenomenon now-adays—everyone had a paperback and was stretched out in the sun. It was afternoon and no one seemed to have class.

In fact, we couldn't find a class in our stay at Goddard. Not a legitimate one, at least, desk and blackboards. Teachers taught where they were: in dormitories, offices, lounges, the library, anywhere at all.

Goddard is a close collection of brown shingled buildings, parts of an old farm hovering on a hill, overlooking the Onion River and a long valley of woods and farm land. There are twelve dormitories, doll houses, designed, it seemed, by Levitt and spaced out on a bare hill. The president's house, white and unimposing, is mixed in with the dorms. The last structure on this campus is the Design Center, put together in all sorts of strange shapes, designed and built by students themselves.

Beyond the Greatwood Campus and reached through a cool, damp, wooded path is the brick and glass Eliot D. Pratt Library. It's hidden in the trees, hooked onto a cliff, and, next to it, the Sculpture Building under construction.

Goddard's second campus is Northwood a half mile away. It's new and luxurious, six wedges of solid garden apartments situated on a hilly mound, with a pond and concrete paths.

That's all there is to Goddard, except for the crafts shops down in Plainfield near the post office, in an old house and several sheds. Obviously, one doesn't go to Goddard for the buildings.

But why do they go, spending at least $4,600 a year? We kept asking this question, and no one gave us the same answer twice, and usually those answers were vague, cloudy, forgotten or unimportant.

What was important was why they were there, or why they were leaving, for students leave Goddard. Only two out of ten graduate, and they transfer in from other colleges as if they were on bus schedules. As one student put it: "If you come from somewhere else you graduate, if you come as a freshman, you won't." The trouble is one of disenchant-ment. It follows the euphoria of beginning at a college, enrolling in a place where there are no grades, no requirements, no rules or regulations about how students live, or with whom, and where there are courses like: Javanese Gamelan; Neo-Marxist Analysis of Advanced Capitalism; the

Creation of Revolutionary Feminism; Cosmic Quest; Basic French; Ceramics; Jewelry; Guerilla Warfare in the Videosphere; Polymorphous Reality; El Realismo Mayego; Madrigals; Household Electricity; Novels of Ayn Rand; Introduction to Eastern Religions. You can, at Goddard, take a little bit of everything.

You can also get at Goddard opinions on everything. It's a tight community; no more than six hundred at a time, and strangers are noticed. People sought us out to give statements, but when all the sides are straightened, ordered, a simple set of sides are offered. Students are either "freaks" or "hippies"; faculty, "touchy-feely" or "subject-matters." There are a few other types—the Black–Third World folks; Goddard has fifty-five but only eight were on campus when we visited. And they keep to themselves.

This phenomenon of the freaks and hippies as two different types is something we noticed at Goddard and have seen at other schools. We do not think it is accidental. Colleges are about to experience a new kind of student.

Visually there is little difference between the freaks and the hippies, though at Goddard we noticed hostility between them. The freaks talked disparagingly about hippies tinkling bells over brown rice, and dumped on the commune living. The freak is a private person who has taken from the hippie's counter-culture his dress, style of life, flexibility and is using the college to gain skills. He has a realistic view of the world and realizes just because he *wishes* certain results they are not going to be immediately gratified. Goddard's faculty is beginning to sense this new student who is looking for competence and who is appearing in larger numbers on their campus. They say students are coming into offices, looking for books to read, information.

The faculty itself is divided between subject-matter and touchy-feely types. This is an oversimplification we realize, but everywhere we went some faculty member would mention the division. And the president seems to be the greatest touchy-feely of them all.

We kept looking for someone to say something nice about Jerry Witherspoon, the president, but no one would, except a few administrators, insiders on his staff. During the long winter session Witherspoon had been fighting with faculty and students. The focal point was the Hanover Plan, written by the president and his administration during a week retreat. Almost everyone not at Hanover resented this document printed on what one faculty member called "Presidential Pink." The forty pages outlined Goddard's future, the shape of things to come, as Witherspoon envisioned it.

But before going on with this document, a little about Jerry Witherspoon, because he dominates most conversations at Goddard. Witherspoon had been at Goddard three years, was a compromise candidate, selected after a twenty-month search. He succeeded Tim Pitkin, a grand old Vermonter who designed Goddard and ran it for thirty years.

Witherspoon, who is thirty-nine and looks, as one student said, like a weathered Paul Newman, was Vermont's tax commissioner and has a political, not educational background, though he did teach a couple of business and law courses at Dartmouth and Berkeley. When he arrived at Goddard in 1967, he began immediately to make changes, creating an impression. First was an elaborate governance system, a set of councils of equal representation by faculty and students. Dissectors of Witherspoon said he was afraid Goddard would go the way of Berkeley and Columbia and wanted to stem the radical thrust, but few students at Goddard are radical. Next, he needed money and moved to increase tuition and students balked. He also arranged an elaborate trimester system and increased enrollment. Then he moved into educational development, creating what he called "100 flowers," diverse experimentation. Some of these were: Radical and Humanistic Studies; course 304; off-campus projects in Taos, San Francisco and San Miguel; the Bread and Puppet Theatre; SKETE; the Design-Construction Project.

All these "100 flowers"—called weeds by dissenters—produced controversy on campus, because they cut drastically into existing budgets and were created "arbitrarily" by Witherspoon.

Another aspect of Witherspoon that grated on people—particularly subject-matter faculty and students—is how he "bought" the youth culture. Witherspoon went to Goddard, one older student said, "to relive his youth."

The only academic requirement is the senior study. There is talk of developing a program and a plan of course study. Witherspoon in his Hanover Plan arranged it in three stages to fit in his nine-trimester Goddard education.

Stage One is exploratory, putting the student in touch with his world. When students can *unlearn* and then begin *to learn*. Stage Two is "extension of perceptions, skills and arts or knowledge," and Stage Three is "devoted to synthesis, application and projection."

A normal four-year program would look like this:

	FALL	WINTER	SPRING
1	Residence	Residence	Non-Residence
2	Vacation	Residence	Residence
3	Non-Residence	Vacation	Residence
4	Non-Residence	Residence	Graduation

People now, as one student said, "go to Goddard instead of going to college." There is endless free-flowing. One can graduate after four years without taking anything academic, for there are no accumulations of credits, just the senior study, and that, according to Tom Absher, in a memo to the faculty, suffers from Goddard's looseness.

"We encourage Omni-Think and All-Speak among our students, course after course, allowing intellectual *hubris* to go unchecked, unchallenged by regular paper writing or simple humility and then, over and over again as students approach their senior studies they want to kill themselves because they can't write a *Summa Everything*. Our students think it beneath them to write on something 'modest' like Joyce's *Ulysses*, or World War I, they want to write a novel in one trimester, or they take on topics like Alchemical-Jungian Epistemologies in the Work of Blake, Nietzsche and Proust in the Light of a Tarot Reading of Beethoven's Ninth Played Backward. Submitted in *Partial* Fulfillment. . . ."

No one flunks at Goddard or loses a semester's credit. As long as a student is there, pays tuition, breathes, he progresses. Writing about this concern of subject-matters faculty, Witherspoon says:

> *The question of sanctions or standards inevitably arises: shouldn't a student who is not performing at an acceptable level be "flunked out" of the college? The question assumes, of course, that the purpose of college is to qualify students to live and work in the adult world. Goddard is not preparation for life, but a special way of living it which recognizes that education will, and must, continue as long as one is alive. People do not "succeed" or "fail" with that kind of life and education, but their rate of growth may vary significantly with the settings in which they find themselves and with the way they relate to those environments.*

The environment at Goddard has its own committee to manage it, and the problems are many. Notes from Environmental Council Meetings outline the concerns:

> *February 18, 1971*
> *The Environmental Council convened last Thursday, morning and afternoon, to hold a long and moderately heated discussion on several issues concerning people on the campus. An impromptu discussion of pets began the meeting, in response to a report from Belmont that an unidentified dog had seriously bitten a student on Greatwood, and that there was only one hour left to determine whether or not the woman should begin the 21-day rabies series. A girl at the meeting said she knew the dog, and she and Ken King left to see if it was inoculated. It was pointed out that any untagged dogs are a serious hazard as the annual fox-carried spread of rabies rises rapidly. A number of students were annoyed about the sudden lack of wildlife, and*

dogs were felt to be a significant cause of the scarcity of local fauna (rabbits, squirrels, chipmunks, deer). The afternoon session was a discussion of guests and college guest policies. A position paper of Allen Cobb was juxtaposed with an older paper generated by an ad hoc committee of the council. The former emphasized the positive aspects of guests and their contributions to the community and the necessity of visits from friends, while the latter primarily outlined a three-day policy which could be extended on request or in special cases. The discussion centered around the fact that some people (in Giles, where ten unknown or long-term people were living in the lounge and one room) are unable to control their own living situation without some support from the administration (or somewhere).

Then, in a memorandum to the Community from the president on October 4, 1970, titled "Cops and Robbers":

Last night Kimberly Cheney, the Washington County prosecutor or "State's Attorney," and his deputy Bob Gagnon, dropped by the college to have a cup of coffee in the community center with Cary Smith. He let us know in advance that they were coming so that no one would make the mistake of thinking that their purpose was to make a bust on the college. When Cheney returned to his car in a Greatwood parking lot a few minutes later, he found that all four of his tires had been slashed and that two raincoats had been stolen from the car.

And, in a note distributed in the community last year:

Dominingo exploits women by forcing himself upon them sexually and otherwise. Women have demanded that he leave Goddard immediately. He was told of this demand last night (Friday night) by a gathering of women. If he is not gone by Sunday night, a large group of women will meet in King basement to decide further actions.

Dominingo did not leave; the women met and beat him up.

The males set the tone of the social life. There is pressure for everyone to conform and pairing up on the small campus is nearly mandatory. Women do not have much freedom, though a dozen have formed their own Lib dormitory.

There is not much sex among housemates of a dormitory. "It would be like sleeping with your sister," one student put it. As a result, close family relationships are established in the dorms. We spent a delightful afternoon in the kitchen of the organic food dormitory on Northwood campus. The elaborate kitchen of the Northwood campus, built by the Design Construction students, is the gathering place for the building. Students wandered in and out through the afternoon, preparing bits of lunch, snacks, talking about themselves and the SKETE program they are part of.

"It means we just take care of ourselves, buy our own food, organize ourselves, that's all." A transfer student at Goddard, short, chubby and obviously the den mother of the collective was explaining, "It's an African term, meaning collective or something." She was shelling peanuts as she spoke, losing half of the bowl to quick hands that darted into her work when she paused. "We were together last year and its kinda groovy being back on campus, here. We hope to find out from the college how much our dorm pays for electricity. We want to pay that, too. You know, get a good sense of how much money it takes to manage."

And all the Northwood dormitories are this satisfied, we asked.

"Oh, no," a half dozen others doing chores around the kitchen commented. "Some of them . . . wow . . . real bummers," a student in overalls, bearded and barefooted and finishing off a jar of honey, answered.

"You got to have something to hold you together. Like this organic garden we're starting. You've got to have that. I mean, you've got to have a community. A purpose, I mean. You might as well eat in the cafeteria if you're not into something. Anyway, why you guys asking all these questions?"

We explained about the book and he listened carefully, nodded and said as farewell, "Okay, but have them print it on recycled paper."

Other groups on Northwood are trying to "create a flowing and loving community." They want to abolish the positions of president, educational director, environmental and financial directors, and establish eight to ten half-time teaching, half-time administrative positions. "By having faculty and students sharing we will transcend the fear of power plays, put no one in the position of being scapegoat, give everyone the opportunity to work in the college and effect change. Every employee will receive basically the same salary, varied according to the number of people dependent on the salary."

Many students are not happy with the community concept, the sharing—or failure to share—responsibility. A letter in one of the campus newspapers reflects this concern and wishes for something more in campus life.

IF I RAN THE ZOO

Did any of you ever wish simple things like an end to burnt nauseating mattresses from AL? Simple things like humanity among individuals in a land where those who give the most lip service to love and peace continually shit on their neighbors or protect freeloaders who shit on their neighbors.

You all know what I mean. It's everything from strychnine mesc to loud music while others are trying to sleep, to library and bookstore rip-offs.

It's the result of a Goddard Laissez Faire given at most of those who understand it the least. It comes from a good majority of the people here not knowing when they are well off! And because they don't know when they're well off, they feel no particular patriotism for (i.e. love and community for) Goddard.

Because of this, the ones who came expecting to find community and only find mess-ups, become cynical and angry and while they're doing their work, they think Goddard should just bump-off.

If I had any control over the curators' office, the main requirements would be geared toward those who had spent some time away from home paying rent, cooking, and cleaning, and working basically on their own. Or else they had spent some time in some pig university recognizing the fact that they weren't getting an education there and the value of an education. NOT just the sort of whimpering I used to hear in some quarters back there. The "I don't like it here, the homework's too hard, I can't read all these books shit."

But alas I'm dreaming. Goddard couldn't do such things—the personification of Goddard is a junkie so strung out that he can't even wipe his or her own ass. What I would like is a dorm for students on Northwood that is similar to the Third World dorm, where people could study and live and develop a community within the walls of one lousy building so that its members can do to the world what they will.

This is a call for solidarity, with the other freaks around believing that clean dishes and pots and pans isn't too much to ask.

This sense of community is found in several places at Goddard, particularly the Design Center, the most interesting educational innovation they have, due largely to David Sellers and John Mallory who believe people learn by making decisions and even pounding a nail is making a decision. Students at the center do much more than just pound nails; they conceptualize, design and produce a product. And their products are not small: they built the Sculpture Building, their own studio, the SKETE kitchens and have plans for low-income housing, structural engineering programs, new materials and new concepts in habitation, and study social design and its influence on the environment.

The center is also more than building projects or learning skills with tools. It is involved with the art of architecture. "Architecture is organic and ecological: buildings are brought into being to enhance the activities they shelter, but beyond that, they represent an articulation of living and doing with land, climate, trees, wildlife—man's given environment, his sharing in which makes his life whole." Students and teachers live in, work with and visit the building they've designed and constructed. This is, as they say, "education of a very fundamental kind."

All students at Goddard are in the Work Program. It's eight hours a week and required. The purpose is to save money, as much as $160,000 a year. But it is also more. "It's a worthwhile extension of the self for the benefit of others." Students work in the cafeteria, clean their own dormitories, work in the library and offices. The Work Program has always been a part of Goddard. And the money saved helps to finance aid. Goddard gives grants amounting to almost five hundred thousand dollars.

Goddard's other programs are, briefly:

Chicano. Students work with the Crusade for Justice, a militant Chicano organization in Denver. A community school in Denver has 130 students and Goddard students teach there.

Dance. Modern dance, ballet, folk, happenings, games, etc. The dance relates to theater, psychology, general semantics and anthropology.

Ecology of the Southeast. Twenty-five students and a faculty member have a bus, camping gear, bicycles and boats, and are studying the ecology of the southeastern states. It covers everything from agriculture and arts to cafe life.

GIFAS: Goddard Institute for Anthroposophical Studies. A community of students who live on a farm in the Vermont hills half an hour from campus. They are "people who share a strong concern for personal growth or 'self-actualization' and spiritual understanding." The focus of the Institute is on such themes as reincarnation and karma. It also provides a setting for individual experimentation relating to spiritual science.

Off-Campus Field Service. The field program develops a college without walls within a radius of some fifty miles around Goddard. Students work with different agencies—children, youth, and adult organizations—in such programs as mental health clinics, museums, free schools, the state government, environmental education, etc. It usually lasts one trimester.

Third World Studies. It is autonomous and for blacks only. There are fifty-five full-time students, five full-time resident staff and seven part-time faculty. It publishes its own calendar and course listing.

304. This is involved with the medium of print—304 symbolizes the triangle, circle and square. Students and teachers concerned with writing and journalism, printing and publishing, poetry and photography.

Goddard also has a repertory theater company, teacher education—with its own pre-school on campus, a local Head Start and day care program and students teach in Vermont and New Hampshire schools. Visual Arts is not organized in a formal way, but a broad range of visual media is available, from painting to film to weaving, plus studio space, a glass furnace and a dozen harness looms. Not bad for a small school.

Non-residence Program. The non-residence terms are a large part of a Goddard education. One student explained it by saying: "You pay the college tuition so you can go somewhere else and collect unemployment while you look for a job." It's not quite that bad. Not quite. At the moment there is little support—financial or otherwise—for students away from school. There is also little feedback or organized reflection after students return to campus. Students now just "go away" and spend a trimester learning or doing something. Goddard's administration and faculty talk about making adjustments in the program and Witherspoon in his Hanover Plans has elaborate proposals. It will take work to make the non-residence program work.

LESSONS OF GODDARD. Trying to catch the pulse of Goddard is difficult. Like anyone or anyplace, no simple sentence sums it up. The college resists stereotyping. But aspects of the place are general enough for comment. There is a certain sameness of the student body. Not many straight people around. This is a problem for any small experimental school. The campus lacks heterogeneity. Students need contact and contrast with others who are involved with different kinds of academic programs, have other ideals and lifestyles.

We found only the occasional student happy with Goddard and they invariably had been on the campus just a few weeks. And they were usually transfer students, who had come from a worse location. Those who had been around awhile were bitter, disappointed and withdrawing from the scene. They sealed themselves up and were defensive. Like most students at experimental colleges.

We did not find great leadership or even much leadership in the administration or faculty. The Adult Degree Program—which makes it possible to obtain a non-resident degree—directed by impetuous Dick Hathaway had the closeness and order of development to ensure measurable results, and gave a frame of reference to students.

The regular Goddard undergraduate education is structured for learning in units of work. The students design their own program. The opportunities at Goddard for learning are many, but students often are frightened by the possibilities. With the whole world before them it is hard to select. They make mistakes and go off on broken ideas; they waste time getting themselves together. This slippage is highly visible at the school. Students do not have the protective shield of classroom routine, college functions and manufactured activities to hide behind. Their academic sins are readily exposed.

Judson Jerome in his excellent *Culture Out of Anarchy* (Herder and Herder, 1971) writes about what happens to students in such situations:

> *Young people are not prepared by their home lives or schools to make decisions and often are nearly incapable of discovering within themselves the grounds for order, discipline, direction and purpose. They have dreamt of what they would do if it weren't for the limits and demands imposed upon them; but when they are free they are likely to unzip and find nothing inside. If you believe you would be creative, industrious and productive except for external restraints, you can retain some hold on dignity, though you feel continually frustrated. But if you discover that you do not, in fact, spontaneously create—or even read, that you are not really very interested in cultural or political events, in ideas, in intellectual issues, that you have little drive to achieve, that there is nothing in particular that you want to do with your life, and that you cannot blame these things you perceive as deficiencies upon some system beyond your control, you are likely to suffer waves of guilt, self-hatred and paralysis of will.*

We did at Goddard find these waves of guilt, self-hatred and paralysis of will, and all this resentment was in May being focused on the president and his plans for Goddard. Everyone, students and faculty, were blaming Witherspoon or Goddard for what was happening to them. But, then, Goddard has been blamed for educational innovation over the years. Much of what is happening in colleges and universities today was started years ago by Tim Pitkin. Whether Witherspoon can handle the situation, pull the forces back together, is not clear. We think he will. But do not expect to hear glowing words about the college; as we said, everyone bad-mouths the place. A year or so ago the villager who ran an illegal bar on campus got drunk one night and killed himself driving home. His last words, fixing the blame, were, "I got it at Goddard."

RECOMMENDATION. We like Goddard, like its setting and its history of innovation in education. Goddard is away from the rush of things and it can be a lonely place unless you have reason for being at school. The openness of the dormitories presents problems, especially the problems of uninvited guests. That situation can be handled if roommates are responsible. There are good people teaching at the school, though Goddard—like all small colleges—doesn't have great resources. If Goddard can straighten out its non-residence program, then you can get what they used to call a good liberal education.

Goddard College
Plainfield, Vermont 05667

HAMPSHIRE COLLEGE

We got the feeling walking about the Hampshire College campus that someone there wants to save the world. Students and faculty are always doing those old Peace Corps things: playing touch football on the meadows, having a kite-flying contest at the inaugural festival, rappelling off the library building in preparation for a mountain climbing trip, and speaking gravely about themselves, as did Archibald MacLeish at the first Convocation: "I think we may be present at a greater moment than we know."

The students have long hair and the usual assortment of overalls, faded jeans, leather, patchwork pants, but we got the feeling they had purchased everything. Hampshire students are monied. They are also friendly, have a nice easy confidence and a certain assumed guilt at their specialness. They are the first class at a school which *Time* magazine called, "the hardest college in the U.S. to get into." Perhaps.

It all began in 1958 (or according to some, in 1762, but more about that later) when faculty gathered from the four other valley schools: Smith, Mount Holyoke, Amherst and the University of Massachusetts. It was called New College—what else?—and the planners in 1966 took over farm buildings on 550 acres of country three miles south of Amherst. The first class came in 1970: 259 freshmen from 2,002 that applied.

The college breaks the "academic lockstep" as they say with four features:

1) delayed admissions and sanctioned leaves;
2) first division seminars and a January Term;
3) three divisions in place of four-year progression;
4) comprehensive examinations as a measure of progress.

This was revolutionary in 1958 and even in 1966, but many colleges today have much of the same. Hampshire will have to hurry to catch up.

Hampshire's three divisions are arranged this way:

I. Courses in seminar form. All students study a variety of areas in the three schools. Takes about two years.

II. One or two disciplines are studied in depth. Work is "carried out in accordance with a particular study plan in concentration designed by the student and his advisors."

III. Concentration on a single area and the production of a thesis or special project. Takes about one year.

The schools are: Humanities and Arts; Natural Science and Mathematics; Social Science. There is also the Program in Language and

Communication which will be the college's "deliberate use of education to improve its students' understanding of communication." Undergraduates can also study law.

Students move from division to division by passing comprehensive examinations, which the students help design. There are no grades, semester hours or course credits. The first year's program looks like this:

2 WEEKS	12 WEEKS	4 WEEKS	12 WEEKS	3 WEEKS
Fall Colloquy	Science Seminar, Workshop or Lectures	January Term	Science Seminar, Workshop or Lectures	Reading and Exams
	Humanities Seminar and Tutorial		Social Science Seminar and Tutorial	
	Lecture-Seminar in Human Development		Lecture-Seminar in Language and Communication	

Courses are varied and, as they say at Hampshire, "relevant." Some are: Alternative Environmental Structures; Cuban Revolution; Utopias: Ideal and Experimental Communities in Theory and Practice; N. O. Brown, R. D. Laing. H. Marcuse: Views of Human Nature; De Rerum Natura; Game Theory; Dimensions of Consciousness. And then some straight stuff: The American Literary Landscape, Plato's Earlier Dialogues, Organic Chemistry in 3-D.

The January term gets students away from isolated Hampshire, the cold and snow. Many colleges have similar systems, but as Carolyn Atkinson, the coordinator points out, "Hampshire thought of it first!" It was proposed in 1958 as part of the experimental curriculum. (In your heart you know Hampshire's No. 1.) The month sessions respond to what is currently "in." Samplings:

EXPERIMENT IN CHRISTIAN LIVING
SHIELA HOULE

For four weeks a group of 8 students, men and women, still live the Benedictine rule. Adopting this life style will entail community living on a smaller scale than Merrill House permits and will include times of prayer, both personal and group, work, discussions, and recreation. The work will be both physical (primarily cleaning, painting, and making livable the old house we will be staying in) and intellectual and creative. Members may want to study in a particular area, write, or practice music. The project requires those involved to live, eat, and sleep in the same dwelling and to have no outside responsibilities. The exact cost to each participant for housing, food, and basic furnishings will be determined by the final number of the group.

WHY THE SEA IS BOILING HOT: FANTASIES
CAROLYN ATKINSON

Alice's Walrus suggested we have many things to talk about—cabbages, sealing wax, whether pigs have wings. The sorts of fantasies that led the Walrus to this statement are what we will talk about and create in this course.

As a beginning, we will read together a few of the best-known fantasies, looking specifically at those written for children, but important to adults. Alice in Wonderland and Through the Looking Glass, The Wind in the Willows, The Little Prince, Winnie the Pooh, Charlotte's Web are high on this list. We might consider others as well, such as The Hobbit and E. B. White's new The Trumpet of the Swan.

After we know these stories and each other a little better, we may choose to create our own fantasy worlds, either singly or collectively. Our fantasies could be realized in many ways—through narratives, graphics, dramas, histories, maps.

What the stories that we read mean, how or if we choose to realize our own fantasies, what importance they have for us—these are questions we will consider as we work together. And we may consider the question of why the sea is boiling hot.

GOING WITH THE DOGS
RAYMOND COPPINGER

There is a mystery animal which appeared in New England during the last fifty years. No one knows quite what it is or where it came from. All we know is that it belongs to the genus Canis which includes dogs, wolves, coyotes, jackals, and dingos. This course will set out to study all aspects of the biology of this genus, using the mystery animal in its natural habitat as the point of inquiry.

Since the course will be conducted as a research project there will be need for people with different talents, e.g., business managers, directors, literature reviewers, technical writers, journalists, photographers, lab technicians, sourdoughs, and track stars. Long-term wilderness tracking by some members of the course will be conducted under the direction of Charles Sheldon, who is well qualified in teaching the basics of cold weather survival and biology. Other outdoor activities will include comparative locomotion of canidae through snow, using an Alaskan Husky team as a model. . . . Persons anticipating Outward Bound-type activity should start getting in shape immediately. The Course requires each student to think "DOG" seven days a week, twenty-four hours a day for one month.

Hampshire College sees itself as a "laboratory for educational change." New ideas tried at the school are to be picked up by other colleges. "Hampshire would like to be," Chairmen of the Board Franklin Patterson says modestly, "a pioneer in shaping education for a new age." Others at the college share Patterson's dreams. Francis Smith, Dean of Humanities and Arts: "Hampshire's impact on education will be felt for two centuries. It's the third great event in the history of U.S. education." The other two? "The founding of Harvard and President Lincoln's federal aid to education."

The truth is Hampshire's a straight school, not very far in front of the academic world. What they call innovative is being done in places like Ottawa, Kansas and New College, Alabama. In areas where they might be free and experimental, they've put on the brakes and write about what they are not. In almost every piece of the many and expensive brochures is the Hampshire disclaimer. Read it!

WHAT HAMPSHIRE COLLEGE IS NOT
(FROM THE HAMPSHIRE CATALOG)

1. Hampshire does not assume that a student can pursue only his self-defined interest in the College. Many of the comprehensive examinations will require the integration of materials from a wide number of fields, and passing those examinations will require a reasonable mastery of those fields. Though there are no "required courses" in the conventional sense, there are required examinations and most students will find it advisable to take a full program of courses in order to prepare for them. In short, the College sees its obligation as encouraging the expansion of a student's definition of relevance, not pandering to it.

2. Hampshire does not assume that a student is the only reasonable judge of his own educational progress. The rigorous, periodic examinations, requiring hard work in preparation, will provide feedback essential for any education.

3. Hampshire does not assume that learning is a relaxed or casual experience. The system of not assigning grades in courses is a means of achieving higher standards, not a guarantee that any minimal amount of work will do.

4. Hampshire does not assume that the intellectual tradition of the West is irrelevant to the growth and development of its students or to the solution of pressing social problems. To the contrary, the College is committed to the proposition that engagement with this tradition is essential for any person wishing to obtain a liberal education.

5. Hampshire will not assume that all of its students are capable of full independent work from the first day of their stay at the College. Rather, Hampshire assumes that all students can become capable of such work, but that it takes time and a great deal of effort.

6. Hampshire does not assume that field work is separate from theoretical work. Field work makes sense only when it is coupled with an obligation to abstract from the data defensible generalizations.

7. The Hampshire governance arrangements will not be egalitarian. They will be hierarchical. To be involved, informed, and participating will be the responsibility and right of every member of the community. But experience, past performance, and a definition of role will determine the decision-making arrangements.

We had found a woman student to show us around and she was explaining Hampshire's paranoia.

"Patterson must have had nightmares Hampshire would become another Old Westbury, some far-out place with students groovin' on the grass. Actually, the place is a drag; I'm leaving." She was one of the twelve students quitting after one year. We asked why. "Oh, no single reason. I'm not getting what I had expected. The place's a disappointment. There aren't enough students around for one thing."

Next year there will be another 390 students, won't there?

"True. That's 100 more than they wanted, but the school needs the bread. They've raised the tuition. It's now $4,300. Money's a problem. I don't know about those new students. They'll have a problem fitting in. Everyone in this first class is cliquish. Brothers and sisters. Not much sex. It's been a bad scene for women. We're just *older*, you know, than these guys. That's one reason I'm leaving." We had reached Johnson Library, one of the college's new buildings, an odd-shaped structure, resembling a turtle. We asked her what state she was from.

"California, but most students are easterns. New York, New Jersey, Mass., Pennsylvania, those states. Admissions Office says they have them from forty states, but it's just token, one or two from each. There're about twenty blacks, but they're middle class. Oh, the bookstore!" She displayed it with a little pride and it deserved it. Someone had put thought into the store, made it a pleasant place with music, space and displays. The store was into natural foods and ecology books, and the usual abundance of textbooks. But it did not have the handy household supplies and toilet articles found in the bookstores of Goddard and Franconia.

Down the hall was the library. A work-study student behind the desk gave a short spiel about the place: thirty thousand books, open stacks, an art gallery, post office, film and television studios and INTRAN, the Information Transfer Center. We asked about INTRAN.

"Well, let's say a student is researching crowd behavior and wants to study primary source material. Okay? He calls the library from his dorm room. He has a pushbutton phone and he asks what footage is available on recent demonstrations. The librarian, me maybe, keypunches the request and a computer readout shows that the library holds videotape of five demonstrations. The student says he wants to see the tapes and the librarian tells him in half an hour there will be a channel ready.

"Okay, thirty minutes later the student, still in his dorm room, turns on the television, selects the channel, and the slide comes into view telling him the tapes are ready. He uses the pushbutton telephone and views the tape. He can also slow the tape down, run it a second time and even enlarge a portion. Not bad, huh?"

How do you know all this, we asked.

"Oh, I read the college propaganda."

The Hampshire propaganda is indeed impressive. It's not only numerous, but also it's quality work, multicolored and full of dramatic pictures. The language is pretentious. Reading it, we had the feeling they were building a new nation, rather than a small, liberal arts college in western Massachusetts. Who do they think they are, Harvard?

Actually, they could have been another Harvard, perhaps called "Queen's" College fourteen years before the Declaration of Independence if the Overseas of Harvard had not persuaded the Governor of Massachusetts to recant the charter given to Hampshire Country in 1762.

The staff and faculty of Hampshire are trying to catch up with that past. Every gesture they make is done with historical implications. Forty pages alone are devoted to "Reflections of an Inaugural Convocation, 1970." Then there's the application information with a pensive photo of Van Halsey, Director of Admissions, done on quality gray grain paper. Patterson, first president of Hampshire, has his speeches printed in small booklets. They have another thick green booklet which with typical modesty they call, "A Model for Innovation in American Colleges and Universities." And on everything is their one line of Latin: *non satis scire*—to know is not enough. (Latin, incidentally, is not taught at Hampshire.)

Students we met also shared this bit of smugness. Having been accepted into Hampshire, they think something must be special about them. But they're not sure what. They are not radical, nor unusually bright. Van Halsey says he's looking for students, "with some self-confidence, self-direction, curiosity, self-discipline . . . perhaps some special talents, a spirit of adventure."

Applications for the 1971–72 class ran over 2,700, but Van Halsey said, most were looking for freedom. "They thought this would be some kind of lotus-land where they could sit around smelling the dandelions for four years." Van Halsey is one of those tall, tweedy, sports-jackets-with-patches sorts of guys found around small liberal colleges. He spent fourteen years at Amherst—almost everyone, if they didn't come from the

Peace Corps, comes from Amherst (or both). He holds a Ph.D. in American Studies from Pennsylvania and teaches at the School of Humanities and Arts. In the Admissions world, he's well known.

Van Halsey is easy-going, non-directive, doesn't push himself or the applicant. He tries to create, he says, "an air of mutual exploration, easy-going communication, and empathy." The Amherst College Record calls him "low-keyed and level-headed." Selection of students is made by Van Halsey and his assistants. He is *really* setting the tone for the college. In such a small place, with few students, Van Halsey's decisions are paramount.

He has been cautious. Students are those healthy middle-of-the-roaders. Over half come from private schools, most of them wealthy and moderate. The first class of blacks met and decided not to have a separate student union. Students come to Hampshire because they want small classes, friendly faculty and a community where nothing is too way out. They've got it!

Students have found Hampshire academic. A student cannot move forward unless a series of examinations are passed. The questions for these examinations are formulated with his advisors. Hampshire, according to Barbara Turlington, Assistant to the Dean of the College, "is in the business of education, not the socialization of students."

It would be unfair to say the personal growth of students is not a consideration of the college. A student has an advisor with whom he meets throughout the year. The advisor is to help plan his program, but is also available to discuss "any matter of campus life about which he may wish to have advice." Actually, the advisor system doesn't work. Some students at the end of the year said they hadn't seen their advisor once, weren't sure who he was.

So far the Hampshire community is close and small. Serious problems of drugs, depressions, etc., are everyone's concern. The college also has the advantage of having in their Health Services Barbara Schimmel who is wise and understanding and though young herself, something of a mother figure on campus.

To have older students and experience on campus, the college had what they called Hampshire Fellows. They were students finishing the last year. At the first commencement, then-President Patterson told them, "You have helped give Hampshire poetry and science, art and computer literacy, history and mathematics, some humaneness in campus life and a sense of quest and contribution in communities beyond the College." Our woman guide called them. "Senior Freaks." "We felt sorry for them." They were under the direction of former Peace Corps member David Smith, the Master of Merrill House, the first residential college on campus. (Dankin House, the second residential, dining and academic complex has just been completed.)

Buildings at Hampshire are hospital-like. Bricks gathered in uneven piles around a central yard. Hampshire got hurt by the federal loans they used to build the dormitories. The rules require that college functions not be mixed. So sleeping, office and academic functions are not associated in any useful fashion. The same law accounts for the phenomena of built-in furniture one finds in the typical college dormitory built in the fifties and sixties. If the furniture is attached to the floor or wall, the government will give a loan for it. Hampshire didn't go for that, but they made the mistake of letting an architect design the room furniture. It seems architects do not like people: they don't want them to be comfortable. The clever modular units are resented by the students. We mention this only as it's another example of overplanning that we feel encumbers Hampshire. (Hebert also has a thing about the lawn benches, which are unsittable. He claims this tells one something about a place. We're thinking about this.)

Besides the failure of the furniture and the Fellows (two of the first seventeen failed to graduate) the college had other problems its first year. Patterson at the commencement summed up the difficulties:

> Trying together to steer a creative, more humane course between two extremes—the solipsistic "doing your own thing" approach which assumes that self-validation of learning is all that counts, and the older authoritarian model which assumes that marks and grades of prescribed performance are the way to go in education—we have sought to provide enough academic structure to insure quality and stability while at the same time providing maximum freedom for creative learning. All of that turns out to be easier to say than to do, as you well know.

Another of Hampshire's problems is to raise twenty million over the next few years. Having been five years in planning, they have used up much of the seed funding. The greatest single chunk was six million from Harold F. Johnson, a graduate of Amherst, who has the library named after him. Because of tight money, few additional faculty will be hired in the next year or two, but students have the advantage of putting together an academic program using courses taught at the other four schools. A five-college bus operates hourly among the campuses and Hampshire students are free to attend other schools. Twenty percent of the classes taken by Hampshire students in 1971 were at the other four colleges. This percentage should grow. Students also can take advantage of the recreation, films, dances and special events of all schools. This is important to Hampshire and eases the problems of limited facilities and students.

Another advantage of Hampshire is the philosophy. Although we don't agree with all those words, the college has a philosophical base of some depth. Many schools begin over cocktails, in one-month crash meetings, as outgrowths of sensitivity sessions, or in office memoranda from deans to chancellors.

Hampshire goes beyond their one line of Latin. Patterson and new President, Charles R. Longsworth, drafted *The Making of a College.* It's Hampshire's *magnum opus.* The idea of Hampshire College—past, present and future—is in this book. It states the college is "concerned with the creation of self-consciousness in relation to tradition" in its students "and expects to give a liberal education" where the student has "a greater sense of himself in a society whose meaningfulness and quality depend in significant degree on him."

The college is concerned about the alienation and "anomic response in youth" and "pits itself to help students find acceptable meaning in both society and self." They do not want students "who feel that self can have little meaning or satisfaction in the acceptance of social responsibility." Hampshire College is the Peace Corps, VISTA, the Massachusetts Service Corps and the Protestant Ethic all together in new red-brick buildings on old land and deeply in debt.

LESSONS OF HAMPSHIRE. The faculty at the college likes to say: we're not experimental, we're experimenting. That's the *Catch 22* clause to keep them above the pithole of real experimental schools. As we said, most of what was visioned as educationally startling in 1958 has already been done. The question is: can Hampshire with more brave words try something else or are they already, as one student said, "becoming less and less flexible"?

It is the nature of the beast to husband property and we feel *rigor mortis* has reached the Connecticut River Valley. That is not to say Hampshire College is bad. It's a damn fine school, a good state college for the seventies, free enough to keep the folks happy and muscle enough to keep students at the grind. It will give that liberal education, with a slight twist. But what more could one expect from a college founded by people who worked so many years at colleges like Amherst? Reading the list of administrators and faculty is like reading alumni magazines of the sponsoring schools. Doesn't anyone leave Massachusetts?

RECOMMENDATION. This school is rushing to establish itself, become a legend, as the ad said, in its own time. It wants to be old and revered, like its neighbors. Besides this idiosyncrasy and its feeling of preciousness, the college works. We think you'd get an education at Hampshire, nothing startling, innovative or adventurous, but worthwhile, certainly tougher than you might want. They are not messing around with those yearly examinations. After four years, you'll know you've been to school, have the rewards of that achievement. Those are good feelings, and Hampshire will give them to you. A new college doesn't have to be all things to all people and Hampshire has chosen what it wants: a small liberal arts college. There are many who will love it. We recommend it. In fact, we recommend it highly.

Hampshire College
Amherst, Massachusetts 01002

THE UNIVERSITY OF THE NEW WORLD

In the winter of 1971 there began to appear on the bulletin boards of colleges, universities and some high schools an artfully designed poster announcing the opening of a new university in Valais, Switzerland.

The university promised to do away with admissions, competitive examinations, grades, irrelevant specialists, I.D. zombies, trustee powers, course lectures, stifling bureaucrats. It would be a "learning, doing university for futuristics." To enroll, a student had only to fill out a card, pay fifteen hundred dollars for the first three months and take a charter flight to Europe. Everyone was selected.

In the foreword of the first general bulletin, published in January, 1971, it stated simply, but with eye toward posterity:

> *The University of the New World is being born like some great American and European Universities were born. A man is moved by a crisis of ideas and society to offer whatever he has to those who are searching. He welcomes whatever help is offered. He compromises only when direct progress without compromises is absolutely barred. In the end, we have a great University or we leave some monument or memory.*

The man was Doctor Alfred de Grazia, lecturer, professor at Stanford, NYU, the University of Chicago and author of *Public and Republic* and *Republic in Crisis*.

In his press release of January 13, 1971, de Grazia said innovations would characterize the university. Among them were "the abolition of classes and the substitution of studios in all subjects, a machine-assisted intensive language-training systems, year-round education . . . free entrance and exit from the University, accreditation by an independent commission, absolute minimization of examinations, of grades and of other alienating features that have become familiar burdens of academic life."

The University of the New World was to be independent, coeducational, nonsectarian and open to persons of all ages and for all general degrees. Instruction was to be in English.

Besides all this, the University of the New World promised something different with governance.

> As far as possible we try to get everything to run by itself and everybody to govern themselves. The University is a democracy in fact as well as in name.
>
> At the University of the New World, power is organized simply and distributed widely among those persons for whom the University is important.
>
> When we speak of the University Community we mean all of those to whom the University is immediately important: the students, the faculty, the workers, and the Friends.

Anyone at the university could be elected to the assembly. The assembly legislates for the university, elects the Rector, approves the election of faculty and studio leaders by the studio, etc.

The studios were to be the center of educational life at New World. Writes de Grazia:

> A Studio is oriented in its own way toward the beneficial construction of the future world. The orientation is conveyed somewhat in its title, usually in its description, and regularly in its operation. The studios may be grouped according to their dominant process, of which there are five: Growing; Making; Meaning; Creating; and Governing. The "ing" is stressed because education and learning are active, not passive processes, and because the desired result from such active learning is practical action: doing. This idea is as valid for physics as it is for the dance.

The faculty listed as planners and/or teachers to lead these studios was impressive. A partial list includes:

> Professor Carl Schildkraut, molecular biologist, of the Albert Einstein School of Medicine; Dr. Immanuel Velikovsky of Princeton, N.J., famous author of works on ancient civilization and catastrophes; Dr. Harvard Arnason, author of the History of Modern Art; Dr. Anthony Weiner, research chairman of the Hudson Institute and co-author of The Year 2000 and other scientific studies of the future; Dean Nasser Sharify of the graduate School of Pratt Institute of Technology, one-time chief of UNESCO's library programs and organizers of New York State University's library system; Robert M. Hutchins, former President of the University of Chicago and presently Chairman of the Center for the Study of Democratic Institutions at Santa

Barbara, Calif.; Francis Pray of the university development consulting firm of Frantzreb and Pray; E. Sherman Adams, Senior Vice President and Economist of the Fidelity Bank of Philadelphia; Peter Tobia, consultant for the Young President's Organization; Sir Michael Fraser, Deputy Director of the Conservative Party of Great Britain; Richard Cornuelle, New York consultant who headed the Presidential Task Force on Voluntary Action.

The studios would consist of an apartment for conference, consultation and study, with pertinent books, audio-visual aids and other equipment, together with auxiliary furnishings for the comfort of the group. The studio is the class. Students enter and leave at will, from "early morning till midnight, all through the year."

The "class" consists of those who make the studio their point of reference. Students, for example, who are specializing in a subject mingle with students who specialize in other fields, who are doing less concentrated work in this one. The January, 1971 bulletin gave information about how this would work.

> . . . *Suppose a student arrives in the month of June; she knows French moderately well and wishes to postpone advanced study in that language. Rather, she wishes to begin promptly learning to become a professional writer. Perhaps she has indicated in advance that she wishes to enroll in the Studios of Poetry and Fiction, Communication, Futuristics, and Ideology. She visits the Poetry and Fiction Studio, where she discusses with a professor what she might do. Observing that her interests tend toward science fiction, he suggests a program of readings and reviews in Utopias and classics of science fiction, to last for a period of three months, with weekly conferences. After that, they decide that she should begin to write a story of her own, over another period of time.*
>
> *Next she visits the Studio of Communications, where it is discovered that her interest lies in story material about plants . . . mushrooms, perhaps. The professor and she may conclude that the Communications Studio ought not occupy her at this time, but rather that she should use the Life Studio, where her biological preparation may be advanced. So she visits the Life Studio, and there arranges a program of readings, reviews, and conferences on plant physiology and the rapidly developing literature in botany and psychology on fungi.*
>
> *Her choice of the Studio in Futuristics is deemed relevant, and she develops there a program dealing with agricultural trends and the variety of science fiction work about extraordinary plants. In the Ideology Studio she strikes the different "isms" that have associated themselves with sacred plants throughout history and even today.*
>
> *In every case, she builds a timed and specific program, and there is as much coordination among the studios as possible. She is not torn and confused by compulsory, unrelated courses that follow the special bent of a*

given professor. This now is "liberal education" in fact. It is not known whether she will go on indefinitely along these lines. She may find that her original interest is evolving in science fiction into an interest in agricultural planning. And so she may shift her studies accordingly, focusing upon a particular culture, such as Spain, whereupon she learns Spanish and does field projects in Spain.

The University of the New World would also have a Center For Rapport Psychology and a Center For Language and Linguistics, and Special Studios: Studio of Civilizations and Catastrophes, Studio For University Friends, Studio For Advanced Study, The Studio of Next University. The University of the New World was also to "hold the best and most accessible collection of English language works in Europe." Six thousand books were to be available for the opening in summer, 1971. Also a printing press and an information system tied into the Geneva computer complex.

Students were to be housed in luxury. From the general bulletin:

The University is centered in three physical locations which are called the Valaire campus, the Haute-Nendaz campus and the Super-Nendaz campus. University Members generally live, sleep, and eat at the campus where they study. Thus, students of language and linguistics live at the Language Center complex of Super-Nendaz. The Members of the Center for Rapport Psychology live at the Haute-Nendaz complex. All others live around the Valaire campus, mainly in old Sion. On all three campuses, wives, families, and friends can be accommodated in the apartments of Members. If not themselves students, they will be charged 60% of the total comprehensive fee or $300 per month, which includes the lodgings, meals, travel credit, and certain other privileges of Members in respect to swimming pools, tennis courts, concerts, movies, etc.

This was all written in the winter of 1971. By summer, 1971, the college had opened and eighty students had arrived (New World had hoped for an opening class of four hundred). Bill Fordham, a friend from New York, was teaching in Switzerland and visited the University of the New World in late August, six weeks after the opening of school. He found these conditions.

• The university was near bankruptcy.
• The university was being evicted from its location because the Belgian owner did not want blacks, long-hair whites, living in his buildings.
• The university had no new location in mind.
• Racism had flared up. Blacks were being discriminated against. Fights had started among the students.

- The graduate assistant/teachers were fighting with de Grazia about the direction of the university.
- Little equipment or books were available. Students and faculty supplied the only library.
- The only studio working successfully was the Women's.
- The assembly met daily in long, involved, tense sessions.

The Sion is a breathtaking location, high in the Alps, above the Upper Rhone River. A medieval town, ancient. It is now, however, a tourist trap, crowded with new constructions, a resort area for rich Swiss, French and Belgians. In a remote location it is a conservative town and frictions between town and gown began almost immediately. Plus there was trouble within the University of the New World. Students arriving from America expected to find a university operating and instead discovered the first educational assignment was to build the college, from the ground. Personalities began to clash, as did idealities. But the trouble had actually begun in New York City, in the village, where Alfred de Grazia began his dream.

De Grazia had gathered a half-dozen young graduate students, some from NYU, others from Boston and Brown who were attracted to him and his dream. These graduate students quit their studies, began to work full-time without pay, all of them sharing in the dream of a new university. The little operating money that they did have came from de Grazia himself and a few friends.

They recruited in the eastern colleges, often hitting five colleges in one day, but enrollment went slowly. It was late May of 1971 before the applications began to arrive, and more importantly, tuition money. The university lives off its tuition and money problems have been the crucial problems of the University of the New World. There has not been enough money and if this handicap is not overcome, the university might not live.

Throughout the spring other problems began to appear. It became clear that the staff of young graduate students and de Grazia did not have the same type of school in mind. The graduate students wanted to emphasize a communal college, de Grazia wanted a community of scholars. This gap in philosophies widened further when everyone arrived in Europe. De Grazia, who had promised these graduate students teaching positions at New World, was unable, because of lack of funds, to hire them. He also began to think in late summer, 1971, that they had turned against his dream of the university. The other central problem was over the question of governance.

Students and the young graduate teachers felt de Grazia wasn't sharing power, that he held onto the final authority at the school and that the governance policy, which as one student put it, "is the only experimental aspect of the university" mentioned in the General Bulletin of 1971 did not exist. De Grazia denies that the college has in reality drifted from its intent.

A twenty-member assembly was selected, not by election, but by lot so as to avoid politics. It turned out to be representative, with at least half the members women and blacks. (Ten percent of the first class were black, mostly Antioch students from Ohio.) De Grazia at one point gave the assembly his checkbook so they could see who and how much money was spent on the university.

Nevertheless, de Grazia loomed on campus as the domineering figure. He said himself that the university would only be independent when he had left the place, for students distrust authority, and he is the authority at Sion. One way or the other students and the young graduate assistants have felt cheated by him. Faculty whose names he had listed as coming were not in the summer of 1971 at New World, equipment and supplies, books, etc., promised, were not available. Buildings did not exist. And there was no money to pay a faculty of forty. (By the fall of 1971 more than twenty faculty members had left; studios were being conducted by graduate students.) According to Bill Fordham the only thing accurate from the original bulletin was the comment about the scenery.

There were other problems as well. The blacks found not only were the Swiss racists, but also so were some of their fellow students. Fights broke out in the apartments. Two white women left after a fight with one black woman. And few—black or white—were getting along in town. Suddenly everyone realized French was essential. Students demanded more intense language courses (and got them), but because of the inability to communicate in French the Americans were cut off from the local people.

Many Americans were experiencing culture shock, had trouble with the altitude, change in time and weather. It took several weeks to adjust. Only a few of the studios were functioning and the Women's Studio was the only successful one. Among teachers, Dr. Velikovsky had made the only impression. Most of the early months was taken up with endless sessions of the assembly. The campus was tense and few were friendly. Bill Fordham in trying to conduct interviews found only the occasional student or graduate student willing to talk about the place. Paranoia was everywhere.

By fall the graduate students and the less than eight students who remained were looking for better, brighter days. They would not leave because they had, as one said, "made an emotional investment in New

World" and were hoping new students would bring new hope and enthusiasm. But more importantly, new students would bring money. The future of the university depended on how many paying students stepped off the charter in Europe.

LESSONS OF THE UNIVERSITY OF THE NEW WORLD. One man's dream can be another person's nightmare and this university has for many been nightmarish. Beyond the general and ideal blueprint for a new university which would offer freedom, Europe and excitement, nothing concrete was available. (In all fairness, we surveyed this college less than two months after opening. It was barely alive and more time was needed to see how it would develop.)

It is hard to expect much from fledgling institutions, especially ones that are tied to the personality of single individuals. Also it is too much to expect that one place on earth will provide once-and-for-all the educational needs of the young. The General Bulletin of 1971 which many students said lied, really committed the fault of only promising. Changing from a dream of such a place to the living school requires talent, time and money. How much of these ingredients the University of the New World has remains to be seen.

De Grazia, however, will need more financial help to pull this off. He will also have to make the university operate on a daily basis. There is little structure at the place and no general agreement on educational philosophy. While de Grazia has been dreaming so have others and the conclusions they have reached are not the same. It appears de Grazia was in a hurry to begin—he needed additional money to keep the dream alive—and that haste has only created problems.

RECOMMENDATIONS. The University of the New World is an opportunity for anyone interested in building an alternative learning situation. Only a third of the charter class in 1971 wanted that experience. It is not a place for serious scholars or students who have difficulty handling ambiguity, or those who have special and sophisticated educational interests. It is also not a place for the poor. The fee is fifteen hundred dollars every three months, but that does include round-trip transportation.

It is an exciting, demanding place, New World, and the first class, even after only a few weeks, felt they had "been here a year." Many thought they would have trouble adjusting again to placid American colleges.

It is too soon to tell if the University of the New World is viable. It depends simply on the number of new students the place attracts. Anyone interested should proceed with caution.

University of the New World
8 Avenue de France
Sion 1950
Switzerland

OR

University of the New World
2 Washington Square
Village, New York
New York 10012

3. New and Experimenting Schools

CALIFORNIA INSTITUTE OF THE ARTS, CALIFORNIA

LOCATION. This school is situated on sixty acres in the new community of Valencia, north of Los Angeles and beside the Golden State Freeway. The Institute's six schools and administration offices are located in a three-story, 588,000 square foot structure. There are workshops, studios, practice and performance rooms, an exhibition gallery, modular theater, sound and video stages, and space and laboratory theaters. There is also housing for 350 students and a cafeteria, library and resource bank.

SIZE. The Institute opened in 1970 with 630 students; 300 more students were added in 1971–72. By 1973, the maximum enrollment will be 1,500.

WHAT KINDS OF STUDENTS. Over 5,300 students have already applied to the Institute. The median age is twenty and men outnumber women two to one. Half of the student body is from California, but thirty-seven states and thirteen foreign countries are represented. The Institute only wants students serious about their art. Students must submit samples of work and students in the performing arts must audition. The goal of all schools is "recruitment of students whose instincts are alive to what they are after and who not only have the imagination and conceptual gifts but are capable of their realization."

RULES AND REGULATIONS. The Office of Institute Affairs states that "our relationships with one another will emerge from our working together." They will not enforce rules, but keep them up to date. The California Institute of the Arts is a community, and as a community, everyone is a member. "If you're in, you're IN." All students are considered artists.

COSTS.

Tuition	$2,500.00 a year
Room	550.00 a year
Board	750.00 a year

GRADING SYSTEM. No grades. Progress is measured as it is in the arts themselves: by what's done as it's done. During his college career, the student develops an Experience File, making at least one entry a term. His file is also "validated" by his mentor once a term. At the end of his stay at the Institute, a student creates a record of his experience. This "curriculum vitae" is certified by the Institute.

WHAT'S SPECIAL ABOUT CALIFORNIA INSTITUTE OF THE ARTS. The Institute consists of six schools: Art, Design, Music, Theatre and Dance, Film, and Critical Studies. There is no established curriculum, for the emphasis is on projects or individual work under faculty guidance. The work guides what is studied. "Classes and lectures revolve around workshops and playing spaces so that craft informs knowledge and knowledge works its way into craft. The training program is thought of as a context of experience in which solutions to real problems can be discovered. The Institute is a laboratory and a performance center. Students and faculty perform as collaborators."

Interaction among the students and faculty is fundamental to the Institute. Physical facilities and faculty resources are available to everyone.

Following are some brief statements about each of the schools taken from the first bulletin:

SCHOOL OF ART: *A basic assumption of the School of Art is that from the day he enters, the student is an artist. . . . Instruction bears upon his capacity for image-making and opens up resources he requires or of which he is unaware, including his own. . . . The student is assigned working space in well-equipped shops. He is not merely floating from class to class. His responsibility is to himself and his work, and to the acquisition of skills to sustain this responsibility. He works under the supervision of professional artists in painting, sculpture, graphics, structural principles, stage design, technology projects, environments, happenings and techniques yet to be named.*

SCHOOL OF DESIGN: *Areas of study include visual and physical phenomena, design strategy, morphology and structure in nature, production processes and technology, the history of invention, principles of ecological design, computer-assisted design, economics and distribution strategies, human factors engineering, environmental shells, visual communications, learning environments, community planning, simulation and gaming, photographic communications, product design. This subject matter merges with concerns of the other schools of the Institute, experiments in life-styles, enviro-structures and social architecture, movement and non-verbal communication, mass-media techniques, urban affairs, social institutions. A self-instructional resource bank of basic skills supplements the faculty in the form of information on film, tape or in publications, an "experience bank" to be drawn upon as needed. The aim is to form the faculty and students into task forces bent on solving concrete problems in the natural and social environments.*

SCHOOL OF MUSIC: *A crucial source of energy is the student himself. He is to be at all times a shaping force in the musical life of the Institute. There are as many individual curricula as individual needs. The student plays, sings, composes, and to assure the quality and variety of what he does, there are instrumental, vocal and compositional training and a full range of ensembles under leading professional artists. . . . Historical, theoretical and compositional studies are directly connected to performance. There is an eye/ear laboratory of tapes and films where the student himself can acquire at his own pace the necessary professional skills. Among the innovations of the program is a strategy of ample time for each performer and composer to practice his art. Research, analysis and performance of world music are pursued with leading artists as faculty participating with students.*

SCHOOL OF THEATRE AND DANCE: *The theatre, an art of many voices, has a language all its own. That language begins in the body and moves through space and time. The actor learns to think with the body. The stage designer learns, with all the visual and plastic means at his disposal, to think through space with the actor. The playwright gives the pretext, his mind upon the shape of action. In a true play, even the properties will appear to act. All particular techniques, from stage mechanics to emotional memory, will converge in the ensemble, growing organically into performing groups. The aim is an expanded and flexible craft that comes from exploration of common ground. . . .*

What has been said of theatre is true of dance to the extent they derive from a common source and, on the contemporary stage, direct their energies to merging ends. . . . The dance program tries to cut behind these orthodoxies to original disciplines and motives in movement, whether in ballet, modern dance, design, multi-media or in unknown forms. . . . In both theatre and dance, faculty and students train together. Exercise and performance are inseparable in classroom, laboratory and in a wide variety of playing spaces, indoors and outdoors, including one of the most versatile theatres in the world.

SCHOOL OF FILM: *In the making of a film, choice may be distributed through a team—writer, director, editor, cameraman—or it may be a com-*

pletely individual venture. The program in film allows for both: the collaboration of diverse talents or the solitary individual who uses a camera as a sculptor uses clay, or thinks of editing as a personal poetic art. In either case, the stress is on the inquisitive and evocative power of the medium through cinematography, lighting in studio and on location, sound recording and mixing, editing techniques, optical camera effects, film graphics and animation, live video, taping and video editing. . . . Whether the film-maker is storyteller or a social critic, abstractly graphic or politically engaged, the program is conceived to give him the instruction he requires under practicing film-makers. Whatever he is, whatever the size of his vision of stylistic bent, we give him the means to realize it and let him follow the logic of his imagining eye.

SCHOOL OF CRITICAL STUDIES: *There are four main areas of inquiry: literary studies, political studies, symbolic studies and intermedia studies. The school is a retrieval system at the disposal of anyone at the Institute who wants access to a body of knowledge, from myth and totem to the physical sciences, that would ordinarily be covered in a liberal arts college. Courses are initiated as required. Relevancy isn't topicality but determined by the urgencies of students and faculty. When the School of Music teaches percussion in an African or Indian context, then something has to be done by anthropologists and social historians, as well as musicologists, to follow up the needs of craft.*

RECOMMENDATION. This is the most exciting college on the West Coast. Its staff and faculty are skilled, experienced and famous. Some of them: Mel Powell (music), Alexander Mackendrick (film), Robert E. Brown (music), Mark Harris (writing), Dugald MacArthur (theater), Sally Jacobs (theater design), Marni Nixon (voice), Terry Sanders (film). The list is nearly endless.

The Institute also has money. Walt Disney money. And its Board of Trustees is impressive. The school is accredited by the Western Association of Schools and Colleges.

This institute is hard to get into. You have to be talented, but once in, the possibilities are many. It's new, fresh and well worth your time and money.

California Institute of the Arts
24700 McBean Parkway
Valencia, California 91355

COLLEGE OF THE ATLANTIC, MAINE

LOCATION. It is on Mount Desert Island, in Maine, fifty miles east-southeast of Bangor. Some people consider the island the most beautiful one in the world. There are freshwater lakes and ponds, granite mountains, marshes and bogs, acres of forests and saltwater shorelines. It's surrounded by Frenchman's Bay and the North Atlantic. Most of the island remains underdeveloped. The College is located on a twenty-five acre estate bordering Frenchman's Bay in Bar Harbor.

SIZE. The College will admit its first class of fifty students in 1972. Top enrollment will be six hundred by 1976.

WHAT KINDS OF STUDENTS. The College says they are "seeking male and female students with the same level of intellectual ability as those enrolled in highly selective colleges." They think they will attract students with Scholastic Aptitude Test (SAT) scores in the middle ranges, 500–600, and are looking at personality and other factors, as well as grades. Over two thousand applications have already been received at the school.

RULES AND REGULATIONS. No formal rules have been established because the administration is waiting until the students arrive on campus. Students will for the most part establish their own governance. They will be full members of the college community with all rights and responsibilities. The College does not plan on "taking the position of watch" with students.

COSTS. Tuition is approximately $2,700 and another $1,000 for room and board. It's a private college, therefore, expensive. A few scholarships are available and the usual loans and work-study possibilities are available from the state and federal governments.

GRADING SYSTEM. Not yet established.

WHAT'S SPECIAL ABOUT COLLEGE OF THE ATLANTIC. Rather than offer various disciplines, the College is organized around one theme: Human Ecology or the interrelationship of man and his environment. "The understanding, appreciation and ability to view wisely the complex interaction of nature, people, technology, government and beauty is what this college is all about," they say.

Problems are selected by a group of students and staff who discuss them in broad terms, then decide upon an area of special interest. Panels form into groups and assume responsibility for certain points. A group might decide to study a problem of land use. Panels would organize and investigate various aspects of a problem: economic, biological, social, aesthetic, etc. Upon completion of one group project, students and staff move on to another.

Students also have course work in the natural sciences, humanities and social sciences. Much of the detail development of the curriculum will take place when students arrive in September, 1972. The College offers a Bachelor of Arts in Human Ecology.

RECOMMENDATION. For the first several years this college will be fluid, unstructured, loose and learning will be in the planning of a college. Everything will be limited, courses and facilities. Through 1973 the College will be four buildings: classrooms, administrative offices, library, dining area and some dormitories. The school hasn't even begun to build. Students have to be extremely flexible, willing to rough it. Students will also have to be committed to the study of ecology and have an interest in science. For those people, College of the Atlantic is something new and something worthwhile. It is the first of its kind and could be famous. If you're interested, write quickly. We think just about everyone will want Bar Harbor, Maine.

College of the Atlantic
Bar Harbor, Maine 04609

MOUNT ANGEL COLLEGE, OREGON

LOCATION. Forty miles south of Portland in a town of 2,000 is Mount Angel. It's a small place, a few brick buildings and lots of land. The college once belonged to the Catholic Benedictine Sisters and became independent in 1965. Some of the sisters and fathers are still around.

SIZE. The college has 325 students, is coed. They want to grow, but not too quickly or dramatically.

WHAT KIND OF STUDENTS. The college uses high school records. Scholastic Aptitude Test scores, letters of recommendation and, if possible, a personal interview to make decisions, but there's no clear Mount Angel type. Half of the students are from Oregon, the majority of others from California. It is not a hard school to get into, but its reputation as a fine college is spreading. Hurry.

RULES AND REGULATIONS. The Dean of Students at Mount Angel writes: "Roughly speaking our attitude is something like this: If you want to smoke dope in your room that is up to you. It is against the law in Oregon and might screw your head up in all directions. But you can make your own decision and we won't do too much to stop you. If you get caught, though, we won't do much to help you out, either. We have no rules in the residence halls other than 'try to respect one another.' " In some cases the Business Office, who leases rooms to the kids, has been more specific relative to pets, double occupancy, noise, etc. But these rules are only enforced haphazardly.

"My basic concept is that kids will eventually learn to make the right choices if they are given enough chances to make mistakes. . . . The bulk of my work, then, has been that of trying to remove rules, trying to keep administrators, teachers, parents, public, and other students off the backs of kids so they were free enough to make the mistakes necessary. Probably my personal philosophy of human behavior and of education is the one element most responsible for the general approach to student life around here more than anything else. This is not necessarily due to the intrinsic worth of my ideas but rather to the fact that I have been around longer than anyone else and am persistent as hell."

COSTS*

TUITION AND FEES

Matriculation (new students only)	$ 10.00
Tuition	1,305.00
Insurance	21.00
Student Association Membership	36.00
	$1,372.00

HOUSING

Room and Board	$ 936.00
Social Activities Fee	9.00
Breakage Deposit (refundable)	40.00
	$ 985.00

* 1970–71 figures.

GRADING. The standard ABC, but individual teachers are using the pass/fail system and it's gaining favor at the college.

WHAT'S SPECIAL ABOUT MOUNT ANGEL. It is an experimental college, continually reevaluating; we think it will expand, grow, not revert. The college offers five programs: Behavioral Sciences, Creative Arts, Humanities, Elementary Education and Liberal Arts. The influence of the Benedictines means the academic base is tough and straight, not restrictive: when nuns go liberal, they go liberal!

Facilities are limited and there is not much money. The Creative Arts program does wonderful things with little funds, and the Behavioral Sciences program, new and small, is solid. The college has independent studies, but does not provide support when students are off campus. The faculty is just too small. No organized overseas ventures; students go on their own.

Mount Angel is a touchy-feely—perhaps because of the Behavioral Sciences people—but we think more because of Tom Sullivan, Dean of Students. He writes, "We keep a pretty close tab on those students having real trouble in dealing with their freedom and give them help and support. We don't necessarily know ahead of time what the answer will be with each kid nor do we have pre-determined goals in mind." The Community Handbook has four pages devoted to types of counseling services available.

The community is close and bitchy. Lots of gossip and no lives are private. Some of the faculty—and the president—live with the students and everyone is on a first-name basis. At times this community is tense and uptight, though no worse than any other place trying to achieve the same sort of lifestyle and education.

RECOMMENDATION. We are pushing Mount Angel. We like the people and the philosophy and think it's a helluva lot better than famous Reed (to the north), and one of the better small places west of the Mississippi. Or east. Students are hearing about Mount Angel and the rush will be on these next few years. We think you should apply. Their beautifully arranged catalog is worth the postage.

Mount Angel College
Mount Angel, Oregon 97362

NEW COLLEGE, FLORIDA

LOCATION. Between Bradenton and Sarasota and on the Sarasota Bay is New College. Built on the former Charles Ringling estate, the college has twenty-seven buildings, is good-looking, isolated, private and new. It opened in 1964.

SIZE. The college has 550 students. One hundred and sixty-six new students were accepted in 1971. By 1975 the college expects a total enrollment of 800 students. There are fifty-six faculty members, some living in dormitories with the students. The dorms are comfortable.

WHAT KINDS OF STUDENTS. Students with strong high school records. The 1971 class had SATs from 580 to 800 verbal, and 550 to 800 math. The average student ranks in the top 5 percent of his high school class. It's not easy to get into New College. You need good recommendations. And you need money.

RULES AND REGULATIONS. The students themselves produce a lengthy handbook full of who, what and where questions and answers. Their Student Code's a tough one: no booze, no drugs, no pets, quiet hours and no guests of the opposite sex. "Common sense and good taste generally suffice as guidelines for conduct at New College," they write, and have a Student Bill of Rights, Student Court and Student Code to back it up.

COSTS. The basic requirement for the degree is nine terms in residence, and billing is by the term. Three terms to the year.

Tuition and Independent Study Fees	$ 930.00
Room and Board	400.00
Student Activity Fee	10.00
	$1,340.00

GRADING SYSTEM. An evaluation by the teacher is used—a paragraph or so on the student's aptitude, work, progress, etc. If the work is considered satisfactory, the student gets credit on a transcript.

WHAT'S SPECIAL ABOUT NEW COLLEGE. Students determine their own program at New College and have the option of completing a B.A. in either three or four years, using two different methods:

CONTRACTUAL PROGRAM

The student develops, with two faculty members, a program of courses, tutorials, and independent study projects. At the end of each semester he is certified that he has met the contract agreement. The student also has to pass a qualifying examination and complete a senior project.

NON-CONTRACTUAL PROGRAM

The student in this program does not declare a field of concentration, and has no senior project. He does, however, complete five Independent Study projects, and each term three undertakings—seminars, lecture courses, tutorials, special projects.

Off-Campus, Overseas. New College encourages off-campus travel, study and work, and has worked out some programs with other colleges and government agencies, and students have studied in Europe, Latin America and India. But it's not a major part of the curriculum.

RECOMMENDATION. To the academic student, this place is academic. (1) It has a sound B.A. program in natural sciences, social sciences and the humanities; (2) small classes, opportunity to design your own program; (3) you can finish school in three years; (4) it already ranks fifth in colleges whose students win Woodrow Wilson fellowships.

If you want a straight education at a small, friendly and loose school in the warm south, New College.

New College
P.O. Box 1895
Sarasota, Florida 33758

PRESCOTT COLLEGE, ARIZONA

LOCATION. Seven miles outside of Prescott, Arizona, on 620 acres of flatlands and sagebrush, in a land of clear air, warm days and cool nights, is Prescott College. The campus was once an Indian battleground and there are Indian ruins on the land.

SIZE. The college opened in 1966 and has 350 students. It will never have an enrollment larger than 800. Prescott wants to keep itself small and close. Student residences are in clusters with no more than eleven students in a building. The teacher/student ratio is one to nine. One to eighteen is normal.

WHAT KINDS OF STUDENTS. Prescott is not looking for anyone exceptional, nor do they require that students have had certain high school courses. There is no language requirement, but they want students who have mastered English and are capable of taking college level courses. SAT and ACT scores are in the 600's.

The admissions process is "personal" and they try to interview applicants, either at the college or during trips made by representatives from March to April. They have an early decision plan, accept transfer students and Special Students who enroll for one or two courses per quarter. It helps if you can visit; they like to see that much interest.

COSTS

Tuition for the academic year	$2,000.00
Room and Board	1,200.00
Student fees	100.00
	$3,300.00

RULES AND REGULATIONS. Prescott doesn't lay down lots of rules. They state simply: "A student is regarded as a responsible person with individual integrity and individual responsibility for his education and his actions." There's a Community Advisory Committee, an elected body of students, faculty, administration and trustees who make recommendations to the president. You can do almost anything if you're quiet about it. However, new, tighter rules have just been written by the Student Affairs Committee. There has been infighting over this at the school.

GRADING SYSTEM. Students are graded "satisfactory" or "unsatisfactory." Very good work receives "honors." Grades, however, are recorded on transcripts for graduate schools.

WHAT'S SPECIAL ABOUT PRESCOTT. The aim of Prescott's curriculum is "to help each person develop his own strategy for his intellectual and personal life style." To achieve this, they've organized into five Teaching and Research Centers. The student chooses a center and concentrates, though he can take courses in the other centers.

Center for Contemporary Civilization: concerned with the problems of civilization on the local, national and international levels. Students plan their work under the supervision of a faculty member, are credited according to the amount and value of their work. No majors, only short courses, seminars and tutorials. The Program Director chooses a theme the student will study. Some of these themes have been: Equality, Freedom and Justice; Religion in Confrontation; and Violence, Revolution and War.

The Teaching and Research Center for Language: concerned with man in communication. It reaches "beyond verbal and non-verbal forms to the creative use of symbols"; "seeks to understand, not only what man says about himself, to himself, and on behalf of himself, but also the symbols he uses in doing this." A student can also develop a program in literature, philosophy, history, the arts or a combination of these areas. Advanced courses in French, German, Russian and Spanish are offered. At the moment there are beginning courses only in Russian and Chinese.

The Teaching and Research Center for Man and Environment: concerned about the ecological relationship of man, his society and his environment. It offers four major programs in anthropology, biology, environmental science and geology. The laboratory is the Southwest and northern Mexico. Some of the themes are: Man as an Organism; the Culture of Man; and Man's Relation to His Natural Environment.

The Teaching and Research Center for the Person: helps students "design and accomplish a strategy for their academic and personal lives." It offers four basic programs: the Introductory Process, Community Life, the Self-Progression Program and the Outdoor Action Program. In the Outdoor Action Program all new students undergo a three-week orientation in the wilderness. It's tough.

The Teaching and Research Center for Systems: "devoted to man's continuing search for order in his natural surroundings and his attempts to create order in his social environment." The disciplines of this center are chemistry, mathematics and physics.

RECOMMENDATION. Prescott College is new, young, innocent and moving in the right direction—a strong academic program, independent study, lots of personal freedom, quiet atmosphere. But Prescott can be a lonely place, there aren't many people around; the campus is desolate and not much activity is organized. What does take place is planned by students. The college has tennis courts, basketball courts, riding stables, a heated swimming pool. These are benefits not usually found in a new school. The centers offer new ways of looking at traditional subjects and freedom in which to pursue a topic.

Prescott College
Prescott, Arizona 86301

STATE UNIVERSITY OF NEW YORK, PURCHASE COLLEGE

LOCATION. Purchase College is forty miles from New York City on a five hundred acre estate in Westchester County. It's a beautiful campus, scenically and architecturally. The administration and faculty are trying to make this college the prestige place of the State University of New York system. And they may do it.

SIZE. Purchase opened in 1971 with two hundred transfer students. In the fall of 1972, five hundred freshmen will enroll in the College of Letters and Science and the School of Arts, which offer programs in music, dance, visual arts, and theater and film. The college will reach its maximum enrollment of six thousand by 1980.

WHAT KINDS OF STUDENTS. Purchase talks about accepting students of "high potential regardless of their ability to meet traditional admissions standards." But they're really looking for academically bright students. If you've done well in school, have strong SAT scores (over 600), then you're okay. You're also okay if you're talented in the creative arts, *i.e.*, dance, film, music, theater, television and photography. Talent and potential of professional achievement are the criteria of admission in the School of Art.

RULES AND REGULATIONS. Purchase is a residential college, 75 percent of the students live on campus, providing a community of artists and scholars. It plans on creating "an adult atmosphere" where students will be independent and responsible. It's too soon to tell whether any of this will work. Hopes are high and students have a say in decisions.

COSTS.

In-state tuition	$350.00 per semester
Out-of-state tuition	550.00 per semester

GRADING SYSTEM. Purchase College has developed a set of examinations and reports (oral and written) called *benchmarks* to test independent study and creative work. It also uses pass/fail for regular classes.

WHAT'S SPECIAL ABOUT PURCHASE. After everything is said and done, Purchase is still a traditional place with a couple of differences. It's community concept, shaky and limited in the first years, offers a chance for artistic and literary people to gather, informally and formally, in a rural setting close to New York City. Students interested in dance, music, theater and literature will be surrounded by like people.

The School of Arts within a couple of years will offer almost unlimited facilities for instruction and studio work. Students earn a B.F.A., and, if they want to spend an additional year, a B.A. from the College of Letters and Science.

The faculty of the School of Arts is first-rate, and students have the advantage of ongoing residential companies, a museum and instruction based on a master teacher/apprentice concept.

RECOMMENDATION. For students interested in literature and the arts who want an inexpensive, solid education, traditional but loose, we recommend Purchase. There's one major problem. Buildings will be limited the first few years.

State University of New York
College at Purchase
Purchase, New York 10577

RAMAPO COLLEGE, NEW JERSEY

LOCATION. In northwestern Bergen County, at the foot of the Ramapo Mountain Range and on three hundred acres of wooded land, is the new campus of Ramapo College.

SIZE. The college opened in September, 1971 with seven hundred students. One thousand students are expected to be enrolled by 1972. Besides the estate mansion (used naturally by the administration), there is a set of one-floor, multi-purpose buildings for lecture rooms, seminars, laboratories, student lounges and a cafeteria. These are ingenious buildings and can be altered as the campus grows. Dormitory space will be available in 1972.

WHAT KINDS OF STUDENTS. Ramapo isn't looking for exceptional students and is easy to get into because it's a new college. No one has heard of the place. The student body is from the immediate area; therefore, middle class and white.

RULES AND REGULATIONS. The governance of students is a series of rules written by students and administration. It's a conservative school, Ramapo, and the rules reflect this.

COSTS.

Out-of-state tuition	$350.00 per semester
In-state tuition	175.00 per semester
Fees	75.00 per semester

GRADING SYSTEM. They use A, B, C and U. The U grades are not recorded on the transcript, only the number of credit hours attempted.

WHAT'S SPECIAL ABOUT RAMAPO. Ramapo has organized itself into "schools." Each has a focus, and a student enrolling selects one.
The schools are:

The School of Human Environment: major programs in environmental science, urban studies, economics, sociology, mathematics, and business and public administration. Students are involved with field work and internships.

The School of International Studies: initial programs in Europe and Latin America with the concentration on comparative literature, history, anthropology and international relations. Not much interest in this program.

The School of American Studies: concerned with the American experience as related to European and Afro-American influences. The school has interdisciplinary majors and programs in traditional liberal arts subjects.
Additional schools are planned. They are: School of Theoretical and Applied Sciences, opening in 1974; School of Contemporary Arts, opening in 1975; and School of Humanistic Studies, opening in 1973.

RECOMMENDATION. It's a state school and has the advantage for New Jersey residents of being inexpensive. In the last few years New Jersey has begun to spend money developing new colleges. Ramapo is one of these. It's a straight school with a predominance of local students; a provincial place. There is much structure built into the curriculum and environment, and a student has support when needed. The campus is remote so a student will be trapped in those woods and hills unless he has a car. Bergen County is the middle of nowhere. For New Jersey, Ramapo is a step. We think forward.

Ramapo College of New Jersey
P.O. Box 542
Mahwah, New Jersey 07430

REDLANDS' JOHNSON COLLEGE, CALIFORNIA

LOCATION. Johnson College is part of the University of Redlands in Redlands, California. It is in the San Bernardino Valley, a campus of one hundred acres of orange groves and palm trees. Johnson College campus, separate from the main college, has its own commons, residence halls and lifestyle.

SIZE. Johnson opened in 1969 with 183 students. It has about 450 now and will grow to a maximum of 600 with a student-faculty ratio of fourteen to one. It's a Baptist-related, privately supported college.

WHAT KINDS OF STUDENTS. They say they are concerned with the whole person "including the development of intellectual, emotional, creative and behaviorial dimensions of each person." In selecting students they look to factors not measured by achievement tests, such as creativity, inventiveness, judgment, individual initiative and consistency of commitment to something outside oneself.

Seventy-five percent of Redlands students are from the immediate area, but Johnson College has attracted students from all over California, and from all over the country. Twenty-five percent come from out of state. These students are looser, freer and more progressive than the average Redlands student.

All students are interviewed, either on campus or near the applicant's home. Students need to submit Board scores, transcripts, etc. It's an academic place, Johnson.

RULES AND REGULATIONS. Students are directly involved in governance, curriculum planning and the community of the school. Johnson believes in a living/learning situation and though the main campus of Redlands is concerned with the living of students and their activities, Johnson is continuing to operate with a large amount of freedom. The first president of the college resigned after a showdown with Redlands over the total freedom of the place, but we expect to see Johnson continue its fine academic program. And no one will change the living patterns of the students. However, in the books it says: no drinking, no drugs, no cohabitation on campus.

COSTS. Tuition and fees are slightly more than two thousand dollars a year. Room and board are one thousand two hundred dollars for a double room. There are also additional costs for the off-campus Interim Seminar and other special field projects. The normal loans and grants are available, plus part-time employment.

GRADING SYSTEM. There are no letter or number grades. A comprehensive and personal critique is developed for each student over four years. This file of written evaluations is the student's record.

WHAT'S SPECIAL ABOUT JOHNSON. Johnson is one of those places educators mention when the topic turns to experimental colleges. It was much heralded in 1969 when everyone dreamed of finding the perfect experimental school, the Camelot of colleges. Johnson is no Camelot, but it's trying hard with its close living/learning community, the emphasis of T-Grouping and other sensitivity training. It was this particular aspect of the curriculum that troubled the main campus; still Johnson is continuing with its program. And that program is:

The college foundation is based on four dimensions of relationship —interpersonal, intercultural, international and environmental. In developing his "contract" toward graduation, a student is asked to expand his knowledge through these four dimensions.

The "contract" is the agreement between the student and his faculty. It's a "renegotiable" contract, if necessary, and works like this: a student has an area of interest and "contracts" to complete certain readings, papers or projects over a period of time. He might also agree to appear regularly at seminar meetings to share what he is learning. The faculty person agrees to provide leadership, new insights and some direction. This contract arrangement works for each student and faculty, and for the whole community of Johnson College.

Another major part of Johnson College are personal growth laboratories. The academic year begins with an all-college Community Laboratory and throughout the year training takes place in various "encounters," "sensitivity training" and "T-group" sessions. These intense relationships established through personal and social growth laboratories are what Johnson is seeking. "A capacity for interpersonal relationships is valuable in all aspects of the academic program: in classroom involvement, in community process, in the field and in the planning of individual projects as well as in long-range 'contracts.'"

Johnson College also has what they call "a total laboratory method of learning." This means a mix of seminars, tutorials, independent study, personal growth labs and field projects. All students are encouraged to do field work, either for a semester or a year. Usually in a culture other than one's own.

The college does not have requirements for graduation, but "works with each individual student to help him discover and agree upon graduation criteria appropriate for him within the college guidelines."

RECOMMENDATION. Johnson College will be adjusting during the 1971–72 academic year with its new president, and some changes will take place, but we believe this academic program will continue, though the reliance on the personal growth labs might be altered. The college has helped Redlands and its thrust on the whole campus will (and is) being felt. We like this college. It's sound, has a well-constructed and imaginative curriculum. It is definitely for the student who wishes to explore his personality as well as gain academic experience. If you're not up to this, stay clear.

Johnson College
University of Redlands
Redlands, California 92373

ROYALTON COLLEGE, VERMONT

LOCATION. The college is in the town of South Royalton in eastern Vermont. Situated on the banks of the White River and surrounded by New England woods, lakes and rolling hills, the campus is scattered through the small town. Its twenty buildings include residential dormitories, efficiency apartments, classrooms, art and crafts studios, a College Inn and a library with a large stone fireplace.

SIZE. Royalton is small, independent and coeducational. It opened in 1966 and now has an enrollment of less than five hundred.

WHAT KINDS OF STUDENTS. As a new and developing college, Royalton wants students "who have the independence, initiative, academic skills and maturity to take advantage of the opportunities offered." All students are interviewed and are asked to take the College Boards, but scores are not used in making decisions. What is important to Royalton is the maturity and independence of the student, his motivation and attitude. Students are admitted twice at the college, for the lower division and again for the upper division.

RULES AND REGULATIONS. All living arrangements are controlled by students. They establish standards for quiet and privacy. A faculty couple or housemother lives in the women's residences, however. One rule is that students have to be twenty-one or have parent's permission to rent an efficiency apartment. Students are not substantially involved in curriculum planning, though they make decisions about their own college career and selection of courses.

COSTS.

Residential School	(3 terms)	$3,000.00
Day School	(3 terms)	$2,100.00

The college has limited scholarships and a work-study program. Normal loans and grants from the state and federal government are available.

GRADING SYSTEM. A system of ABCD is used. Very tough on credits and evaluations. Courses are required and there are even prerequisites. Academically old-fashioned here.

WHAT'S SPECIAL ABOUT ROYALTON. It's a college with a program in International Relations. Study centers are located in Italy, East Africa, West Africa and Hong Kong. A student can spend as many as three terms overseas (if he does, the college picks up the cost of travel). A student is required to work out and do a major research paper while overseas, learn the language and become involved substantially in the country, such as doing a voluntary assignment or teaching school. He is not to be a tourist.

The other unique aspect of Royalton is its two divisions. Students are accepted for two years, then have to apply for the upper division, which makes its own selection.

The lower division offers liberal arts courses, provides a period of time to gain skills for advanced work. A Royalton College Certificate of Studies is received. The upper division has three programs: (1) International Business and Economics; (2) International Relations; (3) World Literatures. A graduate of the upper division receives a Bachelor of Arts degree or the Diploma of Higher Studies in International Affairs.

A four year program might look something like this:

Lower Division

6 credits — English composition
6 credits — Science with laboratory work
27 credits — Three Core courses
9 credits — Foreign language
12 credits — other elections

Upper Division

27 credits — Area of concentration (major)
33 credits — Other elections
10 credits — Overseas project

RECOMMENDATION. Royalton College is another one of those small schools Vermont has so many of. We like its program of international relations and general philosophy. Its faculty is not highly accredited, but experienced. Courses are, as at all small institutions, limited. A student can only begin to taste the variety of education possible. The overseas experience opens up selection and opportunities and the college makes those tricky scheduling arrangements and provides support once overseas. This aspect of Royalton is fine. The college itself—in the woods of Vermont—is a lovely place to go to school. The college also has a center in Florida in case students want to get away from the snow and long winters of Vermont.

On the whole, we don't feel there's enough at Royalton to overcome its limited program, its quasi-freedom. You can do better elsewhere in Vermont, at Goddard, for example. But it does have an International Relations program for students wanting to go overseas with an institution.

Royalton College
South Royalton
Vermont 05068

STOCKTON STATE COLLEGE, NEW JERSEY

LOCATION. This new college is located in Galloway Township on 1,585 acres, part of the south Jersey pine barrens. The campus surrounds a large lake and no formal landscape development is planned. The land will be let to remain informal and natural. It is bounded on the north by the Garden State Parkway and on the south by Jim Leeds Road.

SIZE. Stockton opened in 1971 with a charter class of slightly more than 1,000 students, 600 of them freshmen, the rest junior transfers. It will grow to a top enrollment of 7,500, adding 500 new students every year. Four buildings were scheduled for completion in September, 1971. The dormitories scheduled for opening by September, 1972 are "garden style" apartments for four students including two bedrooms, bath, living-dining-study room and full kitchen. Stockton is planning housing for only 50 percent of its students.

WHAT KINDS OF STUDENTS. Stockton sets out clearly what they want, using tests and academic achievements as their guide. A freshman applicant will be automatically admitted as long as space is available if:

1) in the top 20 percent of the high school class and has a minimum composite score on the ACT's of 18 or combined scores on the SAT's of 800, or

2) in the top 40 percent of the high school class and has a minimum composite score on the ACT's of 19 or combined scores on the SAT's of 850, or

3) in the top 50 percent of the high school class and has a minimum composite score on the ACT's of 20 or combined scores on the SAT's of 900, or

4) in the top 60 percent of the high school class and has a minimum composite score on the ACT's of 24 or combined scores on the SAT's of 1,130.

Others—older, professionals, veterans, etc.—will be selected on an individual basis.

COSTS.

	New Jersey Students	Out-of-State Students
Tuition	$ 350.00	$ 700.00
Room and Board	$1,000.00	$1,000.00
Fees	$ 131.00	$ 131.00

RULES AND REGULATIONS. The college operates on an institution-wide governance system that the first class put together. It is liberal, but has the usual disclaimer on dope and violence on campus. Too soon to tell how this governance will work, but first sessions had the expected mixture of ego-tripping and demands for personal rights any new college in the sixties to seventies has felt.

GRADING SYSTEM.

Stockton uses: H = high achievement
S = satisfactory
N = no report

To graduate, students have to complete thirty-two courses with an "H" or "S."

WHAT'S SPECIAL ABOUT STOCKTON. *Calendar:* It's called "3-2-3" for the number of months and courses in each term. The two-month winter term can be taken off campus doing a special project, but a full program is offered on campus. There is also a two-week "preterm" in the fall for students to meet advisors, faculty, staff, each other.

Collegium: Consists of six Preceptors (faculty) and their students—ninety-six in all. It is to promote intellectual, social and recreational activities of this group. Selection is made by lot, but students have the opportunity to change collegiums.

Preceptorial Groups: Each faculty member (within the Collegium) is assigned fifteen students. He operates as chief advisor, meeting regularly with the students and developing with them their academic program.

Academic Organization: The thrust of the college is "toward disciplinary interdependence and the interrelatedness of knowledge." A student can study one of the disciplinary subjects—political science, economics, sociology, anthropology or psychology—or one of a number of interdisciplinary programs designed by the student himself with the help of an advisor. The major themes so far have been Urban Environment, Ecology and the Human Environment.

There are, however, divisions: arts and humanities, general studies, management sciences, natural science and mathematics, social and behaviorial sciences. Students earn either a B.A. or B.S. degree.

Instruction: A wide range of alternatives, from classroom and labs to independent study and special projects. Students also have the opportunity to study overseas. Not much planned here.

RECOMMENDATION. For New Jersey this is a major college. It has money, vision and a program. Don't expect freedom, however. New Jersey is a straight state and nothing too innovative can be expected. Stockton, however, is an example of the "new" state college being built around the country. This type of college has flexible academic programs and is making attempts to keep the school small, using such things as the Collegium. If you happen to live in New Jersey, want to attend a state college, try here.

Stockton State College
Pomona, New Jersey 08240

THE EVERGREEN STATE COLLEGE, WASHINGTON

LOCATION. At Cooper Point Peninsula, five miles northwest of Olympia on 990 acres bordering on Puget Sound, Evergreen is the first state supported college in this century. Campus buildings are clustered together and connected by a central plaza. It looks like a small city in the center of the woods. Everything but the trees are new.

SIZE. The college opened in September, 1971 with 1,200 students, mostly freshmen and will grow by the 1980's to a top enrollment of 12,000. There are fifty-four faculty members.

WHAT KINDS OF STUDENTS. Because this is a new school, with an innovative curriculum, and inexpensive, Evergreen has more applicants than they can handle. Evergreen is looking for students who are serious about education; students willing to be taught, not radical or intent on "doing their own thing." Students should be in the upper half of their high school class, no other requirement, except, "drive and determination, a capacity for hard work, and a sense of purpose." You have to be together for Evergreen.

RULES AND REGULATIONS. Students do not run Evergreen, nor is there a close, sharing-authority, community. Lines of leadership are drawn. Campus life is similar to any state school, perhaps a bit more humane, but not loose. Students made most of their own dormitory rules.

COSTS (APPROXIMATE)

Tuition:	
State Resident	$ 420.00 per year
Non-resident	$1,000.00 per year
Room	$64.00 per month
Board	$85.00 per month

GRADING SYSTEM. There are no grades, no pass/fail system. Units of credit are given for work fulfilled and a cumulative portfolio prepared on each student. This contains descriptions of projects, evaluations by faculty, student's self-evaluation and samples of work done.

WHAT'S SPECIAL ABOUT EVERGREEN. The school has two ways of earning academic credit: Coordinated Studies and Contracted Studies. A student spends time in both programs.

Coordinated Studies: These are small, cooperative learning communities involving about one hundred students and five faculty members. Instead of studying a particular field—Sociology, Economics or English—the group studies a central problem or theme. The coordinated studies offered for 1971–72 were: Causality, Freedom and Chance; Contemporary American Minorities; Human Development; The Individual in America; The Individual, the Citizen and the State; The Play's the Thing: Then and Now; Political Ecology; Problem Solving: Games and Puzzles; Southeast Asia: Transition and Conflict; Space, Time and Form: Common Problems in Art and Science; Environmental Design; Communication and Intelligence; The Nature and Use of Media Technology; Man and Art: The Renaissance and Now.

Each Coordinated Studies program has a common schedule of group meetings and a common required reading list. The emphasis of the program is on seminars and writing. A student spends sixteen to thirty-two hours in any week with the faculty. The week of academic work includes most of the following: general assembly, lectures followed by discussions, a symposium, film, slide show, play and poetry readings and field trips.

Contracted Studies: One student or a small group of students sign a contract with a faculty member to earn credit by doing a specific project, carrying out a specific investigation, mastering a specific skill. Some of the fields contracted in 1971–72 were: Biology, Physical Science, Mathematics, Computer Science, Public Affairs, Law, Literature, Creative Writing and Journalism. The contract is the total academic assignment until it's completed and the student agrees with the sponsor to achieve a certain amount of work in a given time period.

Evergreen students also have available self-paced learning (machines), work-and-study, internships, study abroad (particularly Japan and Southeast Asia), foreign language.

A program would look something like this (taken from the Evergreen catalog):

For a student interested in public affairs, law, management:

FIRST YEAR: *Coordinated Studies, "Causality, Chance Freedom."*
SECOND YEAR: *Contracts in political science, philosophy, journalism; one quarter Coordinated Studies in American culture.*
THIRD YEAR: *Advanced Coordinated Studies in political systems, including internship in a law firm.*
FOURTH YEAR: *Contract for two quarters of internship in a state governmental agency; then helps to organize and lead a one-quarter group Contracted Study in Washington State government.*

A student interested in literature, music and perhaps teaching:

FIRST YEAR: *Coordinated Studies, "Human Development."*
SECOND YEAR: *Continues "Human Development" and internship as a teacher's aide in a primary school, helping with reading and music.*
THIRD YEAR: *One quarter Coordinated Studies, examining the similar and different roles of men and women in the arts; one month contract reading novels by women; one month contract on creative writing; one month contract, master classes in dance; one quarter Coordinated Studies, leading to the production of short operas by Menotti.*
FOURTH YEAR: *One quarter Coordinated Study in problems of exceptional children; two quarters group contract in advanced educational psychology, with teaching internship in public schools and in classes for exceptional children.*

RECOMMENDATION. This is a new school and a fine one. The planners of Evergreen have come from the experimental schools of the sixties, particularly San José and Old Westbury, some from both places. They have had experience with experimental colleges and are good teachers. Larry Eickstaedt, Richard Jones, Bill Unsoeld and Bob Sluss are outstanding teachers.

For the next few years facilities are going to be limited at Evergreen; they are just building and the state budgets have been cut drastically. This should keep them small and give them time to organize. We think it's a school particularly established for students interested in ecology. The location couldn't be better.

The Evergreen State College
Olympia, Washington 98501

THOMAS JEFFERSON COLLEGE, GRAND VALLEY, MICHIGAN

LOCATION. This college is in the western part of Michigan, northwest of Grand Rapids in the Dutch Reform area of the state, and in the town of Allendale. This is the first experimental college of Grand Valley State College. It opened in 1968.

SIZE. It has 315 students and thirteen faculty members. Students can take courses at the main school (School of General Learning) or at the newer William James College which will have a series of famous men in temporary residence.

WHAT KINDS OF STUDENTS. Thomas Jefferson College is not an "honors" school and they want students to fulfill two requirements: (1) diligently pursue course work entirely on their own with a minimum of external prompting, and (2) contribute substantially to the progress of a group engaged in a learning situation. They are looking for students who "view their education specifically, or life in general, as providing opportunities . . . by which they can advance their personal and academic growth and development." They want students who are bright, but do not base selection on high school grades or tests. A student must first be accepted by Grand Valley, then Thomas Jefferson. Thomas Jefferson requires that all applicants write about themselves and their interests, experiences, education and aspirations. Applicants can request an interview and sometimes the Admissions Committee will want to see a student if material on him/her is limited.

RULES AND REGULATIONS. Students determine their own academic program and have equal power on college policy decisions. No problems here.

COSTS. Tuition for a full term is $152 for Michigan residents, and $400 per term for non-Michigan residents. Room and board is $380 per term for both Michigan and non-Michigan residents.

WHAT'S SPECIAL ABOUT THOMAS JEFFERSON. This is one of the better schools in the Midwest and certainly the best in Michigan. The driving force behind the college is psychologist T. Dan Gilmore who some call "the benevolent despot" of the place.

There are seven modes of learning available at Thomas Jefferson: Examinations, Seminars, Special Studies, Group Special Studies, Personalized General Studies, Independent Projects and Senior Projects. They work this way:

Examinations: Students take examinations in specialized areas of study. If exams are passed they get 5 credits.

Seminars: Organized when a student or faculty member proposes a subject that attracts a group. 5 credits.

Special Studies: One student studies a particular subject which usually results in a major paper. 5 credits.

Group Special Studies: A small group pursues a specialized area in depth. 5 credits.

Personalized General Studies: To overcome initial trouble with wholesale independence of the experimental college, this curriculum option is a 15-credit seminar for first-year students. Usually all working with one faculty member.

Independent Project: A time for social service, or experiencing another culture, overseas or at home. Worth 15 credits.

Senior Project: In-depth study designed by Academic Affairs Committee and student. Worth at least 5 credits.

Students receive either a Bachelor of Philosophy or a Bachelor of Science degree and are able to complete their certification requirements for elementary or secondary teaching, if they want, within the college.

Not much of a community at the school for those who want it, but Thomas Jefferson is making efforts to change this. It is also thinking of changing degree requirements. All of this is still in the air.

RECOMMENDATION. This is an excellent college. A. S. Neill has written of Thomas Jefferson, "the whole setup sounds delightful." Thomas Jefferson receives about one thousand applications a year, usually takes in 150 new students. There is some talk of breaking the college into 250-student units, thereby keeping the whole place small. If you can stand the cold weather and the isolation of Allendale—which, believe us, is isolated—go here. You'll be hearing more from Grand Valley; it's coming on strong. The motto of the place is "KEEP ON TRUCKIN"!

Thomas Jefferson College
Grand Valley College
Allendale, Michigan 49401

UNIVERSITY OF CALIFORNIA, SANTA CRUZ, CALIFORNIA

LOCATION. This campus is the largest of the California state system, some two thousand acres three miles from Santa Cruz. It is seventy-five miles south of San Francisco, at the northern end of the Monterey Bay. The campus is one large park of woods, meadows, flowers. Hard to find a lovelier place.

SIZE. Santa Cruz opened in 1965 and has about 4,100 students in six cluster colleges. There is also a small graduate school. Santa Cruz will grow to about 25,000, but not for awhile, and the additions will be made through new colleges with 600 to 800 undergraduates. The newest college, number seven, opened in 1972. UCSC is the largest employee in the county; its annual payroll is eleven million dollars.

WHAT KINDS OF STUDENTS. Very selective. Average SAT's are in the 700's. Students are into nature and liberal politics, not very hip. Students applying from California schools must have an overall high school average of "B." In 1971, 3,747 applications were received for 1,000 openings. Students going to Santa Cruz want to go on to graduate school, are idealistic, are creative. Bright folk.

RULES AND REGULATIONS. The rules and regulations are imposed by the Board of Regents and apply to all nine campuses of the University of California. UCSC has a liberal interpretation of the regulations and the campus runs smoothly. The "no politics on campus" ruling by the Regents has not stopped various movements on campus. Personal rules regarding the dormitories are set up by each college. There are visiting hours, but they are never enforced.

UCSC, in response to students wanting more freedom in their living, has taken action to offer cooperative cleaning arrangements, natural foods in the dining halls, cooperative cooking options, use of some empty rooms as art studios, more colorful painting of rooms and halls, greater freedom for students to decorate their rooms, inclusion of a privacy clause in the room contract, etc.

COSTS.

(Quarterly)	Resident	Non-resident
University Fee	$100.00	$100.00
Educational Fee	100.00	100.00
Other Fees	30.00	30.00
Room and Board	400.00	400.00
Tuition	0	500.00

GRADING SYSTEM. Students are graded passed/no credit. Evaluations are written for the file by the instructors. Students also take a comprehensive examination in their major.

WHAT'S SPECIAL ABOUT SANTA CRUZ. This college was established to give a variety of opportunities for learning. The plan was a series of colleges of moderate size, residential living, close student-faculty relationships. Its collegiate structure is the most important aspect of the school. Briefly, they are:

Cowell College: Opened in 1965 and has 700 students and 43 faculty members. It has no single direction or curriculum, but is considered on campus as the humanistic college.

Crown College: This is the science college, but teaches science fiction. Wide selection of classes and a free atmosphere. It has about 770 students.

Merrill College: Offers a series of interdisciplinary courses on civilization and cultures of the Third World. There are no required courses.

College V: This is an arts college. The college offers courses in theater, ceramics, dance, writing, metal sculpture, printmaking, light, jazz, etc. All freshmen take a core course.

Kresge College: Opened in 1971 with 270 students and 18 faculty members. The theme of the college is "Man and His Environment."

Stevenson College: The social sciences college of Santa Cruz. Only one required course and everything is taught by seminars.

The new colleges being formed are problem-oriented colleges. College Seven will focus on the problems of cities and minorities, with special attention to Afro-Americans and Mexican-Americans. College Eight will be non-residential.

Each college has a provost who lives in the school and fellows, or faculty members, drawn from all related areas concerning the curriculum of the particular school. Students can take courses in all the colleges.

RECOMMENDATION. Santa Cruz is certainly the best state college in California. It is attractive, free and experimental. Lately it has been able to "adjust" to the new students who are not taking to residential living—would rather live in houses off campus—and Santa Cruz is trying to make their residential schools more attractive. Also, with College Eight being non-residential, they are providing an alternative to campus living. We had a letter from one student who wrote "On campus I hear some people complaining about the freedom we are supposed to have, but don't. Well, after spending two quarters here, after comparing notes with my high school classmates who have gone to different schools, I have to conclude that UCSC is by no means the 'perfect experimental' college but it is decisively better than the schools my friends are attending." We agree. One of the best in the West.

University of California, Santa Cruz
Santa Cruz, California 95060

P.S. The only problem is they sell their General Catalog . . . $1.

UNIVERSITY OF GREEN BAY, GREEN BAY, WISCONSIN

LOCATION. This university has four schools within a sixty-mile radius of Green Bay. The main campus—Green Bay itself—is on the northeast of town on six hundred wooded acres. The site includes a nine-hole golf course, playing fields and about twenty new buildings. The college opened in the fall of 1969.

SIZE. All four campuses have a total enrollment of 4,100. Green Bay has the largest chunk, 2,891. Green Bay is a four-year college, and the other campuses, Fox Valley, Manitowoc and Marinette, are all two-year schools. Green Bay has new apartment-style dorms for 550 students. By 1972, they expect to have housing for 1,500 students, all apartment style.

WHAT KINDS OF STUDENTS. Most students are from Wisconsin and all students are interested in the study of man and his environment. They are serious and reasonable, but nothing unusual. Not at all radical. Politics so far hasn't touched this campus, and it shouldn't. Students are intense about their study of the environment.

RULES AND REGULATIONS. Students sit as "advisors" on most committees. But certainly don't have a final say. Living is left to the students who either commute from family homes or from off-campus apartments. Usual rules for a midwest school and students can't be too obvious about breaking them. Otherwise, everything is okay.

COSTS.

	In-State	Out-of-State
Tuition for the academic year	$ 550.00	$2,000.00
Room and Board	$1,250.00	$1,250.00

GRADING SYSTEM. Most courses can be taken on a pass/fail basis, except the four years of Liberal Education Seminars and courses that are part of a concentration. Some courses can be passed with taking a special examination.

WHAT'S SPECIAL ABOUT GREEN BAY. All campuses of the University of Green Bay offer the same curriculum, which is: Man and His Environment. It is one of the few colleges to have such a total program, and the only place we know that is devoted to the study of ecology, in all its aspects. The college structure is based on themes, rather than disciplines; majors are called concentrations. For example: the College of Environmental Sciences emphasizes the problems of the natural environment; the College of Community Sciences is concerned with the process by which man relates to his social (man-made) environment; the College of Human Biology emphasizes human adaptability to the social and physical environment; the College of Creative Communication centers on human identity—man's impact on his social environment.

The students have four years of Liberal Education Seminars that help focus the ecological theme and tie the academic program together. They also have an Off-Campus Experience where students work on special projects, using the Northern Great Lakes region as a laboratory. Recently Green Bay received one of the first nine ACTION grants to develop this off-campus experience. Tool Subjects are such courses in foreign language, data processing, mathematics, performing arts. Students can take special exams to write off these required courses.

Students at Green Bay spend much of their academic time off campus, out of the classroom. Independent study is stressed and students have great flexibility. It is a college that's producing highly trained people for careers in environment, and immediate relationship with the world. Nothing could be more relevant.

RECOMMENDATION. The best college for ecology going. We recommend it highly, but students need to be committed to this cause. No easy, freaky place. A lot of hard, dull facts and figures are given their due. These people are producing here.

University of Green Bay
1567 Deckner Avenue
Green Bay, Wisconsin 54302

WASHINGTON INTERNATIONAL COLLEGE, DISTRICT OF COLUMBIA

LOCATION. Housed in a couple of offices and classrooms of Hearst Hall, on the grounds of the National Cathedral in northwest Washington. The college is non-residential and private. It is not affiliated with any religion.

SIZE. In the fall of 1971, the first year of the college, few freshmen were admitted. The college expects to grow to a maximum enrollment of one thousand students, adding a new class every year until it reaches four-year status.

WHAT KINDS OF STUDENTS. The equivalent of high school graduation is required, but beyond that Washington International College has an "open door" approach to admissions. Any student who wants a college education will be given the opportunity, the only limiting factor being the maximum number of students.

No examination scores are required, but students (after acceptance) take a series of CLEP (College Level Examination Program) General Examinations to determine the student's academic needs.

COSTS.

Application Fee (refundable)	$ 10.00
Non-refundable Deposit	100.00
Tuition	1,650.00

GRADING SYSTEM. ABC system used, but only passing grades appear on permanent records. Sixty credit hours for the Associate in Arts degree, 120 hours for Bachelor of Arts. One half of the credit hours may be earned through credit taken by examinations, such as CLEP. At the end of each course a nationally standardized examination will be given and the results included in the student's permanent record.

WHAT'S SPECIAL ABOUT WASHINGTON INTERNATIONAL. To justify the word *international* in its name, students spend six weeks every year overseas. Ten locations are available and the costs of transportation and room and board are covered in the tuition. In 1971 courses in Spanish, history, sociology, studio art and geology were offered.

Also every year students may enroll in six weeks of full-time work in an Academic Internship. Students work in hospitals, government agencies, poverty areas, etc. Internships "are planned to interrelate academic course work and associated occupational experience."

Students have two scheduling possibilities for their time "on campus": Modular Option and Self-Pacing Option. The *Modular Option* allows a student to enroll in only one course at a time. He could complete a 3-credit hour course in three weeks, then move to another course. In the *Self-Pacing Option,* a student progresses as he wishes, highly accelerated or slowly. Courses begin about every three weeks; therefore, the student can pick and choose as he wishes.

The college has courses available in arts and humanities, social and behavioral sciences, natural sciences and mathematics. Advanced courses in all these areas will be added as the school grows.

A tremendous amount of the "classroom" work will be done through program-learning machines and individualized instruction. There will be little teacher-student interaction, as Washington International has few faculty members.

The college is not accredited, but this is not unusual. Licensing is not available to a new college until after it graduates its first class. Washington International has taken the preliminary steps toward accreditation and is incorporated as a not-for-profit institution in the District of Columbia.

RECOMMENDATION. Washington International was started by two life-long junior college educators, the Kuhns, and their friends. It is a self-directed and self-learning place, little physical facilities available. Classes take place often where the students are living. Washington International really "administrates" an education, but they don't give one: a student picks his up on his own, using the facilities, the tape recorders and computers, the program-learning provided by the administration.

As is to be expected, it will take several years of developing, learning and planning before Washington International arranges their college. It's a college for students who want and can learn on their own. No tight community or campus. You're on your own! Good luck.

Washington International College
Wisconsin and Woodley Road, N.W.
Washington, D.C. 20016

4. Small and Innovative Colleges

ALTERNATIVE ONE   *State*
Keene State College   *Coed*
Keene, New Hampsire 03431   *Semester*
                                                   60 students

Alternative One is the small experiment of small Keene State College
(1,842 students). It is a two-year program for freshmen and sophomores
that began with less than a dozen faculty members and sixty students in
1971. At the end of two years the students return to the regular college
curriculum.

The program is a series of workshops in Natural Sciences, Social
Sciences, Humanities and Arts. Each student takes two of four workshops
each semester. The direction of these workshops is left up to the participants. Students also do independent study, off-campus projects, and work-
study. All grading is on a credit/no credit system and each faculty
member submits a written evaluation of the student's performance.

Students in Alternative One live in their own dorms. Kennedy
House for men and Strafford House for women. The existing housing
rules and regulations apply to these two houses, however, and there's
little mixing of the sexes. Alternative One has obtained a rooming house
near the campus where sophomore students will be able to live. Alternative One wants to provide "a sense of community activity among a small
group engaged in coordinated learning activities."

Any student who is admitted to Keene State is eligible for Alternative One but must write saying why he wants to participate in it. The letter must be received by July 15 and there is an interview on campus.

It is too soon to tell how successful the program will be. It is still closely tied to the main campus and students take part of their program in regular classes. Some waiving of requirements has taken place. We expect as Alternative One develops on campus it will begin to expand and become more independent. These first years will be trying and exciting; they always are when making up a new educational form for a school. At the same time they are extremely unstructured and demanding. Take that into consideration when thinking about Keene State.

Write us about Alternative One. We'd like to see how it goes.

ANTIOCH COLLEGE   *Private*
Yellow Springs, Ohio, 45387   *Coed*
                                        Quarters
                                        2,131 students

Antioch tells their students not to bring many belongings to Yellow Springs because they'll be away from campus most of the time. Students spend thirteen weeks in the winter and twenty-six weeks over the spring-summer away from campus. Only half the student body is on campus at any given time.

Yellow Springs is not much of a place; it's lost in the flat farmlands of Ohio eighteen miles east of Dayton on Highway 68. A town of 5,000. The campus covers one hundred acres and has forty-three buildings. It's pleasant, but dull. Students don't mind being away from Yellow Springs.

While on campus they run their own lives. Antioch is a free place. Dormitories are divided into units of sixteen to twenty-five students and each hall is responsible for itself, establishes its own rules and regulations. Most dormitories are coed, all of them are open. An Administrative Council runs the college and students have three of the five positions. Students are included in all policies of the school.

Antioch admits slightly less than 600 students each year and over 3,000 apply. They look for students "who are ready to assume responsibility for their own lives" and say they never have enough room for all the qualified people. At the moment they are trying to recruit more low-income and working-class students, but still like students who have had a college-preparatory high school program. Antioch is expensive. A total year, covering tuition, room and board would be about $4,150. Last year 40 percent of Antioch students received some form of financial aid from the college and other sources.

It takes five years to get a degree. Students enroll either in July or October and spend two quarters studying, two quarters off campus working in the Co-Operative Program. They spend the time learning how to work in business, industrial plants, research laboratories, agencies, newspapers, schools, museums, etc. Over the five years a student must earn 85 co-op credits and 165 academic credits. A student can graduate within four years by taking special examinations and showing some evidence of high standard of performance. An Antioch degree has always been a prestigious one.

Antioch's faculty is competent and diverse. It is particularly strong in humanities and the social sciences. Most instruction is by small seminars, tutorials and independent study. The academic demands are high. Students can also spend a year overseas, expenses paid, at a European, African or Asian college. Antioch students have been to places most college students haven't heard of.

In the United States, Antioch has three other major centers: the Baltimore/Washington Branch, a new Law School in Washington, D.C. and a graduate school in education located in Putney, Vermont. Besides these "campuses" they have programs in several major cities and students everywhere. John Coyne was once served hamburgers and french fries in Seattle, Washington by an Antioch sophomore earning five credits working in a diner.

Antioch provides over five hundred job opportunities for their students and some structure in the assignment, but students are nevertheless on their own. It's a first-class work-study college, but we are not sure it is worth the money. Some other colleges have picked up the plan and gone farther, and they have been state schools where expenses are less. We are not sure whether Antioch can respond as they have often done in the past: come up with a plan that has altered the course of education. We hope they can. They're talking about the Antioch System, a federation of Antioch activities across the country.

AQUARIAN UNIVERSITY　　　　　　　　　　　*Private*
2405 Ruscombe Lane　　　　　　　　　　　　*Coed*
Baltimore, Maryland 20209　　　　　　　　　*Semester*
　　　　　　　　　　　　　　　　　　　　　　175 students

This *free university*, opened several years ago by Bob Hieronimus and his friends at their spiritual commune called Savitria, is dedicated to "sowing the seeds of the Aquarian Age." We've included it because Aquarian is moving toward accreditation and students at the school have been able to transfer credits. It looks like a free school that has made it.

The university has over twenty-seven courses and a part-time faculty of twenty-plus. Its students range in age from fourteen to seventy-five with lawyers, dentists, teachers, etc., studying also at Aquarian. Tuition is twenty dollars a course.

The four major fields of study are: Atlantis, Astrology, Reincarnation and Meditation, but it also has courses in existential writings of Kierkegaard and mathematics, among others. There are no grades and none of the other trappings of academia. Also, there are no drugs, no alcohol on campus, and not much noise either. Shoes are not allowed inside the carriage house, the home of the university.

Some course titles are: Qabalah; The Eastern Way; Study of Carl Jung I; Symbology I—The Apocalypse; Esoteric Science I; Sidereal Astrology. All professors must know their material and present it, according to Bob Hieronimus, "in a logical, organized and interesting fashion." Most of the university's faculty teach elsewhere.

The university is open to anyone, but Bob writes us: "The younger kids think we're into all kinds of weirdo things, including drugs. When they find out we're straight, that we're operating on intellect, not emotion, they become disillusioned and drop out. The best students are middle age—twenty-five to forty. What we're trying to do here is to promote brotherhood through the worldwide expansion of consciousness and extension of mental power. We believe the world faces terrible times ahead and the only way man will be able to adjust to the hardships of the future is to look within himself."

Write them or call (301) 664-6959.

BARD COLLEGE   *Private*
Annandale-on-Hudson New York, 12504   *Coed*
                                                     4-1-4*
                                                     643 students

Bard is not a new school—it was founded in 1860 as St. Stephen's—but it has for many years been involved with innovative programs. Its most recent venture is: *University Without Walls.* Twelve students in the fall of 1971 started working toward Bard degrees while living away from campus, being involved with other work. *Women's Studies,* a student-run class organized by several members of Bard Women's Liberation, is graded pass/fail and class attendance and contribution to the class establish the criteria for credit. *Inner College* is a group of fifty students and

---

* Four months of study, one month free (usually February), then four months of study, etc.

four faculty members who are living/learning together. *Ecology and Environmental Biology* uses the 550 acres of Hudson River shoreline that Bard owns as its lab. *Major in Film* is oriented toward film-making rather than the spectator or critic.

Bard's curriculum is derived from the Oxford system: a Lower and an Upper College; an oral and written examination—the Sophomore Moderation—as a test of the student's ability to do Upper College work; and independent work. Bard is highly academic and high scores are needed to get in; but once in, Bard takes care of its students.

The campus is two hours north of New York City and is made up of old estates, gray limestone Gothic buildings, acres of woods and fields and a few modern concrete and glass structures. All classes are small, mostly seminars, tutorials, and the contact with faculty is close and friendly, but Bard is no touchy-feely place, except in the Inner College. A comprehensive fee at Bard is somewhere around $4,150. Unless someone else is paying, it's not worth it. Education shouldn't be that expensive. Few scholarships. In 1971 about twenty freshmen got aid. But in fairness—one gets educated.

The Winter Field Period is four weeks long, a chance to get off campus, earn credit. The first two years are spent doing "something vocational, intellectual or creative," then reading and/or creative projects, and a final year on a Senior Project. All of these programs are closely supervised and tend to go well. But Bard is not committed to experiential learning; it's still by the book at Annandale on the Hudson.

A first-rate, small, liberal arts college. We wish we could afford it.

BELOIT COLLEGE   *Private*
Beloit, Wisconsin 53511   *Coed*
                                                   Trimester
                                                   1,800 students

Beloit College is an independent, coeducational, liberal arts college one hundred miles northwest of Chicago that since 1847 has been doing its own thing. In 1964, it began to do "its thing" bigger and better. It introduced a three-stage plan toward a degree.

The three stages are, briefly:

Underclass Year: Three 15-week terms spread over one year. Students take a two-term underclass common course which is an interdisciplinary investigation of some topic.

Middleclass Period: Five terms of on-campus study, off-campus field experience, overseas work or study, and vacation.

Upperclass Year: Three terms on campus finishing work on field of concentration. Students also take a final common course.

Beloit's underclass common course has students living and studying together. Classes are often held in lounges and dorm rooms and the idea is to get everyone together, living and learning. It's not that innovative, but for Beloit. . . .

All Beloit students are required to spend one term off campus. It's not for credit, but to *widen* the student's experience. Since 1964, the college has placed more than 1,900 students in forty-one states and forty-five countries. Beloit also has a World Outlook Program (they're big on names at Beloit) and students attend seminars in London, Taipei, Vienna, Belgium and Germany. Students live in private homes and work under the direction of Beloit professors. They also have exchange programs with other colleges and students can do field work in Costa Rica, the Quetico–Lake Superior wilderness or at the Newberry Library.

Tuition is $3,100 a year and room and board $510 a term. It's a small school, even smaller because one-third of the student population is off campus all the time. The college is tough and solid, not much wasted time and the terms are intense. Students are middle class and from the Midwest, but don't hold that against them or the school. It's first-rate.

BEREA COLLEGE	*Private*
Berea, Kentucky 40403	*Coed*
	4-1-4
	1,421 students

It costs less than nine hundred dollars a year to attend Berea College. No tuition is charged. Berea is a four-year liberal arts school founded in 1855 in the foothills of the Cumberland Mountains. It has a campus of 1,100 acres, including lawns, gardens, experimental farms and livestock and poultry. Nearby there are 6,000 acres of forest owned by the college.

Eighty percent of the students come from the 230 mountain counties of Alabama, Georgia, Kentucky, the Carolinas, Tennessee, Virginia and West Virginia. The other students—about eighty new freshmen a year—come from all over the United States and overseas.

Berea offers a bachelor of arts degree in twenty-one areas, a bachelor of science degree in six fields. Students take one-third of their college career in required subjects. They are: Issues and Values, Man and the Arts, Physical Education, Health, Religious and Historical Perspectives, and Christian Faith in the Modern World. Berea is in Bible Belt country in case you haven't noticed. But it's also possible to take courses in Black and Appalachian Culture, and the Third World.

It is not academically tough—though 55 percent go on to graduate school—and it is not difficult to be accepted (students from the mountain territory have preference) if you can show a financial need and have had a sound high school background.

Berea is famous for being a college without tuition and for educating many mountain people. Their students in the past have worked, while in school, as VISTA and Appalachian Volunteers. It is a liberal citadel in the backwash of conservatism. Students are radical, but only in the context of this area. They are also hard-working farm people. Most hold extra jobs on campus, everything from stacking books in the new 300,000 volume library to serving beer in Boone Tavern, the college hotel.

If you haven't the money for college and want to get close to nature, write Berea.

BERRY COLLEGE   *Private*
Mount Berry,   *Coed*
Georgia 30149   *Quarters*
                                       1,003 students

Berry College is a small work-study school in the woods of northwest Georgia. Students can work off campus or on to help pay for a relatively inexpensive college education—$2,400 comprehensive fee—while obtaining a B.A. in Art, Science or Music. The college was founded in 1902 and though it's non-sectarian, Berry is a Christian institution; but chapel services, etc., are optional.

Berry College is close to the land. It's among 30,000 acres of forests, fields, mountains and lakes. A quiet, peaceful place where one can almost hear the grass growing. The campus buildings are Georgian and Gothic and even log cabin. The campus is near the city of Rome, the business center of northwest Georgia and has a population of 68,000.

This college offers a traditional education. There is little innovative work being done, but classes are small, the campus is attractive and the work-study program makes it a fine choice for Georgia. The work opportunities are seen as a chance for students to pay for their education, and designed to develop skills in community living, building self-reliance and self-respect, and to provide experience for vocations or avocations. Scholarships, grants-in-aid, loans and awards are also available to students.

This college attracts students from all of the southeastern states, but has a handful of foreign students and students coming down from the North. We suggest it as a college worth considering for students who do not have the funds to go elsewhere, and for those who want a quiet campus and a solid but not extensive academic program. It is not difficult to get into Berry, an average high school record will do. Berry also takes mature students at the end of their junior year of high school, if recommended by a counselor. All academic programs are arranged to meet the individual student's needs.

Think of Berry if you're thinking of Georgia. It is, by the way, only seventy miles from Atlanta.

BLAKE COLLEGE *Private*
200 N. Jefferson *Coed*
Eugene, Oregon 97402 *Term*
30 students

Blake College began in Mexico in 1960. It was "discovered" by the American Embassy and Mexican government in 1965 and the students were deported. In 1966 they established themselves in Eugene, Oregon. They wanted, according to Ray Peat of Blake College, "to create a community for learning and discovery that wouldn't be under the control of politicians, businessmen, trustees and conservative academic 'intellectuals.' " They wanted a community that would offer mutual support for discovery, and an institutional history—for diplomas and transcripts —so students wanting jobs or acceptance to graduate schools could have an educational reference.

Blake is accredited by the American Association of Experimental Colleges and offers a degree after two to nine terms of resident study, based on the student's field of study and its acceptability to the faculty. Tuition is two hundred per three-month term and living costs about a hundred dollars a month. Most of the students live in the Blake commune, but housing is available elsewhere. Students can enroll at any time. The term begins with the arrival of the student at Blake.

All study is individual or tutorial, with seminars and community discussions. Blake College believes "learning occurs only with participation in problems, questions and arguments." It also encourages students to "evolve greater self-consistency through organismic or phenomenological integration." The tutors determine the "curriculum": art, art history, mathematics, biology, biochemistry, biophysics, philosophy, psychology, music, music composition, dance, choreography, history, logic, sculpture, organic gardening and nutrition, political science, anthropology, economics, Russian, French, German, Spanish and linguistics.

Blake College wants its students to learn to see things whole, and to use their knowledge to go beyond what is already known. "We need," they write, "to work together to create new and humanly usable knowledge, to become all we can, to enjoy as intensely as we can. If we are satisfied with phony, superficial and stylized answers, the old culture is going to survive in us."

Blake is another of those small, intense places where education is close and personal. A hard, unstructured education, mostly self-taught, but valuable. If students are interested, they should write at length about themselves, send grades if applying from high school, otherwise just the statement of what they're about. Blake wants students who are intelligent and would feel comfortable within their community. Write or call (503) 345-4598.

BOWDOIN COLLEGE   *Private*
Brunswick, Maine 04011   *Coed*
                                          Semester
                                          967 students

Bowdoin is beginning to accept women. Its class of 1975 had entering freshmen numbering 319: 65 were women. Bowdoin also in 1969 eliminated the College Boards examination requirement for admissions. All test scores were considered optional. It also established Independent Study, one course a semester working under tutorial supervision. For these reasons, and the fact that we have several close friends who went to Bowdoin and "insisted" we include their school, we've included the place. But we like it very much besides. Nathaniel Hawthorne and Henry Wadsworth Longfellow graduated from Bowdoin and they did okay. What else good can you say about the place?

Bowdoin is a New England college, no way else to cut it. About 65 percent come from there, but it recently began to spread its wings, attract students from the rest of the United States, concentrating on the big city ghettos. Ten percent of the undergraduates are black. It is getting increasingly popular. In 1971, 2,923 students applied, 319 got in. People like Bowdoin because it's in the woods and snows of Maine; 110 acres with thirty very old and very elegant buildings on the banks of the Androscoggin River. It has that "college feel."

College life on this isolated campus is tied in with fraternities (and, we guess, now sororities), for the campus and Brunswick offer little else. The result is that students come into a tight community. All senior students live together in a separate center. This again reinforces the feeling of a "class." How the women will change this all-male society, we can't say, but our guess is they'll all become sisters and be taken care of by big brothers. So much for sex at Bowdoin.

Sex or any other diversion takes place thirty miles away in Portland or three hours away in Boston.

On campus it's just that ole liberal arts education, and lots of it. If you've got the money—a comprehensive fee of about $4,250—apply here. One other nice thing about Bowdoin: no grades, they use pass/fail.

CALIFORNIA COLLEGE OF ARTS AND CRAFTS   *Private*
5212 Broadway   *Coed*
Oakland, California 94618   *Semester*
                                           1,326 students

There are a hundred professional programs of art and design at the college level in the United States. Forty-five of these hundred are accredited to award B.F.A. and M.F.A. degrees. California College of Arts and Crafts is one of twenty that is private and independent. It is also one of the best. And one of the least expensive of the private schools. Tuition for 1971–72 was $1,450.

CCAC has three major functions:

1) training of professional artists—painters, sculptors, printmakers, craftsmen, industrial, interior and commercial designers, film-makers;

2) developing art teachers for public and private elementary and secondary schools, and for junior college and college positions;

3) supplying supplementary training in the arts, crafts and design for students who do not desire a degree.

CCAC is organized into eight divisions: Basic Studies, Fine Arts, Crafts, Design, Humanities and Sciences, Education, Ethnic Studies and the Graduate Program. Students take a Basic Studies program the first two semesters. This program is the same for all students. Everyone is taught skills in drawing, painting, three-dimensional design and another craft. Also the student is required to take introductory courses in history, English, philosophy and the physical, biological and social sciences. The second year is directed toward a major division (courses are carried over from the first year and requirements completed). In the third and fourth year a major is selected and concentration of area completed.

Life at California College of Arts and Crafts is relaxed, informal and free. Many classes are held outside and everyone is on a first-name basis. There is no feeling of "classroom." The campus is a four-acre hillside garden in Oakland with views of the San Francisco Bay, the Golden Gate and the mountains of Marin. The Berkeley campus of the University of California is only two miles away.

CCAC faculty is first-rate. Some are: Michael McClure, writer and one of the editors of City Lights Press; Bella Tabak Feldman, lecturer in Fine Arts; Trude Guermonprez, professor of Textile Arts and winner of the 1970 National Craftsmanship medal presented by the American Institute of Architects; Glen Wessels, lecturer in Fine Arts.

First-rate school for arts and crafts in a wonderful location. Can't be beat.

CAMPUS-FREE COLLEGE
Box 161
Arlington, Massachusetts 02174

Private
Coed
External Degree
Handful of students

Campus-Free was begun in 1971 by a few former Franconia College grads as a non-profit undergraduate college with students and Program Advisors throughout the United States. The college has no physical campus. It employs teachers for individual students. It is designed "to offer maximum flexibility in educational resources and learning experiences, high quality of guidance and instruction, and a variable but relatively modest cost." It works this way.

A student contacts a Program Advisor—Campus-Free College has over two hundred Program Advisor candidates. They are faculty members of other colleges, university and research institutes, artists, etc. The Program Advisor and students plan a curriculum for the individual needs, skills, interests, budget, etc., of the student and present that to the Academic Council for review. In the course of study a student might take courses, do tutorials, on-the-job learning, lab work, foreign travel. Progress is evaluated every three months by the Academic Council, and, of course, the Program Advisor. When the curriculum goals have been met, the student applies for a degree which is granted by the Board of Trustees.

Cost for this education varies, but expect to spend about two thousand dollars per year. Students have to pay for their own room and board, supplies, etc. Students can, however, pay with services rather than cash. There is also limited scholarship aid.

This kind of education is the type we support, knowing that it takes a special mature student to live on his own and learn without much physical or emotional support from an institution. Campus-Free has turned the learning process over entirely to the student, where it belongs. We wish them well and we suggest you write them.

CARLETON COLLEGE
Northfield, Minnesota 55057

Private
Coed
4-1-4
1,392 students

Carleton College has always been one of those schools mentioned when people talk about good, small liberal arts places in the Midwest. Everyone gives it okay ratings. Even the students like the place. Students are a ductile bunch, but smart. Average SAT's are in the 700's.

Carleton has a bunch of innovative programs, though the college is straight with no experimentation. Among their special programs are: American Studies, Black Studies, Junior-Senior Year Program, Senior Colloquia, Independent Reading, Off-Campus Programs, Asian Studies, Independent Study Overseas. There's a lot there for the taking, but it costs. At least $3,500 for everything, per year.

On campus students are guarded closely. Students have a Freshman Seminar and required humanities courses. It continues like that all four years. But classes are small, faculty friendly. And students, in attempting to add some of their own ideas to the school, have organized Bald Spot University, a free school that should grow.

Carleton is having money problems, like all those small liberal arts places, but it will hang on, and with the continuing pressure of students, open up some more. The college attracts students from all over, nearly three-fourths are from out of state, It has a campus of 945 acres in rural southeastern Minnesota, about forty miles south of the Twin Cities. The college has twenty-five buildings, the first built in 1872.

The college has some courses that are graded satisfactory/unsatisfactory. Students can select the courses they want, up to eighteen hours each year. But students want grades; they want to go to grad school. Most rules and regulations are strict, little personal freedom for students and everyone lives on campus . . . no experimenting here.

Nevertheless, we like Carleton, but you have to like to grind, nothing free.

COE COLLEGE
Ceder Rapids, Iowa 52402

Private
Coed
4-1-4
1,286 students

Coe College, like a first-class whorehouse, has something for everyone's taste. It is a college education one can assemble from a variety of pre-packaged programs. The school offers two bachelor degrees: Arts and Music.

Very little is required at Coe. Students take a freshman year Introduction to Liberal Arts, then complete thirty-two to thirty-six courses with a concentration of seven to eleven courses in some coherent interdepartmental sequence. And there are options:

Work Study: Students work off campus for a term as interns in urban and rural health, education or some governmental agency.

Exploratory Term: Four weeks in January where a student follows a special interest, is graded satisfactory/unsatisfactory and produces a report. The selection of study project, travel, special seminars or even classroom work is a student's own decision.

Independent Study: Projects are offered in all departments and arranged between the student and some professor.

Occasional Courses: Offered usually only once, especially during the Exploratory Term, and are not listed in the catalog. They come about because of some interest of students and teachers.

Off-campus Programs: A series of possibilities, usually just for outstanding students at places like: Argonne Labs, Newberry Library, New York and Washington. Students are engaged in research projects during these terms and are selected by individual professors.

Overseas Study: Coe College has programs through different auspices in France, Germany, Austria, Spain, Mexico, Sweden, Norway, Israel and a few countries in Asia, Japan and India to name just two.

Coe College is located in downtown Cedar Rapids, a town of 111,000 about 225 miles west of Chicago. It is related in its history to the United Presbyterian Church, but is independent and liberal. The campus is new and has fourteen modern buildings on eight blocks of land. It is a dormitory school, almost everyone lives on campus. Students are academic and straight. Drugs are not an issue, though the college was busted a few times last year. Students have voting members on the faculty committees and share in all student-life organizations and committees. Not much campus politics, not much politics at all, but the students have protested against the draft and Nixon and their administration.

Coe is expensive. A comprehensive fee, covering everything at the college is $3,200. Aid is available and the college makes it a practice to support students who wish to attend, but do not have funds.

In any state, Coe would be a fine college. In Iowa, it's outstanding.

COLBY COLLEGE
Waterville, Maine 04901

Private
Coed
4-1-4
1,532 students

In 1969 Colby opened its *Center for Coordinated Studies,* a tiny innovative program with three objectives: (1) create, through interdepartmental programs of study, more coherent patterns for a liberal arts education; (2) create and sustain a greater degree of responsiveness between students and faculty in the design and conduct of curriculum; (3) create a more pervasive learning environment for students. It's a living/learning situation where students and faculty select courses of study. Some of their current areas of interest are: Intensive Studies in Western Civilization; Bilingual and Bicultural Studies; Hegiran History; Darwinism; Classics.

Colby also has two other innovative programs: *Junior Year Abroad* started in 1970 in cooperation with the Université de Caen and a *January Program of Independent Study.* Students receive pass/fail in the Independent Study, but otherwise the program is tightly controlled by the faculty.

Colby is no slouch of a college. When it experiments, it takes its time and develops slowly, no rushing after fads at this place. It has a fine reputation, inside and outside of Maine. It started back in 1813 by a group of Baptists, but now is independent and non-denominational. It has a new campus on Mayflower Hill with thirty-four modern, Georgian colonial buildings, and room to grow. Tuition and room and board run about $3,500.

Students are involved, but have no voting rights at faculty meetings. They do arrange their own social lives, though Colby is a straight place here . . . no official experimentation with living patterns beyond the Center for Coordinated Studies. Students haven't made demands here, we suspect.

Colby has always attracted those solid students who do well in high school and on Board scores: the all-American kind of student. Very few way-out folks. As a school it is concerned about the development of the whole person and trying to keep life from becoming too difficult. Therefore, sports, entertainments, partying are important to the college. Because of the small student body and a rather large faculty, students and faculty know and like each other. And we like them.

COLLEGE AT OLD WESTBURY   *State*
SUNY   *Coed*
Box 210   *Semester*
Old Westbury, New York 11568   *450 students*

College at Old Westbury is in its second attempt at being the innovative and experimental branch of the State University of New York. It began first in 1968 with the hope of developing a more humane college, a college with full partnership for students. That venture stopped when the first president, Harris Wofford, moved to Bryn Mawr. The second president, John David Maquire, a Baptist minister and teacher added to the original mandate from the Board of Trustees the theme of human justice. He proposed four objectives for the college.

1) *To seek to educate those traditionally by-passed by higher education;*
2) *To establish Old Westbury as a community college which serves the greater New York area;*
3) *To organize a curriculum around a critical analysis of fundamental issues in American society;*
4) *To establish a form of college government which involves mutual responsibility and action among faculty, students, and staff on a broad range of decisions basic to the life of the college.*

Old Westbury has gone further than most colleges in America in deliberately gearing the admissions of students for a racial balance. The college admits 30 percent blacks; 30 percent whites; 30 percent Puerto Ricans; 10 percent Third World. The faculty is also divided 50–50 between black and white and women hold 50 percent of all staff and faculty positions. This could be the most revolutionary undergraduate college in America.

It is located on a beautiful woods and fields Long Island estate twenty miles from Manhattan. The campus is new, students move into the first complex of buildings in fall, 1972. The buildings resemble a small European village with plazas and shops, restaurants and residential halls.

Old Westbury offers two academic programs: education and health. All students also take a Core Program, weekly discussions, seminars, lectures, films, reexamining the "nature of American life and society." Students are involved in at least one semester of Field Studies projects in Nassau County or New York City. Overseas studies is not a feature of the school. Grading is on a pass/fail system, there are few examinations and a genuine attempt is made to get as many people as possible through an education.

This is the college for blacks and Puerto Ricans in the New York area. Old Westbury wants, according to President Maquire, "to make opportunities available for people who have never had a chance at higher education." Students do not need to have any previous academic records or achievements to get into Old Westbury. Students should telephone for application material: (516) 333-7800.

Naturally at such a college there have been many clashes of ideologies and it appears the political dynamics of the school means President Maquire will be leaving and a new black president appointed. No black is president of a SUNY college or university and the need for such an appointment is overdue. Old Westbury looks like a natural place to begin and Maquire can take the credit for making that possible.

COLLEGE OF THE PERSON	*Private*
626 East Capitol Street	*Coed*
Washington, D.C. 20003	*Unstructured*
	No students

College of the Person is a school we came across on the streets of Washington, D.C. It was put together by Bonnie and Dan Sillers, Ph.D-ers in psychology and education from California. They were talking up their college in DuPont Circle. The student is the curriculum. Each student decides what is important and what he/she wants to study. The first year is a residential year to help students transfer from traditional educational experiences to learn how to live/learn on their own. Students learn by: apprenticeships, experimentation, seminars, travel, work, independent study and research. Even classrooms!

One of the major functions of the college is to validate living/learning experiences. The Office of Records assists the student in developing and recording experiences, but no attempt is made to evaluate the learning. "What the student gains from the experiences is known only to him. He may wish to convey this to others by describing the experience and/or displaying the learning in his file. It could be a poem expressing insights and/or feelings, pre- and post-experience test results, a journal, recommendations by fellow workers, a film, a project, or whatever."

The Sillers believe in a learning community. "Though learning is an individual process, it does not necessarily take place in isolation. Since you will be experiencing a great deal of freedom in a new setting, this lack of structure may create in you a desire to have others, who are part of this living/learning experience, share with you in a deeper relationship. A relationship that will provide for emotional involvement and support, an opportunity to share feelings, perceptions, insights, love and concern." Both Sillers have had training in human awareness workshops. They have also studied the Human Potential Movement in this country with its emphasis on individual development and responsibility through bodily awareness exercises, confrontations, encounters, Gestalt therapy, meditation, massage and yoga. All of these activities will be part of the College of the Person.

Beyond all this not much more is available about the new college. Write them or call: (202) 547-1640. But watch it, this place could be all bullshit. On the other hand we suspect that Sillers may be right when he says, "We've found more interest among adults than young people, older people with soul." That's what we figure.

COLLEGE OF THE VIRGIN ISLANDS	*Territory*
St. Thomas	*Coed*
Virgin Islands, 00801	*Semester*
	1,362 students

The campus of the college of the Virgin Islands is located on 175 acres overlooking Brewer's Bay in the Caribbean. It's a new school— opened in 1963—and spread over hilly terrain three miles west of the town of Charlotte Amalie. It is a four-year college similar to a small school on the mainland, but located 40 miles east of Puerto Rico and built on an island where the average temperature is 78 degrees.

The selection of courses is limited because of size, but basic liberal arts majors are available: Biology, Chemistry, English, Mathematics, Social Sciences, Spanish, Teacher Education and a new undergraduate program in Marine Sciences, a natural for the location of the school.

Most students come from the islands of the Caribbean, but the college is seeking more students from the mainland and other parts of the world to "create an international cross-cultural experience for all students."

Admissions is not difficult. A C average is required and anyone serious about attending would be accepted. Students applying from the mainland should allow plenty of time for the process. It is not expensive: tuition is about $350, room and board $390. The college has new residential halls for 140 students.

A new 130-acre campus is being built at Golden Grove in St. Croix and the college sponsors the Caribbean Research Institute, environmental laboratories in St. Thomas and St. Croix and the Virgin Islands Ecological Research Station at Lameshur Bay on St. John.

Although the faculty is not outstanding and the facilities are limited, this is a particularly choice college for undergraduates interested in the marine sciences and the Caribbean cultures.

COLLEGES-WITHIN-THE COLLEGE	*State*
University of Kansas	*Coed*
Lawrence, Kansas 66044	*Semester*
	20,000 students

This is a big, wild and wooly place, the University of Kansas. In the last few years it has been the next thing to a battlefield. In February, 1970 students marched for the Chicago Seven; in April a bank was bombed, the student union was set on fire; the National Guard was called on campus and there was gunfire. Students and faculty smoke dope in and out of the classrooms. And all alone people like Jerry Lewis, an Assocate Dean, are trying to break down the "bigness" of this campus on the plains.

Their plan is residential colleges. A series of five "colleges" that have three basic goals:

1) More intimate administration-faculty-student contact;
2) Educational experimentation and innovation;
3) Inclusion of organized living groups in the academic process.

The hope is that the colleges will bridge the gap between the student's academic and social lives and provide an administrative center where all questions—academic, social, personal—can receive individual attention. These colleges were established for the first and second years, but plans are being made to make them four-year semiautonomous units.

The trouble is: students prefer to live off campus. Dorms cost about $900 for room and board, apartments are a lot less, a lot more freedom. This program of Colleges-within-the College has to stand in front of a wave of general resentment (in all colleges of the U.S.) toward dormitory living. Although the program has built into it independent study, seminars, field work, etc., students want to live off campus, on their own. University of Kansas people aren't that impressed with having an identity with a special "college."

Tuition is $550 for in-state and $1,050 for out-of-state students. Kansas has mostly midwestern students, and they are radical. It is, as we say, big, wild and wooly, but little sense of a community, little experimentation in academics, but trying. Students, however, aren't that interested in education. Dope yes, books no.

COLORADO COLLEGE
Colorado Springs, Colorado 80903

Private
Coed
Modular
1,600 students

Colorado College is the first and only school using a full-time modular course system. Schools closest to this program are the scientific university at Marseilles-Luming, France and San José State, but both of those are partial attempts. Colorado College breaks the academic calendar into modules of time three or three-and-a-half weeks long. Nine modules of time complete the year, four in the fall, five in the spring. Courses run sequentially, depending on kind and content. *Principal courses* vary from one to three modules of time—that is, from three to ten-and-a-half weeks. There are four *principal* types:

Single: full time on any subject. One faculty member and students (15–20) take just this one course. Full academic load.

Interdisciplinary: two or three teachers and student—a full academic load for both teachers and students.

Extended Half-course: for subjects which are particularly demanding or require considerable time for absorption of material. Two half-courses are a full-time load.

Adjunct Course: These are dance, instrumental music, choir, etc., usually will cover the full semester or the year. Students take two adjunct courses in addition to their main courses.

The design gives students a chance to intensely study one subject, then move into another area. A typical day might be two hours of work with a professor, followed by an assignment of reading. After lunch and until sometime around three o'clock research in the library. Evenings free.

Colorado has 1,600 students, 120 faculty members and is private. It costs $2,000 for tuition and fees, another $950 for room and board. It's located 75 miles south of Denver, in the city of Colorado Springs and at the foothills of Pikes Peak and the Rocky Mountains.

The modular system is new at Colorado College—voted in by the faculty in October, 1969. It is on a trial basis at the school and has had opposition. The system provides an intense way of learning: total immersion in one area with only one or two professors. It is not for everyone. The college talks about flexibility of the courses, but we don't see much. If you don't think such learning would be limiting and demanding, then Colorado College should be fine.

DEEP SPRINGS COLLEGE   *Private*
Deep Springs, California   *Men*
via Dyer, Nevada 89010   *Semester*
                                         24 students

Deep Springs College was started in 1917 by Lucien L. Nunn the lawyer and pioneer of Telluride, Colorado. Nunn also started the Telluride Association. Deep Springs is located in a pocket of the Inyo-White Mountains of California, a valley twelve miles long, four miles wide at 5,200 feet of elevation. It is dry desert country. The nearest town is Big Pine, 28 miles away.

Deep Springs is, as they say, an idealistic institution. It provides a liberal arts education, a community of students, professors, and ranch workers, and a solitary environment for independent study. Students earn sixty credits in two years of study and working. Most students transfer on to other colleges. All students receive full room, board, and tuition scholarships. They enter during the summer semester, attend the fall and spring semesters, have a summer off, and, subject to reinvitation, return for three more semesters, through the third summer. All students work at least twenty hours a week on the ranch. Everything from washing and ironing student and college laundry to breaking horses.

Students are self-governed. They regulate smoking and no one is allowed to drink or use dope. Also students are restricted to the valley and no social ties with neighbors in adjacent valleys are permitted. These restrictions "are intended to free the student from distractions and promote a degree of self-discipline. They are long-standing traditions which must be accepted by every student coming to Deep Springs."

But Deep Springs is a free place. Very little time is spent in class— and classes are never more than nine students, often only one or two— there are no dormitory hours, no housemothers. Students are free to sleep in the desert, to live off in a cabin as a hermit. To study by himself. He must only fulfill his work responsibilities. As Nunn said in 1922, "Deep Springs aims to place the small weight of its influence where it will tend to develop men of fixed purpose and character, who will dedicate themselves to the higher cause of service." And that's what they do at Deep Springs.

EARLHAM COLLEGE
Richmond, Indiana 47374

Private
Coed
Trimester
1,145 students

Indiana has Indiana University, Notre Dame and about thirty small, religiously affiliated colleges, that give strong liberal arts educations. Earlham is one of these and we think it's the best in the state.

It's not experimental or innovative. To them, changing to a 3-3 (three courses—three terms) calendar is a major step forward. The school is Quaker and straight, but Earlham is not another Bryn Mawr or Haverford moved west, though it has many of those high standards of that long line of Quaker schools. Students are friendly, even to each other, and they all call everyone, even the president, by first names. In many ways, it's a fifties college campus, but it has worth.

There are several interdepartmental programs: Afro-American Studies; Human Relations; Fine Arts; Environmental. And they have Independent Study—over 350 projected were okayed in 1970–71. Overseas work is encouraged. Earlham belongs to a Great Lakes Association that sends students to Asia, Africa and Latin America. Students can go to Europe or Jamaica during the winter term. But these ventures are usually overorganized, togetherness junkets.

Students can also enroll in a voluntary pre-term, before the start of classes. This might be a series of seminars on campus, an outward-bound trip or the study of a particular topic, like marine biology in Boothbay, Maine. For a small school, Earlham offers enough courses to last a lifetime of studying at Richmond.

Richmond, however, is a drag. It's 50,000 people working in industry and they don't like the college. But there's nowhere to go. Dayton, Ohio is 40 miles west and who wants to go to Dayton?

There are other disturbing things about Earlham: rules and regulations are everywhere. Students can't smoke in the classrooms or the johns and sex is unheard of. Lots of brother/sister routines. Students at the college are straight, even to short hair, not radical or outspoken, but have that Quaker concern for their fellowman and they want an education.

Earlham is giving them one.

ELBERT COVELL COLLEGE   *Private*
University of the Pacific   *Coed*
Stockton, California 95204   *4-1-4*
                                         243 students

Everything is taught in Spanish at Elbert Covell, the second of three cluster colleges of the University of the Pacific. It opened in 1963 and prepares students from all the Americas for careers in foreign service, international business, bilingual and bicultural education and community development and nutrition.

Students live together, eat together, and are separated from the rest of the university, which tends to have straighter students (with the exception of Raymond College) than at Elbert Covell. Students of Covell call themselves *covelianos,* and promote their own Latin identification. They play a lot of football (soccer) around their dormitories. Half the academic work at the college must be in the Spanish language, but beyond that Covell has few requirements. A few basic courses, that's about it.

To be accepted a North American student must be competent in the language. Otherwise it is not difficult to be accepted. Students have to be committed to Covell's program "Interamericanismo." Naturally. Students can take advantage of other courses in the university outside of Covell, covering areas not touched by this Spanish-speaking school. Covell offers sixteen different majors itself and has students from sixteen countries. About 42 U.S. citizens are enrolled.

Elbert Covell is the first Spanish-speaking college in North America and because of its diverse student body it does offer a unique opportunity for an undergraduate studying Latin America. The 4-1-4 calendar gives students the chance also to travel to Spanish-speaking countries during the year and the college does sponsor trips. The month is considered a time to do Independent Study; the whole university is involved.

As a private college tuition, room and board runs about $3,900. Financial aid is provided and there are loans and other job opportunities at the college. Apply early. We might also mention that Covell might be Latin, but it is not revolutionary. Students here from Central and South America are not radical. Very little at Stockton is radical. The administration itself is friendly and first names are used, in Spanish.

EMPIRE STATE COLLEGE   *State*
SUNY   *Coed*
Box 6096   *External Degree*
Albany, New York 12206   *1,000 students*

Empire State College is the new non-campus, non-residential school of the future. It's an undergraduate college chartered by New York State where students obtain either A.A. or B.A. degrees by gaining academic credit through correspondence work, educational television, counseling and occasional seminars, on-the-job and volunteer experiences, proficiency examinations, summer colloquiums and independent study.

A student enters college at any time and "contracts" a program lasting a month, a semester or a year, full time or part time. He studies with a small faculty at one of twenty "learning centers" around New York. The academic work is done at home or using the laboratories and libraries of nearby established campuses of SUNY. Students are tested by written examinations, research papers, oral examinations and can achieve a bachelor's in the normal four-year length of time, or shorter.

Empire State opened in the fall of 1971 with centers in Albany, Rochester and Westchester Counties. In fall, 1972, additional centers open in Rockland and Nassau Counties and in Syracuse. A center is scheduled for January, 1973, in Buffalo and in Binghamton by April, 1973. Tuition is $550 a year.

One thousand students were initially enrolled on a first-come, first-served basis. By 1973 it is expected 7,000 to 10,000 students will be enrolled, with each center handling approximately 400 students.

Empire State is patterned after England's massive Open University which is college by television. Empire State provides more than Open University. It offers the personal contact with instructors and all the opportunities of being on one's own. Chancellor Boyer in an article in *The New York Times* was quoted as saying, "We've had a recent upsurge in inquiries from younger people who don't want to be locked into the acreage of a campus and we hope the college will be appealing to this group." We think it will. High school students we have seen have been looking for this kind of independent education. Empire State gives it to them.

EXPERIMENTAL PROGRAM
University of Montana
Missoula, Montana 59801

State
Coed
Quarters
90 students

During the academic year 1970–71 Montana began its Experimental Program, tentative steps for freshmen and sophomores. The program concentrates for a year on studies "which speak to the moral concern of students and explore the range of meaning which responsibility and freedom have assumed in the Western World." Three faculty members from the Philosophy Department teach in the Experimental Program. They cut across department lines of the humanities and social sciences in studying the material.

Students entering the program divide into three groups of thirty, each with an instructor devoting all his time to them. They meet together two or three times a week. Twice a week seminars meet with fifteen people. And each student meets for individual consultation once every two weeks. Every student is expected to write in a journal an hour or more every day on the readings and discussions. There are also short papers, running about four to eight pages, due every two weeks. A total of ten hours a week is spent in lectures, classes, seminars.

The strength of the program is in the reading list. And the reading list is like the Great Books, but not quite as lengthy as that program. The fall quarter list is: *The Odyssey, Greek Lyrics,* and *The Bible.* There are also contemporary books, *Soul on Ice,* for one. Students are expected to begin reading during the summer and have the list done by the opening of school.

Students have been invited to enroll, selected at random from all those in the upper 50 percent of high school classes. If one wants to get into the program, he/she can. Students earn twelve credits each quarter and are allowed to take one course outside the program. Grading is pass/fail.

Montana is a cheap place to attend college: $140 for in-state and $400 for out-of-state students, per quarter. Dorms are about $285 per quarter for room and board. You have to be twenty-one to live off campus. Montana has a total campus enrollment of just less than 8,000 students. It's lovely in the mountains and may be worth it. The Experimental Program, however, is only beginning and has a long way to go.

EXPERIMENTAL PROGRAM
University of Vermont
Burlington, Vermont 05401

State
Coed
Semester
232 students

The University of Vermont has a cautious little experimental program for its freshmen and sophomores that is based on the living/learning residential college concept. It started in 1969 and is operating on a trial basis. Students are selected at random from the freshmen class and invited to join. A normal academic load is three seminars from the Experimental Program and one conventional course from the university. (Vermont has a total enrollment of 5,243 students.)

The objectives of the experiment are: (1) to test the value of the small living and learning community within the framework of the larger university; and (2) to test the effectiveness of less structured and more individualized forms of instruction.

Grading is pass/fail and students have an advisor who develops with them an academic program for the two years amounting to 60 credit hours that have the distribution requirements of the College of Arts and Sciences. Therefore, the student doesn't have much freedom of selection. Courses offered are straight; the kind of subjects offered almost anywhere.

The living/learning environment is special. Students now live in Coolidge and Mason halls and are responsible for their personal lives. The living is intense, hairy at times, but the most "education" at Vermont goes on in these dormitories. Students can remain in the halls for their four years. It's the one part of the program which we like very much. Close friendships with faculty and students develop because of the living arrangements.

Tuition for Vermont residents is slightly more than $600 per year; $2,000 plus for non-residents. Room and board is another $1,000. It is not necessary to live on campus, however. Students are beginning to seek places in town, away from school.

Over the first two years the Experimental Program lost 24 percent of their students, the largest percentage were in-state students. This dropout is higher than the normal University of Vermont attrition. A sure sign the program isn't promising. Don't expect too much from the university's experiment and you won't be disappointed.

FAIRHAVEN COLLEGE
Western Washington State College
Bellingham, Washington 98225

State
Coed
Quarters
526 students

Fairhaven is the residential cluster college of 9,000 student Western Washington State College. It's new—1968—and outstanding.

Students of Fairhaven live in a tiny valley one-half mile south of the main campus in twelve residence halls, housing fifty students each. The buildings are four stories high, have large lounges, small seminar rooms, cooking facilities, and are coed. There is also a separate building housing academic, administration and recreation facilities. The campus has already won several design awards and resembles a winter resort.

There are no grades at Fairhaven, written evaluations by tutors are used as marks. Students work out a program of study with their advisors, putting together a liberal education of Sciences (12 credits) ; Social Sciences (12 credits) ; Humanities (20 credits) ; Composition (3 credits) ; and 27 credits of Elective Seminars, Independent Study and off-campus and overseas study. Students have studied and traveled in Greece, Japan, Germany, England and Mexico.

Students are involved in the planning of the curriculum and the development of the cluster college. They are represented on all major committees. They also have the responsibility for the governance of their residence halls. At times these halls become intense and bitchy places and students have few alternatives. They have to live in the dormitories. Anyway, there is little to offer off campus. Bellingham is a hick town of 40,000. No place to live.

No courses are established at Fairhaven. Seminars and courses develop because of special interest of the faculty and the students. Some electives offered in the last few years were: Organic Gardening, Existentialism, Primitive McCluhanism and Non-Linear Man, Economics and the Novel, The Politics of Norman Mailer, Riding the Ovarian Trolley.

Costs are low. Total expenses—tuition, room and board—are $1,410 for Washington residents and $1,770 for non-residents. (We expect the figures to go up by fall, 1972.)

The college is looking for very mature students, academically well qualified and able to work with little guidance. Most students are accepted as freshmen, but a few transfers are accepted each year, usually at the sophomore level. Fairhaven has more applications than places. In 1970, eight hundred people applied for two hundred openings. Every year it gets tougher to get in. We think you should apply early. There are not too many Fairhavens around.

FRANKLIN PIERCE COLLEGE   *Private*
Rindge, New Hampshire 03461   *Coed*
                                           4-1-4
                                           1,143 students

This liberal arts college opened in 1963 with two objectives: (1) provide a liberal arts education for students who demonstrate motivation and capability; and (2) provide the opportunity for learning through inquiry and discovery to any student who wishes to pursue academic areas of individual interest.

It does both well.

On a new campus of 650 acres an hour and a half from Boston, it's a rural place and remote. (In 1973 an extension campus will open in New Mexico.) Although small it does have a $1,200,000 science building and a modern Library-Resource Center which has a unique resource file called locally, "Who Knows What" file. This catalogs non-academic subjects in which faculty and staff are proficient.

The campus buildings range from colonial to contemporary. Students themselves have helped in some building. They constructed the ski tow, base hut and have refurbished an old barn for a theater. Students come from over twenty-five states and half a dozen foreign countries, but most students are from New England and the East Coast. The comprehensive fee is about $3,500 and the usual financial aid is available, but limited.

The college is divided into three divisions: Humanities, Natural Sciences and Social Sciences. A core curriculum must be taken by everyone. Independent Study is just for seniors and P/F (pass/fail) works only during the January Term. Not much is available for overseas study, though faculty members take students overseas during the summer. Everyone knows everyone at the school. There is a low student-to-faculty ratio and the faculty is there to teach. A few years ago a professor walked with a group of students from the campus to Nova Scotia as an experiment in deeply personal learning experiences.

Franklin Pierce also has a special admissions program, which includes a Summer Laboratory, for students of potential who have not met the requirements of the college, though Franklin Pierce is not difficult to get into.

GOUCHER COLLEGE
Towson, Maryland 21204

Private
Women
4-1-4
2,205 students

This tiny college on 330 acres in the Dulaney Valley twenty minutes from Baltimore is included for two reasons: (1) we support women's colleges; (2) it's innovative and imaginative.

For a small college Goucher has an impressive list of statistics: 389 courses, eighteen departments, students from thirty-four states and ten foreign countries, 35 percent of the classes with less than eleven students in them. But what makes Goucher rather special are: Freshmen Seminars, Independent work, Inter-Institutional programs with Johns Hopkins University, pass/fail, Junior Year Abroad, Mills College Exchange program and January Term.

Goucher's January Term courses verge on experimentation in the real sense. Some offerings in 1971: The Fairy Tale; The Keyboard Sonatas of Beethoven; Man and War; Non-Euclidean Geometry; The Tarot as Philosophy; The Turbulent Spring in Paris; Aggression and Ecology.

Living is restrictive, however. Unless you're twenty-one or from the Baltimore area, you live in small residences of fifty students each and a faculty family living-in. But students do share in the running of the school in many innovative ways. Students are voting members of the majority of the standing committees, including Admissions, Curriculum, Independent Work and Honors. This is not a practice seen everywhere.

Goucher is off in the woods and that should be taken into consideration. Washington, D.C. and Baltimore are close. But who wants to go to Baltimore? And Washington is just another tourist town. The college tries to overcome this isolation by importing speakers, cultural events, even men, but a college can only stretch that sort of activity so far. The weekends are bummers . . . but then most college weekends are bummers.

Goucher, naturally, is expensive: $3,700 is a rough comprehensive fee to pay for all students living on campus. Get their classy bulletin, women, and give them consideration.

HUTCHINS SCHOOL *State*
Sonoma State College *Coed*
Rohnert Park, California 94928 *Semester*
109 students

Hutchins College opened in 1969 as the first cluster school of Sonoma State. It offers a broad, non-specialized, interdisciplinary B.A. degree. It controls its own internal affairs and curriculum, and has its own community. Sonoma State is the freest school of the California State system and Hutchins is an important program, and experimental!

The lower division is a series of four seminars that focus on specific themes or topics. Each seminar of ten students meets approximately five hours per week. Students also meet once a week with their tutors to go over papers and each student makes an independent study contract with his tutor and is responsible for completing a project of some kind every term. The subject matter of the first two years fulfills the college general education requirements. In the upper division course work the emphasis shifts from the seminar to independent work. Each student is expected to pursue his own specific interests. Students can either do study of a single problem or topic over a long period of time or deal with several smaller issues. All students complete a Senior Project.

The seminar is the primary means of instruction and they are always small, no larger than ten students. All the faculty is close to the students and they have been selected because of their interest and support of interdisciplinary orientation and that approach to learning. In the first years the faculty has, however, divided over issues of method of instruction. The central problem was the balance between "do your own thing" and "flexible structure." This controversy has spread to the student body.

Sonoma State does not have dormitories, but students of Hutchins gather in apartments, often for classes, and a spirit of community is shared, though with its usual tensions. Of the first one hundred students in September, 1969, sixty-seven returned as sophomores. Sonoma State is a popular college, offering a lot for its total enrollment of 3,562. If a student drops out of Hutchins he can continue in the regular program without difficulty.

Grading at Hutchins is pass/fail and every term the student receives written evaluations of his work. He also has the opportunity to study off campus and to go overseas.

Sonoma itself is isolated in the short hills of California. Rural farming on all sides. A nice place for a college, but apply early. This is another one of those colleges a new generation of students has discovered.

INNER COLLEGE   *State*
U-167   *Coed*
The University of Connecticut   *Semester*
Storrs, Connecticut 06268   *61 students*

The Inner College is an accredited alternative program within the University of Connecticut for honor students. Students can take fifteen credits of work every semester in independent studies. The entire curriculum of the Inner College is composed of student-initiated and student-taught courses with some courses offered by faculty of the university to Inner College students. Some courses have been: E.S.P; Fantastic Literature; Journal Writing; Meditation, Master Game, Yoga, etc.; Leather-working.

Students have also earned credits living in teepees and growing their own food, working on the Hudson River Sloop restoration, studying the education system in the Philippines, and making films. Students are not limited to Inner College and may take courses at the university, which has a total enrollment of some 15,000 students at Storrs.

The University of Connecticut at Storrs isn't much. It is famous for its school of agriculture and natural resources, that's about all. Students. have been radical in the past and demonstrated against the ROTC. But most of the students are into old-fashioned college routines, sports. It is also an isolated campus, off in the town of Mansfield in eastern Connecticut. Boston is two hours away, New York three.

The university also has an Experiment College with an enrollment of some seven hundred students. It offers about thirty-five courses—Basic Weaving, Witchcraft, French Cooking—without grades and without credits. Some of the Inner College folk teach at the free school.

UConn is inexpensive: $165 per semester for in-state students, about $550 a semester for out-of-state students. Dorms run over $500 a semester for room and board. And it is not difficult to get enrolled. They take the top fourth of graduating high school classes. One problem. Inner College only takes sophomores. (You can transfer into UConn with a C average.) Students have to apply directly to the Admissions Office.

Inner College is growing. It now has its own office and meeting place. Students and administrators are beginning to see its value. Around Mansfield, it is a step forward for the university. It makes UConn livable.

INTER AMERICAN UNIVERSITY
San German, Puerto Rico 00753

State
Coed
Semester
4,000 students

Puerto Rico may appear to be a bonanza for the student who doesn't want to venture beyond the protection of the U.S. flag while getting the most air fare for the dollar and still be in another country. Unfortunately, all is not palm trees and sandy beaches for any Continental who matriculates at the University of Puerto Rico (the public institution) or any of the four or five private institutions.

One must be prepared to make a commitment, not so much to the subject matter, as to an attempt at understanding the island culture and an appreciation for the anticulture that surrounds those activities involving the unacceptable aspects of Americanism. There is always the hidden agenda of "Yankee Go Home." One of the most difficult adjustments is for the student of Puerto Rican origin who has grown up in the States and returns for his higher education only to be pegged as a "New Yorican" who has cast off all that is good about Puerto Ricans and has brought back to the island all that is bad about the mainland (poor Spanish, poor manners, dress, etc.). But the country is a rewarding experience for the student who wants to understand the present mood of the island and will make every effort to achieve bilinguality during the course of study. This is not as easy as the Berlitz ads make it appear, but a major effort will enrich an otherwise bland traditional classroom experience.

The greatest opportunity for a bilingual type of four-year program is at the San German Campus of Inter American University. This emerging institution has been ruled by a Puerto Rican administration since 1969 when the first native son assumed the presidency after fifty-eight years of Continental management. One of the natural tendencies has been toward a more provincial program with less emphasis on the Inter American ideal.

A student should expect a more strict parietal rule than one would expect to find on a mainland campus, but if the person can make the cross-cultural experience part of the total educational experience, then this setting is for him. San German is one of the old Spanish colonial towns 120 miles from San Juan.

Other colleges.

In Ponce (the second largest city to San Juan) on the south-central coast is located the Catholic University. Within the last two years a Catholic layman has been named president, a first for this private institution. They have a limited bilingual program. The college integrates well with this growing, commercial and industrial center. The city is cosmopolitan and has several fine examples of tropical architecture, the museum of art being the most prominent. A large number of Cubans have made Ponce their home. Inter American University and the University of Puerto Rico have regional colleges in Ponce.

The Puerto Rico Junior College and the Sacred Heart College in San Juan are two other colleges on the island. The Junior College is coed and run by a dynamic woman. Sacred Heart is Catholic and for women.

The public University of Puerto Rico which was closed in late spring of 1971 with several days of rioting has been the most successful in siphoning off the intellectual talented students on the island by giving them scholarships. The average student, who is usually the poorer student, struggles along academically and financially through the private schools. At the Inter American University at San German the students who come from the other Caribbean Islands and the Continentals always seem to be at the top of the class.

We suggest that a student interested in Puerto Rico consider studying one or two years on the island and obtain a degree on the mainland.

USEFUL ADDRESSES
University of Puerto Rico System
Rio Piedras, Puerto Rico 00931

Puerto Rico Junior College
Rio Piedras, Puerto Rico 00928

Catholic University of Puerto Rico
Ponce, Puerto Rico 00731

INTERNATIONAL COMMUNITY COLLEGE   *Private*
1019 Gayley Avenue   *Coed*
Los Angeles, California 90024   *Quarters*
                                                  150 students

International Community College opened in October, 1971 with initial campuses in Dublin, Ireland; Salzburg, Austria; Viborg, Denmark; Avignon, France; and Florence, Italy. Programs will be started in two years in Yugoslavia, Israel, Japan, Mexico, Spain and Greece. It's a two-year college chartered in California and uses as an educational base the Great Books approach. Students study the Greek classics in terms of Freud and current philosophy.

The theme for all campuses in 1971 was "Man and His Relationship to the State" along with the language and culture of the country the student was in. Each country campus has its special emphasis: Salzburg: music and history; Viborg: archaeology and cinema; Avignon: French history and western culture; Dublin: creative writing and theater; Florence: fine arts.

The curriculum is structured, but not spoon-fed. According to Dean of Students, Charles Rosewell, "We don't teach anybody anything—we establish an environment that encourages people to learn." The students meet twice weekly in seminars and twice a week in smaller groups for reading programs and critiques of written assignments.

The college costs $3,850—tuition, travel, room and board—for the year. Limited scholarships are available. The school is new and untested, though the people who started the college are experienced. The president founded Hawaii's Maui Community College and was a dean at Haile Selassie I University in Ethiopia. International Community has good intentions, a good idea, but needs some seasoning.

In 1973–74, the college will accept third and fourth year students for independent-study programs leading to Bachelor of Arts degrees.

JUSTIN MORRILL COLLEGE	State
Michigan State University	*Coed*
East Lansing, Michigan 48823	*Quarters*
	910 students

Justin Morrill is the experimental liberal arts college of huge (38,000) Michigan State University. It has been called locally, a "hippie" college with a cafeteria for a curriculum. But it's a lot more. Although not an honors college, Justin Morrill graduates have done very well. Out of the first 157 graduates, Justin Morrill had 33 Phi Beta Kappas, 4 Woodrow Wilsons, a Marshall Fellow, a Danforth winner and the highest GPA (Grade Point Average) in the university. On the Graduate Record, the seniors scored "superior" in humanities, social science *and* natural science. The college is also famous for its language program. Students take one year of intensive foreign language in a special program. Freshmen are required to take Inquiry and Expression. This three-term course "is to cultivate in the student an awareness of important personal, national, and international questions."

The college opened in 1965 and is "experimental" in that programs are used to test new forms and content for undergraduate education, but not for much more. Students have a Field of Concentration, either a traditional major or a typical or thematic major. The choice and variety are wide.

There is a sense of community. Students live in Snyder-Phillips dormitory. It's one of those ivy-covered, woodwork, small-lounge dormitories that creates an intimacy, but it's too small for the whole college. Only a third of the college's classes are taught in Snyder-Phillips' four classrooms.

Students at Justin Morrill are liberal and moderate. Dean Gordan Rohman says a third of the students "might as well be in any dormitory of any college." Students are involved with the running of the college, mostly in an advisory form of governance. Fifteen students are employed as advisors to freshmen and students do teach courses in the college.

Students also spend at least one term off campus involved in some kind of cross-cultural field-study program. The field study actually covers three terms: a preparation seminar, the term in the field and a follow-up seminar. Students have lived with families in France, served as staff members in a social service agency, been assistant teachers in Head Start and worked in senator offices.

Justin Morrill is straight and tough and small. A good experimental cluster college at impersonal Michigan State.

LAWRENCE UNIVERSITY   *Private*
Appleton, Wisconsin 54911   *Coed*
                                              Terms
                                              1,311 students

Colleges look better if they're liberal in a conservative atmosphere, than if they're liberal in a radical setting. Liberal Lawrence looks good in conservative Appleton. It's a hick town two hundred miles north of Chicago, a small industrial place that produces paper and pollutes the Fox River. Lawrence is, nevertheless, perhaps the best small place to be found in Wisconsin. Perhaps the best place in the Midwest.

It is involved now in a five-year study to revamp the curriculum. Over the last few years Lawrence has cautiously begun to stretch itself, introduce an overseas program to Europe and the Middle East, try off-campus and Urban Studies Programs. Students are demonstrating, on campus and off, but mostly off. Still no pass/fail or student run classes, but. . . .

Booky students at Lawrence, the kind that are alway third or fourth in the high school graduating class, real plodders, but full of that friendly, warm midwestern feeling you hear so much about . . . and rarely see. No sulky Madison types here. Lawrence students behave, want to learn and are damn bright! Like the boyfriend in *Sterile Cuckoo*, always bookin'.

We expect Lawrence to move quickly in the next two or three years.

The winds of change are touching the Midwest and, as we said, Lawrence is liberal. They'll see the handwriting on the wall and adapt. The Admissions Officers are going to continue to look for that straight plodder, but they won't find them much longer. The cold fields of that kind of attitude are changing. The Midwest has only been radical at a few places, now the small campuses—so many of them in these states—are beginning to roll. But besides that, Lawrence *feels* something is amiss with their program and this study, slowly and carefully done, will produce dramatic changes. The advantage of small schools is that they have the opportunity to change, to alter lifestyle and have that adjustment felt and seen by all. Watch what happens in Appleton.

In the meantime, since you have four years that you want to spend wisely, try here . . . look them over. Tuition, fees and room and board is something around $3,300. You'll know you've been to college.

LIFE STUDIES PROGRAM	*State*
University of New Hampshire	*Coed*
Durham, New Hampshire 03824	*Semester*
	152 students

Life Studies is a two-year program in basic education at the University of New Hampshire. It was begun by a group of students and several disaffected teachers in 1969. Lift Studies is a series of innovative seminars open to all freshmen and sophomores. They take at least three courses per semester and all general education requirements are waived.

There is a large range of courses, generated from student interests. Some taught are: Spirituality—mysticism, energy systems, astrology, Zen; Education—internships for freshmen at local high schools; Leadership Skills in Higher Education—developing projects in university reform; Contract Workshops—independent study on almost anything. Students write out a "contract" on what they plan to accomplish, a UNH faculty member "sponsors" them.

Life Studies has three major advantages:

1) students have a broad range of abilities, backgrounds, interests.

2) community people are used—artists, innovative public school teachers, upperclass students, clergy, community action people.

3) participatory nature of classroom and course organization, structure, decision-making.

The program has had its troubles trying to develop a true learning community, overcoming skepticism from traditional faculty, and development of self-government within the program, but it is growing and has a life of its own. Tuition is cheap: about $750 per year for in-state, $1,600 for out-of-state students.

Life Studies has some important "structure" built into the program. We particularly like their Freshman Learning Skills Labs. This provides students the chance to develop skills needed for college work and helps them adjust to the freedom of the program. They have a young faculty in Life Studies and if you go to New Hampshire make sure you take a course from John Coe who last fall taught a course in Liturgical Music. He's outstanding.

LINFIELD COLLEGE   *Private*
McMinnville, Oregon 97128   *Coed*
                                            Semester
                                            1,212 students

Linfield in their statement of educational philosophy says, "the Linfield community is an ivory tower in which the student is temporarily removed from immediate involvement with the social and economic problems of modern urban America in order to get some perspective on them. The freedom from involvement is not provided as an escape, but to provide the freedom to investigate the problems of the world and acquire the skills needed to understand and solve them."

Linfield is located forty miles from Portland on eighty acres of lawns, oak groves and parks. It has thirty-five buildings, one thousand plus students from fifty states and overseas, a first-class faculty and an academic program that's demanding and committed to the liberal arts.

Students begin with an interdepartmental and interdisciplinary core curriculum which provides a base for study. Students then select a major to be completed in the junior and senior years. Students also are encouraged to spend at least a year overseas and language majors are required to study overseas. Recently Linfield introduced an Environmental Studies major. The program is based in the natural and social sciences.

The academic year is two sixteen-week semesters with a two-week reading period in January when the dorms are opened and students can do anything they like, academic work, ad hoc seminars or read independently. This is an unique idea; we like it. It is a residential college and students need special permission to live off campus, and campus living is tight, though the college doesn't stand in *loco parentis*. It does, however, provide head residents.

Linfield was started and is run by the American Baptists, but it is not a religious school. It is, however, one of those fine small Oregon colleges that year after year provide liberal educations for students who are straight, but certainly not square. They are also smart students. Linfield leans toward academic grades when selecting. $2,750 plus is the comprehensive fee.

LYMAN BRIGGS COLLEGE	*State*
E-30 Holmes Hall	*Coed*
Michigan State University	*Quarters*
East Lansing, Michigan 48823	*600 students*

Lyman Briggs College began in the fall of 1967. It was established by Michigan State for students interested in a broad liberal education in the biological and physical sciences and mathematics. Located in Holmes Hall, one of the living and learning units of Michigan State, there is some feeling of community. This arrangement helps break down huge Michigan State (40,000 plus).

It is not a college of all things for all students and only makes sense for students who want scientific training. The fields of concentration are: Biology, Computer Science, Earth Sciences, Environmental Sciences, General Science, History and Philosophy of Science, Mathematical Sciences, Physical Sciences. The college is not experimental, but being small, it allows for the individual advising and some curriculum flexibility, but everyone has to complete a common core program, and each field of concentration has its requirements.

If accepted to Michigan State, a student can apply to Lyman Briggs. Therefore, its students self-select themselves. There are no specific requirements, but students should have a minimum of three years of high school mathematics and two years of science beyond general science.

The faculty of Lyman Briggs is taken from the departments on campus. Only about eight are full time. The others come and go. This hurts the feeling of a separate college. There are almost as many secretaries as there are full-time teachers.

We can't get overly excited about Lyman Briggs. It is a residential college on a campus which resembles a small city. Michigan State is "rethinking" all their residential colleges in 1972. Students aren't buying living/learning arrangements. They want to be off campus. Michigan State, and other big schools, are having trouble filling their dormitories. Lyman Briggs offers some special advantages for science students. It gives them equipment for one. Holmes Hall has its own computing facilities, five laboratories, etc. Lots of goodies. But it's still that dormitory living!

MARK HOPKINS COLLEGE   *Private*
Brattleboro, Vermont 05301   *Coed*
                                                        Semester
                                                        50 students

Walter Hendricks has been starting colleges all his life in the hills of Vermont. He was involved with Marlboro and Windham and in 1964 began Mark Hopkins, naming it after the man who was president of Williams College from 1836 to 1872. President James A. Garfield once remarked, "The ideal college is Mark Hopkins on one end of a log and a student on the other."

Mark Hopkins is far from an ideal college. It has less than a handful of faculty, a few old barns and houses on sixty acres, no sense of community and costs $1,200 a year.

Why go?

It does have a workable tutorial independent study program and students who know what they want to study can have time and their own teacher. About 75 percent of the students use this method of independent study, though other forms and group seminars are available. The college really means what it says when it writes: all educational goals are individually set. There are, of course, no grades, tests or other such requirements. The only scheduled courses are in the basic skills of reading, writing and speaking. And they, too, are often taught as tutorial.

Most of the students are high school dropouts or educational renegades. Even some foreign students, from places as far away as Nepal and Japan. Most students come and go, using Mark Hopkins for what it has to offer, which is limited, but loose. The college is not accredited, but students have had no trouble transferring credits to nearby Antioch-Putney and other schools. They also can use the facilities of the nearby colleges. Mark Hopkins doesn't have much of its own. It's a good place to attend if you want time to write, paint, weave or work with leather and need justification. If people ask what you're doing, you can always say you're going to college.

MONTEITH COLLEGE   *State*
Wayne State University   *Coed*
Detroit, Michigan 48202   *Quarter*
                                                        1,000 students

Monteith College—named after an early Michigan educator—is a product of the Sputnik days. Every college at the time wanted to become scientific. With the aid of Ford Foundation money, Wayne State started in 1959 "an experiment in reforming and reorganizing undergraduate curriculum."

The Monteith plan "offers a broad-based four-year general study program, concerned with the development of major ideas in the areas of humanistic studies, natural sciences, and social sciences." Students are required to take basic courses, a senior colloquium and do a senior essay. About half of a college career is given over to "electives." Monteith believes that "there is a body of knowledge everyone should possess."

The college which operates inside downtown Detroit and huge (35,000 plus) Wayne State University is opened to undergraduates but admissions is selective and applicants have to have at least a B average.

Monteith College is a healthy and viable attempt to break down large state schools, but it is not by our standards an experimental college. It still suffers from fifties academic thinking and students only have representatives on the Student-Faculty Council. They do none of the planning. The college is meant for those students interested in Engineering, Law, Medicine, Nursing, Library Science, Teacher Preparation and Social Work. Students who want structure and small classes.

We have included it in our review of schools because it is a small college and offers a solid education. Being a downtown Detroit school it does not provide a campus and students when they gather go to Monteith Center. It's about all they have to give a "sense of community." The center is used for discussions, social events, readings, etc.

Wayne State's Monteith College offers an inexpensive education, and for the academically bright, an excellent opportunity to learn.

NEW COLLEGE   *Private*
Hofstra University   *Coed*
Hempstead, New York 11550   *Semester*
                                                         350 students

New College of Hofstra University is a small innovative liberal arts unit attached to the larger university, and one of the older experiments in education which started in 1958. But New College is certainly not very experimental. There are elaborate sets of academic rules and regulations, course numbers and requirements, grades. Just to read and understand the esoteric New College Bulletin requires a B.A.

New College changed its curriculum in 1970, titling it Changeover Program. The academic year is divided into four eight-week sessions, two or more courses are taken each session. A flat tuition fee of $2,300 is paid for the year. The school also has an Encounter period up to a year where a student leaves campus for another college, social work, work-study, foreign study, etc. Nothing too unique.

Students with faculty advisors work out programs within one of four concentrations: Humanities, Social Sciences, Natural Sciences and Liberal Arts. The required courses are: First Course, preparing students for college work; Problem Centered Program, involving current problems of education; and a Final Course summing up a student's career.

On campus, classes come thick and heavy. This school is more honors than innovative. Students have high SAT scores and like doing academic chores. The faculty is uptight and tedious. Social contact between students and staff is formal. Not much feeling of a community. Most of the students are scattered through high-rise dormitories and once on Hofstra's 12,000 student population campus, they look like everyone else.

Young Dean David C. Christman thinks New College is, "one of the comparatively few truly creative departures in higher education." We don't see it. But like football teams, everyone thinks his experimental college is the best. If you can't get off Long Island then New College is one of your few innovative opportunities. Not much, but better than nothing.

NEW COLLEGE   *State*
Oakland University   *Coed*
Rochester, Michigan 48063   *Trimester*
                                                     100 students

New College is the academically tough cluster college of academically tough Oakland University. New College replaces the general curriculum requirements of Oakland and allows for individual creativity. All freshmen take a course titled World Civilization. This is the study of both western and eastern civilizations, the religion, politics and art. It's comprehensive and serves as the unifying element of the first year's work. The course is taught like all New College courses through seminars, and group teaching from faculty in all departments. Freshmen also take a required Performing Arts Workshop. This is taught to "develop some part of the student's creative ability." More colleges should have such a course.

Two approaches to a degree are offered in the sophomore and junior years. There is little difference between them and the major part of this time is spent on a Field Term. Students in the past have done everything from technical research to working as a longshoreman. After the Field Term, students concentrate on science and complete one of four options:

Senior Colloquium, Independent Research, Apprentice Teaching or Oral Examination on a reading list.

There is little community, students live where they want and tend to spread themselves thin in Rochester. Resident students live in Vandenberg Hall, and it's the site of many of the college's activities, from classes to concerts. New College helps to break down Oakland University (7,000 plus students) and gives personal attention not likely to be found elsewhere on the campus. The work is tough and restrictive. It is very much an honors school, and a fine one. We would not recommend that you seek out New College, but if you have to stay in Michigan, this college is an alternative. And it is innovative . . . if only in a small way.

NEW COLLEGE   *State*
University of Alabama   *Coed*
Box 6211   *Semester*
University, Alabama 35486   *100 students*

There's not much innovation in this state, but one excellent attempt is the New College. It's a school of one hundred students within the 13,000 at the University of Alabama. New College is trying an interdisciplinary approach, using seminars, off-campus experience, independent study and the Learning Contract.

With the Learning Contract a student develops a program of study in the form of a contract and presents this to an Advising Committee, of which he is a voting member. Other members are a Core-Tutor and at the student's option two others. Members can be faculty, other students or someone from off campus.

The Advising Committee guides the student's development and is concerned about the total person, not just his academic performance. The contract can be changed and modified, but generally each student will be responsible for the completion of the interdisciplinary seminars, a number of electives, a depth-study program, and an off-campus learning experience. Twenty-five percent of a student's work is at the New College. The remaining 75 percent is taken at the university, in their departments and divisions.

Students are involved with the evaluation of their own program and progress, but most of the evaluation is based on normal examinations and a grading system. Not much flexibility here. The normal length of time for an undergraduate degree is four years, but the total hours will fluctuate, depending on the academic experience and progress of each student.

New College was chiefly designed by Neal Berte, the Dean, who also planned a similar program at Ottawa in Kansas. David Mathews, the president of Alabama University, hired Berte without faculty approval to start New College.

Mathews was tired of years of discussions at Alabama on experimentation without anything happening. Both Mathews and Berte think New College will be the model for other undergraduate schools.

There is some fear of New College at the university. It is seen as an honors college and as a competitor for funds. Berte says New College will not be "an enclave for the intellectually elite" and is looking for non-academic qualifications on applications. Students are required to pass an entrance examination and present an outline of educational experience and future plans. There are no special costs to attend New College and Alabama is not expensive.

If you live in Alabama then the New College program is the best available. In fact, it looks good enough to travel for.

NEW COLLEGE   *State*
University of Hawaii   *Coed*
2001 Vancouver Drive   *Semester*
Honolulu, Hawaii 96822   *324 students*

New College was developed by a group of faculty, students and administrators as an outgrowth of a Humanities Council Project in 1969. The experimental program was approved and classes began in the fall of 1970. The University of Hawaii has something like 35,000 students and this inexpensive—tuition cost is $116 for residents and $371 for non-residents—and innovative New College is okay. It's a bit straight and lower division has all required courses, but there's pass/fail and a lot more. But briefly:

Students take two courses per semester for the first two years. These are run by a committee and broken into a number of seminars. The courses proceed sequentially along three tracks. First, three of the eight courses deal with the Modes of Thought in: (1) the Humanities; (2) the Natural Sciences; (3) the Social Sciences. The second track resembles traditional World Civilization and Humanities courses, but an attempt is made to give a sense of the lifestyle of some of the great cultures in man's past and present. The third track offers the student a chance to study a culture other than his own. He studies another language and lives in another culture.

The junior and senior years are used for independent study, overseas study or taking courses at the University of Hawaii. A program is worked out with a faculty advisor. The student has two goals: passing the comprehensive oral and/or written examination and the completion of a project, creative or otherwise. It could be possible for a student to finish in less than four years, or to take as many as six years.

Students are selected by a Student Selection Committee. This committee is run by students themselves and they are responsible for selecting students after the person has been accepted by the university itself. New College wants all types, but so far has been getting those overachievers. Its faculty comes from the university itself. They have their own building and a feeling of community is beginning. If you go there take courses from Asa Baber and Arnold Edelstein. Good people.

OBERLIN COLLEGE   *Private*
Oberlin, Ohio 44074   *Coed*
                                                         4-1-4
                                                         2,491 students

This place out in the flat country of Ohio, a nothing kind of area thirty-five miles southwest of Cleveland, has been yearly graduating students who listen to a different drum. They're eccentric, given to a strange individualism and idealism. We're not sure what came first—Oberlin or the students—for Oberlin is a freaky place, one we like and recommend.

Oberlin has a new, young president, Robert Fuller, who is edging the college along. One of his innovations was coed dormitories that got wide publicity in the winter of 1970. Since then the college has liberated their school through a series of small actions:

October, 14, 1970—The College of Arts and Sciences faculty introduces non-traditional grading systems. A series of credit/no entry, pass/fail, etc. grading.
of Trustees.

October, 28, 1970—Election of three recent graduates to the Board of Trustees.

February 10, 1971—Dropping the dean's list and Latin distinctions at graduation.

April 1, 1971—A new Music Education Program that reduces required courses and lets students shape their own programs.

Oberlin has a wide selection of off-campus work. Students can study overseas, do an urban semester in Philadelphia, work on an arts program in New York, take correspondence study, or participate in an exchange program with Fisk University or Tougaloo College. Students earn a Bachelor of Arts degree at Oberlin or can study at Oberlin's Conservatory of Music, one of the oldest and best schools of music in the country.

Students also have a Winter Term, one month long, but no credit is given. Students can pursue programs of independent study or do research.

All of this education runs over $3,850 for tuition, room and board.

Oberlin is not certainly for everyone. We think students who are into books and ideas, who like long philosophical arguments, but don't mind quiet countryside and little to do but study will like Oberlin. Oberlin has had, however, its moments of radicalism and demonstrations. They marched over Cambodia and Kent State and have gone to Washington, but SDS has not been operating in years. Everyone is too busy reading and writing.

OFF-CAMPUS COLLEGE	*State*
SUNY AB	*Coed*
Box 7000	*Semester*
Binghamton, New York 13901	*6,583 students*

Harpur College was a small liberal arts state college until it became an undergraduate unit of the State University of New York at Binghamton. It has grown from less than five hundred students to more than six thousand. In 1957 Harpur divided itself into three residential subcolleges, each with its own master, staff, dorms and dining facilities. Off-campus students (about 1,600) felt they were not getting enough services for their money. In May, 1970 a group of them wrote a constitution for an Off-Campus College and set up a seven member executive committee election. They began working on programs designed by off-campus students to meet off-campus student needs. They were able to achieve a bus service, community store, legal aid and new courses.

The executive committee established an academic council composed of six students and three faculty members. The council has sponsored credit and non-credit courses—automobile theory (2 credits), introduction to science fiction (4 credits), kundalini yoga, mysticism in music, drug counseling (4 credits) and individual innovative projects that range from 4 to 16 credits. Off-Campus managers are receiving 4 credits for their work each semester.

The Off-Campus College also sponsors a wide range of educational and social activities—political speakers, debates, films, theater, readings and macrobiotic picnics. They also rent a farm a few miles from the college and operate a small organic farm. Produce is sold in their own store.

Decisions for the Off-Campus College are made by the seven-student executive committee at weekly open meetings. All activities are voluntary. No demands are made of off-campus students, some live off campus to be entirely alone, and they are.

This plan allows students who live off campus not to become forgotten folk in the university community. It is the first attempt at such organizing that we have seen and it helps make a large state school very small and supportive. Write them.

OTTAWA UNIVERSITY   *Private*
Ottawa, Kansas 66067   *Coed*
                                            Short Terms
                                            875 students

What can you say about a school 106 years old that has a picture of its chapel in the catalog? That it's free, loose and open? No, but it's experimenting.

Ottawa University is a Baptist school fifty miles from Kansas City that in 1970 reorganized their educational program in several innovative ways to make it a residential college worth considering. It has eight key elements in its new plan.

Calendar: a 2-2-1-2-2 pattern (numerals refer to the number of courses taken during each session). A student enrolls in four seven-week terms per year, and either the January or the June four-week term.

Advising: A student has a Primary Advising Committee made up of a faculty member, fellow student and someone from outside the campus, if he wishes.

Contract: Students work out with their Primary Advising Committee a statement of four-year goals and a program. It is subject to revision at the end of the sophomore year. Within the contract, students have to satisfactorily complete a core curriculum, a number of electives, an in-depth program and some off-campus experience.

Interdisciplinary seminars: Students complete eight Core Seminars. They deal with "man as a problematic creature, whose attempts to understand himself, to learn his place in the cosmos, to learn to live with others, provide recurring themes and open avenues to both truth and value."

Depth-Study: Similar to a departmental major or a field of concentration.

Electives: Selected by the student, usually in the first two years, to follow special interests.

Off-Campus Experience: Some sort of "cross-cultural field experience" either in the U.S. or overseas. Could last at least a year.

Evaluation: Done by normal examinations in the core program, but also means discussions and assessments by the Primary Advising Committee on how well the student is doing in completing the four-year contract.

Ottawa is a straight school. Chapel attendance is required every Wednesday and they have the traditional ABC system, plus classroom attendance. The students also are straight, not particularly bright (it's easy to get accepted) and pay a comprehensive fee of $2,930.

However, Ottawa (like New College at the University of Alabama) has a new and valid curriculum. They are being innovative where so many others aren't. An old college friend who teaches at Ottawa wrote, "The place is exciting—now if only we could get some students excited about coming to flat, dry, lackluster Kansas."

PACIFIC OAKS COLLEGE
Pasadena, California 91105

Private
Coed
Semester
425 students

In 1945 seven Quaker families joined together to found what is now Pacific Oaks College and Children's School. Today, although the responsibility for running the school has passed from the hands of six of the seven families to a state chartered Board of Trustees, the educational style and philosophy which spurred the founding of the school still reign.

Stated briefly, that philosophy holds: (1) that each human being has a fundamental worth and a unique and important identity and human potential; (2) that learning and growth are lifelong processes; (3) that each person, no matter how young, can make an important contribution to the world and to those around him.

Pacific Oaks is one of only four institutions in the United States which specializes in preparing teachers for the very young child. The Pacific Oaks College and Children's School are on the same site, and college students and pre-schoolers share the same buildings, classrooms, etc.

Since the college was founded as an upper division college in 1951 (fully accredited in 1959) research in the field of early childhood education has been one of its great strengths. Research conducted during the past eight years in the fields of day care and the construction of environments for young children have made Pacific Oaks the leading information center in the country in those two fields.

For at least one full academic year all college students as part of their course load work in the yards of the children's school observing and studying individual children and their behavior in group and social situations. The administration of the children's school is independent from that of the college. It is largely run by parents working through twenty-two permanent committees which handle everything from curriculum to laundry. The Pacific Oaks and Children's School has 180 children and a waiting list from birth.

The college recently added a master's degree program. Both bachelor's and master's candidates study the full range of human development, from conception to death, concentrating on the early years. Degrees granted are the B.A. and M.A. in Human Development. Tuition is six hundred dollars per semester (part time fifty dollars per unit). Limited financial aid in the form of fellowships, tuition aid grants, loans, College Work-Study Program and time-payment plans.

Admission to the degree program is based on completion of transfer requirements for junior standing: sixty or more semester units of college work and a C average. A few highly qualified students may be permitted to enroll on the basis of completion of thirty or more units, plus work experience related to Pacific Oaks curriculum.

For students interested in pre-school, we can't recommend a better place.

PENDLE HILL   *Quaker*
Wallingford, Pennsylvania 19086   *Private*
                                                       Coed
                                                       Terms
                                                       75 students

Pendle Hill describes itself as "a learning center not concerned with grades, credits, degrees or such commodities; but with the ongoing search for integrity, a place to stand, and joy in being human—a search both individual and corporate, drawing upon the roots and raw materials of religious experience."

Pendle Hill was founded in 1930 by the Quakers to benefit, "men and women of all faiths, races and nationalities." It is located on twenty-two acres twelve miles southeast of Philadelphia, a rural setting. Students range in age between eighteen and seventy and preference is given to applicants who have been out of high school for at least one year.

The purpose of Pendle Hill is to provide time "in which life is lived for its own sake, a time in which the individual may freely and without pressure seek to commune with his fellowman, and to understand from that communion what it means to be human." Each student, working with a staff advisor, tries to find out what his individual search is.

Some courses offered in 1971–72 are: The Journal of George Fox; Poetry—A Dialogue; I and Thou; Tales of the Hasidim; Crafts; Community. Pendle Hill has its own library and students can use the libraries at nearby Swarthmore College. Students are encouraged to enroll for three terms, but if space is available, will be accepted for only one. Tuition is two hundred dollars a term, room and board is another six hundred dollars.

Pendle Hill is also the center for a wide range of conferences, some have been: Gandhian Non-violence in India with Narayan Desai; Retreat with Christine Downing; Marathon in Honesty-Responsibility-Involvement with Keith Irwin; Seminar with Maurice Friedman.

We have known several students—all non-Quakers—who have spent a year at Pendle Hill. And all have loved their year in Wallingford. The school curriculum has been accepted by many other colleges, and credit arrangements should be worked out before enrolling, if you want credit for the experience. Students are discovering Pendle Hill and as they take only forty-five new students each term, room is limited. In 1971 they began turning away as many students as they accepted. Apply early.

POMONA COLLEGE
Claremont, California 91711

Private
Coed
Semester
1,346 students

Pomona is one of the five Claremont Circle Colleges in southern California. It is the freest school of this collection of colleges. It is also another one of those many beautiful California campuses: gardens of palm trees and pines, ivy-covered adobe buildings, all on acres of land thirty-five miles south of downtown Burbank. Pomona, like everything else in California, is expensive: $3,750 for tuition, fees, and room and board. But it's worth the money. Pomona has a handful of worthwhile special programs and is, as they say, an all right place to attend college.

Freshmen students have available to them a series of short courses, lasting a month or so. Students have a chance to sample several fields through this method. Independent Study is part of all student programs. (They range from "reading and research" courses to honor programs.) Study abroad is done with the cooperation of The Experiment in International Living. In 1970 sixty-five students went overseas in the program, living in fifteen countries. Students also have the opportunity to study in Pomona College's special program in Taiwan. Student Exchange Programs are with Fisk University in Tennessee and Swarthmore. Only a limited number of students are involved. Washington Semester Program is done at American University. Students study the government process. In the Undergraduate Research Participation Program in Science qualified students work part time during the year and full time in the summer on research in biological and physical sciences. Pomona with the other Claremont Colleges has a Human Resources Institute that has a Center for Black and Mexican-American Studies open to all students.

Pomona is only looking for academically bright students. At least a B average from high school and high Board scores. They can be choosy, and are. Students are open, friendly and have a sense of community. Twenty students and a faculty member live together in one dorm in an experiment called, appropriately, Experiment in Living. Dorms are separated, but there's lots of living together. No one minds. You could do a lot worse in southern California. You could have to go to UCLA and spend a semester just looking for a parking space.

PROJECT TEN   *State*
Southwest Residential College   *Coed*
University of Massachusetts   *Semesters*
Amherst, Massachusetts 01002   *300 students*

Project Ten is an attempt to humanize huge University of Massachusetts. It offers between thirty and forty courses taught by faculty drawn from all over the university. Courses such as: math, physics, economics, history, anthropology, sociology, literature rhetoric, etc. All courses are taught in small, informal classes. Project Ten also has "Non-Academic" courses: cooking, jazz, human sexuality, conservatism, fantasy literature, altered states of consciousness, etc.

It is a coed community of students, faculty and staff, most of whom live in Pierpont House in the Southwest Residential College. About 150 new students are admitted each year. They write, "we are working to create a home within the large University; a forum on a human scale which will make personal discovery—intellectual, social, ethical— possible."

All new students take freshmen seminars. The students meet in groups of ten to fifteen with a faculty member, graduate student and one or more upper classmen. It's a 3-credit course to advise and orientate the new students to the university. Survival skills is the goal, along with offering a chance for the new student to locate himself and his values within a small group experience.

To apply is simple. A mutual selection process. Project Ten wants "intellectual energy, a commitment to building a community, a willingness to experiment, and the belief that happiness is possible."

Project Teners for the most part are creative and expressive people, few "joiners." They have been active on campus in antiwar activities and edit and write for the campus publications and broadcast on radio. A few are even in the Honors Program. In 1972 they begin tutoring in the Hampshire County jail and the Springfield Street Academy.

This Project Ten is one small step . . . very small. It's hard to "overcome" U of Mass—that sprawling mass of concrete and glass and highway. Nevertheless Charles Adams and the others involved in Project Ten are good folk.

RAYMOND COLLEGE   *Private*
University of the Pacific   *Coed*
Stockton, California 95204   *Terms*
                                                   250 students

Raymond College of the University of the Pacific opened in 1962 with an intense seminar—tutorial liberal arts curriculum. Its academic year is arranged so students take three courses a term and can earn a B.A. degree in three years.

Raymond offers no majors, but provides a broad range of subjects. Students take a core of twenty-two interrelated courses and five electives that take three years to complete. A fourth year of electives and practical work experience can be added.

Grading is pass/fail and written evaluations by faculty members make up the transcript. With a small student body and a faculty-student ratio of one to ten, seminars often have no more than twelve students. Acceptance to Raymond is the same as at the University of the Pacific. Pacific looks more toward straight academic achievements than anything else. Not too tough, however, and not too expensive! A comprehensive fee is about $3,900 for the three-year program.

Raymond has not changed much since opening in 1962 and that has caused problems. We had a letter from Provost Berndt Kolker, who writes: "Raymond College is in fact not now either experimental or innovative. After its inception in 1962, it became institutionalized so that it has become difficult to recapture its original spirit of innovation.

"Students, faculty, and administration are now engaged in a major effort which will allow the college to reconstitute itself. We hope this will give Raymond the kind of flexibility which will be needed during this decade, if this school is to serve adequately." We wish them well and think Raymond College right now isn't a bad place to be. Not when it has a provost who's thinking ahead.

The university as a whole is a straight place, nothing radical happening on campus. Dormitory living is old fashioned, but Raymond has its own dorms and students at this college are freer than most on campus.

REED COLLEGE
Portland, Oregon 97202

Private
Coed
Semester
1,221 students

Reed College lost its president in 1970 after a year of campus turmoil over granting of tenure. At one time in American education Reed was *the* radical college in America. Not so any longer. Those liberal giants have turned conservative with age. As if that's surprising.

A new president took over in the fall of 1971 and we're not certain how Reed will change, if at all. Reed opened in 1910. Besides being radical, it also is famous for its high academic standards and its bright students. Although Reed doesn't use grades or examinations as "cutoffs" for admissions students need to be impressive to be accepted. Reed graduates have received more Woodrow Wilson recognitions than graduates of any other college or university. Two-thirds of Reed graduates go on to grad schools.

Classes are small—fifteen to twenty—and learning, "depends on group discussion, frequent papers and paper conferences with teachers, and independent study." Grades are ABC, but no grades are given out, unless a student is doing poorly, then he's advised of his progress. Students are bookers.

Reed is located five miles from downtown Portland and has that ivy-walled "model-campus" look, though hurt some because of Portland's pollution problems. The campus spreads over ninety-five acres, covering two sides of a canyon, divided by a river and a built-in wildlife sanctuary. Most students live on campus, paying $400 per year. (Tuition runs another $2,500.) The lives of students are free with no college regulations. Students do what they want, within reason.

Reed is not for everyone, their bulletin says. We agree. We recommend it to students who like to study, are academic freaks and want a liberal arts degree. The atmosphere is sullen at Reed. There is not much community feeling. Friendships are limited to small groups, couples. It is not a college for friendly flower children, but is perfect for those few excited about studying say, Greek or Latin. Over 50 percent of the students who enter don't graduate.

Still it's not what it used to be. Reed's reputation is beginning to fade in the West.

RIPON COLLEGE
Ripon, Wisconsin 54971

Private
Coed
Semester
1,121 students

Ripon College is one of those solid small schools in the woods of Wisconsin. It's outlook is totally academic, with little course flexibility. It does, however, provide twenty-one different fields of study, in the U.S. and overseas, and for a small place that's a lot. We recommend it to students who always do well in academic environments and want a liberal arts education with some possibilities for adventure.

As a student at Ripon, you can study off campus at the American University in Cairo, Central America, Cuttington College in up-country Liberia, Waseda University in Tokyo, in Poona, India and in Europe. On campus, you are enrolled in a four-course, four-credit curriculum system, which means each year a student takes more of less subjects. Ripon begins school in late August, leaves a wide break at Christmas and the spring semester runs until June. No summer school.

Not much freedom with grades, a straight ABC. Courses are required and some juniors and seniors (if doing well) are encouraged to do independent study, but the reins are tightly held by faculty.

The student body is midwestern conservative and smart. There is little campus politics or radical movement among the students. They study at Ripon. A comprehensive fee—$3,428.20 in 1971–72—pays for everything. Some scholarship money, work/study. Ripon has a Transitional Year Program.

Campus life is limited to big bands, dances, guest lectures and organizations from Free Universities to Pi Kappa Delta. Students ski when they're not in the library. They even have ROTC.

Then why Ripon? It's a beautiful campus (the kind you've always wanted to attend) and it offers four years of close faculty contact and an institution that cares about its students. In fact, they worry over them. The teaching is personal and demanding. You'll respect the degree you get from Ripon.

ROCHDALE COLLEGE
341 Bloor Street West
Toronto 5, Ontario
Canada

Private
Coed
Unstructured
850 students

Canada has the most notorious of the experimental colleges. It is called Rochdale—from the English town where the worldwide cooperative movement began in 1844—and started in 1965. It is located in an eighteen story building near the University of Toronto. This building is home for 850 students and the crash pad for as many as five hundred more. It was at one time the New Jerusalem of the northern youth culture. People were sleeping in elevator lobbies, in broom closets, stairwells, in garbage rooms. In October, 1970 a Toronto newspaper wrote: "Think of all the filth, rot, decadence and immorality that has infected this world during the past five thousand years. Put them all together and you have only the surface of the biggest cesspool the world has known: Toronto's Rochdale College."

Henry Tarvainen, director at the St. Lawrence Centre for the Arts, who has lived in Rochdale with his family for four years, says, "Rochdale is the most misunderstood and misinterpreted place in the world." It is a place that offers no degrees, is not recognized academically, has no faculty as such, and courses come and go quickly. But it is alive!

Rochdale is trying hard to establish its community. To be a voting member of the corporation, the applicant must work a minimum of forty hours without pay at something within the college—sweeping floors, painting communal areas, organizing cooperative movements on his floor. For this the college provides educational resources and space. Some items they list: Bookbinding, Yoga Seminar, Paper Making, Music Room, Weaving Studio, Farm Seminar, Silk Screening, Leather Workshop, Carpentry.

Living at Rochdale costs about eighty dollars a month for a single, about fifty-five dollars for a double room. The building is owned by its residents who annually elect a council who hires administrators. There are no restricted rules; limits are defined by the personal relationships of the residents. If there's room, Rochdale accepts you.

Life should be better for Rochdale, the wave of Americans crashing the place, seeking a free place to live is over, we think, and we suggest Rochdale might be a place for you to spend a semester or an academic year off campus from your college, a place where you might begin your college career.

ROGER WILLIAMS COLLEGE   *Private*
Bristol, Rhode Island 02809   *Coed*
                                           Semester
                                           3,421 students

This college in the sixties began to expand and experiment. It is a member of the Union for Experimenting Colleges and Universities and on its Bristol campus in 1971 opened one of the first university-without-walls programs. It also has experiments involving interdisciplinary approaches to learning, work-study programs, student teachers, pass/fail and a lovely new campus on sixty-three acres of Rhode Island shoreline.

The Bristol campus of Roger Williams College offers junior and senior division courses with thirteen majors. It is the liberal arts campus and the center of the college. There is also a campus in Providence which has developed profession-oriented programs and some urban studies.

Tuition for this private school is reasonable. Eight hundred dollars a semester. Room and board runs another $650 a semester.

This is not a wildly experimental place. It is moving carefully and in small steps. SAT's are not required and high school records are not the only measurement for acceptance. Roger Williams is looking for students who want to "discover, and rediscover" that education is a process rather than a product.

Roger Williams has a young faculty, responsive to students and classes are small and informal. It's a friendly place. We think it is also an ideal place for Rhode Island. Students who want to develop their own program, but like structure and advice will be happy here. Bristol is an old town with charm and close to Providence and Boston. The atmosphere is not competitive nor the course material irrelevant. There are requirements and that sort of thing, but you can find a happy home at Roger Williams. And on the ocean too.

SHIMER COLLEGE   *Private*
Mount Carroll, Illinois 61053   *Coed*
                                                 Semester
                                                 375 students

Shimer College publishes a small brochure titled: "It's Our Guess You've Never *Ever* Heard of Shimer College," and then they proudly state they have no marching band, no football team, no fraternities or sororities and that they're the 1,482 largest college in the entire United States. Not bad.

Mount Carroll is in northwestern Illinois, eighteen buildings on eighty-five acres. It's located in an area famous for hunting, fishing and camping and far away from anywhere. Shimer's a lonely place and, therefore, people come and go quickly. On the application form, they ask how long you think you'll stay.

One thing they do at Shimer is study. "Students are expected to read at least five or six hours every day of the week," writes their Dean of Faculty. Academics is the game. In many ways, Shimer is a small University of Chicago, with a strong emphasis on Hutchins' great books. A large number of the faculty come from the U of C and Shimer was chartered in 1896 as the Francis Shimer Academy of the University of Chicago.

Courses are traditional and geared to a series of comprehensive examinations. Students have to be able to perform well on exams and in written themes. "The College is," their catalog says, "a place where ideas come together." There is not much interest in anything else, the socialization of students, or a community of people. Shimer doesn't manufacture activities for students; "they must initiate and maintain their own activities as their interests and needs dictate." All that is on campus are weekly films, intramural sports, but they keep the classroom buildings open twenty-four hours.

Shimer does have the advantage of being one of those ivy-covered walls and columned buildings college off by itself where one can get a fine liberal education. It's not for everyone, but they do take students who have not graduated from high school. A fifth to a quarter of each entering class has only completed two or three years of high school. Board scores must be high. We recommend Shimer to students who like to study and want that classic college in the woods.

SIERRA NEVADA COLLEGE   *Private*
Box 264   *Coed*
800 Campbell Road   *Quarter*
Incline Village, Nevada 89450   *60 students*

Part of the Objectives of the College states: "Sierra Nevada College is a proponent of responsible capitalism. The college recognizes our society is money based—that goods and services are exchanged for money and not for goods and services. What the college hopes to accomplish is to teach the student to offer worthwhile services and to expect reasonable payment for them." It's an odd college, started by a lawyer, Friedrich von Brincken, who wanted to use the place as a tax write-off.

Courses are limited and mixed. Business and communicative arts are the best. The emphasis is on success. A student in creative writing, for example, is expected to be published by the senior year. Classes are small, no more than fifteen students each and instruction generally good, though no professor is paid. The president teaches half a dozen classes himself, all in business. Everyone is called by first names.

Sierra Nevada is not seeking freaks or way-out folks. They look over grades, SAT scores, the application and then invite the applicant to Nevada for a personal interview.

It's a small college, not overly close, no touchy-feely place in the mountains. Students are "into" the outdoors. Lots of skiing and camping.

Squaw Valley is down the road. The campus is three connected wooden cabins kept cosy during winters by large fireplaces. Sierra Nevada is isolated, forty miles from Reno, but no one feels away from things.

The school is overrun by women and local people taking business courses. Sierra Nevada is not an academic retreat. Classes are geared for results and are productive. Standard grading, but students can plan their own courses. Nevada has two state colleges and we think Sierra Nevada leaves them both behind.

SIMON'S ROCK COLLEGE   *Private*
Great Barrington, Massachusetts 01230   *Coed*
                                                4-1-4
                                                216 students

Simon's Rock has a policy of admitting students after only two years of high school. The average age of the freshman class is sixteen. It's a four-year college and offers an Associate of Arts degree. The college is working on further accreditation, but for the moment students have to go elsewhere for the B.A.

The college is on two hundred acres west of Great Barrington. The land was a private estate of the parents of President Elizabeth Hall and is new—built since 1965—with small classrooms, coeducational residence halls, lakes and ponds, and miles of Berkshire pines. Students come from nineteen states, but most are easterners. The school is expensive: $4,000 tuition, room and board.

Simon's Rock is traditional—it originally was a women's college—and strict. First year students cannot have automobiles and need to check out on weekdays or overnight. There is also class attendance, but Mrs. Hall says, "We stop treating students like children because they are not children, and we give them adult choices to make." The college has over 130 courses and the only classroom requirement is that a freshman take one of thirty English courses. Students have the majority in the community council and share equal representation with faculty on the academic affairs committee. Students are not for the most part treated like high schoolers.

It's a small, woody and safe college that offers a fine liberal arts program. Anyone now in high school and unhappy might consider changing for the last two years. Simon's Rock is not a make-believe college. The academic work is tough and students have transferred without trouble to places like Hampshire, Sarah Lawrence, Prescott, Reed.

High school students are beginning to hear about Simon's Rock and applications have quadrupled in the last year. Present students are also learning it's a nice place to attend college and they're not leaving, therefore, it's hard to find a place at the college. Apply early, perhaps in your freshman year of high school.

ST. JOHN'S COLLEGE
Annapolis, Maryland 21404

Private
Coed
Semester
345 students

Tom Hebert says St. John's is the college he always wanted to attend. He likes the green campus on the Chesapeake Bay, the eighteenth-century Georgian colonial architecture, the reverence they have at St. John's for books, discussions and lengthy discourse.

St. John's College in Annapolis is the third oldest college in the United States. In 1937 Scott Buchanan and Stringfellow Barr developed a four-year program based on a hundred-odd Great Books that are studied and discussed in seminars. As they say at St. John's, "what Saturday football is at some colleges and fraternity parties elsewhere, the seminar is at St. John's." Besides four hours of seminars, each student has eight hours of language and mathematics tutorials, six hours of laboratory sessions and weekly formal lectures.

There are no grades, and examinations are oral and individual. Students work closely with their tutors, but there is no individual program. Everyone takes four years of the same material, the same Great Books. It is one of the very few (if only) colleges that requires Greek, two years of it.

St. John's is academically tough. Students like to read and deal with ideas. If you tell a student it's three o'clock, he is likely to respond: what do you mean by three o'clock? Status on campus, means you're good in the seminars. At St. John's everyone works, and they work hard.

About three thousand students apply every year and 126 are admitted. SATs are high. St. John's is looking for that "St. John's type." They look like students on any campus, and the usual problems with the administration persist, but these students aren't radical nor do they have the time for campus politics.

The new Santa Fe campus (opened in 1964) has 290 students on the slope of Monte Sol, 260 acres of wooded land in New Mexico. It's a different state, but the same Great Books. That means: a freshman year studying Homer, Plato, Aristotle, Aeschylus, Herodotus, Hippocrates; a second year with Vergil, the Bible, Dante, Chaucer, Plotinus, Machiavelli, Copernicus; a third year with Rabelais, Milton, Cervantes, Voltaire,

Locke, Rousseau; a final year with Goethe, Balzac, Nietzsche, Marx, Freud, Einstein. All of this costs $2,450 in tuition and $650 for board. It's well worth it. St. John's gives one of the few truly "pure" liberal educations. Hebert may be right, but he wouldn't have lasted a day.

ST. OLAF COLLEGE
Northfield, Minnesota 55057

Private
Coed
4-1-4
2,611 students

The Paracollege of St. Olaf's has some 135 students. Its purpose is to be innovative and experimental. There are no courses and progress is determined by examinations that take place when a student thinks he's ready. All students move at their own pace, and all learning is interdisciplinary. Students have a tutor who guides the academic program.

The four areas of study that St. Olaf conceives as a liberal education are:

1) Language studies: mathematics, logic, English and foreign language study;

2) Natural sciences: physics, chemistry, biology;

3) Social science: sociology, psychology, economics, political science;

4) Humanities: history, philosphy, religion, literature, visual and plastic arts and music.

Students take General Examinations and Comprehensive Examinations, plus do a Senior Project. Besides these requirements, they attend a Freshman Seminar and a Senior Seminar, but nearly half their college work is in independent studies. The seminars are the only graded part of the course work.

Students meet their tutors at least once every two weeks and he evaluates their program. Students also keep daily logs of their ideas and experiences and tutors have access to them. But the logs are resented and ignored by many students and the Paracollege is considering abandoning them. All Independent Study is done under the direction of the tutor and is for the most part highly structured.

Paracollege students are trying to establish a separate place on campus. They want coed dorms, a gathering place for themselves. The faculty feels that Paracollege students are "politically more liberal, academically less cautious, and physically more hairy" than the whole St. Olaf student body. Very true.

St. Olaf in cold Northfield is an academic place. Students study, but they also have fine opportunities for overseas study and the January Interim allows another chance to get away from the snow, or into it. Paracollege has had its troubles, but generally is making it. It is not so much a free place as it is an honors college. Don't look for an easy ride. St. Olaf is tough. It is also expensive, $3,850 covers it all.

STUDENT CENTER COLLEGE   *Private*
610 Little Lake Road   *Coed*
Mendocino, California 95460   *No Schedule*
                                           Handful of students

We have had several long letters from Bonard Wilson who conceived of this college and we'd like to reprint them in part. They explain what the school is about.

> We hope to have a truly student-centered college—one in which the student is self-directive in his learning and living and really shares in all decisions that affect him. Printing a catalog, hiring faculty, going in debt for land, building buildings and doing all the usual things are the antithesis of what we are trying to do. . . . We hope to attract people who are moving toward more freedom rather than people who are only running away from what is.
>
> We have no catalog. We are not yet accredited and will try to be only if we can without losing our integrity as a student-centered college. We have not set a tuition; we hope to operate on a cooperative basis as cheaply as possible. My guess is that our costs will be much less than other private colleges. We have a staff potential superior to any I know of. From over four hundred applicants, we have a surplus of well-qualified people who, without reservation, are eager to help establish a student-centered college. We would like to have students who are moving toward being self-directed in their learning-living and who want to help create a college environment in which they can continue to move in that direction. We do not want to recruit students; we want them to hear of us, to ask questions, to visit us and to decide for themselves about joining us.
>
> Learning Centers now envisioned are:
>
> *The Person:* Knowing and accepting oneself and growing toward one's potential.
>
> *Communication:* Verbal and non-verbal self-expression in languages, art, music, drama, dance and media and receiving the expressions of others.
>
> *Community:* Knowing and accepting others and forming interdependent relationships from "one-to-one" to "nation-to-nation."
>
> *Environment:* Knowing and enhancing the environment through using it creatively and constructively.
>
> *Learning:* Learning how to learn and how to facilitate learning.

We sincerely hope we hear more from you and that we see you in the near future or whenever you can come. Our way—our dream is to establish this college on a shoestring so that it can be duplicated all over the country. We are convinced that this is the direction for education and a way must be found to move it with our own resources, at least until others agree and want to help. We hope you can join us in some way.

That's all we know about them. Write if you're interested. We wish them well and share their dreams.

EXPERIMENTAL COLLEGE   *State*
Fresno State College   *Coed*
Fresno, California 93710   *Semester*
                                                    323 students

This Experimental College encourages experimentation with course content, interdisciplinary courses, experimental programs in teacher training, altering the academic calendar and the unit value of courses, new grading systems, freshmen seminars, tutorial courses, independent study programs, etc. Its courses and program are designed to be incorporated into the general curriculum of Fresno State. If after one year an experimental course or program does not appear to justify such inclusion, it is normally dropped from the offerings of the Experimental College.

The Experimental College is part of the institutional structure of Fresno State. It is guided by the faculty—with provision made for student participation—and functions as an academic department. All Experimental College courses are available for elective credit and open to all students, regardless of grade point average or major.

Some of the course offerings in 1971 were: Love and Violence; Basic Mountaineering; The Students' Role in the Governance of the Campus; The Second Sex: On Women's Liberation; Alchemy; Practice of Yoga; Algebra for Elementary and High School Teachers.

This is a limited little Experimental College. Fresno State has something like twelve thousand students. It sprawls at the edge of Fresno, a campus of some 1,400 acres, in the middle of California farmland. The college offers degrees in almost everything. It's just a big state school.

Fresno, however, has something of a liberal orientation. All committees have student representation, and there is off campus, overseas and other special programs for the students. It's an easy college to attend, they're not looking for any high grades. But there's not much community. Less than 10 percent of the students live in dormitories. Most of the undergraduates have apartments in town or live at home. There are fraternities and sororities, but they attract few students.

If you have to go to Fresno State then check into the Experimental College, otherwise, avoid.

EXPERIMENTAL COLLEGE   *Private*
Tufts University   *Coed*
Medford, Massachusetts 02155   *Semester*
                                              960 students

"X College" as it's titled at Tufts started in 1964. It has no residence halls, extra-university offices, special classrooms or full-time students. It's not committed to any political philosophy nor does it have a program or grant a degree. What does it do?

It grants credit toward a degree and is an independent, but integral part of Tufts University. Experimental College is open to undergraduates, graduate students and faculty members of the university. At the moment it has four programs:

1) Auditing for Breadth: A student audits three courses instead of being regularly enrolled in one. He submits written evaluations of the experience when he completes the series.

2) Self-Achievement: A student completes a course from the regular curriculum without attending lectures or being formally enrolled. A professor establishes the conditions for evaluation.

3) Individual Studies: A student works on a one-to-one basis with a faculty member. Students can also take a "student sabbatical" and study off campus.

4) Combined Degrees Program: Students undertake an accelerated program combining undergraduate and graduate courses, leading to both degrees within a maximum of five years.

A student can do only part of his undergraduate work in "X College," but he has wide selection. In the first seven years of operation, it has offered over three hundred seminars. They were divided between freshmen and upperclass, none larger than twenty students. The subjects are varied and fall into four groups:

1) Subjects that are departmental in nature: *i.e.,* "The Napoleonic Wars. A Military and Political View" and "Elementary Dutch."

2) Interdisciplinary and other subjects not in one department: *i.e.,* "Cinemarxism" and "Astrological Studies."

3) Studies that further an individual's personal development: *i.e.,* "Choreography," "The Transcendental Experience," "Photography."

4) Subjects that relate to current social and political problems: *i.e.,* "The Military-Industrial Complex" and "Black Politics."

Grading is "pass/withdraw" in the freshmen seminars and "pass/fail" for upperclass seminars.

Plans are developing for coordinated courses in three additional areas—Black Studies, Earth Studies and Media Studies. The Experimental College continually changes and develops, but will not dramatically effect life at Tufts University. It is, however, a place where you can spend time and learn.

WESTERN COLLEGE   *Private*
Oxford, Ohio 45056   *Women*
                                                   Modules
                                                   400 students

The Vice President for Administration, Donovan Auble, wrote us about Western College, "a committee of students, alums, and faculty was appointed in the fall of 1969 to examine the activity of this historic institution and make recommendations for updating the program. 'Freedom with Responsibility' was the result." This program means students design their own courses under the guidance of tutors, grades are replaced by evaluations, all departmentalization is eliminated and faculty teach what they want.

This program is the result of President William C. Spencer who went to rural Western College from Columbia University. He thinks that Western in the seventies will recreate the medieval university in which students will seek out teachers to learn what they want to know. The academic year is divided into four modules of twelve, four, six and ten week lengths. Module II of four weeks is an Independent Study period. A student can travel, do a group project, a research paper. During the other modules, she takes three learning units. What she wants to study is decided with her tutor and since there are no requirements, her course of study is extremely flexible. Some courses offered are: Swahili; Cupid and Psyche in Literature and Art; The Female and the Novel; Sleep and Dreams; Anti-War Opinion and Activity During American War Periods; Calculus.

Tuition is $2,624 per year and room and board is another $1,216. Students come from thirty-five states and forty-one countries. The campus of 208 acres of woods and lawns has fifteen buildings and is over 118 years old. Oxford is a college town, large Miami University (12,000 plus students) is also there. Actually within two and one-half hours driving distance from Oxford there are eighty-six other colleges and universities.

Students are selected carefully and admissions are based on general intelligence, motivation and ability to become self-directed in an atmosphere as independent as Western. Students fill out a lengthy application form, submit SAT grades, personal recommendations, but no interview is necessary.

Besides the module system, Western has a number of unique special programs. A Multi-cultural Emphasis. Each year the college emphasizes one of the four major non-Western areas of the world. The program includes a series of lectures, films, recitals and exhibits, and a travel seminar to the area. Western also has Teacher Education, Medical Technology, Cooperative Programs, Junior Year Abroad and any special study a student might want to attempt.

President Spencer has predicted that at least two-thirds of the country's 750 private colleges and universities will be forced to shut down because of lack of students and funds, but thinks Western's experimental program and high quality of academic work will survive. We think he's right.

UNIFIED SCIENCE STUDY PROGRAM	*Private*
Education Research Center	*Coed*
Massachusetts Institute of Technology	*Semester*
Cambridge, Massachusetts 02139	*110 students*

The Unified Science Study Program is an alternative freshmen and sophomore program sponsored by the Education Research Center. Students in this program work with the faculty individually or in small groups to plan and carry out their studies. It's purpose is to encourage students to spend much of their time working on projects they formulate themselves. It began in 1969 and proposed, "to blur disciplinary lines, to start with projects constructed around real problems, to engage the issues raised by the organization, structure, and function of physical, chemical, biological, economic, and social systems."

With the help of an advisor, the student develops a written plan telling what he wants to do, how and with whom he will do these things, how his work will be documented and evaluated. The student also indicates what facilities he will need for his project and how much it will cost. The advisor puts the student in touch with other people who can work with him. When a student's interests lie outside the areas of competence of the faculty, or when he needs specialized facilities, arrangements are made so that he can use the resources of the remainder of the institute or of other organizations in the area.

USSP is located in a ramshackle wooden building on campus. Computer facilities, laboratories, a shop, a small library, a lounge, seminar rooms, faculty offices and working space for each student are mixed together. The place is cluttered with coffee pots, posters and artifacts from various projects; many people spend most of their days there.

Some of the projects have been: programming a computer-routed minibus system for inner city transportation; making a film on the religious community of the Hare Krishna sect; bibliographic research on radioactivity in drinking and recreational waters for Ralph Nader.

Any student accepted to MIT can opt for USSP and after two years (at the present) return to the traditional program of the university. Requirements still have to be met at MIT, but for the first two years it is independent studies at its finest!

UNITED STATES INTERNATIONAL	*Private*
UNIVERSITY	*Coed*
P.B. 2909	*Quarters*
San Diego, California 92112	*4,121 students*

The United States International University has eight of the loveliest campuses we've seen and a program that takes students as early as the eleventh grade and provides degrees through a Ph.D.—if you can stand it. The university is conservative and uptight. President William C. Rust has a crew-cut mentality, the student body is straight (for California), traditional, but the university has a wealth of opportunities and the facilities are luxury.

The campuses of the Middle College—equivalent to two years of high school and two years of college—are: *Elliott,* 400 acres of rolling hillside and eucalyptus trees on the northern edge of San Diego. Opened in 1968, it's plush. The residence halls are completely equipped apartments—not dormitories—and are clustered around swimming pools. The seminar rooms have recessed carpeted "conversation pits" and all of them are circular or oval; *Colorado Alpine,* is 175 miles west of Denver in Steamboat Springs. Eighty acres overlooking Yampa Valley and near Mount Werner, famous for skiing; *Ashdown Park,* in Sussex, England, on 180 acres near the Ashdown Forest. It is thirty miles from London and in some of the most beautiful countryside of England; *Mauna Olu,* on the island of Maui near the lower slopes of Mount Haleakala. The nearest town is Makawao, three miles away. The campus is isolated.

The curriculum of the Middle College is broken into four main themes: Life In Contemporary Society, Self and Community, Nature and Ecological Systems, Meaning and Value. There are electives (not many) and students can accelerate their own program.The third year is an International Year, on campuses in Kenya, Mexico or England. Three or four quarters are spent learning a language overseas, understanding another culture. Other courses relate to the particular area of the college. When the student returns to the United States he finishes his B.A. at any one of the campuses or begins work on an advance degree in: Business Administration, Law, Human Behavior or Performing Arts.

For all of this, students pay a lot. Quarter costs are $1,070 tuition, room and board.

It is not difficult to be accepted, if you have the money. It provides an adequate college education. Their teacher preparation is respected, as are their law school and business courses. But remember, you're not going to have much freedom.

UNIVERSITY OF ALASKA *State*
College, Alaska 99701 *Coed*
Semester
6,843 students

Why go to Alaska? It's certainly not innovative or experimental, but it is small—only 2,274 students on the main campus. The campus is four miles north of Fairbanks on 2,250 acres. The University of Alaska is new—most of the thirty buildings have been constructed in the sixties. And Fairbanks is easy to reach—three hours by plane from Seattle. As a state college it's inexpensive—about $870 a year for tuition, room and board. It is not a difficult college to get into—a B average in high school if you're non-resident, a C average for in-state students. (The university, through various programs, enrolls one out of every twenty Alaskans a year.) Besides all this, the University of Alaska isn't a bad school.

Academic colleges of the university are: College of Arts and Letters, College of Behavioral Sciences and Education; College of Biological Sciences and Renewable Resources; College of Business, Economics and Government; College of Earth Sciences and Mineral Industry; College of Mathematics, Physical Sciences and Engineering.

It is the major world center for arctic and subarctic research and the study of the environment of the Far North. Besides these colleges, the university is the base for ten research units, everything from the Alaska Cooperative Wildlife Research Unit to the Musk Ox Project. All these projects have field sites.

Housing is provided for 882 men and 421 women. Most single students live on campus, but students can live off campus. Students are on the University Assembly. The student government has successfully lobbied in the State Legislature for a new campus activities center and the purchase of a huge air-inflated structure that provides indoor facilities for hockey and tennis, among other sports. Outdoor sports are snowshoe softball, harpoon throwing and Eskimo blanket tossing. The university also has a winter carnival.

In winter the temperature averages minus eleven degrees, but there's no wind or humidity. Nights are long—Fairbanks is only 130 air miles from the Arctic Circle, but in the summer the temperature is in the mid-seventies and the days average twenty-one hours of sunlight.

Alaska is a young pioneering state. Half of the population of 284,000 are under twenty-three years of age. The cities have a frontier atmosphere and the people are what they used to call rugged individualists. It is a fine school for students wanting to work in the behavioral and biological sciences and are looking for their own new frontier. While there's still a chance.

UNIVERSITY OF GUAM   *State*
P.O. Box EK   *Coed*
Agana, Guam 96910   *Semester*
                                            2,467 students

The University of Guam is the only American college in the western Pacific. It is a four-year school offering degrees in Arts and Sciences, Nursing and Education. The university also has a masters degree program in Education.

The campus is outside of the capital city of Agana on a hundred acres of sloping hillside overlooking Pago Bay and the Pacific Ocean. It is a new campus with the three dormitories, Student Center and Robert F. Kennedy Library all built since 1968. The campus is built amid palm fronds and tropical forest. A lovely place to attend classes. The university is also well equipped: microfilm library, audio-visual studios, "little theater," air-conditioning, etc. It has just about all the facilities to be found on a college campus on the mainland.

The university is inexpensive. Free for residents of Guam and only ten dollars per credit hour for non-residents. A B.A. degree can be earned for less than $1,250. Guam is traditional academically. There is an ABC grading system, a "Dean's List" and requirements for graduation. It is also academically quite easy. Students come from Guam itself and the Trust Territory. English, the language of instruction, is often a second or third language for the students.

It is a particularly appropriate school for students interested in Micronesia. The university is the base of the Micronesian Area Research Center and the western Pacific repository of information on the cultural, political and scientific data of that area. The university is advantageous for students interested in the linguistic and cultural situation of Guam or the Trust Territory.

In most respects it is a "foreign" school, but still an American one. Anyone wanting to learn about "our" relationship to the Trust Territory could spend a valuable year at Guam. The school is naturally geared to providing an education for its people and "giving an accelerated program for training of local teachers," but American students on independent studies or off-campus programs could settle for two semesters at the University of Guam and learn a lot about a U.S. presence in a foreign country. And more should.

UNIVERSITY OF PUGET SOUND   *Private*
1500 N. Warner   *Coed*
Tacoma, Washington 98416   *4-1-4*
                                                        2,106 students

This college of thirty Tudor buildings on seventy acres of lawns and woods in residential Tacoma has a half-dozen programs going for it.

Its new short Winterim is for the intensive study of one course and these courses are revised repeatedly to meet the students' requests. The University of Puget Sound has study programs overseas in Rome, Vienna, Breukelen and Rennes. Most of these are language-oriented ventures. (The university recently took over the Weyerhaeuser Estate on Commencement Bay in Tacoma for intensive language study near their campus.) Puget Sound has some pass/fail, but extremely limited. Their Honors Program is selective and based on grades. They also have a Cooperative Education Program where students in the same curriculum area are paired off. While one member attends classes, the other works full time at a job related to their field. At the end of each semester the students switch positions, continuing this format until graduation, which requires about one year longer than normal studies. This work-study approach provides practical experience with classroom work. And it's very good.

Puget Sound is selective and students need to be smart. They come from forty-eight states and about twenty-two foreign countries. Over 90 percent of their students are in the top half of their high school class. Total expenses, tuition, room and board are slightly more than three thousand dollars.

The University of Puget Sound is carefully moving toward a more liberal program at their school. They are not rushing things here. And their students are not demanding. The university can get away with taking their time. It has some of the qualities of a traditional college: those football teams and dances, but that's not all bad.

The university won't trouble you much, you can live off campus, and they'll give you an education. What more could you want? Lots, but we'll have to wait awhile for Puget Sound to catch up . . . however, what they have is honest.

UNIVERSITY WITHOUT WALLS	*Private/State*
Antioch College	*Coed*
Yellow Springs, Ohio 45387	*Semester*
	1,000 students

The University Without Walls is a project involving seventeen institutions under the auspices of the Union for Experimenting Colleges and Universities located at Antioch College. The schools involved are: Shaw University, New College at Sarasota, University of Minnesota, Antioch College, Skidmore College, Loretto Heights College, Goddard College, Friends World College, University of Massachusetts (School of Education), Roger Williams College, Staten Island Community College, Howard University, Bard College, Stephens College, University of South Carolina, Chicago State College and Northeastern Illinois State College.

It is called the University Without Walls because "it abandons the tradition of a sharply circumscribed campus and provides education for students wherever they may be—at work, in their home, through internships, independent study and field experience, within areas of special social problems, at one or more colleges, and in travel and service abroad. . . . It abandons the traditional classroom as the principal instrument of instruction, as well as the prescribed curriculum, the grades and credit points which, however they are added or averaged, do not yield a satisfactory measure of education. . . . It places strong emphasis on student self-direction in learning, while still maintaining close teaching-learning relationships between students, teachers and others. It aims to produce not 'finished' graduates but life-long learners."

Some of the institutions admitted small pilot groups in the fall of 1971, but full-scale semester operations involving fifty to seventy-five students on each campus begins in the fall, 1972. The degree offered is awarded from the sponsoring institution.

The University Without Walls provides a highly individualized and flexible approach to education, using a wide array of resources and relying heavily on self-directed independent study. The first students are also involved in developing plans for greater use of the concept at their school and other colleges and universities. For further information, write Dr.

Samuel Baskin, President, Union for Experimenting Colleges and Universities at Antioch. And if you run across any of their students let us know.

WASHINGTON-BALTIMORE CAMPUS *Private*
Antioch College *Coed*
1709 New Hampshire *Quarter*
Washington, D.C. 20009 *321 students*

This is one of the Antioch, Ohio franchises, growing up, it almost seems, along the beltway between these two cities with one detour at Columbia, Maryland, that new planned town. Students earn interdisciplinary B.A. degrees from Antioch College and they study, for the most part, urban problems (and at Columbia, ecology). Some recent course titles: Diagnosing Community Needs and Information Techniques; Principles of Economics II; Environment: A Challenge to Modern Society; Understanding the City—Introduction to City Planning.

Besides this the Washington-Baltimore campus runs a number of programs and studies that fluctuate according to faculty and student interest. They are: American Indian Studies; Environmental Design Program; Appalachian Study Center; Center for Humanistic Education; Center for the Study of Basic Human Problems; Center for Social Research; Human Ecology Center; Work/Study Program; and Center for the Arts.

Tuition for all this is based on a sliding scale anywhere from seven hundred to three thousand dollars, depending on parents' ability to pay. Students live where they can and in Baltimore there are plans to take over a downtown hotel to be shared with other students from the area.

Students are involved with all aspects of the running of this college. And as a small college, everyone knows everyone else. There are only about sixteen full-time faculty members. Some students also teach. Students have to be mature for this school, for there is little, if any, personal support for students. Everyone is very much on their own. The work-study program—where money can be earned for payment of tuition—puts students into social action kinds of jobs. Often in the inner-city.

Washington-Baltimore has little sense of community, spread out as they are between three cities. This arrangement has caused trouble and in-fighting and several times the school has come close to closing. But it hasn't and we think it won't. Antioch College always has had the ability to bounce back from trouble. The college now is suffering from growing pains and changes of directions. Not any sure place with predictable answers, but if you can handle ambiguity, you can handle this place.

WHITMAN COLLEGE
Walla Walla, Washington 99362

Private
Coed
Semester
1,100 students

This is not an experimental college, not really innovative (except in new living arrangements), but it's the best liberal arts college in the West. It's better than Reed, but it just isn't well known outside of the state.

Walla Walla (or W²) means "many waters" and the campus has its own creek, plus forty-five acres and twenty-one buildings. The town of Walla Walla is 26,000 and it's 160 miles southwest of Spokane. The college is over 112 years old and produces graduates who go on for further degrees. Between fifty and seventy percent enroll in grad schools. This is a hard academic place.

Inclusive budget for Whitman is around $3,400 for the year. Anyone accepted can obtain some sort of financial assistance from the college. Getting accepted is a problem. Whitman takes about 350 new students every year, and they're exceptionally bright. In 1970 all but 5 percent of the freshmen had 3.00 and above point averages in high school. Eighty-six percent of the entering students ranked in the top 20 percent of their graduating high school class.

At Whitman classes are small, never more than thirty-five students in any one, often less than fifteen. The student-teacher ratio is thirteen to one. Not bad. Faculty and students also know and like each other, classes are sometimes at the homes of professors. But no grades are given away. Tests and papers are common on this campus. There are some pass/fail, but only for upperclassmen. The college has a few exchange programs with black colleges and send students overseas with the Experiment in International Living, nothing else innovative is tried.

In 1971 the college loosened its residence halls, made three coed and allowed more students to live off campus, responding to some of the demands of the students. But people going to Whitman are straight folks. They are also wealthy. They get a solid education here, a liberal arts one. The college is strong in English and History, not outstanding in the natural sciences. It gives a student a lot. One problem is isolation. Students have to make up their own social activities and Walla Walla is remote. Everyone seems to have a car, however. It's a college close to wheatfields and the Blue Mountains and worth the money, but you have to play by their rules. Remember.

WILLIAM JAMES COLLEGE
Grand Valley State
Allendale, Michigan 49401

State
Coed
Three terms
750 students

This is the newest college of a cluster of colleges in western Michigan at Grand Valley State. Two colleges are already in operation and William James, which opened in 1971 is a person-oriented, future-oriented and career-oriented school. It seeks to revive James' approach to psychology and extend his individual psychology to the realm of social psychology; the psychology and sociology of small groups, the sociology of knowledge, of institution, of religious groups, of the family, of political societies, etc.

During the first years the curriculum will be composed of four parts: Synoptic Program: furnishes "skills and discipline every informed man finds useful." It's central element is the Synoptic Lecture Series. A distinguished lecturer resides on campus for two weeks. His lectures, delivered on ten consecutive class days, concern his area of interest, his vision of life. These are then discussed in small groups during the remaining weeks of the term. Other programs are Environmental Studies: investigates the physical and biological milieu in which man lives and acts; Administration and Information Management Program: analyzes various factors that enable man to live a life beyond that of pure nature; and Social Relations Program: investigates the more frequently observed kinds of social units.

William James College uses honors, credits and no credit. The student's transcript does not record those courses for which no credit has been awarded. The college is on a three-three plan. Every student takes three courses in each of three terms. A Bachelor of Science degree is awarded. Students at William James can also take courses in the other two Grand Valley colleges: Arts and Sciences and Thomas Jefferson.

William James' specialness is its *career orientation*. By this they mean a practical pragmatic approach to educating students, the same approach James would have recommended. The college plans its subject matter and teaching methods in such a way that knowledge gained through studying at the college is relevant to both a student's life and to his place in history. Courses are not watered-down nor do they disregard post-college experience. It's a tough tightrope to walk, but William James is confident. Costs at this state supported school are low: $152 a term for Michigan residents.

WINDHAM COLLEGE   *Private*
Putney, Vermont 05346   *Coed*
                                               Semester
                                               850 students

Windham College is in its twentieth year, a school of sixty-seven faculty members and 850 students. It has a new campus on the banks of the Connecticut River and they write in their 1971 catalog "it must ensure that its graduates have learned to see things whole, that the young of a deeply troubled society acquire the saving subtlety to distinguish between that in our heritage which is to be preserved and that which is to be discarded."

This is a protective school. Students have to live in dormitories, are taken care of, nurtured. Everyone knows everyone else and there's a lot of community. Students are allowed some freedoms. They can produce or publish what they want, no censorship, and representatives of the students sit as voting members of all faculty committees. There is pass/fail on the freshmen seminars and upperclassmen can take one course each semester as pass/fail. But that's about all the freedom with the academic program. Lots of requirements.

Windham is one of those tiny Vermont Colleges where one can obtain a fine, but not flashy, B.A. degree. The college has limited resources and offers just basic stuff. Nevertheless, its faculty is outstanding for a college of its size and the school does have an ambitious overseas program, but mostly to Europe. No Independent Study or stuff like that.

All of this education is about $3,670.

The college has little more to offer. Students can take courses at nearby Marlboro College and Putney itself is also home for the Experiment in International Living, the Putney School and the Antioch-Putney Graduate School. Windham is only an hour from Dartmouth, and an hour and a half from the Five Colleges of Amherst. And, of course, there's the skiing and rural Vermont all within reach.

Consider Windham College for all those reasons. They may be enough.

WORLD CAMPUS AFLOAT
Chapman College
Orange, California 92666

Private
Coed
Semester
5,200 students

Chapman College is one of those many religious, privately controlled, residential, coeducational, four-year, liberal arts schools.

The major difference is World Campus Afloat. Since 1965, Chapman has sent five hundred students each semester around the world, studying on the way. The ship touches ports at places like: Pago Pago, Bali, Mombassa, Caracas, Casablanca, Singapore and the whole thing costs about three thousand dollars.

The floating campus really is a school. Over sixty courses are offered and there's room for laboratories, a theater, and physical education on ship. Once in ports there's trips to places like Machu Picchu in Peru, the Medici Tomb in Florence, the Palace of Versailles and people to meet: His Holiness the Pope, the Prime Minister of Malaysia, Her Royal Highness Princess Margriet of the Netherlands, and others as well, beggars in India, the Hyena Man of Harar, a Ceylonese Parliament member. As one student put it: "I can tell you what it's like to examine the Sphinx and pyramids of Egypt, to participate in an audience with the Pope, to visit Casablanca's Casbah, to buy Hong Kong bargains, to be entertained by the Prime Minister of Malaysia, to walk in the footsteps of Socrates and Caesar, to meditate at the birthplace of Christ."

The Campus Afloat is fairly straight and the other colleges associated with it are also traditional: Adams State College, Bloomfield College, The Defiance College, Drake University, Hofstra University, McPherson College, Northeast Louisiana University, Oklahoma State University, Otterbein College, Phillips University, Springfield College, Whitworth College and the University of Wyoming.

Students can't drink or use drugs on ship, but this rule is violated. The cabin areas are divided according to sex and a student needs permission from the Dean of Students to cross over. This rule too is violated. It's a straight place, Chapman, on land or at sea. But an education is possible, plus the opportunity to see a wide range of places and at the same time, gain academic credit. Chapman has had trouble filling their ship—most students realize they can get most of the same kind of education traveling by themselves, but if you want a semester away from your present school, World Campus Afloat is one way to go.

YANKTON COLLEGE
Yankton, South Dakota 57078

Private
Coed
4-1-4
670 students

There is not much in South Dakota that's experimental or innovative. Of the less than twenty colleges in the state, we like Yankton. It's old—1881—and small, and they are using the 4-1-4 calendar system that is becoming popular. They divide the year: September–December; January; and February–May.

During the month Interim, students work intensively in a group project, a seminar, some independent project, or do an internship. The faculty members are used as guides or fellow-inquirers, not as teachers. It's not very revolutionary, but it's *something!*

The college has just started a new freshmen program. It's an integrated-course approach that concentrates on the environment. Students spend an academic year dealing with as many phases of the problem as possible. It is the subject matter of almost all disciplines—from Political Science to Philosophy. Not all students have to take the program and it is selective.

Yankton is a church-related school, but non-sectarian. It costs less than $2,500 for all fees and is located on fifty-five acres of land on the banks of the Missouri. The school is the center of Yankton itself, a city of 12,000. Most of the land in southeastern South Dakota is used for farming.

The college is famous for its conservatory of music and worth attending for that reason. The school also offers opportunities for overseas study in France, England and Mexico. The programs are very straight and tightly controlled.

It is not difficult to get into—a C average will do it—and it's not an outstanding or demanding place. But Yankton is close to the country and for South Dakota, it's good.

5. Special Programs

SCHOOL FOR INTERNATIONAL
TRAINING OF THE EXPERIMENT IN
INTERNATIONAL LIVING
Kipling Road
Brattleboro, Vermont 05301

Private
Coed
Modules
Not announced

This is an upper level B.A. program involving students in a multi-cultural environment that will "actively apply the philosophy that an individual's primary loyalty should be to humanity." Students share the campus for one semester with students enrolled in the International Students of English Program, the International Career Training Program and the Masters of Arts in Teaching Program.

There are intensive modules of two and one half to three weeks in each of the four major areas—ecology, mediation, population and development. All students participate in each module. Midway through the first semester a one-week cross-cultural field experience highlights a semester-long seminar on cross-cultural studies. Cross-cultural studies, along with languages, are semester-long courses. During the month of January students are encouraged to study at another institution that follows the 4-1-4 calendar.

From February onward through the second semester of the junior year and the first semester of the senior year each student works on either an individual or small-group basis following plans developed in cooperation with the staff of the school. For example: a small group of students might concentrate on social and economic development in

Mexico; an individual majoring in ecology might do field work with the local Windham Regional Planning and Development Commission; a student interested in population and family planning might be apprenticed to an organization such as Zero Population Growth or Planned Parenthood Association.

All students during the final semester will be measured against the goals of the program. In most cases such measurement is informal and part of a continuing process. A pass/fail grading system is used. Students will have to reach a Foreign Service level in one foreign language and have knowledge in one major problem confronting society: Ecology and the environment; Mediation and conciliation; Population and family planning; Social and economic progress in the developing nations. They must demonstrate ability, through actual practice, to carry out assigned work responsibilities (in volunteer work, an internship or a career position) in either an international or domestic organization.

The all-inclusive fee for this upper level B.A. program is about four thousand dollars.

UNIVERSITY YEAR FOR ACTION
806 Connecticut Avenue, N.W.
Washington, D.C. 20525

Government
Coed
Year Program
1,000 students

ACTION brought together several government agencies: Peace Corps, VISTA, SCORE, ACE, Foster Grandparents into one super volunteer service organization. Its first program to aid low-income people in the United States was University Year for ACTION which places college students in full-time jobs of service to poverty communities for one year of college credit work. Volunteers are paid a small stipend ($35 per month) for living expenses and are given a room and board allowance of perhaps $160.

Any student—undergraduate or graduate—enrolled in a participating university could apply for the program. Each student is involved with a training program that includes skills training, cultural understanding, project discussion and analysis, administrative procedures all related to the target poverty community.

The first colleges and universities to receive grants for this ACTION program were: University of Nebraska, University of Massachusetts, Wisconsin State—Green Bay, Howard, Federal City College, Morgan State. The community sponsors of such programs would be organizations like: Indian Tribal Councils, Community Action Programs, hospitals, Urban League organizations, Head Start and Job Corps projects. etc.

In their program description, ACTION wrote, "University Year for ACTION will move somewhat beyond past volunteer programs in several ways. It is more than an opportunity to serve for the volunteer, since he will receive educational credit and the guidance of the university during his term of service. It is more than low-cost manpower for the community sponsor, since through the volunteer the sponsor will have a unique access to the knowledge and talents of the university. And it is more than an educational innovation for the university, since the volunteers will become a new form of 'extension agents' providing the university with a new level of contact with the people, particularly those of low income, in the immediate environment."

UYA is holding steady at 1,000 volunteers and twenty-five universities for 1972–73 in order to tighten up existing programs. It will probably expand later. The basic assumption of UYA is that universities and their students can help America solve its problems of poverty and injustice. This is probably fallacious. But UYA programs do have a high percentage of minority students (33%) and students are "played back" into the sorts of environments they came out of. So there won't be white kids using poor and black communities as training grounds. The principal problem of UYA is that each volunteer will be with the community agency for only one year. There won't be much impact at that level.

But we know two things: (1) the colleges and student volunteers will change from the experience and (2) if we were students today, we would try to get a UYA project for our school.

III. Foreign Study

GHANA
University of Ghana
GUINEA
École Nationale des Arts et Metiers
KENYA
University of Nairobi
LESOTHO
University of Botswana, Lesotho and Swaziland
LIBERIA
University of Liberia
Cuttington College and Divinity School
MALAWI
University of Malawi
MAURITIUS
University of Mauritius
MOROCCO
University of Mohammed V
NIGERIA
University of Ibadan
University of Ife
University of Nigeria
University of Lagos
Ahmadu Bello University
SENEGAL
Université De Dakar
SIERRA LEONE
Fourah Bay University College
SUDAN
University of Khartoum
TANZANIA
University of Dar-es-Salaam
UGANDA
Makerere University
UNITED ARAB REPUBLIC (EGYPT)
The American University in Cairo

7. STUDYING IN SOUTH AMERICA
ARGENTINA
Catholic University Santa Maria
BRAZIL

Federal University of Bahia

CHILE

Catholic University in Santiago

COLOMBIA

Universidad Javeriana
Universidad del Valle

COSTA RICA

University of Costa Rica

DOMINICAN REPUBLIC

Universidad Autonoma de Santo Domingo
Universidad Nacional Pedro Henriques Urena

MEXICO

Center for Intercultural Documentation (CIDOC)

PARAGUAY

Universidad Catolica Nuestra Senora de la Asuncion

8. STUDYING IN THE MIDDLE AND FAR EAST

INDIA

JAPAN

Waseda University
Sophia University

LEBANON

American University of Beirut

NEPAL

Tribhuban University

THE PHILIPPINES

University of the Philippines, Diliman Campus

REPUBLIC OF SOUTH VIETNAM

University of Hue

TAIWAN

Tunghai University

TURKEY

Middle East Technical University
University of Ankara
Robert College

We have gathered this information about living and studying overseas from our experience overseas, from friends and associates, embassies, and even strangers who heard about our research and wrote us. The costs and grade averages required of college programs in Europe come mostly from the schools' Directors of International Education. We know that these specific figures are continually changing, but our estimates will give you some idea how much it will cost to study in these programs.

1. Europe, Going and Coming

. . . Let us view the disadvantages of sending a youth to Europe. To enumerate them all would require a volume. I will select a few. If he goes to England he learns drinking, horse-racing and boxing. These are the peculiarities of English education. The following circumstances are common to education in that and the other countries of Europe. He acquires a fondness for European luxury and dissipation and a contempt for the simplicity of his own country; he is fascinated with the privileges of the European aristocrats, and sees with abhorrence the lovely equality which the poor enjoys with the rich in his own country: he forms foreign friendships which will never be useful to him, and loses the season of life for forming in his own country those friendships which of all others are the most faithful and permanent; he is led by the strongest of all human passions into a spirit for female intrigue destructive of his own and others happiness, or a passion for whores destructive to his health, and in both cases learns to consider fidelity to the marriage bed as an ungentlemanly practice and inconsistent with happiness; he recollects the voluptuary dress and arts of the European women and pities and despises the chaste affections and simplicity of those of his own country; he retains thro' life a fond recollection and a hankering after those places which were the scenes of his first pleasures and of his first connections. . . . It appears to me then that an American coming to Europe for education loses in his knowledge, in his morals, in his health, in his habits, and in his happiness.—FROM A LETTER OF THOMAS JEFFERSON TO JOHN BANISTER, JR. 1785.

Our first advice is to tell you not to go during the summer. Europe is too crowded. Keeping alive, finding a place to crash, hitchhiking, et cetera is an endless hassle. During the summer of 1971 eight hundred thousand or more young Americans went to Europe, taking advantage of student rates on international airlines, special school charters and group rates. Overseas airline offices looked like student unions. In Europe one couldn't see the monuments for the young. Tent-cities were set up outside major cities, housing four and five thousand a night during the peak months. Students stretched out in every park, bundled together in sleeping bags. There were no rooms left in Europe. Youth hostels, taking the youngest first, had enough twelve- and thirteen-year olds to fill their dormitories. There were no free park benches. Students wandered the wet dark streets of London, slept in the underground, in doorways, in lobbies of airports (the best place to crash), on the banks of the Seine. In Ibiza they slept in the small plazas of Santa Eulalia del Rio until the night of July 16 when the Guardia Civil moved in on one hundred, killing one and injuring more. Few traveling to Europe in the summer of 1971 had a good night's sleep.

We warn you about summer in Europe. Any summer. But we know you'll go anyway, for that is what everyone does. So if you have to go, go right!

PASSPORTS

Apply immediately. You'll need the passport before obtaining visas (if going anywhere that requires them). The busy time for getting a passport is from February to April. It takes about three weeks. In 1970 the Passport Office issued 2,219,159 passports and 661,480 were for people twenty-four and under. In 1971 the number of people going overseas was even greater. From April to August of 1971 the total number of travelers going to Europe jumped 45 percent over the same months from the previous year. In May, 1971 alone the change was 23 percent.

You'll need the following:

- birth certificate
- personal identification
- two photographs
- $10

We did hear in the summer of 1971 local passport offices were requiring young students to bring their parents with them to verify it was okay for the teen-ager to go overseas.

STUDENT IDENTITY CARD

Your own high school or college I.D. is okay—if it has a picture and birthdate on it—but still get the International Student Identity Card.

This will take care of you everywhere. *Don't leave America without it.* It will save you money and time and it only is one dollar. Write:

Council on International Exchange
777 United Nations Plaza
New York, New York 10017
(212) 661–0310

OR

Overseas Flights for Americans
1560 Broadway
New York, New York 10036
(212) 587–2080

WORLD HEALTH CARD

You need a World Health Card. This can be picked up from the U.S. Public Health Offices, most doctors also have them. We think you should take at least these shots:

Smallpox, Typhoid and Paratyphoid, Tetanus, Poliomyelitis. If you're going beyond Europe, you'll need more. Allow at least three months for all shots.

GUIDE BOOKS

Let's Go: Europe published by the Harvard Student Agencies and distributed by E. P. Dutton. Fifty thousand copies were printed for 1972. They sell out every year. *Europe on $5 a Day* by Arthur Frommer. It's ideal because you can tear the book apart, throw away the countries you've seen or aren't interested in. Best for restaurants and hotels. *The Hitchhiker's Guide to Europe* by Ken Welsh, published in England. Besides hitchhiking it's good for cheap hotels and restaurants.

You might also want to get the Council on International Educational Exchange (C.I.E.E.) "Survival Kit." It has lists of intra-Europe flights among many other items. The C.I.E.E. people are the best in the field and you should consult them if you want to study, live, work or travel overseas. Good folk!

PACKING

For traveling use just a pack. Take a few pieces of clothes and nothing much more. Sandy Goldsmith, a friend of ours touring Europe in the summer of 1971 found, however, she was wearing everything from T-shirts to sweaters to raincoats, the weather varies if you're moving around. If you're planning on spending a summer traveling, then settle down, drop your luggage someplace and travel with a day-pack. We're down on knapsacks. They're awkward, heavy, stereotyped and can only be carried one way. We suggest something like a Sling-Pak made by Atlantic Products, Trenton, New Jersey. They have a Knap-Pak that sells for twenty-five dollars and carries four ways. This lets you take it into the hotel like a suitcase. Sleeping bag, yes, we guess you'll need one. Hotel rooms in summers aren't going to be easily found.

OVERSEAS FLIGHTS

Expect to pay between $195 and $225 for a round-trip ticket between New York and London. If you join with a group from school or some charter you will do slightly better. Icelandic gives the cheapest rate, takes the longest. Shop around. Try to travel to Europe off season for you want to save as much as you can flying overseas: it's your one single big expenditure. You don't want any flight/tour combination. This limits your movement, doesn't take into consideration whimsical ventures. One problem with charters: you return when the plane leaves, not before or after.

Try and fly to Europe on non-American or non-European lines. Air India is always less crowded, likes to get the business. In Europe fly Ethiopian Airlines, or Middle-East. They are always empty. We particularly recommend Ethiopian Airlines, think it's the best in the world.

FREIGHTERS

Only a few available, but if you've got the time, go this way. Freighters take ten to twelve people and it's first-class travel. Figure on twelve days crossing. For information write either of these publishers for books. About the only information available.

Harian Publications
Greenlawn, New York 11740

Ford's Freighter Travel
Box 505
Woodland Hills, Calif. 91364

TRAVELING IN EUROPE

Well, there are planes. You can obtain flight schedules from C.I.E.E. but the trouble with student flights is dealing with student offices. They're crowded and understaffed, often mismanaged. More than one person we know has arrived in Europe ready to pick up a ticket and nothing had been arranged. These offices also serve as a clearinghouse for other information. *i.e.,* people selling tickets, wanting riders, hotel rooms, etc., but the lines stretch around the block.

We like the *student railpass.* It's good for western Europe and a two-month ticket is about $125. These tickets are not sold in Europe, therefore you have to decide before leaving if this is the way you want to travel. Sandy Goldsmith writes: "I had a railpass which in some ways is very good—makes you feel free to go wherever you feel like since it's prepaid; saves waiting in lines to buy tickets, etc. But unless you move around a lot, I doubt it is actually a financial savings." We agree.

Railways in Europe aren't like U.S. ones. They're clean and they work. Most of Europe travels by rail. It's an excellent way to be tossed into another culture. Travel second class. Only American tourists and rich Europeans travel first class. The railway stations are noisy, vibrant places, actually small cities under a ceiling. In Catholic countries you can go to Mass there. All stations have English-speaking guides.

Buy bread, wine, some cheese, maybe a couple of bottles of beer for the trip. (Then you can say you did it!) If traveling with friends send a scout ahead to find a compartment. It's too difficult to search for a seat and carry luggage. The competition is fearsome. Europeans are expert. Especially Italian women over fifty.

Traveling by train you see the country in a leisurely, relaxed way and going by night saves hotel money. But night trips in full compartments wipe one out. One trick Coyne used in East Africa and Europe was to clear the luggage off the overhead rack and stretch out. You can sleep that way. It works, really. A friend of ours writing from Europe had another suggestion. "You can get a couchette for a buck more so you can lie down; otherwise you'll arrive as exhausted as if you had hitched. Just buying a train ticket doesn't guarantee you a seat and its usual to spend a six hour ride in the aisle. Between Savona and Pisa I commandeered a toilet and spent the trip in there."

The pleasure of second-class train travel is sharing meals with strangers you meet. Everyone takes out their provisions, spreads the food on top of overturned suitcases, cuts up the cheese, passes the wines and chunks of black bread. Food never tastes better than this way.

To obtain a student railpass write one of the offices of European railways in the United States. A few addresses:

Scandinavian Railways
630 Fifth Avenue
New York, New York 10020
(212) 757–0146

French National Railways
323 Geary Street
San Francisco, California 94102
(415) 982–1993

Italian Railways
333 N. Michigan Avenue
Chicago, Illinois 60601
(312) 332–5334

HOTEL HUNTING

Another advantage of railway travel is that trains take you into the center of town, near the old and cheap pensions. Here's how to search for a room: store your bags at the railway station or if you're traveling with someone leave a person behind. Pensions are within walking distance, a block or two. Get a room early in the day, before nine o'clock. They get up early in Europe. Forget youth hotels, YMCAs and YWCAs. They have rules and regulations and in most places you have to be inside by ten or eleven. But writes Sandy Goldsmith: "We stayed mostly in youth-hostels and student hotels; I was pleasantly surprised by them—very adequate places and it was nice to have other kids (a lot of Americans) to talk to, go places with. I go to bed early, though, so the curfew didn't bother me. We stayed in a couple of small hotels/pensions; it was a nice change to have ones own room and be able to come back to rest in the afternoon. Hostels often close during the day." As we said, stay away from hostels, even if you go to bed early.

CAMPING

Europe is better equipped and more enthusiastic about camping than Americans. Camps sites are located outside of almost all major cities, near resort locations, just about everywhere. They're well equipped, most have water, supplies, electrical outlets. For information get hold of *Europa-Camping and Caravaning*. It costs about four dollars. Write:

Campgrounds Unlimited
Blue Rapids, Kansas 66411

CARS

The best place in Europe to buy a used car or van is Dam Square, Amsterdam. Folk are always arriving here broke and need to sell their vehicle cheap to make it back to the United States. Renting cars is a hassle. You have to be at least twenty-three, sometimes twenty-five. We know of one organization called Car-Tours in Europe that rents to students, but you have to buy coupons for rooms—usually at universities—but if there's three or four traveling together this is an inexpensive and comfortable way to tour. Write:

Car-Tours In Europe, Inc.
555 Fifth Avenue
New York, New York 10017

If you're staying in Europe for the year try and buy a car. It will be cheaper for you in the long run.

HITCHHIKING

Roads are overcrowded with young people hitching, or *autostopping* as they call it. Hitching is accepted everywhere. Students eat and sleep in hostels when they're on the road, or outside if the weather permits. Expect to cover 200 miles a day. It depends on what part of Europe. Holland is easy, northern Germany and Denmark difficult, southern Germany good. France is either exceptionally bad or very good. Italy is better and Belgium is terrible. Spain and Portugal poor. Britain okay, Ireland excellent.

Follow the same practices you use in the United States. Get a sign, get outside of town (local bus will handle this), leave early in the day and make yourself interesting looking there on the side of the road, someone worth picking up. Women should double up. Pick someone on the plane overseas, travel with him.

DRUGS

You might be interested in some of the penalties for dealing in drugs overseas.

France	1 to 5 years
Spain	up to 6 years
Italy	3 to 8 years
Sweden	1 to 2 years
Greece	5 to 20 years
Lebanon	3 to 15 years
Turkey	10 years to life

We have this letter from a student at Old Westbury College about the attitude of some young Americans going to Europe and smoking dope. Here's part of it:

> *. . . By pure coincidence, there were a total of eight Old Westbury students, including myself, on the Icelandic flight. . . . As you probably can imagine the scene on the plane was Old Westbury all over again. At one point, we all sat on the floor in a group speaking of the good old days at old Old Westbury and, of course, passing a joint around to the consternation of the stewardess and the envy of the other young passengers who were doubtless wishing that their plans were so far-fetched as ours—little did they know! The general effect of that scene on the plane—upon reflection—is rather depressing. We all felt a childlike satisfaction in being able to smoke the illegal weed and with an audience present to multiply our self-satisfaction. The dream of a peasant revolution seemed realizable and the unmentioned group recognition of this idea reinforced naïveté as a potentially viable life style. Of course, at heart these dreams are quite immature. We all know that if there was any problem with the authorities we could cry home to our parents, call our lawyers and return to Old Westbury and the society that idolizes the young.*

It wouldn't have been that easy for this person or anyone dealing with drugs, regardless of the school you're attending or your parents' position. Sure, folk in the parks in Amsterdam, in downtown Dam Square, on the island of Amager or in Tivoli, on both banks of the Seine, in Nice, everywhere overseas are smoking dope, but if they get busted they're going to jail and the American Embassy isn't able to get them out. In Iran, by the way, it's death for pushing. Expect to be searched on the borders, in airports, going through customs, anyplace there's a crowd of young people. Good luck!

MONEY

Everyone runs out of money in Europe so plan ahead. Make up a budget control sheet to keep track of how and where you're spending your money, something like this one.

• Put your money in travel checks—and do those complicated things about recording the numbers. Get your checks in small bills—tens and twenties—checks can be cashed everywhere, often at a better exchange rate than "green."

• Buy a roundtrip airlines ticket. You can at least get home again. This is important.

• Hide away (even from yourself) a ten dollar bill. Put it in your wallet and forget it. Don't spend it until you get to the airport going

BUDGET CONTROL

AMOUNT BUDGETED _____

TOTAL SPENT _____

SURPLUS (DEFICIT) _____

Date	Currency	This Item	Spent to Date	Date	Currency	This Item	Spent to Date

home. You'll need at least two dollars for the airport departure tax, the other eight you can spend at the duty-free shop.

• Try and obtain an American Express card. You'll have to get it through your parents, unless you happen to be independently wealthy. An American Express card solves money problems. You can write a check overseas up to five hundred dollars (but make sure you bring your checkbook).

• Hint around for a farewell gift of a passport case. (Or buy one yourself.) Ideal for carrying traveler's checks, passport, I.D., and large enough for foreign currency, which in some countries comes in bills the size of wallpaper.

• If you're staying in one place and studying, open a bank account. This takes about two months to do and your local bank at home can help you. Most universities, for example, won't take American checks, therefore, you'll have to pay cash or have an account. Do this only if you're staying an academic year. Too much trouble otherwise.

• Some countries—Luxembourg for one—will want to know how much money you have to travel on. Therefore, you'll show something. In cash or traveler's checks you are usually required to have five hundred dollars or a roundtrip ticket out of the country. We expect that European countries are going to get tighter on this regulation.

JOBS

Next to impossible. We know one organization that lines up work for you overseas. But since in Europe you're paid less than in the U.S., you get the feeling you're working for nothing. Write:

Eurojob
102 Greenwich Avenue
Greenwich, Connecticut 06830

The Council on International Educational Exchange also publishes a useful booklet on job opportunities. Write them. Women might consider *au pair* for France. You live with a French family, taking care of the children. Room and board is provided and about fifty dollars a month for pocket money. Have to stay six months. Write:

Accueil Familial des Jeunes Étrangers
23, rue du Cherche-Midi
Paris 6, France

They'll want references, preferably in French.

EATING OUT

The two guidebooks we recommend will help, but here are a few general rules.

- Never eat at a place with tablecloths
- Never eat at those sidewalk cafes
- Skip breakfast
- Buy food in the market or grocery stores, eat in the park
- Once a month (at least) treat yourself to a fine meal in a fine restaurant
- Leave a tip wherever you eat. It won't be expected and everyone will be pleased.

AVOID THE CITIES

Unless you're in Europe just to meet other Americans or you really like seeing the sites, avoid the cities. In 1970 Amsterdam was the capital of the youth trade, in 1971 it was Copenhagen. And every year young people flock to the Spanish steps (because the American Express Office is next door) or to Haymarket (again American Express) or Trafalgar Square, but if you're interested in seeing Europe head for the provinces, travel inland, go to eastern Europe, the islands, North Africa, the west coast of Ireland. You'll have a better time, meet more people. And some of them won't even be Americans.

COMING HOME

Don't bring dope into the United States. If you have long hair, a pack, are under thirty, customs will stop and search your luggage, maybe you. Male or female. It doesn't matter. Fly home on a weekday, avoid the weekends. If you can, try also to avoid New York Kennedy Airport. Land at Dulles. No one ever uses that airport! O'Hare's not bad. But nevertheless you can't avoid the crowds. After a month, a summer or perhaps a year overseas, you may be wondering why your foreign language studies in high school or college weren't better done, made more interesting, and you might be wondering why you weren't trained in cross-cultural communication so you could have encountered Europeans and European society on their terms.

We end with another quote so you can begin training yourself for your next trip overseas. It's from an excellent book by Roger Harrison and Richard L. Hopkins called: *The Design of Cross-Cultural Training: An Alternative to the University Model,* it goes:

COMMUNICATION: *To understand and communicate directly and often non-verbally through movement, facial expression, person-to-person actions. To listen with sensitivity to the hidden concerns, values, motives of the other. To be at home in the exchange of feelings, attitudes, desires, fears. To have a sympathetic empathic understanding of the feelings of the other.*

That's what it's all about, at home or overseas.

2. Studying in the Western World

AUSTRALIA

There are fifteen universities in Australia—five in New South Wales, three in Victoria, two in South Australia, two in Queensland, one each in Tasmania and Western Australia and one in the Australian Capital Territory (Canberra). The universities in Australia have been established by governments. The older universities were established by colonial governments when the states were separate colonies and the more recently established ones have been set up by state governments or by the Commonwealth government. They are all autonomous and secular and most are modeled on the lines of the Scottish and English provincial universities which were established during the nineteenth century.

Tuitions vary widely from one university to another and from one faculty to another. The range is $200 to $650 (American dollars) per year. Room and board will cost about $18 per week. Except for the University of New England, where half of the students live in residential halls, accommodation on campus is limited. About 15 percent of the students live in residential halls. At some universities there is an International House, which handles overseas students.

Students wishing to enroll should get in touch with the Australian Embassy before applying to the university. There is a quota for overseas students and the competition is stiff for some universities. General qualifications can be made by anyone having completed two years of college in the United States. Education here will be traditional. Little innovative programs are being tried. Australia has no special arrangement for students who wish to study only a year in their country.

Some quick facts about Australia: it is about the size of the United

States, English-speaking, and has a population of 12,371,600. The continent has a sunny equable climate ranging from tropical in the north to cool temperate in the south. The countryside is flat or rolling, and the mountain ranges are in the east.

USEFUL ADDRESSES:
Australian Embassy
1601 Massachusetts Avenue N.W.
Washington, D.C. 20036
(202) 797–3167

The Registrar
University of Adelaide
Adelaide, South Australia, Australia 5000

The Registrar
Australian National University
Box 4, Post Office,
Canberra, A.C.T., Australia 2600

The Registrar
Flinders University of South Australia
Bedford Park, South Australia, Australia 5042

The Registrar
La Trobe University
Bundoora, Victoria, Australia 3083

The Registrar
Macquarie University
North Ryde, N.S.W., Australia 2113

The Registrar
University of Melbourne
Parkville, Victoria, Australia 3052

The Academic Registrar
Monash University
Clayton, Victoria, Australia 3168

The Registrar
University of New England
Armidale, N.S.W., Australia 2351

The Registrar
University of New South Wales
P.O. Box 1,
Kensington, N.S.W., Australia 2033

The Secretary
University of Newcastle
New South Wales, Australia 2308

The Registrar
University of Papua & New Guinea
Box 1144, Post Office,
Boroko, T.P.N.G.

The Registrar
University of Queensland
St. Lucia, Queensland, Australia 4067

The Registrar
University of Sydney
Sydney, N.S.W., Australia 2006

The Registrar
University of Tasmania
Box 252C, G.P.O.,
Hobart, Tasmania, Australia 7001

The Registrar
James Cook University of North Queensland
P.O. Box 999,
Townsville, Queensland, Australia 4810

The Registrar
University of Western Australia
Nedlands, Western Australia, Australia 6009

AUSTRIA

There are sixteen institutions of higher learning in Austria. We have listed the ones that we think are most relevant for American students.

University of Graz
(Karl-Franzens Universität)

University of Innsbruck
(Leopold-Franzens Universität)

University of Salzburg
(Paris Lodron Universität)

University of Vienna
(Universität Wien)

Institute for Social and Economic Sciences
(Hochschule fur Sozial-und Wirtschaftswissenschaften)

Academy of Music and Dramatic Art
(Akademie fur Musik und Darstellende Kunst)

Academy of Fine Arts
(Akademie der Bildenden Kunste)

At least two years of undergraduate work in an American college or university are required. Students apply by writing the Rector of the school they want to enter. American students can enroll either as regular or special students. The Rector will want to know what you plan on studying and something about your academic background. Mail him a curriculum vitae, transcripts, copies of any degrees, proof of citizenship and some proof of an adequate knowledge of German. (One of your professors should be able to supply this.) Make sure you enclose international reply coupons; it speeds reply.

The academic year is from October to July, two semesters. Tuition varies, but never more than ninety dollars per semester. Austrian universities do not have dormitories. Students find places in nearby hotels, boardinghouses or with families. The Austrian Foreign Students Service helps in finding lodging. Plan on spending about two hundred dollars a month for room, board and extra. For further help on housing accommodations, write:

Oesterreichische Auslandsstudentendienst
Fuehrichgasse 10
Vienna 1

The only degree offered by Austrian universities is the doctorate. Soon Austrian schools will be offering the M.A. degree and diploma for those planning on teaching, but an American student can plan on anywhere from three to six years before obtaining a doctorate. Therefore, most students plan on spending only one year overseas studying, or enrolling in one of many American programs operating in Austria. They are:

ADDRESS	COST	GRADE AVERAGE
BREGENZ *Wagner College* *Staten Island, New York 10301*	$3,000	C+
INNSBRUCK *Foreign Study Program* *Notre Dame University* *Notre Dame, Indiana 46556*	$3,000	C+ (for sophomores)
SALZBURG *Overseas Travel* *HRCB, 202* *Brigham Young University* *Provo, Utah 84601*	$1,399 (one semester)	C

VIENNA *Department of German* *University of Southern California* *Los Angeles, California 90007*	$2,700	B
Foreign Study Programs *Temple Buell College* *Denver, Colorado 80220*	$3,800	C+
Central College *European Studies* *Pella, Iowa 50219*	$2,300	B
Institute of European Studies *35 East Wacker Drive* *Chicago, Illinois 60601*	$2,800	C+
Vienna Program *University of Puget Sound* *Tacoma, Washington 98416*	$2,300	C+

USEFUL ADDRESSES
Austrian Institute
11 East 52nd Street
New York, New York 10022

Austrian Embassy
2343 Massachusetts Ave. N.W.
Washington, D.C. 20008

Austrian Information Service
31 East 69th Street
New York, New York 10021

BELGIUM

Higher education in Belgium is based on the traditional education pattern of western Europe—Americans need at least two years of college. It is a country that prepares specialists, *i.e.*, lawyers, doctors, teachers, engineers, scientists, etc. Nothing here for the A.B. Generalist.

Students apply by writing the individual university. There are no application forms, everyone is accepted on individual merit. Belgium has four universities: University of Brussels, in Brussels (French); State University of Liege, in Liege (French); Catholic University of Louvain, in Louvain (French and Dutch); University of Ghent, in Ghent (Dutch).

All the universities are practically identical. Each comprises five or six basic schools or departments (faculties) : Humanities (called Philosophy and Letters) ; Law, Political Science; Social Science; Economics; Medicine; Science and Engineering. The University of Louvain also has a School of Theology and Canon Law. Over sixty thousand students attend universities and other institutions of higher learning; about 10 percent are from other countries.

The four major universities offer language courses for foreign students. Write them:

Université libre de Bruxelles
avenue Franklin Roosevelt 50
1050 Bruxelles

Katholieke Universiteit te Leuven
Krakenstraat 4
3000 Leuven

Université de l'Etat à Liège
place du XX Août
4000 Liège

Rijksuniversiteit te Gent
St-Pietersnieuwstraat 25
9000 Gent

Drew University in Madison, New Jersey, has a spring semester in Brussels at the Free University. It is in English and costs about two thousand dollars for everything. It is a semester program for economics majors concerned with the Common Market. Write:

The Brussels Semester
Drew University
Madison, New Jersey 07940

The academic year runs from October 1 to the end of June. Tuition varies, but under one hundred dollars for the year. Living in Belgium is expensive, like the United States.

It takes a bit of work to obtain a Belgian visa. Besides the passport, students need two passport pictures, a letter from the Belgian university allowing the applicant to register, a certificate of health, a notarized declaration signed by the applicant's parents guaranteeing payment of expenses and several other forms filled out and signed. Allow some time for all this processing. Needless to say, you'll need to know either French or Dutch.

USEFUL ADDRESSES

Belgian Government Information Center
50 Rockefeller Plaza
New York, New York 10020
(212) 586–5110

Fédération des Centres Étudiants Étrangers
rue de la Prévoyance 60
1000 Bruxelles

Belgian-American Educational Foundation
420 Lexington Avenue
New York, New York 10017
(212) MU 3–1496

Belgian Embassy
3330 Garfield St. N.W.
Washington, D.C. 20008
(202) FE 3–6900

DENMARK

NORDEN-FJORD WORLD UNIVERSITY. Norden-Fjord World University is an association of small educational centers in northern Denmark. It is the most experimental, open and self-directed "college" in the world. How's that? There are five centers for the university, the oldest and most famous being New Experimental College.

New Experimental College is ten years old and was founded by Aage Rosendal Nielsen, a leading voice in world experimental education. "We thought it would be easy and fun," he writes, "to be in charge of our own studies and to live our lives together. I found it was difficult and practically impossible. When I still go on with my work at NEC, it is partly because I am caught in the establishment of it, and partly because I have not yet completely given up the hope that I can learn to understand and get along with every person I meet."

Aage and his wife Sara are powerful and dynamic people. They are the strength and direction behind New Experimental College. Many of Aage's educational dreams are outlined in his book *Lust for Learning*, which is mainly about NEC. He does sum up the college in a paragraph of a brief pamphlet about the school:

> *When everything is said about our aims and our ideals, and where we are today, each individual at New Experimental College is his own time and money. This means that each person who comes here, students and teachers alike, makes his own way and pays for it. So, your time here is yours. You*

can spend most of it on your own work and study, and with the help of the Ting, you can construct any educational policy or program which the Ting finds desirable. It IS expected that you will take part in kitchen and house-keeping duties on a cooperative basis, the plan of which can be worked out by the Ting.

The Ting is a community meeting where all problems are worked out, personal and academic. It is the governing form of all educational policies at NEC. People do not vote, but "pursue the issue until it is unanimously resolved." The success of the Ting (and New Experimental College) depends on the people at the school. For people come and go at NEC. A friend of ours who spent a year at NEC wrote us a long letter about the place. It's reprinted here in part.

Dear Tom and John,   *7–7–71*

 I don't know where to begin, but let me say first you can study photography, film, ecology, weaving, philosophy. You can study almost anything. There are various centers and many people to work with on independent study projects that you want to do. There are always people here ready to help you when you need it and ask for it. Those people teaching are usually good because they are only teaching if there is a demand for it. . . .

 NEC is an idea constantly being re-defined by each of the persons who live here. You will find your presence here makes a difference. You decide how you spend your time. Other people try and help you. You are expected to help everyone else who is here and if someone does not make it, you will be blamed for it. You will find people who are seemingly no good. You will find your own situation intensified. You will find how you learn and how you don't. Why you do and why you don't. You pay for your time and facilities.

 The country is beautiful and you adjust to the weather. The weather is constantly changing. But you'll need a raincoat, warm clothing in winter, and a towel and washcloth. Everyone dresses loose at the school, but have one nice thing or suit for events. . . .

 We live in a great old barn and everyone has a single room. There's plenty of space. The college is expensive: $1,192 for two 16-week semesters. The summer school is 8-weeks long and costs $626, I think. Write Aage about this. Living is fairly cheap, but cigarettes are thigh. A buck for twenty and booze is out-of-sight. Lots of dope, though, No problem. (Yet!)

 Tell Marcia I think she should come. Good luck on the book. I think it's a great idea. I miss you both.

              Peace & Love,
              Debbie

Everyone is not as happy about NEC as Debbie. We had another letter from a student from Goddard who spent a term in Denmark at New Experimental College and then Højskole, a Danish Folkehøjskole, and part of the World University.

For me NEC was not a supportive community. It was not stimulating or rather conducive to a learning environment as in the context of a college but as just a community existing for no other purpose than to be—it was very much alive. Learning took many varieties or forms—from talking, talking feelings with someone, to watching cows to loving and caring for each other.

Seven hundred people have been to New Experimental College over the last ten years, Nielsen publishes a list of names and we wrote many of the people who had recently been at NEC. Everyone of them had a *reaction* to the college and all felt that if a person had a purpose for going, it could be worthwhile and successful. Writes a student who returned in the spring of 1971.

Living at NEC was a good experience. There were about 20 people living under one roof—old and young—mostly Americans, some Danes, even an Arab. It was a very intensive living experience. Aage set it up with the idea that all people should be able to live together without conflict. Well, this didn't seem to be the case. One had to have pretty good nerves to be together 90% of the time with people you didn't know and maybe didn't want to know either. Besides this, there was no preconceived ideas or meanings to our life together at NEC other than living and being together. Actually some people were doing projects of sorts—one woman was writing a book, another woman came to live for a week to see if it was the type of community that would satisfy her and her two children. Probably most of the people were there to find themselves in a group such as at NEC.

We have been recommending it to students who would like to do one semester or a year of independent study overseas. New Experimental College and the other centers offer ample opportunity for work in the arts and crafts.

Now something about the other centers.

PRAESTEGAARD. This center is set up to study, research and create films and still photography. It's run by David Nelson who writes, "Ours is a conscious attempt to re-discover and effectively work with those ideas and concepts which are the sources of creativity. Ideas and concepts which were discovered by the early Greek civilization but have simply been forgotten."

Praestegaard has no prerequisites for admissions, beyond a serious commitment to the development of photographic concepts. It is housed in the thatched-roof parsonage of the Kettrup Church, both living and working facilities. The fee for each semester is $1,150. That covers room, board and tuition. Fall semester begins September 9 and spring semester February 12. There is also a summer program of eight weeks starting on

July 1. Alan Clark a student at Praestegaard writes: "The photographic motif and the cinematic medium are our tools, human perspective the vehicle and the individual the grounds for the work done here. I would like to spread the excitement we feel in the success and failure of our ideas and work with others, students and teachers, who are interested and want to communicate what they have learned."

Students working in still photography are required to have an adjustable speed/f-stop camera in a format larger than 35 mm. Two and one half by two and one fourth formats are acceptable, a view camera is strongly recommended. Students working in cinema are required to have an adjustable speed/f-stop 8 mm or super 8 mm camera. Other materials can be purchased at the school.

ASGARD. Asgard is the center for art, handcrafts and living. It is really an experiment in living and learning. Facilities are available for work in fine arts, ceramics, textiles, wood, plastics and metals. There is also equipment for the study of sound techniques and photography. Asgard means the home of the Nordic gods and is located on twenty-five acres of farmland in the town of Ydby in Northwest Jutland.

Approximately twenty students live together in indoor mobile rooms. The rooms can be placed together in any arrangement for a communal feeling or separated. Students paint and decorate their rooms to suit themselves. There is also space for living and working, studios, lounges, and bathrooms which include saunas. There are also kitchen facilities to accommodate macrobiotic, vegetarian and carnivorous diets.

The cost for a semester is eight hundred dollars. This includes room, board, tuition and use of equipment. The equipment available is:

Ceramics: all basic tools, wheels and kiln.

Textiles: weaving looms of various types, batiking, tie dying, leather craft, clothing construction, printing and rug hooking.

Wood: basic tools, power saw, lathe. Everything from woodcuts and candle holders to furniture and house construction is possible.

Plastics: polyester and fiber glass construction for furniture, boat making, etc., as well as plexiglass sculpture.

Metals: basic tools for jewelry, copper enameling, metal sculpture and welding.

Anyone over eighteen is eligible for admission to Asgard. There are three semesters, fall, spring and summer. Apply early for space is limited.

NORDENFJORD HØJSKOLE. Nordenfjord Peoples College is "a center for human development and for the development of humanness." It's located in a renovated farm in Thy, northern Denmark. It's a working farm with thirty acres of land and livestock.

Each semester begins with an intense experiential period for the purpose of each person becoming involved in a freeing process. This takes place through activities, partly spontaneous, partly from work and seminars. Everyone lives and studies together, teaches one another and designs their own curriculum. The main language is English. Fees for 1972 and $1,192 for sixteen-week spring and fall semesters. This covers almost everything.

EARTHGAARD. The center for ecology and world systems coordination. Terry Harlow, the Director, writes about Earthgaard; "Institutionally we provide a 'free' environment in which students decide upon independent and group projects which they would like to work on. Staff of the school retain the position of advisors and resource coordinators. We like to see leaders develop from the group, instead of being imposed by the administration. A proportionate amount of each student's tuition is deposited in an account which is managed by the group. Investment and returns are divided equally among participants at the end of each semester." Earthgaard puts out a magazine, *Physiognomy* which is about Norden-Fjord World University. Fees are approximately the same as at the other centers.

THE WRITING FARM. Writes the Writing Farm: "There are a handful of Americans and one Englishwoman who live together in Jylland, in a small community center for writing and the study of literature. Each of them writes, or has written something to their own taste, in their own hand, and at their own speed. Writing Farm operates under the concept (And the concept is a result of their being together) that there are benefits in living and working together as writers, as students of literature, and as people."

The Writing Farm is also involved with crafts, music, drawing and acting. People staying at Writing Farm receive a private room, food prepared communally, companionship and solitude. Everyone is allowed to use time as they choose. "Anyone can give a class, but no one has to attend." The cost for room and board is $150 a month and everyone is asked to stay at least two months.

ADDRESSES FOR NORDEN-FJORD WORLD UNIVERSITY:
New Experimental College
Skyum Bjerge
7752 Snedsted
Thy, Denmark

Earthgaard
Box 12
9690-Fjerritslev
Denmark

The Writing Farm
Svankjaergard
Svankjaer
7755 Bedsted
Thy, Denmark

Asgard
Ydby
7760 Hurup
Thy, Denmark

Nordenfjord Højskole
Gaerup
7752 Snedsted
Thy, Denmark

You can reach Norden-Fjord by flying to Thisted airport. If arriving by train from Copenhagen get off at the station in Snedsted, coming from Europe travel north from Hamburg toward Thisted, disembarking in Snedsted. From England, sail from Harwich to Esbjerg and take the train up to Snedsted. Call the college from the station: area code 07 93 51 11—telephone number (Koldby) 33. But let them know you're coming.

Norden-Fjord World University has five different centers, ranging in size from five to twenty members. You should be able to find something there for yourself.

THE INTERNATIONAL PEOPLE'S COLLEGE. Another excellent school in Denmark is the International People's College in Elsinore. It is a folk high school for adults, residential, with 120 students from twenty countries. The average age of students is twenty-three and applicants must be at least nineteen years old.

Every student plans his individual program with the help of a teacher. This teacher meets with all his students once a week in a seminar to discuss some reading or criticism. All students take part in three additional activities:

1) Bi-weekly lectures: given by outside speakers on subjects of current interest selected by a student committee.

2) The Manual Work: a tradition of the college. It consists of not more than one hour's work a day.

3) International Orientation: given by students and teachers.

A command of either Danish, Norwegian, Swedish or English is required, but no other formal academic qualification is needed. Students are asked to leave if their academic work does not satisfy the requirements of the teaching staff.

Courses fall into three general areas:

1) The Humanities: Religions, Philosophy, Literature, Art and Music;

2) Social and Economic Studies: ranges from Political Theory to News of the Week;

3) Linguistic Studies: The European languages and Esperanto.

There are no examinations or prescribed material to cover. Students decide where the courses will go. Students are not accepted for less than one term, and each term is self-contained. Costs and starting times are:

October 1, 1972	6 and 9 months	Danish kroner 2.430 = U.S. $324.00	
January 1, 1973	6 months	" " 2.430 = U.S. $324.00	
April 20, 1973	3 months	" " 2.130 = U.S. $285.00	

All prices include boarding, lodging and tuition. For further information, write:

The International People's College
3000 Elsinore – Denmark
Principal B. Mølgaard Madsen

HESBJERG PEACE RESEARCH COLLEGE. The general idea of a science of peace started after the World War II and Hesbjerg, among others, is experimenting with the application of this new knowledge in schools. They are currently building a Pentagon of Peace in Fyn. The college has about one hundred students, at least twenty years old, and offers courses in a wide range of subjects, some are: Peace and Conflict Theories; Game Theory; Peace and Revolutionary Movements; Developing Countries; Danish; Education; Ancient Civilizations; Oriental Languages; Psychology.

Fees are two hundred dollars a month for tuition, board, lodging and it is possible to arrange a work-camp payment to reduce costs. Three-month terms start on October 1, January 6 and in the middle of April.

For additional information, write:

Hesbjerg Peace Research College
DK–5573 Holmstrup
Denmark
Principal Jørgen Laursen Vig

It is becoming difficult to obtain study visas after you are inside Denmark. Therefore, apply at the Danish Embassy or Consulate before entering the country, if you plan on staying more than three months.

There are only two other long-term courses available to English-speaking students. Scandinavian Seminar, which is discussed elsewhere in the book, and The Danish International Student Committee organized by Dean W. Newson, Whittier College, Whittier, California and Arthur Engelebert, Washburn University of Topeka, Kansas.

USEFUL ADDRESSES
Danish National Tourist Office
Scandinavia House
505 Fifth Avenue
New York, New York 10017
(212) 687–5609

Danish Information Office
280 Park Avenue
New York, New York 10017
(212) 697–5107

FRANCE

We had a long letter from a friend at the Centre Universitaire Méditerranéen, Université de Nice and have reprinted it.

Dear John & Tom,   *May, I think, 1971*
Came back from classes and found your letter. I'm off to Monaco this afternoon, so let me pull out the Smith-Corona and type you some thoughts. Use them as you want. What to tell undergraduates about Nice? It's hard to know what someone would want to know about France, especially after a year here. I can't remember what I wanted to know when I came. In fact, I can't remember what I was like when I arrived here! I use to think in English, now I think in French. That's a major change.
I'll begin with some facts. Centre Universitaire Méditerranéen (CUM) costs $50 a semester. A room in the dorm runs about $35 a month and meals at the university around $6.50 a week. I live off campus with a Swedish girl I met since you were here, John. We have a furnished place with a view of the Bay of Angels for sixty a month. Got it through C.R.O.U.S. (18 Ave des Fleures). That's the local student rental agency. All French students use it. We eat here or at a place called Chez Jackys by the Port. A steak meal runs 90¢. All the students eat at Chez Jackys.
Students at CUM come from all over—Africa, Middle East, Asia. Everyone speaks French. Tell them they have to know French! But you know that, anyway. Most of our friends (and almost everyone else) tries to live outside of Nice. On the east it's Villefranche (where we live), Beaulieau, Mont Alban, Cap Ferrat and on the west Cagnes-Sur-Mer, Juan-les-Pins, Antibes. These are places about 15–25 minutes away by solex or mobylette (small motorized bikes that can be bought for $25 (used) and are cheap). Living

out here (away from the resorts and tourists) you get a feeling for the country. The provencal *people live out here.*

I have been lucky with two good French teachers. M. Joyeaux teaches an intro course and is the best prof at CUM. Great actor and unbelievably easy to understand. The course is completely in French. M. Joyeaux is good for the ego, builds up his students. Then Mme. Villain-Fullman. She's hard at first—written and oral expression in the course—but patient, kind and extremely helpful providing you want to learn the language.

Besides that I am studying the Philosophy of Modern France (not in capital letters) but an attempt at gaining an insight into French society—a look at its early thinkers: Rousseau, Descartes, DeTocqueville, etc. and some modern men: Camus, Sartre, Levi-Straus, Gide, etc. Read some history of France and have been traveling with Monica around the country, just talking to people. The French are, generally speaking, eager to talk, to discuss, to argue. Living in Nice is conducive to learning this way as it offers all the advantages of a large city, yet it is relatively quiet. It has a fine set of libraries (English ones too, rare in France) bookstores, museums, cultural events. What have you. The student population is large and aware (in a recent survey by the government the University of Nice was said to be the second most political campus in France, after the University of Paris.) All the quality of instruction is high. They tell me.

Books to read? Monica recommends Michelin Guide to France, *but she's got a thing for guidebooks, reads them like comics. I don't know, anything by Camus or Sartre, I'd say.*

What else? The academic year is November through mid-June and the address is: Centre Universitaire Méditerranéen, 65 Promenade des Anglais, 06 Nice, France. We're splitting here in a couple weeks, going to visit a friend in Menorca. Home sometime next fall. Hope this letter helps and finds you both.

Cheers,
Billy

P.S. *Forgot. There's about 175 Americans here now. It's too many as it is, tell your students to go someplace else. I don't want company.*

Going to school in France is easy to do, but looks complicated. The French are great believers in forms and procedures, but they are also very helpful. If you follow along now, step by step, it will make sense. This, however, is not a chapter of the book where you can skip around, you can do that with Third World countries, but not here . . . now by the numbers . . .

1) *Credits:* French universities operate on a yearly basis and award *diplomas.* There are three official government diplomas for foreign students: (1) Certificat Pratique de Langue Française (ler degré), (2) Diplôme d'Études Françaises (2eme degré) and (3) Diplôme Supérieur d'Études Françaises (3eme degré).

If you have two years of college and a very sound command of French, you can enroll in the regular French university courses. In both situations, the student has to arrange credit with his American college. It is not automatically transferred.

2) *Admissions:* If you're old enough—16 at some colleges—you will be accepted. It's as simple as that. The French government wants you to apply to only one program and university. They supply in their university publication the form to use. Cut it out, fill it out and get three International Reply Coupons (obtainable at any post office) and mail the letter off. Within two months you'll have heard.

3) *Visa:* A student staying in France longer than ninety days needs a student visa. This can be done in person or writing a French Consulate and even in France within three months of arriving. Best to do it before leaving the United States. Take your passport, two passport-size photographs, the letter of admissions from the French university, a notarized statement of financial guaranty (your parents or guardian can sign), $3.60, and fill out two visa application forms (available from the Consulate) and mail or take to the nearest French Consulate. The $3.60 should be paid by Postal Money Order and all forms are available from the French Cultural Services. Write:

Cultural Services of the French Embassy
972 Fifth Avenue
New York, New York

4) *Living Arrangements:* The Cultural Services also provides a form and you provide three postal coupons (and another passport picture) and mail it to the school that accepted you. Every university provides a *Service du Logement* that helps students find a place to stay. This works everywhere. In Paris rooms at the Cité Universitaire are reserved for graduate students. It is nearly impossible for an overseas student to obtain a room. Housing is hard to find in Paris, the Service du Logement in Paris can help, however. Elsewhere, you can find a room in a boarding house for $110 a month (full board) or a room as a paying guest with a French family for $100. An apartment (if available) costs from $25 to $50 depending on location.

Other living expenses are hard to gauge. The Cultural Services estimates $150 per month. Students aren't allowed to work, but women between eighteen and thirty can live and work *au pair* in a French family. She receives a room, board and a small allowance for exchange of daily baby-sitting or light housework. It's a unique opportunity to learn about another culture and family life, if you like kids.

5) *Universities:* Over twenty universities offer programs for American students. We've listed them briefly, with basic information. The selection is up to you.

AIX-EN-PROVENCE: *Old capital of Provence. A city for students interested in art and archaeology. Good skiing in the French Alps.*
> MINIMUM AGE: *18*
>> DATES: *End of October to the end of May*
>> FEES: *$60 a year*
>> COURSES: *Language, French history and literature*
>> ADDRESS: *Secrétariat de L'Institut d'études françaises*
>> *pour étudiants étrangers*
>> *23 Rue Gaston-de-Saporta, 13*
>> *Aix-en-Provence, France*

BESANÇON: *The Université de Besançon is a large city in the old Duchy of Franche-Comté.*
> MINIMUM AGE: *18*
>> DATES: *November 1 to June 15*
>> FEES: *$60 a year*
>> COURSES: *Language, French civilization (art, literature, history)*
>> ADDRESS: *Professeur Conseiller*
>> *Centre de Linguistique Appliquée*
>> *47 rue Mégevand*
>> *25 Besançon, France*

BORDEAUX: *A major port of France and the export center for Bordeaux wines.*
> MINIMUM AGE: *17*
>> DATES: *October to mid-June*
>> FEES: *$60 a year*
>> COURSES: *Audio-visual and audio-lingual courses in French*
>> ADDRESS: *Monsieur le Directeur du Centre*
>> *d'études françaises pour étudiants étrangers*
>> *Faculté des Lettres*
>> *Complexe Universitaire, 33*
>> *Talence, France*

CAEN: *On the river Orne, a few miles from the English Channel. The university was founded in 1432.*
> MINIMUM AGE: *18*
>> DATES: *October 1 to June 30*
>> FEES: *$80 per year*
>> COURSES: *Audio-visual language instruction. Students also allowed to attend classes at the Faculté des Lettres et Sciences Humaines*
>> ADDRESS: *Cours pour étudiants étrangers*
>> *Université de Caen, 14*
>> *Caen, France*

CLERMONT-FERRAND: *A tourist city, and the center of tire-making for France.*
   MINIMUM AGE: *18*
      DATES: *October 25 to May 20*
      FEES: *$20 a year*
   COURSES: *Language and French civilization*
   ADDRESS: *Cours pour étudiants étrangers*
         Faculté des Lettres, 29
         boulevard Gegovia, 63
         Clermont-Ferrand, France

DIJON: *A section famous for its art and monuments, its history, cuisine and wines.*
   MINIMUM AGE: *16*
      DATES: *October 26 to June 17*
      FEES: *$160 per year*
   COURSES: *Audio-visual language instruction and French literature and history*
   ADDRESS: *Centre International d'Études Françaises*
         Faculté des Lettres
         2 boulevard Gabriel, 21
         Dijon, France

GRENOBLE: *Principal city of the French Alps. Beautiful location.*
   MINIMUM AGE: *17*
      DATES: *October 15 to February 15* (first semester)
         February 15 to June 15 (second semester)
      FEES: *$140 per semester*
   COURSES: *Language and regular French courses in literature and French civilization*
   ADDRESS: *Comité de Patronage*
         Palais de l'Université
         place de Verdun
         B.P. 237–38
         Grenoble

LILLE: *An industrial center eighty-five miles north of Paris.*
   MINIMUM AGE: *18*
      DATES: *November 1 to June 30*
      FEES: *$35 a year*
   COURSES: *Language, history, economics, philosophy*
   ADDRESS: *Institut d'expansion universitaire,*
         Office des étudiants étrangers, 9
         rue Auguste-Angellier, 59
         Lille, France

LYON: *Second largest city in France in the valley of the river Rhône. One of the major cities of theatrical production in France.*
   MINIMUM AGE: *18*
      DATES: *November 3 to June 30*

FEES: *100 per year*

COURSES: *Language by audio-visual instruction, contemporary literature, history*

ADDRESS: *Secrétariat du Cours
aux étudiants étrangers
18 quai Claude-Bernard, 69
Lyon 7e, France*

MONTPELLIER: *In southern France, near the resort of Palavas-les-Flots, and the
Mediterranean.*

MINIMUM AGE: *18*

DATES: *November to end of June*

FEES: *$190 per year*

COURSES: *Wide offering of courses, language to demography*

ADDRESS: *Faculté des Lettres et Sciences Humaines
Secrétariat de l'Institut des Étudiants Étrangers
place de la Voie Dominitienne
34 Montpellier, France*

NANCY: *A quiet place, once the capital of the Duchy of Lorraine.*

MINIMUM AGE: *18*

DATES: *November to June 1*

FEES: *$50 per year*

COURSES: *Language, French civilization, history*

ADDRESS: *Cours permanents pour étudiants étrangers
Faculté des Lettres
23 boulevard Albert ler
54 Nancy, France*

NANTES: *A commercial port and an industrial city. Near the mouth of the Loire
river.*

MINIMUM AGE: *18*

DATES: *October to June*

FEES: *$30 per year*

COURSES: *Language, not much else*

ADDRESS: *Secrétariat de la Faculté
des Lettres et Sciences Humaines
Chemin de la Sensiva du Tertre
B.P. 1025
44 Nantes, France*

NICE: *On the Bay of Angels. A leading resort area.*

MINIMUM AGE: *18*

DATES: *November to mid-June*

FEES: *$50 a semester*

COURSES: *Language, French history and civilization*

ADDRESS: *Centre Universitaire Méditerranéen
65 Promenade Des Anglais
06 Nice, France*

PARIS: *You've seen the movies*

    Institut de Phonetique et de Recherches sur le Langage, Université de Paris

    MINIMUM AGE: *19 (need three years of college, fluent French)*
        DATES: *November 2 to June 5*
        FEES: *$40 per session*
      COURSES: *Theoretical and practical French Phonetics*
      ADDRESS: *Secrétariat de l'Institut de Phonétique*
           19, rue des Bernardins
           Paris 5e, France

    Alliance Française, École Internationale de Langue et de Civilisation françaises

    MINIMUM AGE: *19*
        DATES: *September 1 to June 30*
        FEES: *$14 a month*
      COURSES: *Language*
      ADDRESS: *Monsieur le Directeur*
           de l'École de l'Alliance Française
           101 boulevard Raspail
           Paris 6e, France

    Cours de Civilisation Française à la Sorbonne, Université de Paris

    MINIMUM AGE: *18*
        DATES: *October 15 to June 15*
        FEES: *From $70–$230, depending on course*
      COURSES: *Language, literature, art and history*
      ADDRESS: *Secrétariat des Cours de Civilisation Française*
           à la Sorbonne
           47 rue des Écoles
           Paris 5e, France

    Institut des Professeurs de Français à l'Étranger, Université de Paris III

    MINIMUM AGE: *19* (two years of college required)
        DATES: *November 1 to end of May*
        FEES: *$90 per semester*
      COURSES: *Geared for graduates and fluent speakers of French*
      ADDRESS: *Institut des Professeurs de français à l'étranger*
           46 rue Saint-Jacques
           Paris 5eme, France

RENNES: *A beautiful city of botanical gardens, museums and archaeology.*

    MINIMUM AGE: *17*
        DATES: *October 20 to May 25*
        FEES: *$37 per year*
      COURSES: *Language and literature* (contemporary literature)
      ADDRESS: *Secrétariat des Cours pour les Étrangers*
           Faculté des Lettres
           avenue Léon Bernard, 35,
           Rennes, France

ROUEN:

   MINIMUM AGE: *18*

      DATES: *November 1 to May 21*

       FEES: *$50 per year*

   COURSES: *French language and literature*

   ADDRESS: *Monsieur le Directeur*
              Cours pour Étrangers
              Université de Rouen
              Faculté des Lettres et Sciences Humaines
              rue Lavoisier
              76 Mont Saint-Aignan, France

ROYAN: *Located by the sea and capital of the Côte de Beauté, a modern city.*

   MINIMUM AGE: *18*

      DATES: *New program every six weeks*

       FEES: *Six-week course: $115*
            Four-week course: $80

   COURSES: *Intensive language using audio-visual methods, also German taught*

   ADDRESS: *Monsieur le Directeur du C.A.R.E.L.*
              Palais des Congrès
              17 Royan, France

STRASBOURG: *A medieval-looking city and a network of canals.*

   MINIMUM AGE: *18*

      DATES: *Mid-October to the mid-June*

       FEES: *$140 per year*

   COURSES: *Language*

   ADDRESS: *Monsieur le Directeur de l'Institut d'études françaises*
              Cours pour étrangers
              Université de Strasbourg
              Palais Universitaire, 67
              Strasbourg, France

TOULOUSE: *Very large city. Site of Basilica of Saint-Sernin.*

   MINIMUM AGE: *15*

      DATES: *November 1 to June 30*

       FEES: *$75 per year*

   COURSES: *Language*

   ADDRESS: *Centre Régional des Oeuvres Universitaires, 76*
              Monsieur le Directeur
              boulevard de Strasbourg, 31
              Toulouse 01, France

TOURS: *Near three hundred rivers, the center of chateaux country.*

   MINIMUM AGE: *16*

      DATES: *October 3 to June*

       FEES: *$26 per month*

COURSES: *Language, lecture courses in French civilization*
ADDRESS: *Monsieur Grenard*
Secrétaire Administratif de l'Institut de Touraine
1, rue de la Grandiere
37 Tours, France

C.R.O.U.S. The university service known as "Centre Regional des Oeuvres universitaires et scolaires" can be found at each university. It can give you information and advice on almost anything.

AMERICAN COLLEGES. Three American schools are operating in France; they are private institutions similar to a U.S. college. Addresses:

The American College in Paris
65 Quai d'Orsay
Paris 7e, France

American College of Monaco
Avenue de l'Hermitage
Monte-Carlo
Principauté de Monaco
or
1212 Lewis Tower Building
Philadelphia, Penn. 19103

Institute for American Universities
27, Place de l'Université
13 Aix-en-Provence, France

USEFUL ADDRESSES:
Services Culturels Français
972 Fifth Avenue
New York, New York 10021

Centre Régional des Oeuvres Universitaires
84 rue Mouffetard, Paris 5e

French Embassy
2129 Wyoming Avenue, N.W.
Washington, D.C. 20009

FINLAND

Finland has limited opportunities for American undergraduates. It does not seek them out as students. The best way to study in Finland is through Scandinavian Seminar (explained elsewhere in this book), but if you know the language, Finland has something to offer. They have seventeen universities—five new since 1967. All of them are small, except for the University of Helsinki. It takes three to four years to earn a bachelor's, the first degree. All degrees are earned through passing a series of examinations.

It is possible to study Finnish during the summer at the University of Tampere. The cost is about a hundred dollars. Write:

Finnish Ministry of Education
Korkeavuorenkatu 21
Helsinki 13, Finland

Otherwise, Finnish is needed everywhere. All the universities have faculties, *i.e.,* theology, law, philosophy, medicine, social sciences, and agriculture and forestry. The faculty of philosophy is divided into two divisions, humanities and science. Swedish-speaking students can study at Abo Akademi. It offers a wide selection of courses, including theology.

Finland has an active student service organization in Helsinki which provides flights from America and travel programs in Europe, as well as detailed information about Finland. Their address is:

Student Service
Kampinkatu 4 B
Helsinki 10, Finland

The main universities and enrollments are: Helsinki (29,543), Turku (8,203), Tampere (4,541), Lappeenranta (2,341), Jyvaskyla (2,589), Joensuu (1,200), Kuopio (2,100), Vaasa 3,000), Oulu (2,300). For additional information on visas (only required after three months) write:

Embassy of Finland
1900 24th St. N.W.
Washington, D.C. 20009
(202) HO 2–0556

GREAT BRITAIN

All universities in Britain accept overseas students but the number is small, and British universities want American students who have had one or two years' study at an American school. To avoid months of delay and disappointment, we suggest you apply as an "occasional student." This is for a one-year or two-year course in most of the universities. Apply directly to the university you want, they're listed below:

UNIVERSITIES	SUBJECT AREAS
ENGLAND	
Aston in Birmingham *Gosta Green* *Birmingham 4*	Engineering, Science, Social Science
University of Birmingham *P.O. 363* *Birmingham 15*	Arts, Commerce and Social Science, Law, Science and Engineering
University of Bradford *Bradford, 7*	All subjects
University of Bristol *Senate House* *Bristol 2*	Arts, Social Sciences
University of Durham *Old Shire Hall* *Durham*	All subjects
University of East Anglia *Earlham Hall* *Norwich*	Arts, Sciences, Social Studies
University of Exeter *Exeter*	Arts, Sciences, Social Studies, Law
University of Hull *Hull, Yorkshire*	Arts, Music, Theology, Pure and Applied Science, Social Sciences, Law
University of Keele *Staffordshire*	Arts, Social Sciences, Law, Natural Sciences (one year only)
University of Kent at Canterbury *Canterbury, York*	Humanities and Social Sciences
University of Lancaster *University House* *Bailrigg, Lancaster*	All subjects (they consider only exceptional cases)
University of Leeds *Leeds 2*	All subjects
University of Leicester *Leicester*	Arts, Science, Law, Social Sciences
University of Liverpool *Liverpool 3*	Arts, Science, Law, Engineering Science
University of London *Senate House* *London, W.C. 1*	Write Academic Department of university for list

University of Manchester *Manchester 13*	All subjects
University of Nottingham *University Park* *Nottingham*	Arts, Law, Social Sciences
University of Reading *Reading*	Arts, Social Sciences, Sciences
University of Sheffield *Sheffield 10*	Arts, Pure Science, Law, Social Sciences (except Psychology)
University of Southampton *Highfield, Southampton*	Arts, Engineering, Applied Sciences, Social Sciences, Law and Science
University of Sussex *Falmer, Brighton*	All subjects
University of Warwick *Coventry, Warwick*	All subjects
University of York *Heslington, York*	Arts, Social Sciences, Natural Sciences

WALES

University College of Wales *Aberystwyth*	Arts, Economics, Social Studies, Music, Law
University College of North Wales *Bangor*	Arts, Sciences, Oceanography, Divinity
University College of South Wales *Cardiff*	Arts, Economics, Social Studies, Science
University College of Swansea *Swansea*	Arts, Economics, Social Studies, Science
Institute of Science and Technology *Cathays Park, Cardiff*	All subjects (English postgraduates only)

SCOTLAND

University of Aberdeen *Aberdeen*	Arts, Divinity, Law
University of Dundee *Dundee*	Science, Engineering, Applied Sciences, Social Sciences
University of Edinburgh *Edinburgh*	Arts, Divinity, Music, Social Sciences, Science
University of Glasgow *Glasgow W.2*	Arts, Divinity, Engineering, Music, Science

University of St. Andrews *College Gate, St. Andrews*	Arts, Science, Divinity
University of Stirling *Stirling*	Arts, Science, Social Science
University of Strathclyde *George Street* *Glasgow, C.I.*	Applied Science, Arts, Social Sciences

NORTHERN IRELAND

The Queen's University of Belfast *Belfast 7*	Arts, Economics, Law, Sciences
New University of Ulster *Coleraine*	Physical Sciences, Biological and Environmental Studies, Social Sciences, Humanities, Education

You should begin applying at least a year in advance of enrolling. School begins in October. Tuition is $600 for the academic year, but figure on $2,600 for all living expenses. The universities have halls of residence and approved housing, usually just a room. For general information about admissions write:

Universities Central Council on Admissions
G.P.O. Box 28
Cheltenham, England

From the British Information Services you can obtain books and handbooks that will answer most of your questions. Some useful ones: *Higher Education in the United Kingdom: A Handbook for Students from Overseas. Which University.* Information on first-degree courses. Your college library (or local library) should have a copy of *Commonwealth Universities Yearbook.* It's a 3,000-page annual about United Kingdom universities.

A few American colleges and universities offer year programs, mostly in the arts and social sciences. They are:

ADDRESS	COST	GRADE AVERAGE
COVENTRY *Junior Year in England* *Valparaiso University* *Valparaiso, Indiana*	$3,100	C+

EAST ANGLIA *International Education* *University of Colorado* *Boulder, Colorado 80302*	$1,250 plus (Part transportation)	C+
LANCASTER *Beaver College* *Glenside, Pennsylvania 19038*	$3,350	C
International Education *University of Colorado* *Boulder, Colorado 80302*	$2,000 plus (Part transportation)	B
LONDON *Beaver College* *Glenside, Pennsylvania 19038*	$2,000	B
Drew University *Madison, New Jersey 07940*	$2,660	C+
Tufts in London *Tufts University* *Medford, Massachusetts 02155*	$3,500	B
WROXTON *Wroxton College Semester Abroad* *Fairleigh Dickinson University* *Rutherford, New Jersey 07070*	$1,500	C

USEFUL ADDRESSES
British Information Services
845 Third Avenue
New York, New York 10022
(212) 752–8400

National Union of Students
3 Endsleigh Street
London, England

GREECE

If Greece wasn't such a majestic country, and its people generous and friendly, we'd tell you to avoid it. The regime is repressive and militaristic, but then you've seen the movie Z. A friend from Athens writes:

A certain percentage of the professors are real bastards. They can fail you because your hair is too long and you can do nothing except repeat the course. One person I know has taken a Law course five times. Another friend has to shave his beard every time to go take an exam. The courses are all lectures, no seminars, no dialogue. There are no such things as term papers, quizzes, reports, debates, etc. The entire grade depends on the results of the final test. It takes between 4–6 years to get a diploma. Tuition is free and I pay about $37.00 a month rent and $2.00 a day for food. Although the people are warm, they don't like hippies and it is tough at times living in such a repressive place, but there's always the Parthenon even if we have to live with Papadopoulos.

We also had a letter from a young Greek student studying at Athens University.

Most of the students are not intellectually interesting. This is true for the masses. However, the few who are, shall we say, members of the intellectual elite, are indisputably intellectually superior to their American counterparts. We are also members of the European community. Therefore, we learn, to a certain extent, in a different way from that to which Americans are accustomed, and we do think in a different way. This would probably create certain communication problems between "your" students and "ours."

In subjects such as sociology, economics, in short, all the sciences, American students would probably be very disappointed by Greek methods of instruction, equipment, etc. There are hardly any opportunities for any kind of meaningful research. The liberal arts courses: philosophy, Greek, Latin, literature, are somewhat better for Americans. But generally speaking, the only thing worth studying in Greece for an American would be modern Greek literature (for which fluency in the language is, of course, a requisite). There are no boarding facilities at the University of Athens, but it is quite easy to find a room or small apartment and furniture. Rent is cheap.

For students only wanting to spend a year in Greece and who do not know the language (which is not that difficult to learn) there are two possibilities. There is a College Year in Athens, a privately administered program, that costs about $3,300 for tuition, room and board. Write:

College Year in Athens
Psychico
Athens, Greece

or

Stonehedge
Lincoln, Massachusetts 01773

Or contact Pierce College, P.O. Box 472, Athens, for their program. There is nothing else available at the undergraduate level, except a one-semester program sponsored by Lake Forest College in Illinois.

Try and develop a year independent studies for Greece with the college you're now attending, some study that would allow you to live quietly on one of the islands. You'll never want to go home again.

USEFUL ADDRESSES
Embassy of Greece
2221 Massachusetts Avenue N.W.
Washington, D.C. 20008
(202) 667–3168

ICELAND

Overseas students are acceptable to the University of Iceland, if they are eligible for admissions to a college in their own country. But for Americans that means you must be at a junior level, as Iceland uses the European system of education.

The university has 1,700 students and a faculty of 200. There are only a handful of American students, but it is possible to do a worthwhile year or more of independent studies at the university. We suggest enrolling in the Faculty of Philosophy where there is a course in Icelandic Language and Literature especially for foreign students. The university offers a degree in *Icelandic, Baccalaureatus Philologiae Islandicae.* It takes about three years. Scholarships are available for overseas students wanting to study Icelandic. Write the Ministry of Education for information.

There is no tuition at the University of Iceland, only a registration fee of twelve dollars. The university has two student hostels, but overseas students find it difficult to obtain a room. Accommodations can be found in the city of Reykjavik; room and board for one month runs about ninety dollars.

The semester begins September 15 and ends January 31. Second semester is February 1 to June 15. All application information should be mailed to the Registrar before June 1. There is no application form, just mail a letter of intent together with high school and college transcripts. An orientation session is held in September for everyone. This program is in English (language of instruction at the university is Icelandic) and held at Laugarvatn, a country school center just south of Reykjavik. It's a series of lectures on the history of Iceland, its literature, economy, geology, etc. There are also excursions to Pingvellir and Skålholt, and to Great Geysir in Haukadalur.

Although Icelandic Airlines might be for everyone under twenty-five, the university isn't. We think serious students who want to obtain firsthand knowledge about the country should apply. Reykjavik itself is a wonderful place to live, one of the "freest" places in the world. W. H. Auden once told us if he were picking a country in which to start all over, he'd select Iceland. They read more books per capita than anywhere else in the world.

USEFUL ADDRESSES
University of Iceland
Reykjavik, Iceland

Icelandic Embassy
2022 Connecticut Avenue N.W.
Washington, D.C. 20008
(202) 265–6653

IRELAND

There are two universities in Ireland—the National University of Ireland and the University of Dublin (Trinity College, Dublin). The National University comprises three constituent colleges—University College, Dublin; University College, Cork; and University College, Galway.

Students born outside Ireland are admitted to the constituent colleges only by special permission for which they must apply to the president of the college concerned. Such students are admitted, in limited numbers, to the faculties of arts, commerce, science and law. Students should apply to the college regarding the procedure to be followed.

We think students should apply as "occasional students" and spend a term or academic year in Ireland. This arrangement is open to students whose field of study lies within non-professional faculties. Trinity College only accepts occasional students for one term. Tuition fees for such students ranges from two hundred to four hundred dollars a year. The academic year consists of three terms beginning in October and lasting until the end of June. English is the language of instruction.

Institutions in Ireland, with the exception of Trinity College, Dublin, do not have student residences. All colleges have lists of approved lodgings and student hostels. The yearly cost ranges from $1,400 to $1,800. Employment opportunities are limited and a special work permit is required for foreign students.

Courses on Irish life and culture for foreign students are available during the summer. Information on these programs may be obtained from the Registrars of the International Summer Schools at each of the colleges.

USEFUL ADDRESSES
Embassy of Ireland
2234 Massachusetts Avenue N.W.
Washington D.C. 20008
(202) 483–7639

Registrar
6 Trinity College
Dublin, Ireland

Irish Tourist Information Bureau
590 Fifth Avenue
New York, New York 10036

Registrar
University College
86 St. Stephan's Green
Dublin, Ireland

ISRAEL

In 1971 over 7,600 foreign students studied in Israel. Every year this number grows. It's one of the easiest countries for overseas students to attend and you don't have to be Jewish. Israel has a little bit of everything for everyone.

We recommend two schools: Hebrew University and Tel Aviv University. Both have special one-year programs in English for American undergraduates, beginning with a three-month summer *ulpan* (language study). The nine-month academic year begins in November.

Hebrew University has a beautiful campus in one of the truly beautiful cities of the world, Jerusalem. Just living in Jerusalem is an education. The main campus is on 125 acres west of the city and since the Six Day War, the university has regained its original campus on Mt. Scopus. The university is large, wealthy and expanding.

A special office on the main campus handles overseas students. It's directed by a Canadian, Dr. Cohen. He's a fine person, but his staff is small and harassed by hundreds of overseas students. (In 1970 out of a total enrollment of 15,320 students, 4,000 were from overseas.) Activities are organized to help overseas students at Hebrew University. All sorts of trips, folk dancing, seminars, etc., but most are overorganized and a bore. The Old City of Jerusalem is only a few miles away and a student could spend a semester wandering through those narrow streets and never be tired of the life.

The cost of the one-year program is between $2,600 and $2,800. This includes a round-trip ticket from New York to Tel Aviv, tuition, dormitory accommodations, *uplan* studies and registration. Another $70 a month is needed for food and expenses.

Hebrew University usually takes visiting students who have completed at least one year of college. They have over ninety courses in Jewish or Israeli studies and a wide range of other choices, everything from archeology to English Lit. Most courses are taught in English.

Hebrew University has a number of good teachers, but they are mostly the "old-school" type, heavy into lectures and rote learning. Some outstanding professors:

Professor Michael Konfine—A Bulgarian whose field is Russian History. He's young to have reached the rank of a Professor—forty-five—and is liked by everyone. He makes his students work hard, but they do because they respond to him. Not a difficult grader.

Doctor Ozer Schield—A sociologist who is head of the Psychology Department. He has studied and taught in the United States and is considered brilliant, but eccentric. He is the most interesting lecturer at Hebrew University.

Doctor Rivka Bar-Yosef—Known as Smily on campus, Doctor Bar-Yosef is extremely popular and well known throughout Israel. She is head of the Sociology Department.

Hebrew University is an excellent university, by anyone's standards. They are selective about students and have several ongoing programs with colleges and universities in the United States. But students can apply directly to their office in New York for application material. They'll want you to take a physical, have an interview, but these can be arranged all over the United States. Write:

American Friends of the Hebrew University
11 East 69th Street
New York, New York 10021
(212) 988–8400

Tel Aviv University in Ramat Aviv is just north of Tel Aviv and has an enrollment of 8,800 student, 500 of whom are from overseas. It's a new university, opened in 1963 and still building. The campus isn't much, twenty buildings scattered over rocks and sand, and the city of Tel Aviv is a disaster. It may be the ugliest town in the Middle East (with the possible exception of Amman). However, within a few miles of Tel Aviv's campus are the long, clean beaches of the eastern Mediterranean and that makes the town livable.

Tel Aviv University has an overseas office and has been accepting visiting students in a big way since 1968. Like Hebrew University, students receive little personal attention and often find themselves confused and alone. Tel Aviv, however, has Nira Finkelstein, the pretty and bright Administrative Assistant in their Overseas Office. She's tremendous, understands Americans and knows every inch of the campus, and the country. If you're in trouble at Tel Aviv, see Nira.

The one-year program at Tel Aviv cost $1,945. This covers the round-trip ticket from New York, *ulpan,* academic year, housing in hotels and one meal a day.

Tel Aviv doesn't have the "academic" standards of Hebrew, but in many ways is a much better college. Some of the outstanding teachers are:

Doctor Erik Cohen—He is a young teacher in sociology whose field is urbanization. He came from Hebrew University. He is well liked by his students.

Professor Moshe Lazar—Also taught at Hebrew University and his move to Tel Aviv University caused an academic scandal in the country. He is considered a true "genius," who specializes in Roman languages and culture. Take him also for his class in modern theater and don't miss his lecture on Federico Garcia Lorca.

Professor Chayim Ben-Shachar—Is the Dean of Social Studies and a young, bright star at Tel Aviv University. His field is economics. It is definitely worth taking a course from him while overseas.

Tel Aviv University also has arrangements with American colleges, but students can apply directly to their office in New York. Address:

American Friends of the Tel Aviv University
41 East 42nd Street
New York, New York 10017
(212) 687-5651

Israel is a small country, even after the Six Day War, and can be seen in a weekend. Roads are excellent and everyone hitchhikes, or tramps as they say. Israelis are open and almost everyone speaks some English. Hebrew is not a difficult language to learn. Two weeks in the *ulpan* will give a working knowledge of Hebrew.

The *ulpan* is a tough language course. The Israelis have been teaching thousands of immigrants how to speak Hebrew and they do it through discipline, rote memory and long hours of drill. Not many modern techniques used, but the instructors are young, often university students themselves.

While in Israel, take advantage of the *kibbutzim*, plan on spending a month or longer at one of them. Only about 4 percent of the population of Israel lives on *kibbutzim*, but the spirit of the country and *real* communal living is found there. The work is manual, and hard work during harvest time, but room, board and a small allowance is provided.

A student attending an American college might arrange a one-semester independent study or field project in Israel living on a *kibbut*. To get information, write one of the Jewish agencies for Israel in the United States. Some addresses are:

Jewish Agency for Israel
515 Park Avenue
New York, New York 10022

Jewish Agency for Israel
220 South State Street
Chicago, Illinois 60601

Jewish Agency for Israel
46 Kearney Street
San Francisco, California 94108

Hebrew and Tel Aviv Universities operate on the European system of large lectures, very little contact between students and teachers. To see professors at Tel Aviv University, we've seen students lining up outside office doors at five A.M. Students are several years older than American students, having already been in the army and they are in a hurry to get through college. They are naturally more concerned about a degree than an education. Women usually don't have a problem with this age difference, but males are hard pressed to find Israeli women their age.

Another college worth checking is the American College of Jerusalem. We do not know much about it, but it's a private, non-sectarian college offering a Bachelor of Arts. (They also have one-year programs.) American College is American sponsored, offering almost an "American curriculum" in Jerusalem. It's quite small and expensive: $2,750 a year, plus transportation. Students have the advantage of small classes, seminars and personal attention and the disadvantage of classes full of Americans. (But then this is also true of Tel Aviv and Hebrew: classes are mostly American filled, unless students know Hebrew and can shift into regular classes.) For more information on American College of Jerusalem, write:

The Committee for the American College in Jerusalem
One East 42nd Street
New York, New York 10017

Israel is a country easy to live in and is at the center of major political problems. It is worth getting to know. To understand the Middle East it is necessary to know both Israel and the Arab World. The problems are complex and history is long in this Middle-East struggle. We suggest you begin by learning both sides of the story.

Good books on Israeli higher education: *Higher Education in Israel: A guide for Overseas Students* by Abraham S. Hyman. It's available from Jewish Agencies and was published in 1971; *Facts about Israel:* Jerusalem: Keter Publishing House, 1970; and *Holiday Magazine Guide to Israel,* New York: Random House, 1970.

ITALY

Thirty American colleges run programs in Italy. They are established ventures, but as one woman told us about the Stanford program in Florence, "After the first couple of weeks cruising around the city we just sat all day in the dorm, getting high. We could have been back in California. As far as the eye could see, were other Americans." We've listed the colleges that have programs, but once again we suggest you go to Italy on your own.

It's difficult to enroll in an Italian university—not like France—basic requirements are two years of college, excellent Italian and the Italian Consulate handles the process. You present transcripts, etc., to him and he forwards them to the Italian university. Be prepared for a long delay. Tuition runs ninety dollars a year and nothing much is provided in the way of assistance.

There are two ways of spending a year of independent study in Rome or Florence that we'd recommend: Dante Alighieri Society and the International House.

Dante Alighieri in Rome has courses in language and literature and art. Courses begin every two months and the school is quite conservative. One student we know, wrote: "It's an awful place, stay away!" The quality of instruction, however, is high, but the method is geared to structure, not speaking. International House in Rome comes highly recommended. Another woman we know spent a year there. She writes:

They run a 40 lesson intensive language class that meets three hours a day, either in the morning or the afternoon. They also run a 4 hour a week course following the same book that only meets in the evenings and is made up mostly of older people who work in Rome for American companies. The International House has its own book that they wrote themselves and includes the exercises that are in the lab. They call their method "the direct approach" and limit classes to 12 and under. The main point I think they have in their favor is that within a month one's comprehension of Italian improves dramatically.

Like every school I've ever been connected with, the International House has its problems. Only two Italian teachers have contracts which means that the teacher turnover is great. Some of the teachers are really terrible—I've been lucky.

Unfortunately the International House isn't content with just being a language school, and has set up a social club that you automatically join when you enroll. The "Club" sponsors such events as MISS INTERNATIONAL HOUSE *beauty pageants, international hootenannys, and "rap sessions." The clubby aspect of the school creates a forced atmosphere of friendliness. In spite of this I recommend the International House mainly because I haven't found any place better in Rome, and comparatively their rates are reasonable. About $60.00 a month.*

The most important thing that I think other non-Italian speaking students should realize is that they either have to spend the money for an intensive language school—or forget about even understanding Italian. Also, students shouldn't hesitate to rent furnished apartments in Rome. Most leases can be broken with two months notice. It's cheaper and nicer than living in a pensione.

There's an American library here (bad) and a British library (better). The best bookstore is the Lion Bookshop on Via Babuno. They'll order any British book at no extra charge. Hope this helps.

The International House opened in London in 1964 and has over fourteen others around the world. In Rome you can study the movements in modern Italian literature—Moravia, Lampedusa and Pirandello; the visual arts and the counterreformation in Rome; the social history of ancient Rome; the Etruscan civilization and contemporary Italy. The International House also provides rooms and meals. Address:

International House
Via Marghera 22
00185 Roma

In Florence there is the University of Florence Course for Foreigners. It is a two-semester course that costs about forty dollars a semester, write:

Centro di Cultura per Stranieri
Via S. Gallo
25/A Florence

Some other useful addresses:

Dante Alighieri Society
Piazza Firenze 27
Rome, Italy

Italian Embassy
1601 Fuller N.W.
Washington, D.C. 20009
(202) AD 4–1935

Istituto Italiano di Cultura
686 Park Avenue
New York, New York 10021

American colleges and universities offering year programs in Italy

ADDRESS	COST	GRADE AVERAGE
BOLOGNA		
City University of New York *Queens College* *New York, New York 11367*	$2,225 (everything)	C+
Dickinson College *Carlisle, Pennsylvania 17013*	$3,440 (everything)	C+
Indiana University *Bloomington, Indiana 47401*	$1,175 (tuition only)	B
Johns Hopkins University *International Studies* *1740 Massachusetts Avenue N.W.* *Washington, D.C. 20036*	$1,150 (tuition only)	B
Sarah Lawrence College *Bronxville, New York 10708*	($3,600 (tuition only)	B
FLORENCE		
Michigan State University *Center for International Programs* *East Lansing, Michigan 48823*	$950 (a term)	C+
California State Colleges *International Programs* *1600 Holloway Avenue* *San Francisco, California 94132*	$2,080	C+
Florida Presbyterian College *International Education* *St. Petersburg, Florida 33733*	$600 (tuition)	C
Florida State University *International Studies* *Tallahassee, Florida 32306*	$1,675	C

ADDRESS	COST	GRADE AVERAGE
Gonzaga University *Gonzaga-in-Florence* *Spokane, Washington 99202*	$3,400 (everything)	B
Lake Forest College *Lake Forest, Illinois 60626*	$770 (tuition)	C+
Middlebury College *Graduate School* *Middlebury, Vermont 05753*	$3,500 (everything)	B
Moore College of Art *Philadelphia, Pennsylvania 19103*	$1,550 (plus transportation)	C+
Smith College *Junior Year Abroad* *Northampton, Massachusetts 01060*	$3,630	B
Stanford University *Junior Year Abroad* *Stanford, California 94305*	$1,095 (tuition, room and board)	B
Syracuse University *335 Comstock Avenue* *Syrascuse, New York 13210*	$1,840 (a semester)	B
Villa I Tatti *The Harvard University Center* *Cambridge, Massachusetts 02136*	No tuition, fellowships	B
Villa Schifanoia Graduate School *Rosary College* *River Forest, Illinois 60305*	$3,000	B

PADUA
University of California
Education Abroad Program
Santa Barbara, California 93106 $3,000   C+

PAVIA
Portland State University
International Program
P.O. Box 751
Portland, Oregon 97207   Not given   C

PERUGIA
American Institute for Foreign Study $2,750   C+
102 Greenwich Avenue
Greenwich, Connecticut 06830

ADDRESS	COST	GRADE AVERAGE
PISA		
Oswego State University *Oswego, New York 13126*	$2,100	C
ROME		
American Academy in Rome *101 Park Avenue* *New York, New York 10017*	$175 (tuition)	C
Center for Mediterranean Studies *Via Cadlolo 90* *00136 Rome, Italy*	$3,000	C
Rhode Island School of Design *2 College Street* *Providence, Rhode Island 02903*	$4,100	B
Finch Intercontinental Study *Finch College* *52 East 78 Street* *New York, New York 10021*	$5,350	C+
Intercollegiate Center for Classical *Studies in Rome* *Stanford Overseas Campuses* *1C Inner Quad* *Stanford, California 94305*	$3,300	B
Loyola University *6525 North Sheridan Road* *Chicago, Illinois 60626*	$3,050	B
Albany State University *College of Arts and Sciences* *Albany, New York 12203*	$2,000	C+
Pennsylvania State University *211–12 Engineering C* *University Park, Pennsylvania 16802*	University (tuition)	C+
Rome Center of Liberal Arts *Temple Abroad* *Tyler School of Art* *Beech and Penrose Avenues* *Philadelphia, Pennsylvania 19126*	$3,830	C+

ADDRESS	COST	GRADE AVERAGE
SIENA		
Buffalo State University	$1,250	C+
International Education	(plus tuition)	
1300 Elmwood Avenue		
Buffalo, New York 14222		
VENICE		
Venice Island of Studies	$2,750	C
Liberty Trust Building		
Philadelphia, Pennsylvania 19107		

For information on summer courses write Instituto Italiano di Cultura.

For help in finding a place to stay or finding a school if you are in Italy, here are some organizations to contact:

Centro Italiano Viaggi Istruzione Student
Palazzo Antici Mattei
Via Michelangelo Caetani 32
Rome, Italy

Centro Relazioni Culturali con l'Estero
Via Piemonte 63
Rome, Italy
(branch offices at every university)

NETHERLANDS

Holland has eleven universities. Tuition runs about sixty-six dollars per year and the language of instruction is Dutch. Only one college course makes much sense for American undergraduates. That's a Dutch language course, three months long, at the University of Leyden (Rijksuniversiteit te Leiden). Admission to any university in the Netherlands has to be requested from the Ministry of Education, The Hague.

Male students in business can study (in English) at N.O.I.B. Nijenrode, Breukelen, which has been established by the University of Oregon. Syracuse University in New York has a one-semester program in home economics and related courses (in English) in Amsterdam.

For the most part, American students have to have at least two years of college to be admitted to a Dutch university. The universities operate on the typical European system: no obligatory enrollment, no course credits, few examinations, little contact with professors. Dutch universities do not provide dormitories, but students can easily find furnished rooms or a place to stay with a family. There is also an Office for Foreign Student Relations which is helpful in settling in. No visa is required, but if staying longer than a month, students must check with the American Embassy in Holland.

USEFUL ADDRESSES

The Royal Netherlands Embassy
4200 Linnean Avenue N.W.
Washington, D.C. 20008
(202) 244-5300

The Netherlands Information Service
711 Third Avenue
New York, New York 10020

Netherlands Office for Foreign Students
Pier 40, North River
Amsterdam, The Netherlands

Holland is a nice place to visit, but we can't think of any reason (except learning Dutch) to study there. But if you insist, get *Study in Holland—A Guide for Prospective Students,* from The Netherlands Information Service. It will tell you more than you'll ever need to know.

NEW ZEALAND

There are six universities in New Zealand and one affiliated agricultural college. University education is like the British system, not the American. There is no educational institution equivalent to the Liberal Arts College. The New Zealand student follows specialized rather than general courses. The student attends a number of lectures, tutorials and/or laboratory work per week. There is also independent reading and research with a minimum of supervision.

Students from the United States must be able to prove eligibility for admission to an accredited American university or college before being acceptable for a New Zealand university. An overseas student from America should apply to the Secretary, Overseas Students' Admissions Committee, P.O. Box 8035, Wellington, New Zealand.

All universities offer courses in arts and sciences, although the specific subjects taught vary. Each of the universities in the four main centers—Auckland, Wellington, Christchurch and Dunedin—provides, in addition, courses in law, commerce and music. The academic year starts in March and is divided into three terms usually March to May, June to August and September to November. The long vacation is from

November to March and there is a three-week vacation between terms. Most bachelor's degree courses require three years.

Tuition costs between $150 and $300 per academic year. The cost of room and board in university dormitories is approximately $700 per academic year. Clothes, books, vacation, travel, etc., should come to another $700. There is a shortage of accommodation for students in university cities in New Zealand and a relatively small number live in university dormitories.

USEFUL ADDRESSES
New Zealand Embassy
19 Observatory Circle, N.W.
Washington, D.C. 20008
(202) 265–1721

The Registrar
University of Auckland
P.O. Box 2175
Auckland, New Zealand

The Registrar
Massey University
Palmerston North, New Zealand

The Registrar
University of Canterbury
Private Bag
Christchurch, New Zealand

The Registrar
University of Waikato
Hamilton, New Zealand

The Registrar
Victoria University of Wellington
P.O. Box 196
Wellington, New Zealand

The Registrar
University of Otago
P.O. Box 56
Dunedin, New Zealand

NORWAY

The language of instruction at all colleges and universities of Norway is naturally Norwegian. To study there it's best to begin with the

University of Oslo's International Summer School, which runs from about June 27 to August 7. Classes for the normal year begin in late August, early September.

The International Summer School has 350 participants and over 250 each year are Americans, usually admitted through St. Olaf College in Northfield, Minnesota. Americans have to be juniors in college and have a good academic record.

All courses at the summer school are in English. Courses are limited and concentrate on all aspects of Norway, everything from Norwegian literature to applied arts and crafts. There is a mandatory, non-credit, General Survey of Norwegian Life and Culture which is a lecture course, and I.D.s are checked. This six-week summer session is academic, grades are ABC and the University of Oslo awards Certificates of Achievement only to students who have passed. Credits earned can be transferred to American colleges. To enroll as a full-time student after the summer school, contact the Foreign Student Advisor while on the Oslo campus.

Summer students live in Blindern Studenterhjen and at Nord-Norsk Student-og Elevhjem. These are single rooms, separate dorms by sexes, with quiet hours and no cross-visitation after eleven P.M. Very strict! Classes are held in the Geology, Liberal Arts, Social Science and Mathematics buildings of the university, a short walk from the dormitories and ten minutes by electric car from downtown Oslo. It's a new campus built among trees and overlooking the Oslo Fjord and the hills that surround the city.

If you stay on at Oslo, it will take between five and eight years to receive your first degree which is the *candidatus,* but tuition is free at Norwegian universities. (The summer school fee is $700 for flight, tuition and room and board.) Normal cost of living is approximately $150–$200 per month. Students who want to stay longer than three months need to report to the *fremmedpolitiet* (police) and apply for a residence permit.

We think you should approach Norway via the International Summer School or the Scandinavian Seminar. It is, after all, a cold country and you're going to need all the help you can get.

USEFUL ADDRESSES
Administrator
Oslo Summer School
St. Olaf College
Northfield, Minnesota 55057

Summer School Administration
University of Oslo
Blindern, Oslo 3, Norway

PORTUGAL

You need Portuguese for Portugal. That perhaps is the major stumbling block to obtaining a degree in a country which still is the least "discovered" in Europe and where living is warm and inexpensive.

Portugal has four universities, Coimbra being the most famous. There is also a College of Music and Arts in Lisbon that's noteworthy. It takes at least four years to obtain the first degree, the *licenciado,* however, the faculties of letters and the faculties of science at the universities award a *bacharel* degree after three years. To be admitted apply directly to the university you want and leave plenty of time for international correspondence.

The academic year runs from October to July and tuition is slightly more than fifty dollars per year. No dormitories are provided, but room and board is obtainable and the cost is low. Rent per month for a small furnished apartment is about seventy dollars.

There is a summer school course available at the University of Lisbon, every year from July 5 to August 14. It's an intensive course in Portuguese, history, art, literature, philology, philosophy and geography. They also have a series of lectures, in English, "to demonstrate the position of Portugal in the Overseas Territories." Portugal's colonial rule is the last imperialistic gesture in Africa and continues without justification. For information on the summer course, write:

> Direcção do curso de Férias
> University of Lisbon
> Rua da Academia dos Ciências, Lisbon

Queens College in New York has a short summer course for students who have a basic knowledge of the language, write:

> Summer Program in Portuguese
> Queens College of the City University of New York
> Flushing, New York 11367

Americans need a visa if staying longer than sixty days in Portugal. The visa should be obtained before leaving the United States.

USEFUL ADDRESSES
Portuguese Embassy
2125 Kalarama Road N.W.
Washington, D.C. 20009
(202) CO 5–1643

Casa De Portugal
570 Fifth Avenue
New York, New York 10036
(212) 581-2450

RUSSIA

Before 1970 it was impossible for an American undergraduate to study in Russia. It's still not easy but 260 students study each year at the University of Leningrad under a program of the Council on International Education Exchange. Students in this program study Russian language and culture. Academic standards are not rigorous though competition for admission is. Thirty spaces are available in each of the semester sessions, two hundred are available for the summer.

The tuition for the four-month semester is $2,500 and takes care of almost everything—room and board, books, field trips and transportation. Tuition for the nine-week summer session costs a little less than $2,000 and covers the same expenses.

Students apply to CIEE through member colleges of the council even though they may not attend one of them. Member schools are: Georgetown University, City University of the City of New York, Kansas State, University of Colorado, Dartmouth, University of Washington, Middlebury, and the University of Indiana. With the application is required an autobiography (in Russian), a statement of purpose for the trip (in English) and a tape illustrating Russian language facility. Three years of Russian is usually required, however, more important is a good recommendation from a professor at a member college. For information write:

CIEE
777 United Nations Plaza
New York, New York 10017
(212) MO 1-0310

The University of Leningrad, the second largest in Russia, has 19,000 students. The buildings are spread throughout the city and classes for the Americans are scheduled in the oldest building of all—a baroque structure completed sometime in the 1700s. The classes for language instruction begin at nine A.M. and go until one P.M., five days a week (six days during the summer). Classes in Russian literature are regularly included during this period and lectures in Russian art and history are sometimes added. The Russian instructors are good; they want Americans to enjoy their visit and go out of their way to invite students to their houses and arrange receptions so they may meet interesting Russians.

After classes in the afternoon, many field trips (sometimes too many) are planned by SPUTNIK, the student tour section of Intourist. Trips to the Museum of the History of Revolution and the Aurora Battleship (the first ship to fire in the revolution) are obligatory, others are not and some effort is made to arrange tours according to the interests of the students. One student requested tours through day-care centers and a famous Russian ballet school—she got them.

American students live in a five-story dormitory, a short walk from the university building. In the summer they live pretty much by themselves but during the semester sessions four Americans and two Russians share a room. The Russians picked to live with Americans are economics or political science majors. The bathroom facilities once again illustrate their universality by "being down the hall," and the showers are often one floor up. The dormitory floor is coed but the showers and bathroom facilities are not. Hot water runs three days a week so Americans and Russians bathe at the public baths, a large room with a lot of shower-heads and stalls. It's not bad.

Arrangements are made for Americans to eat together at a cafeteria located on the way to class. Rolls filled with rice, sausage, hamburger patties mixed with dried cereal are regular fare—sometimes for breakfast, lunch and dinner. Don't write Russian food off entirely, the students say the ice cream is the best in the world. Also, you can supplement the meals with food from the markets and *Beriozkas* (dollar stores). For foreign exchange, the *Beriozkas* sell scarce commodities at low prices. American cigarettes and liquor are cheap. In fact, they are usually sold below U.S. prices. Caviar, very scarce in Russia, is sometimes available, though expensive.

The two major influences you feel while in Leningrad are Lenin and World War II. Lenin's name and figure are everywhere—on streets, houses and monuments. (To illustrate how important he is and circumspect you must be, American program leaders sent home a member of the group for drawing a mustache on a Lenin poster.) Although the city has been rebuilt exactly as it was before the war, Leningrad was devastated and a million or more inhabitants died. The memory of this dreadful period is still strong.

Students walk to class but there is a good public transportation system for sightseeing and other excursions. Rides are cheap (five cents) and all routes are easy to understand—even the subways!

There are too many cultural opportunities available to American students in Leningrad to include. For a partial list there is the Hermitage Museum, the Russian Museum of Art and Pushkin's House. In the evenings, there are some of the world's greatest artists performing regularly at the Kirov Ballet and Opera, the Leningrad Philharmonic, and the "Palaces of Culture." Tickets are reasonable by U.S. standards. Expect to pay not more than $3.50 and for eighty cents you can get standing room and move down to the $3.50 seats after admission. Movies in Russian and foreign films are always showing.

You can get news from home from American tourists staying in the big tourist hotels near the university building. Or arrange months in advance with *Newsweek* or *Time* for a subscription to you in Russia. The *International Edition of the Herald Tribune* isn't too expensive and arrives up to a week late. Secondhand and new bookstores are everywhere, but if you're looking for English titles you'll probably come up with only a *Webster's Dictionary* or two.

Americans who have been on the program agree that it is possible and preferable to shed your American appearance. Men should buy Russian clothes and get a Russian haircut. (The program has no regulations as to length of hair or beards.) Everywhere in Leningrad the women wear drab cloth coats with a raccoon or similar type fur collar. American women should take one to Russia with them, they should be lined for cold winters.

Meeting Russians is not really a problem for semester students as they meet the friends and family of the Russian roommates. (Some have met people in the boulevard coffee shops.) In Leningrad, the people are mixed in their reactions to Americans, some hostile, some friendly and many incredulous that Americans are allowed to study here (a strong anti-American line appears in the press daily). American students realize that Russians may not feel too free to get to know them. Many Russians are worried they will be contaminated by Western ideas or they are worried they will appear disloyal to Russia. Consequently, Americans always carry in the backs of their minds the fear that their friendship may be harmful to Russians they know.

In spite of these problems, Americans and Russians date, though rarely on a one-couple basis. Usually a group of people gather at one person's apartment for the evening. Though it is permitted, U.S. students shy away from inviting Russians to their dormitory because the desk clerk requires the visitors to leave identification documents.

In general, participants on the program try to protect the independence of the program by taking care in the ways they act so as not to encourage the general suspicion they are agents of the U.S. Government. For one thing, they try to steer clear of the American Embassy.

USEFUL ADDRESS
Year In Russia
CIEE
777 United Nations Plaza
New York, New York 10017

SPAIN

It's easier to go to the moon than get into a Spanish university. And it makes no sense at all in applying unless you know the language. All universities give a language examination before classes begin. Tuition per year is just fifty dollars. Classes begin in September and are over in mid-July. After the initial year, each year is divided into two *cuatri-mestres* and all subjects of the first part must be passed before a student can continue in second-semester subjects.

There are several steps to enrolling and plenty of time is required to process an application. We suggest you leave at least a year for the process. All documents have to be mailed to a U.S. Spanish Consulate for checking, then returned to you before leaving for Spain. The Spanish like their paperwork. These are the steps: (a) Send birth certificate and high school/college transcripts to the Spanish Consulate nearest your home. They are translated and legalized. Also mail with the transcripts (b) catalogues of the schools attended; and (c) a statement of the source and amount of income you have. The more "official" documents you have, the better it is. Make sure you keep a copy of everything. They can get lost.

Once these documents are "legalized" at home they have to be presented again in Spain, either in person or by a friend. This can be done at the Instituto de Cultura Hispanica, also called Oficina de Gestio. The documents are then taken to the *convalidation* office located at Victor Pradera, 1, Madrid. The student is given a *volante* or certificate allowing him to enroll in the university. He then presents all the documents again at the school. If a student arrives in Spain with his documents in English and not legalized, he can have them translated at: St. Castaneda, Plaza Juan de la Crozz, Madrid.

Spain has twelve state universities. The University of Madrid is the most famous, and the most modern. It is also the most radical. Students usually demonstrate every year. If you do not want to enroll in a Spanish university, it is possible to audit classes. No documents are required, but you must obtain special permission from the university at the time of registration.

Cost of living is about one hundred dollars per month and some help is provided by the university in obtaining housing. All campuses have their *Collegios Mayores,* but it is better to find a room at a pensione.

USEFUL ADDRESSES
Embassy of Spain
Cultural Affairs
1629 Columbia Road N.W.

Washington, D.C. 20009
(202) 462-8736

Mr. Jose Maria Aranaz
Instituto de Cultura Hispanica
Auda de los Reyes Catolicos
Ciudad Universitaria
Madrid, Spain

It is possible to obtain a special Diploma of Hispanic Studies at one of the universities. The course is offered in their Departments of Philosophy and Letters (*Facultad de Filosofia y Letras*). Students take two courses in Spanish and literature and two other subjects in areas related to Spain. The total cost is about ninety dollars.

Students can register any time during the month of September in the secretariat of the university he wants to attend. He can apply at any time during the year for the forthcoming academic year. The final admissions will take place when he arrives on campus.

A number of American colleges have year programs in Spain, we've listed some of the better ones having year programs.

ADDRESS	COST	GRADE AVERAGE
Institute of Languages Georgetown University Washington, D.C. 20007	$1,500 (tuition only)	C+
Junior Year in Spain New York University New York, New York 10003	$2,600	B
Study Abroad Coordinator Ohio Wesleyan University Athens, Ohio 45701	$1,850	C+
Smith Junior Year Smith College Northampton, Massachusetts 01060	$4,340	B
SEGOVIA Segovia Program Ohio Wesleyan University Delaware, Ohio 43015	$2,000	C+
VALENCIA Institute of Spanish Studies 1315 Monterrey Boulevard San Francisco, California 94127	$1,900	B

Of all these possibilities, we suggest the one-year Diploma of Hispanio Studies. Write the Cultural Affairs Office of the Spanish Embassy in Washington about this program.

SWEDEN

We suggest attending college in Sweden through the Institute For English-Speaking Students, Stockholm University. This is a small English-speaking department within the university started in 1959. It runs three programs: Swedish Language, Stockholm Junior Year and the International Graduate School. About fifty students enroll each year in the Junior Year Program. Students from America usually come for the language program, then are assisted in entering the university for a year of study. Tuition for the year is slightly more than $900 and the cost of living around $240 a month.

The University of Stockholm is decentralized. There is no "campus," students are scattered throughout the city in rented rooms or dormitories so attending college means being on one's own. Students are also on their own in academic studies. Most of the courses available are about Swedish and Scandinavian subjects, taught in English. They are usually survey-like lectures meeting twice a week for two hours. The language classes meet between ten and fourteen hours a week, but students need to do twice as much time studying to keep up with the material. Students study at Stockholm! Libraries, such as *Humanistiska Biblioteket,* are so crowded it is impossible to find a seat unless you arrive early in the morning. Professors are interested in facts: numbers, names, details, etc. Professors are also hard to find. Contact is usually limited to classroom meetings and one or two personal consultations a semester. Grading is ABC and based on tests—three major tests a semester—and reports and papers.

In the Junior Year Program students take language and any four of eight lecture courses. They are: Modern History, Government, Economics, Sociology, Literature, History of Art, Social Welfare, Cinema. The course description of one lecture series is:

MODERN SCANDINAVIAN HISTORY
The entire history course awards 4 semester credits.
The first part departs from the time of the Napoleonic wars. These years brought several decisive changes in the political conditions of Scandinavia: Finland was separated from Sweden and transformed into a Grand Duchy under the Russian Czar and Norway was severed from Denmark and became the subordinate partner in a union with Sweden. Liberalism and nationalism in their Scandinavian form are studied in comparison with the corresponding developments in continental Europe. Several lectures are devoted to social and economic changes as population movements (including

emigration) and industralization. Another important aspect is the develop-
ment towards full democracy: parliamentary reform, extension of the fran-
chise and introduction of parliamentary government. This course ends with
World War I.

To be accepted by IES, American students have to have completed two years of college with a minimum grade average of C. In the language programs American students are with other nationalities, Czechs, Polish, Japanese, Greek, etc., but the Junior Year Program is only for Americans.

The teaching staff of the Institute for English-Speaking Students is connected only on a part-time basis. They are teachers from other Swedish institutions and are well qualified, the majority with degrees equivalent to the American Ph.D. The teacher for Economic Integration, a graduate school seminar, is the Director of Foreign Relations for the Federation of Swedish Industries.

Contact with professors, as we mentioned, is limited, but IES has an Ømbudsman who looks after students. He is himself a former student of the IES program and a graduate student within the Stockholm University. IES also has counselors available, but they assume American students are mature enough to take care of their own lives.

It is possible to live in student dormitories, IES will make the initial arrangements, but a place cannot be guaranteed. Dormitories are administered by students themselves and are spread out through the city. Apartments are also available, small places with just a room, lavatory and a shared kitchen. Housing is difficult to come by so let the IES know early what sort of place you'd like.

Stockholm is an expensive city. A beer costs a buck and movies run from one to three dollars. A pack of cigarettes runs about a dollar and whiskey is twelve dollars a bottle. Wine is cheap, however.

Be prepared for long cold winters, rain and snow. Clothes in Sweden are good quality and moderate in price, therefore, you might want to buy overseas. Either way, the Swedes are well-dressed people, fashion-conscious. Women need skirts and pant suits, and men, coats and ties. You'll need a trenchcoat and a warm coat.

The institute warns against Americans coming to Sweden because it's reportedly the world's capital of "sex, sin, suicide, and socialism." *I Am Curious (Yellow)* is as much Sweden as cowboy and gangster movies are America. It is not a country of the easy lay. Also, there is little campus politics. Students are scattered through the city and your university community will likely just be your dormitory or friends you meet in the classroom.

The IES makes it easy for Americans to spend a year (or more) in Sweden and it is one of the better equipped overseas offices we've seen.

They are experienced handling American undergraduates and know what you need, but they are also only interested in students in Sweden to study. You can screw off in Stockholm, but not at their expense. For further information—and they have lots of it—write either of these addresses:

Institute for English-speaking Students
Wenner-Gren Center
Sveavägen 166
S–11346 Stockholm, Sweden

The American-Scandinavian Foundation
127 East 73rd Street
New York, New York 10021
(212) TR 9–9779

Good books to read are: *The New Sweden,* Frederick Fleisher; *Sweden and the Price of Progress,* David Jenkins; and *Travel, Study, Research in Sweden,* (available from the American-Scandinavian Foundation for $3.00).

SWITZERLAND

Swiss colleges and universities correspond to our graduate schools which will usually mean an American student needs at least a B.S. or B.A. degree to be admitted. Students are individually considered and it is possible for an upperclassman to be accepted, if serious and perhaps has the language qualification.

Switzerland has seven universities, three are German-speaking: Basel, Bern and Zurich. Three are French-speaking: Geneva, Lausanne and Neuchatel. The Catholic University of Fribourg is bilingual, French and German.

All colleges are on the semester system, mid-October to mid-March, and mid-April to mid-July. There are no dormitories (with the exception of Georgetown's program at Fribourg) but boardinghouses, student hostels and rooms with families are available. Cost of living is about $160 per month; tuition runs $200 a year.

For specific information write to the secretariat of the college in mind, or write:

Central Office of the Swiss Universities
26 Sonneggstrasse
Zurich, Switzerland

Three American universities and colleges sponsor programs in Switzerland. The University of Pittsburgh has a European American Study Center in Basel. Courses in German, literature, art, sociology and politics. The comprehensive fee is $2,600. Write:

Council For International Education
University of Pittsburgh
Pittsburgh, Pennsylvania 15213

Georgetown University has a program for male juniors at Fribourg. Students must have a B average and a working knowledge of German or French. Costs are $2,000, plus transportation. Write:

Georgetown-at-Fribourg
Georgetown University
Washington, D.C. 20007

Rosary College has a junior year for women at the University of Fribourg. Cost is $2,500, plus transportation. Write:

Director, Junior Year Program
Rosary College
7900 West Division
River Forest, Illinois 60305

The American College of Switzerland is a private college, accredited in the United States and established for American college age students whose families live overseas. It's run like a 1950s' college, only that the location is Leysin, in French Switzerland. Students are mostly Americans, but 30 percent are other nationalities. We don't see much reason for students to go to Switzerland and attend another American school, especially one as traditional as this, but in case you have no other choice . . . write:

Mr. Hans Spengler
330 East 49th Street
New York, New York 10017
(212) EL 5-2219

Then there's The University of the New World at Valais. It's the extremely experimental place being started on top of a mountain. The first class was the summer of 1971. We've described it in detail in another section of this book.

WEST GERMANY

To apply for admissions to one of West Germany's thirty-eight universities a letter should be sent to the *Akademisches Auslandsamt* of the university in mind with the following documents:

1) a school leaving certificate (high school transcript) , certified;
2) a curriculum vitae, in German and signed;
3) proof of having studied at least two years in a college or university, transcript, certified;
4) where appropriate, evidence of previous practical work related to field of study;
5) proof of nationality;
6) a certificate of proficiency in German;
7) a health certificate;
8) six passport photographs;
9) a self-addressed envelope and two international reply coupons.

The *Akademisches Auslandsamt* is the office of the university which is responsible for foreign students and where overseas students can obtain information on the university. A complete list of universities' addresses can be obtained from the Deutscher Akademischer Austauschdienst (DAAD). Write:

German Academic Exchange Service
Dokumentation und Information
5300 Bonn-Bad Godesberg 1
Kennedy-Allee 50

German universities vary, but the semester system is used in all, mid-October to mid-February, and mid-April to mid-July. Recently the universities have undergone reform and the course of study has been structured. Studies are now divided into separate sections: the first section is completed in two–four semesters after which an intermediate examination is taken. Students then plan with advisors their final two years. It takes between three and six years to obtain a degree.

German universities are structured around the lecture system. There are also some seminars, practicals and colloquia. Attendance is compulsory and to graduate, students must prove they have attended a certain number of them. But general education in Germany is largely the responsibility of the students.

Tuition is about $200 per year and the cost of living $140 per month. The universities provide no housing for students, but the *Akademisches Auslandsamt* will assist in locating housing for students.

German universities are exceptional schools, but extremely traditional and impersonal. It would perhaps be best to attend college in Germany through another avenue. Schiller College (described elsewhere in the book) has campuses in Germany at Kleiningersheim, Bonnigheim, Heidelberg and Berlin. Schiller is particularly fine for theater arts.

Other opportunities are through American colleges maintaining programs in Germany. We have listed the more important ones:

ADDRESS	COST	GRADE AVERAGE
BADEN-WURTTEMBERG		
Lawrence University	$2,200 plus	B
Appleton, Wisconsin 54911	(part transportation)	
BERLIN		
World Affairs Center	$2,000	C+
Beloit College		
Beloit, Wisconsin 53511		
BONN		
International Programs	$2,500	B
224 Strong Hall		
University of Kansas		
Lawrence, Kansas 66044		
FREIBURG		
Association of Mid-Florida Colleges	$2,600	B
Box 1357		
Stetson Station		
Deland, Florida 32720		
Wayne State Junior Year	$2,650	B
Wayne State University		
Detroit, Michigan 48202		
HAMBURG		
Foreign Study Program	$3,200	B
Purdue University	(out-of-state)	
West Lafayette, Indiana 47907	$2,320	
	(in-state)	
HEIDELBERG		
Smith Junior Year	$4,000	B
Smith College		
Northampton, Massachusetts 01060		

Heidelberg Junior Year *Heidelberg College* *Tiffin, Ohio 44883*	$2,800 plus (part transportation)	B
Pepperdine College *South Vermont* *79th Street* *Los Angeles, California 90044*	$3,600	C
KLEININGERSHEIM *Dubuque in Germany* *University of Dubuque* *Dubuque, Iowa 52002*	$3,300	B
MARBURG *Millersville State College* *Millersville, Pennsylvania 17551*	$2,150	B+
REGENSBURG *Office of International Education* *University of Colorado* *Boulder, Colorado 80302*	$1,900 plus (part transportation)	B
TUBINGEN *Study Abroad* *Washington University* *St. Louis, Missouri 63130*	$2,700	B+

USEFUL ADDRESSES:
German Academic Exchange Service
1 Fifth Avenue
New York, New York 10003
(212) 220–2616

German Embassy
4645 Reservoir Road N.W.
Washington, D.C. 20007
(202) 331–3000

3. Special Colleges and Programs

EMERSON COLLEGE

Why should a small college in Sussex be named after Ralph Waldo Emerson? The answer, which must at first sound rather enigmatic, is that the college derives its impulse from the work of Rudolf Steiner. Both men—the one in the United States during the nineteenth century, the other in Europe during the early part of the twentieth—spoke for a spiritual ideal of man. The scientific culture of the West, according to them, for all its discoveries and inventions, has burdened the world with a habit of mind which negates the spiritual hopes and capacities of human beings, and denies any real meaning to life on earth. Emerson would have recognized Steiner's endeavor to open "a path of knowledge which would lead the spiritual in man to the spiritual in the universe." Emerson would have appreciated that Steiner's path leads, not away from, but more deeply into the realities of life: Out of Steiner's "Anthroposophy" has sprung a wealth of practical work in education, medicine, agriculture, care of handicapped children and adults, architecture, social work and the arts.

Emerson College was founded in 1962, and acquired its present property, which includes a two hundred-acre farm, in 1967. About 130 students can be accommodated. The majority come from English-speaking countries—including a substantial group from the United States—but ten or more other nations are represented. Most students live in lodgings in the nearby village of Forest Row, but work and eat at the college. The work is intended to call on all truly human capacities, intellectual, artistic, social and practical. Lectures and seminars are an essential part of the college life, but time is given to work in arts and crafts, farming and gardening, eurythmy (an art of movement), speech training, and the domestic tasks of preparing vegetables, serving meals, cleaning, washing up and maintaining buildings and garden. All students normally take the first or Foundation Year course, which can be followed by more specialized Second-Year courses in Education, Agriculture or the arts.

The Foundation Year begins with an introduction to Steiner's life and work, in the context of the critical issues of this century, and continues with a survey of the evolution of human consciousness as seen in science, art and religion. The second term is concerned on the one hand with the environment of man (the earth, the plant and animal kingdoms, races, peoples, social life), and on the other hand with the nature and development of man's inner faculties of thinking, feeling and will. The special theme of the third term is human destiny, and the tasks ahead. As well as attending lectures and seminars in these themes, students are encouraged to gain some intensive experience in painting, sculpture and modeling, music, eurythmy and speech, and later to pursue individual projects in one or other of these. Students can choose to work in a craft (weaving, wood carving, etc.) and in farming and gardening.

Second-Year students follow a common course of studies during the first period of each morning, and then split up for more specialized work. During the first term, the emphasis is on further studies of human nature, including stages of child and adult development, temperaments, aspects of psychology, etc. During the second term, social themes are emphasized—social history, social aspects of education, the family, human communities. The third term takes up further studies of human destiny.

For their specialist work, the Education Course works with Michael Hall, the nearby Rudolf Steiner school which has some 550 students aged five to eighteen. This allows regular collaboration with practicing teachers both inside and outside the classroom, and students spend at least six weeks of teaching practice in one of the Steiner schools in Great Britain.

Students of agriculture can gain practical experience on the college farm, and on two other nearby farms (run by former students). There are laboratory facilities, and a small field program of experimental plots has begun, as part of work now under way in several European centers (as also in the United States) to develop further the "biodynamic" methods of agriculture inaugurated by Steiner.

Second-Year arts students follow individual programs worked out with members of staff, but include some common studies. There are facilities for painting, sculpture, wood carving, weaving, music, speech, drama and eurythmy.

This kind of description of the work is somewhat schematic and abstract, for the reality of the college lies in the living and working together of students and staff, in shared experiences and individual growth and development. Thus one year develops out of the previous one, but is not identical: Each September, eighty to one hundred new students arrive. They meet the forty to fifty students who have returned for a second year, and the members of staff (there are about twelve permanent teaching staff, but together with help from teachers at Michael Hall, the college invites visiting teachers and lecturers from Britain and Europe). The experience of previous years flows into the forming of the courses, but as the year proceeds, and staff and students get to know each other, it begins to acquire its distinctive character, with its own needs, problems and special achievements. All kinds of initiatives spring up in music, drama, study projects and social events.

A special feature of the college life is the celebration of festivals—Michaelmas, Christmas, Easter, Whitsun. "These festivals cannot be truly sustained today out of traditions; they can only be renewed in connection both with the season of the year and with the universal human experiences with which they belong: Courage to meet darkness; the birth of an inner light at midwinter; death and the overcoming of death; the hope for new community. Many can contribute to the forming of such festivals, which are enriched with the arts, and contribute in a fundamental way to the experience of the College year," writes John Deuy, Deputy Principal.

Students are accepted as individuals, but the nature of the work makes it more suitable for those who have completed a first college degree, or who have worked for a few years after leaving school. The average age of the student body is mid-twenties; there are a few younger students, and a proportion of older people, including married students with families (although accommodation for the latter is not easy to find). Applicants are asked to do some preliminary reading in one or more of Steiner's fundamental works, so that they can test in advance whether a college based on Steiner's work promises to meet their needs. The college is a private foundation, and has to charge fees. For the year 1971–72, these are $1,368 inclusive of board, lodging and tuition during term time. The College year begins in mid-September, ends in late June, with three-week vacations at Christmas and Easter. Further details can be obtained by writing to:

Emerson College,
Forest Row,
Sussex, England

SCANDINAVIAN SEMINAR

This program is the most "respectable" way to go to Scandinavia. It's a program twenty-three years old and chartered by the Board of Regents of the University of the State of New York. Over fifty-five colleges and universities regularly send students to Denmark, Finland, Norway and Sweden through the program. It costs slightly more than two thousand dollars for nine months of tuition, room and board, one-way transportation from New York and course-connected travel within Scandinavia. (Limited interest-free loans are available.)

The Scandinavian Seminar has two goals for its students: to acquire fluency in a Scandinavian language, and to become involved in the life and culture of a Scandinavian community. Students spend their nine months—usually one student per school—in Folk High Schools. A Folk High School resembles a small American college. It's a residential school between fifty and one hundred students. No grades are given, no tests, but the seminar prepares a special evaluation of its students for those who want credit from their colleges back home.

The curriculum is mainly liberal arts from literature to economics, and there is special instruction in gymnastics and crafts. An advisor from the Folk High School is assigned to each seminar student. Besides classes and learning the local language, students also do an independent study project. Some of these topics have been: Niels Bohr's Principles of Complimentarity; Kindergartens in Norway; Life in Sigtuna from 1000 to 1100 A.D.; a Study of Pär Lagerkvist; The Ryijy Rug: Yesterday and Today.

A Scandinavian Seminar year operates something like this:

Students leave in late July for Denmark and the Introductory Session. There students are interviewed and a school scheduled and a study program developed for each student. In the fall students go to the Folk High School in one of the four countries and live with a Scandinavian family. The fall program is concentrated on language. At the winter break, students go to the mountains of Norway for evaluation, project planning, discussion and skiing. The spring semester is working on an independent study project. The entire seminar group meets a final time in early May in Sweden for summing up.

Over two thousand students inquired about the seminar program in 1970 and seventy-nine finally enrolled. The majority of these students were at the undergraduate level. Sixty-three of the students finished the year overseas. Next year, Scandinavian Seminar expects to have ninety students in its four countries.

This is a competent, well constructed program. A strong academic year overseas and creditable. There is little feeling of "groupness" because students are spread thinly throughout the countries, but if you can handle yourself alone overseas, then try the seminar. For information write:

Scandinavian Seminar
140 West 57th Street
New York, New York 10019
(212) 247–1043

SCHILLER COLLEGE

Schiller College has campuses in Germany, England, France and Spain. It is a member of the European Council of International Schools and is recognized by the Oberschulamt of the German Ministry of Education and is a member of the American Association of Junior Colleges.

It has students from forty states and twenty countries, over five hundred are enrolled at all campuses. The college uses an American semester system, has examinations, grades and credits, and small classes. An approximate comprehensive fee covering tuition, European travel and student activities fee is $1,800. About half of the students attend Schiller for only one year, but it is possible to enter as a freshman and attend either the Berlin or Bonnigheim campus. Upperclassmen enroll at Berlin, Heidelberg, London, Madrid or Paris.

The basic curriculum is the same, but each campus has several special areas, they are:

BERLIN: *Theater arts, music, political science, history, international relations.*
BONNIGHEIM: *German language and literature, business administration, history, fine arts.*
HEIDELBERG: *German language and literature, political science, philosophy, history, European studies, religion.*
LONDON: *English literature, history, economics, education.*
MADRID: *Spanish language and literature, fine arts, European studies, international relations.*
PARIS: *French language and literature, theater arts, fine arts, international relations, political science, philosophy, European studies.*

Students are able to study at several campuses while obtaining their B.A. (or master's) and Schiller also has travel programs throughout Europe. The college also runs extensive summer programs for other U.S. colleges. Over six hundred students a summer.

Faculty are mostly American and competent. And the facilities are beautiful. Kleiningersheim Castle, which houses the administration of the college and European Institute of Advanced Studies was built in 1580. Other campuses of Schiller are just as lovely.

Students get an education at Schiller, but once again it's an American implant in Europe. The college has structure and experience and tends to be "protective" of students. It's 1950s in outlook and overly concerned about dope and hippies. It is a straight place. We recommend it as a second or last resort. Write:

Mr. U. R. Laves, Director
Schiller College U.S. Office
429 N.W. 48th Street
Oklahoma City, Oklahoma 73118
(405) 842-5979

TRAVEL/STUDY PROGRAMS

Special student travel/study programs, like flowers, flourish in the spring. On high school and college bulletin boards, in the Sunday newspaper supplements, on radio and television, everybody wants you to go overseas and study. The American Institute for Foreign Study and the Foreign Study League alone enroll seven thousand students every summer.

The propaganda is attractive: flashy color pictures of students asking directions of smiling host country nationals; exciting descriptions of how you'll spend your time—"visit old haunts of Hemingway and Fitzgerald, spend an evening strolling through the Latin Quarter" or "in Rome, spend your free time at the tennis courts or in the modern swimming pools built for the Olympic Games."

We think you should go to Europe on your own. But if you want to take advantage of these travel/study programs—and some are excellent and inexpensive—here are points to check *before* signing up. You can lose money and your summer with a phony organization. In the summer of 1970 an agency called World Academy filed bankruptcy and stranded three thousand students in Europe. Seventeen other organizations quit in 1971 because of financial troubles.

WHO SPONSORS THE PROGRAM? If the sponsor is a legitimate college, or a long-standing educational agency like the Experiment in International Living, the American Field Service or the Council on Student Travel, then you are on safe grounds and will get a solid academic summer.

Don't be misled by places that call themselves *schools, institutes,* or *non-profit*—this doesn't mean anything. They are usually "make-believe educational" institutions. The "school" might be nothing more than a post-office box somewhere, or a one-room office. If some travel agency, or an airline is the sponsor, then you'll probably get lots of travel and little study. American International Academy, for example, is owned by Overseas National Airlines. Watch out for academic programs that stress "free time," a chance to seee Europe "on your own." Translated, this means not much education, supervision or support. This is also true if the program doesn't mention *credit;* you'll be getting culture, not academics.

SELECTION OF STUDENTS. If there isn't any selection, or if your application fee isn't refundable, watch out! You may also be recruited by someone—a high school teacher—who signs up twelve or so students and gets a free ride himself. Over twenty organizations use this technique. This is okay, if you know him, and if he's going overseas to look after you; not if he has something else in mind, like doing studies himself.

WHO ARE THE OTHER STUDENTS? Are they your age and do they share your interests? Look out for programs jamming all ages together, you'll have nothing but trouble.

WHERE WILL YOU LIVE? The program might be on the campus of a foreign university, but will you be herded together in an otherwise empty dormitory? You'll never meet anyone then, only spend the summer talking to other Americans. This you can do in the United States and save the money. If you're going to live with a host country family, fine—but make sure it's not a boardinghouse, and find out how these families were selected.

HIDDEN COSTS. Any program will cost money. Therefore, see what you're getting. Break down the figures, compare them to other programs and to traveling to Europe alone. Make sure *all* transportation is included in the stated cost. For example, who pays for the transportation from the airport to school? Who pays for those *special* tours?

INSURANCE—DON'T GO OVERSEAS WITHOUT IT. If insurance is included, find out what it covers. You might want to get your own. Make sure there's some kind of medical arrangement stated in the program, either an American nurse, doctor or an agreement with a competent local medical staff.

OTHER POINTS TO CHECK. Is there an American office? The organization should have an official base in the United States which can be legally responsible for the program.

Is there an in-country orientation program? What is it about, and how long? If less than a week, it's not much of an orientation.

What's the teacher/student ratio? A good ratio is one teacher for thirty-five students.

How long are you in class? Don't count field trips as classroom hours. You should be *in class* between twelve and fifteen hours a week, if the program is worthwhile.

What sort of academic standards are there? Do you take tests, do independent research, have final examinations? If there is no standard evaluation, then the academic part of the program is shaky.

Is a permanent academic record kept and available? Do colleges accept transcripts from this program?

How long has the organization been in operation? If this is the first program, then expect administrative hangups. Within the last few years there have been hundreds of study/travel organizations. They come and go.

Who do you know who has been in the program? Obtain some names from the organization and write or call these people, find out what they thought of the program. They're the best gauge of its worth.

Have you read the fine print? Have others, friends and family, looked over the forms, the program. What do they think?

Does the program sound true? Read the promotional material several times, see if you get a clear picture of the advantages and disadvantages.

Generally speaking, if it's a high school program, traveling from city to city, the European education will be only exposure, not classes. If a high school or college sponsors its own program, then you can be assured of at least academic standards. Here are two lists of some commercial organizations:

SEVEN ESTABLISHED PROGRAMS WORTH CONSIDERING THAT HAVE BEEN IN OPERATION OVER THE PAST FIVE YEARS

ORGANIZATION	LOCATION
Academy of International Studies	*Los Angeles, California*
AIMS	*Washington, D.C.*
American Institute for Foreign Studies	*Greenwich, Connecticut*
American International Academy	*Los Angeles, California*
American Leadership Study Groups	*Worcester, Massachusetts*
Foreign Study League TSI	*Salt Lake City, Utah*
International (Cultural) Exchange School	*Salt Lake City, Utah*

NEW STUDY/TRAVEL ORGANIZATIONS IN 1971

ORGANIZATION	LOCATION
Ambassadors Abroad	*Grand Rapids, Michigan*
International Institute	*Phoenix, Arizona*
International Travel Council (*only offer January programs*)	*Salt Lake City, Utah*
National Foreign Study	*Stamford, Connecticut*
Study Tours (*use ITC fares*)	*Sherman, Oklahoma*
Study Guild International	*Salt Lake City, Utah*
World Encounters	*Santa Monica, California*

In 1971, three more organizations—recruiting students through teachers—for a free seat and/or cash. These are just sightseeing groups with no attempt at academics. Tours are three weeks long.

ORGANIZATION	LOCATION	COMPENSATION TO TEACHER IF FIVE STUDENTS ARE RECRUITED
Co-op Travel International (Division of Happy Travel Service)	*Norfolk, Virginia*	Plus $25 for each student above *one*
Ambassadors Abroad (*Emhage Tours, Inc.*)	*Grand Rapids, Michigan*	Plus $80 for each student above *five*
Study Tours	*Sherman Oaks, California*	Plus $50 for each student above *five*

RECOMMENDATION. We think the Experiment in International Living is outstanding in this travel/study field. They have been sending programs overseas for many years and have almost limitless experience. Write them in Putney, Vermont 05346.

4. Living in the Third World

To go to college somewhere in the Third World is to touch the world firsthand, often to touch it where it burns. We say this as a word of warning. There's nothing easy about getting educated in a non-Western culture. Academic calendars are erratic, living conditions stark and transportation difficult and unreliable. But if you have the ability to hang loose, bypass Europe, chances are the Third World experience will change your life. It did ours.

The first thing that happens to you when reaching a country with few familiar sights, sounds or even smells, is a phenomenon called *culture shock*. It's the abrupt recoiling from the environment. The condition is usually short lived, but vivid. In those few hours and days, everything seen, felt or tasted is pungent. Stories tell of Americans flipping out completely when arriving in a foreign country, but such extreme reactions are rare. You, however, will see the country and its conditions with unique clarity. You'll see the obvious problems of poverty and powerlessness of people. If you are not already, this experience will radicalize you. To realize how most of the world lives is one of the first lessons learned in the Third World, and a lesson that cannot be avoided overseas.

Not much can be avoided while living and studying in the Third World. To live in another culture—particularly a non-Western culture—is not easy. We mentioned culture shock and every foreigner's need to adjust to the new country and people. We hope that while living and studying overseas you'll be particularly sensitive to this "other" culture, respecting its modes and being aware of its prohibitions, adjusting your

American manners to the civilized societies you'll find throughout the Third World.

This is a polite way of saying that at times there will be food you'll have to eat, places you'll have to crash and ceremonies you'd rather not attend. There aren't a lot of simple ways of getting out of such situations.

Holidays and fiestas abound overseas. Spain, which isn't Third World, nevertheless has 3,410 fiestas a year. Sometimes it seems no one works overseas; banks and stores close, so does the American Embassy, and, of course, schools. So join in.

If you're in a small town or village, you may be asked as a guest to join the celebration, to sit at the head table with the local chief or mayor and by all means eat and drink. Everyone will be watching. They know their food and customs are exotic to the foreigner, and they are pleased when a foreigner, an American, enjoys their food. And sitting or squatting up front, it is difficult to fake appreciation.

Cultures and modes of living in Third World countries are as complex (if not more so) than our Western ways. One reason for living overseas is that it sharpens one's awareness of his own culture and background. Living inside and close to other societies teaches a person about himself. One begins to question and evaluate his own beliefs and ways of behavior. This alone is a profound education.

Writing in the *Journal of World Education,* John Rashford, a graduate of Friends World College, talks about his kind of education:

> The person involved in study-travel exposes himself to others. As a guest where cultural differences demand that he view and do things in ways he has never done, he will learn to understand them, for he will have lived with them on their own terms. But more importantly, by putting himself in a new context, he will learn to understand himself. And with this opening, he can and will grow; he can and will stand open to life itself like a flower to the sun.

After her freshman year in Hebrew University, an Old Westbury student wrote:

> This situation served to make me particularly aware of myself and what there was in me to make me an individual. At my arrival, there hardly was a me, because of my past totally conformist attitudes. There was nothing to conform to in Israel; each person was just himself; and what was I? I could say that all thought was in search of conforming to being an individual. But I also had to be someone that I could live with in peace, and believe in, and depend on. Almost the entire year was spent essentially alone because of all this. I had to be a total person before I could get close to, and be accepted by other people. I was terrifically lonely, but I was constantly watching, thinking, and learning!

Then you'll have to deal with bureaucracy and red tape. Ours is bad enough, but some places in the world you'll decide to leave the country rather than deal with it.

Here's a report from a student in Egypt:

> *There is this massive building on liberation square that houses the civil service. I call it the Bureaucracy Building. It is where they stick all the college graduates whom they can't employ. These people have one function only: to stick on one kind of stamp or to sign their names on one special line, or to type one form. They labor mightily from nine in the morning to twelve-thirty in the afternoon when after a long hard day they lock up and close down. There are stories of people who have never emerged once they made the mistake of entering. I pass them in the halls as they run from office to office trying to find the man with the right stamp.*

This story could be repeated in any number of countries. What to do in such situations? There will be times when you'll need a stamp or a signature, some permission or the other. Be prepared to wait. Don't expect to deal with three or four ministries in one day. There are always long lines and people who seem to have been waiting for years. Take a book along. You'll be surprised how fast you get cooperation once they know you're willing to wait.

There are other problems as well. Writing from Nanyang University in Singapore, a student describes his room:

> *We found after a few days that we were really renting our rooms from the ants. They make very good companions; they're in your bed, your books, your clothes, and food, and even in your soap. There are other bugs, not so numerous to be aware of. The cockroaches, which are huge, and the spiders (non-poisonous). But don't panic. Insecticides are available at all the stores on campus. For mosquitoes use either your net or burn mosquito incense.*

It is hard to anticipate what will be tough overseas. Peace Corps Volunteers repeatedly found it was not the physical conditions, the lack of convenience that were difficult about life overseas. They adjusted to living without electricity, sleeping under mosquito netting and taking malaria preventives. What was difficult was the slow pace of life and the routine.

A student at Tel Aviv University wrote:

> *It became more and more a problem to study as the year wore on. The rain poured down day after day and I think everyone began to feel too penned-in and bored with the routine, and with each other. There seemed to be a lack of things to do, and a lack of motivation in almost everyone.*

The classes became less and less stimulating, and a dwindling number of people attended. It became a chore to go through the routine of going outside and catching the right bus to the corner, then standing in the rain for the next bus to go to the University, and then repeating the routine to come back to the apartment and more nothing.

Anyone who goes overseas has to make adjustments; slipping into drugs is a too simple and too dangerous a solution. Around the world, authorities are busting students and other young people for drugs. They're illegal almost everywhere. In Guinea, Peace Corps homes have been raided, in the Old City of Jerusalem at the Damascus gate, the police pick-ups are routine. Hashish at the secondary level is beginning to spread in Israeli schools, and American college students are blamed. Beirut has over twenty Americans jailed for smuggling, and in countries like Spain and Italy the number is in the hundreds. A total of eight hundred Americans are in jail overseas because of drugs. Be careful about drugs. If you're young, have long hair, wear jeans and carry a pack, you'll be stopped and searched at every border, airport and often on the street. About the only exception is Nepal. There they sell drugs in restaurants. But hippies can't get into Nepal.

Living with oneself is the tough part of life overseas. There are very few diversions, pastimes. One must be prepared to find amusement and hobbies from the raw material of the land, whether it is hiking in Nepal, climbing Mount Kilimanjaro in Tanzania, working on an archaeological dig in Peru. Entertainment is not manufactured, is not a product, as it is in America.

The only real way to overcome the strangeness of the country, the loneliness, is to become part of the culture. Learn the language, learn everything you can about the place, study its history, understand the values of the new society, and don't impose your values and ways on them; it's their country.

Culture shock works both ways. Your American habits in many cultures are abrasive. In Ethiopia, for example, pointing one's finger at a person means you consider him a child, or a dog. In Nigeria, to look a person in the eye for a long period of time is considered disrespectful. These are two examples of non-verbal communication. You should understand how non-verbal communication happens. The classic book on the subject is Edward T. Hall's *The Silent Language*.

Here are some types of non-verbal communication in different cultures:

The American gesture of slitting one's throat to mean "I've had it," or "I'm in trouble," means in Swaziland "I love you."

To compliment a friend by saying he is looking thin is normal in America. In Ethiopia it is an insult. To be heavy in most African countries means wealth and importance.

In America, two males holding hands is considered queer, but in Africa and the Middle East, men hold hands all the time, and nothing is abnormal. In fact, a man and a woman holding hands is disapproved of.

In America it is considered rude to hiss or snap one's fingers at a waiter, but that's how it is done in Chilean restaurants.

There are hundreds of other examples of non-verbal communications about which you should be sensitive. The signs and signals from other cultures will, if you understand them, make your life overseas easier.

John Rashford, in the *Journal of World Education,* also comments about his adjustment:

The challenge of travel is not especially to one's intelligence or knowledge; it is a challenge to one's character. All too many travelers carry along a blinding pride, founded on the philosophy of "doing one's own thing." Humility is rarely considered an important traveling companion. I have seen many students stumble shamefully when they had to deal with others not as servants, drivers, guides, or as functional objects for their own use, but as people. It is in this crucial relationship that the road parts between the tourist and the study-traveler.

The willingness to humble oneself rather than use others, to work actively rather than spend lavishly, to step out of the security of one's own background and give up the pre-packaged perceptions, these are the markers for the path we must take for cross-cultural experience, understanding, and true friendship.

EXPERIENCING A NEW COUNTRY

One experiences a new country in stages, and each stage modifies and reevaluates the information presented before. These stages develop this way:

IMAGES. One carries with him on flight to a foreign country impressions gained from books, posters, looking at maps, talking to other travelers. These images have little to do with the impressions one has on arriving at the international airport overseas. The aftermath of a long, time-changing journey, the rush of people, a new, strange language, signs that are unfamiliar, custom procedures, is overwhelming.

To reduce this hassle, try and arrive during the day, avoid local holidays and weekends, and don't be in a rush to leave the airport and reach the city. Take your time, get used to the new climate, the change in altitude, adjust. Change money—not a lot, just enough to get you through a couple of days—and find the cheapest way of getting into town, usually by bus.

PRESENTATION OF CITY. The bus is the best way to see a city. From wherever you are in the city, and you'll most likely be someplace downtown where the cheap hotels are located, ride the bus. The bus will take you the complete route and bring you back to where you started. A handful of such trips over different routes and you'll know the major parts of town.

Once you've done this, and it shouldn't take more than a day, find what services the city offers. This can be best done by going to the lobby of the best hotel in the city, usually a Hilton or International. Hang out there awhile.

First-class hotels are convenient places to cash traveler's checks, send cables, find out (in English) what's happening in the country. It's also simpler to make phone calls in the lobby of a first-class hotel, and making a telephone call overseas is often one of the most difficult things to do. Believe us!

Once you have a couple of safe harbors, your hotel or pensione, and someplace else, like the lobby of a Hilton, venture out, this time on foot, and get another kind of feel for the city, establish familiarity over an area, find a convenient place to buy English newspapers and books, locate a few good, cheap restaurants, learn where to get out-of-town buses.

SETTLING IN AT COLLEGE. Within a couple of days you'll want to see the college or university. It will probably be located just outside of the city, as it is in Rabat, Morocco, or at least on the fringe, as in Tel Aviv, Cairo or Mexico. You may have passed it on your bus tours.

Universities aren't easy places to understand—even in the United States—they sprawl over acres, with lawns and endless assortments of buildings, little identification.

But regardless of the year, students are around. They are your best source of information on the college. Use them.

Find out where students live, eat, what they are into. Students overseas usually occupy a special position in the society. It is quite a distinction to be a university student. Often the tuition is free and stipends are paid by the government. Dormitories are provided, but many students live off campus—which we suggest for you, but try to get a student as your roommate.

Your student roommate will teach you almost everything you need to know about the university. Through him and other American students (if there are any) or American faculty, you'll quickly learn about the college.

To extend your knowledge beyond the campus, begin to use the neighborhood in which you live. Establish a routine, be visible. The quickest way to get to know people is through children; they are friendly, willing to talk in their halting English or help you speak their language. And they will help you get to know their parents.

Be friendly, smile. In Ireland the Germans were continually being harassed by their Irish neighbors. Asked why, a former I.R.A. member responding in a *New York Times* article, replied, "They don't register as personalities."

That's what you have to do overseas: register as a personality. You'll already be known as an American, a Yankee and other terms, most of them derogatory. You can overcome this attitude if you become a person in the community. If you eat at one of the local restaurants, have a beer in the nearby bar, spend a few hours talking to your neighbors. Remember, people don't like strangers.

These opportunities for women are limited. Women are restricted in many ways, particularly socially. It's important that women not live in dormitories; they are regular bastilles in foreign countries, particularly Third World countries. Going out alone is also difficult, but can be done, not late at night but in the early evening. Female university students, though about the most liberated women in the country, will not venture out with you. You'll have to do it on your own. All your normal behavior, your friendliness, will be misunderstood by the males. Male chauvinism runs rampant in the Third World; don't even expect to make inroads into it.

Once you have friends overseas, people to see and talk to, a schedule of classes and afternoon teas, beer in the evening, a routine of life will give you the support needed to make it overseas and away from home.

ACTIVITIES. Jane Coe, who lived for several years in Ghana, developed a series of activities that would help Americans get into the Ghanian culture. We have modified her activities to fit any culture in the Third World. We suggest you try them when you arrive overseas.

FIRST WEEK

1) *Adopt a local first name, use it in introductions.*

2) *If people come to meet you, be sure to return the visit—to their homes— within the next day or so, whether specifically invited or not.*

3) *Visit the nearest doctor so he knows who you are.*

4) *Learn the local resources in terms of food, supplies, etc.*

5) *Learn the following items about the city or town:*

    a. *When market day is.*
    b. *Lorry and taxi fares to nearby places.*
    c. *The name of the district, region and traditional areas.*
    d. *What dialects and other vernaculars are common in the area.*
    e. *Locate stores and market (s) .*
    f. *Locate churches, community center.*

SECOND WEEK

Visit the following places for fairly long periods of time—two or three hours; talk with whoever is there; note who—in terms of age and sex—gathers where and when.

  1) *Attend church services Sunday and during the week.*
  2) *Attend a football match or practice; play in it.*
  3) *See a movie.*
  4) *Visit the nearest health facility.*
  5) *Visit the post-office, get a post-office box number.*
  6) *Make a map of the section you're in, note the gathering points of time, purpose and who, by sex and age.*

You will now know where to find and meet people your own age; you will know something about the college leaders, community leaders, stranger's communities, clubs and societies.

THIRD WEEK

To understand the business of a city or town, do the following:

  1) *Visit the market daily or at various times of the day. Note when it is most active, who does what, when, etc.*
  2) *Select one store item and visit the stores where it is sold. Compare the prices, stores, owners, customers and locales.*
  3) *Learn as much as possible about all the members of one occupation— carpenter, shoemaker, barber, fisherman, butcher, teacher, goldsmith, etc.*
  4) *Visit a few local farms.*
  5) *Seek out the unemployed or the financial dependents and find out how they manage to live and if "unemployment" means the same thing to you as to them.*
  6) *Make a cost-of-living estimate.*

FOURTH WEEK

Whatever society you move into in the Third World, you'll come directly in contact with "the traditional way" of the culture.

  1) *Attend and then discuss with someone, the ceremonies relating to birth, puberty, marriage, divorce, death, disease, "Acts of God."*
  2) *Visit the storyteller or linguist to learn the local history.*
  3) *Discuss names and naming with ten to fifteen people, noting the origin of the names and which names are used on what occasions.*
  4) *Find out who owns various types of property and then who is next likely*

to own them (consider household utensils, personal belongings, houses, farm-lands, trees) .

5) *Ask about kinship terms and assess how they are used. This is best done in the local language, using terms of the language.*

6) *Talk to people from various social levels, according to such criteria as wealth, occupation, education, age, number of children.*

7) *Try to meet all the relatives of one person—your roommate perhaps—and assess how closely related they are, the nature of that relationship.*

8) *Discuss beliefs about such things as lightning, cause of illness, skin color, intelligence, good and evil, "the ideal person," with people of various education levels and ages.*

9) *Find out when the festivals are, who the sponsors are, and the history and background of them. How are they celebrated?*

FIFTH WEEK

Try to learn what happens inside the homes of your friends. How your host country friends live will give you a true picture of the culture.

1) *Make a map of the household; note on it by age and sex where various members spend most of their time.*

2) *Spend as much of one or two days with one member of a typical house-hold. Note the network of relationships of that one person.*

3) *Make two or three local dishes, serve them to your friends.*

4) *Learn a few proverbs and when to use them.*

5) *Learn the non-English names of the material items in a household.*

6) *Buy local cloth and have a dress or shirt made from it. Wear the national dress publicly.*

7) *Learn the local games and play them.*

Besides all these activities, keep a daily journal in which you record what you see, hear, experience. The emphasis should be less on "This is what I did" and more on "This is what I learned about the country, how I learned it, etc." Recording your life overseas will heighten your perception, enable you to check various answers to the same questions and give you a chance to reflect upon your experiences and moods.

APPLICATIONS AND VISAS

It's not easy to be accepted to a school overseas, not at least doing it from America. (We estimate it will take you at least six months of corresponding before you'll be accepted.) If you are in the country, you can avoid months of delay waiting for mail. You can see people personally. There's no better way of doing it. Just have a transcript of your high school or college grades and a letter from your school saying you're doing independent studies. If you are applying from the States, some suggestions:

Always appear official. Use school stationery and type letters. Give yourself a title, that helps. For example: Chairman of Student's International Committee. Don't use red ink. (In West Africa it's an insult to write anyone in red ink.) Mail letters airmail and enclose a self-addressed envelope and international postal reply coupons. (Coupons are exchangeable in any country for local stamps. To get the amount required, write Director, Classification and Special Services Division, Bureau of Operations, Washington, D.C. 20267).

We think the easiest and perhaps most effective way to go to school in the Third World is as an independent student. With letters from your own college stating you're studying such and such and signed by someone, a dean or director of international studies. Try and get them to use the school seal, imprinting it on the letter; that's impressive overseas.

Present this letter when applying for a visa. It will help. Obtaining visas is also a time consuming job. If you do not live near Washington or the foreign country's consulate, then mail a copy of your letter with your visa request. Most countries in the Third World want pictures. Therefore, when you get passport pictures, get a lot. You'll need them for just about everything. Ethiopia wants two, Guinea three, Ivory Coast four; we have no idea what they do with them. Look your best in the pictures, combed hair, tie, no beard (if possible). You could be denied a visa if someone at the embassy doesn't like your looks.

College campuses in America are often small towns, self-supporting islands where students can buy textbooks, magazines, toilet articles, records, tapes, clothes, even groceries. This is not true of schools overseas. Often there is nothing more than classrooms, a few dormitories and a cafeteria. It's impossible to feel "at home" on a foreign campus. Host country students don't feel at home. They're strangers themselves, coming to the capital from remote provinces, from up-country villages, a different state, even other islands. The food, customs and perhaps the language is as strange to the national students as it is to you.

Don't expect luxury. There will be few lounges of soft furniture, no comfortable study areas or handy recreation facilities. Maintenance of buildings isn't one of the strong points of Third World countries. These schools are strapped for funds. Often it has taken all resources just to open a college. Universities often look like they've been bombed, windows are smashed, blackboards hang off the walls, stairs are broken and the electricity is faulty. They are much like what you'd find in any large public high school in America.

HEALTH AND HAZARDS

You'll feel the weather overseas. Air-conditioning is limited and not wasted on classrooms. Central heating is also rarely found. Students go to lectures bundled up, take notes with their gloves on. Most of the time you're either too hot or too cold. Then there are other problems: monsoon rains, snow storms, droughts, hot winds off the deserts. Natural disasters: earthquakes, active volcanos, plagues and epidemics, the outbreak of war. Chances are few of these calamities will occur in the country of your choice, but a few simple words of advice.

Young people think they will live forever. They have not had much personal experience with death, nor have lived in stress conditions. Surprisingly, the Peace Corps has found it's safer overseas than at home. Since 1961 over 49,300 Volunteers have been in the Peace Corps. Only 80 have died and the largest number of these deaths were in traffic accidents, particularly motorcycling. A few deaths have been exotic. Two volunteers lost their lives in the 1970 Peru earthquake, another was killed in the bush of Tanzania. One volunteer in 1966 was eaten by a crocodile. But the majority of deaths have been motor accidents, asphyxiation and the result of not taking preventive medication. The Peace Corps has six basic preventive measures which are good for anyone going overseas.

- Always wear a helmet when cycling.
- Never go swimming alone.
- Make sure gas water heater and kerosene heaters are properly ventilated.
- Take prescribed medication.
- Drive at a safe speed.
- Do not drive when overtired or sleepy.

Before you do almost anything else about going to the Third World, you'll need to get inoculations and have them recorded on the yellow International Certificate of Vaccination provided by the Public Health Service. This document is as important as your passport. Smallpox, cholera and yellow fever vaccinations must be stamped by a certifying agency on this card. For the countries you'll be visiting, this document is nearly priceless. Don't lose it!

You'll need at least three immunizations:

SMALL POX	YELLOW FEVER	CHOLERA
Everywhere	*Africa*	*Asia*
	Central America	
	South America	

HEPATITIS	TYPHOID	TYPHUS
Rural Mexico	*Africa*	*Ethiopia*
Africa	*Asia*	*Burundi*
South America	*Philippines*	*Ruanda*

Asia	South Pacific Islands	Bolivia
Philippines	South America	Peru
Central America	Central America	Colombia
Pacific Islands	Rural Mexico	Mexico

MEASLES

Africa

PLAGUE

Vietnam
Cambodia
Laos

You can purchase almost any medicine you want overseas, therefore, don't worry about a medical kit. Take with you any special medicine you need, at least a four-month supply. If you wear glasses take an extra pair, plus the prescription. Beyond that, you'll need paregoric, Kaopectate or Lomotil. This is for diarrhea, and you'll have that. You'll need anti-malarial drugs. We suggest chloroquine phosphate; it's called Aralen and start taking it a couple weeks before you leave.

You're going to have trouble with bedbugs and fleas, especially in Africa and Asia. Bedbugs you can usually get rid of, fleas never. Sorry about that. Mosquito netting helps. You can easily set one up. If you're on the road, hitching, take along water-purification tablets. They ruin the taste of water, but are needed. *Don't drink unboiled water.* Bottled water is okay, or better yet, beer. *Please don't drink unboiled water.* Remember, we warned you. You can, however, eat off the street, at small shops and cafes. Try anything that is cooked or boiled. Peppered chicken in West Africa, for example. Or in Asia, Chinese soup; it's a meal in itself. Begin slowly, let yourself adjust to the climate and the taste. After awhile, you'll love it.

If you really become very sick and need a physician, contact the American Embassy, British Embassy or the Peace Corps. All have lists of doctors. Other sources are American missionary organizations. They seem to be everywhere. And where you're staying—hotel, hostel, a family— they'll take care of you. Just let them know you're sick. You'll get lots of TLC and perhaps even chicken soup. The world is full of Jewish mothers.

WHAT TO DO IN CASE OF A COUP D'ÉTAT

If you spend any time in Third World countries you'll go through a coup d'état, or, if not that, an uprising, riot or a student strike. You might even be the cause of the trouble. The 1967 May riots at Haile Selassie University were started by two Antioch students who had taken pictures of conditions at a mental hospital in Addis Ababa and showed them on campus, giving the students a reason to demonstrate.

Veteran expatriates will say, "You haven't lived until you've lived through a coup." But you should be prepared, for coups come often and suddenly in the Third World. A friend teaching at Makerere University College in Uganda was unprepared for the January, 1971 coup: "I opened the last can of beer in the house the evening before the firing started." He didn't recognize the sporadic gunfire that occurred that night in downtown Kampala. Thought it was thunder.

Most coups take place at night, or when the head of state is out of the country, or after lunch during those long two- and three-hour siestas favored in warm climates and Latin American countries. A Peace Corps Volunteer we know traveling through West Africa arrived in Nigeria on the eve of the 1966 coup. He slept through the change of government at the Peace Corps hostel and early the next morning was arrested when he innocently went out and started taking pictures of public buildings, unaware of the total curfew in Lagos.

So, in case of a coup, a few handy suggestions:

RULE NUMBER ONE. Have a supply of food and staples ready, enough for several days of turmoil. At the first sign of trouble, all stores will close, iron windows and doors will be drawn down and locked. And they'll remain closed until the fighting stops. Stores will also close unexpectedly and remain locked for lengthy periods of mourning whenever a religious leader, head of state or member of the royal family dies. Count on three days at least and sometimes more than a week.

RULE NUMBER TWO. On your way overseas buy yourself a good short-wave radio. You can purchase one at New York's duty-free shop if you're flying out, but you'll get a better bargain in Shannon, Amsterdam, Aden or Hong Kong.

You're not going to be able to find out what's happened in the country unless you have a shortwave radio. The first executions of coup d'état forces will be to close the international airport, seize the radio and television stations (both state-owned) and take over all telecommunication facilities. You'll be cut off from the outside world. Rumors are always around in Third World countries, especially those with a controlled press. During a coup, you can't believe everything. You may be only two blocks from the presidential palace, but you'll need the BBC to tell what is happening. A shortwave radio also picks up Voice of America, good only for music, and Armed Forces Radio, good for sports. You need BBC for news reports or coup d'état, revolutions and cricket results throughout the Commonwealth. Until the coup is successful or defeated, there won't be any local news, either by radio or television, and no newspaper. To find out what's really happening, you'll need the shortwave.

RULE NUMBER THREE. Stay out of sight. You can get into trouble and hurt if you're too close to the coup or its demonstration. The Peace Corps throughout Latin America issued orders prohibiting volunteers from even watching demonstrations. Too many volunteers were getting hurt taking pictures.

Coup d'états are a time for old scores to be evened. If the street fighting is prolonged, it's easy to knock off an enemy. As a result, there's a lot of civilian shooting, often indiscriminate.

The sudden freedom from laws can turn against you. Anti-American feelings run high overseas. There was a time when Americans were considered chosen people, blessed by endless good fortune. That's no longer true. The Vietnam war, U.S. economic domination, mass migration of Americans, Peace Corps volunteers, military, tourists, thousands of them traveling in packs and young Americans saturating countries like Nepal, India, Afghanistan, Israel, the Caribbean and the Mediterranean looking for drugs, have soured the world's opinion of Americans. Therefore, stay out of sight, you may be the victim of someone's wrath.

RULE NUMBER FOUR. The American Embassy in Third World countries has Emergency Evacuation Plans for Americans overseas. They are elaborate systems built on wardens and section control. When a coup d'état happens, the wardens—American Embassy military and AID personnel—make contact with Americans in their section. This system seldom works.

In the attempted coup of 1961 in Ethiopia, an AID official who had been in the country less than a month and was staying temporarily at a hotel near a battalion headquarters of the Ethiopians received a telephone call from the American Embassy. The embassy told him he was a warden and read a list of Americans he should immediately contact. Outside his hotel, tanks and army troop trucks were converging on the area, gunfire had started in the streets and the hotel windows were sprayed with bullets. He was on the floor, backed into a corner with the telephone and a gin bottle when the call came. His answer to the embassy was to hold the headpiece up to the sounds of the battle, then he hung up. So don't count on the American Embassy.

In 1967 at Hebrew University at the outbreak of the Six Day War, not one of the hundreds of American students left the country, though the American Embassy advised them by letter to do so. The letters reached the students after the war was over.

Keep away from the American Embassy in case they're in the line of fire. If you need help, try the British Embassy in Africa and India, the Swiss Embassy in Latin America. Look for the embassy of a small, neutral country no one dislikes.

Best of all, stay with your host country friends. They'll look after you far better than any other Americans or embassy. You're safest with other students and their families. Most societies outside the West operate on extended family—everyone supports everyone else.

RULE NUMBER FIVE. At the first signs of trouble, fill your bathtub, or any other large container, with water. Also make sure you have candles in case the electricity goes. If you have shutters, close them, or, at the very least, tape the front windows of your house or apartment in case someone starts throwing rocks. Remember, Americans get blamed for everything. Often for good reason.

RULE NUMBER SIX. Once the coup is over, get word home. Your parents will know even less than you about what has happened in the country. Don't count on one letter or telegram carrying the news. Telegrams often lose their meaning in translation from one language to another. Letters, often immediately after a coup, are subject to censor. And codes don't work. If whoever is reading your mail can't understand it, he'll throw it away anyway. Just write that you're okay. Save the coup d'état stories until you return to the United States—they'll get better with time anyway. Ours did.

5. The Radical Traveler

Some negative thoughts about Americans
studying overseas,
or just being overseas,
or maybe just being Americans

We asked Gerry Schwinn, returned volunteer from Nigeria and past Chairman of the national Committee of Returned Volunteers, to write his perspective of American students traveling to the Third World. CRV is "an organization of people who have served as volunteers in countries of the Third World. While overseas, we learned firsthand that our own government was time and again aligned with the forces of reaction, repression, and exploitation of the many by the few, and that our presence was intricately linked with these forces. As returned volunteers, we have come together to study, expose, and organize against United States imperialism and to build support for liberation struggles at home and around the world."

●   ●   ●

In our position of world leadership, we need citizens with a knowledge of foreign countries and fluency in other languages to administer and carry on our global commitments: to run our far-flung aid programs, to enable us to communicate effectively and advantageously with other countries, and to interpret our policies and programs directly to those with whom we deal.
—LYNDON BAINES JOHNSON, 1962

What better reason could there be for *not* going abroad. Hardly do the people of the world, the people of the Third World especially, the Indochinese, the Guatemalans, the Ethiopians, the Palestinians, need to have the "world leadership" of the U.S.A. strengthened and perpetuated. If a lack of people to do America's bidding, as LBJ described it, *weakens* the ability of the United States to wage imperialist and genocidal war, to train police-terrorists to maintain repressive regimes and to perpetuate the profitable rape of the world's resources then in the name of humanity, *stay home!*

Furthermore, Americans, you among them, should not bother to study abroad because you are not going to be touched by the experience and will not be capable of observing or beginning to understand where you go. You will merely come back well on the road to an area studies-major pleasantly burdened with your ignorance and feeling the need to say from time to time "when I was in . . ."

Study for Americans in the Third World is unlikely to be study or schooling in a formal/conventional sense which is probably okay, though struggling to survive in a foreign institution, having to regulate your behavior according to unfamiliar expectations, would be a meaningful experience. But you will probably think it best to choose "independent study" out of your typically American arrogance and bourgeois inability/laziness to cope with institutions more demanding and rigid than American students are familiar with or responsible to.

Once abroad what you will do is seek out other Americans or Europeans, find those places and pastimes that are most reminiscent of "back home" and increasingly pontificate about "These people . . ." in direct proportion as your exposure to the local people and their society goes down.

The people you will "really be able to converse with" will nearly all be members of the local elite, the ones most nearly your peers, and odds are you will be exposed to the most American-oriented of the local elite. Those with the healthy xenophobia of being primarily concerned about their own country are likely to be hostile to Americans.

You should understand that you carry a good deal of national and cultural baggage with you when you go abroad. Your view of the countries you will visit comes through the heavy filter of America's place in the world. If you find yourself, hopefully, put off by LBJ's rephrasing of "manifest destiny," you may have some appreciation that there is no ideology in the world more rigid and self-justifying than American ideology. In many countries things American—its government, its military, its businessmen, its cultural exports—will have an overwhelming presence, and you will be but another from that place that has such inordinate influence on the daily lives of the local people and will be hated for it.

Believing that the best intentioned student is more akin to the most *Babbitt*like tourist than anything else, I hesitate to say that there is a way to go to the Third World as a "student." One person staying home won't, of course, bring the Colossus down and so maybe there is a way to do a little chipping and cracking and even learn during an overseas experience.

The most important thing will be what you do before you go, and that should be a great deal:

• Dip into the history of where you are going, though don't depend only on what foreigners, especially Americans, have to say.

• Read some of the short stories, novels, plays and poems written by the nationals of the country you will visit.

• Learn about the country's past experience with Europe/America. Both the history and contemporary national literature will help understanding here.

• Check *The New York Times* (begin with the index) on what has been happening in the country for the last few months, or year. Get familiar with the names of important local figures and see what the issues of local concern have been/are.

• Try to learn enough to get some clue to what you want to learn by going.

Once there try to be conscious that you are an American and be alert to how you are treated! How do other Americans behave and how are they treated? What form does the American presence take?

As an American you will have access to information (from other Americans) that is often denied to the local people. You will find that the "recreate America" syndrome is so strong that the Americans you will meet overseas are open to other Americans regardless of how closed or even antagonistic they might be if you met them in the United States. Your pursuit of the machinations and attitudes of official and business Americans may mean that you can be a resource to the nationals where you are, who are working to free their country from American dominance/influence. There may perhaps be a constructive role for the American student in the Third World. A few local Americans have found it possible to be useful, albeit in a peripheral way, to radical movements in Japan and the Philippines, perhaps the possibilities exist elsewhere.

You should be clear, before you leave, what you hope to have accomplished by the time of your return. This may well and probably should change while abroad, but such a change is educational only to the degree it is conscious. You should not make rigid plans about what you will do after you return because there should be room for your experience in the Third World to shape your response and behavior once you return, to quote Jose Marti, "to the belly of the monster."

A THIRD WORLD BOOKLIST

ALI, TARIQ (ed.). *The New Revolutionaries*. New York: Apollo, 1969.

ARURI, N., and GHAREEB, E. *Poetry of the Palestinian Resistance*. Drum and Spear Press, 1970.

BURCHETT, WILFRED. *Viet Nam Will Win*. Monthly Review Press, 1969.

*CASTRO, FIDEL. *Fidel Castro Speaks*. Edited by James Petras and Martin Kenner. New York: Grove Press, 1970.

CESAIRE, AIME. *Return to My Native Land*. Penguin, 1969.

CHOMSKY, NOAM. *At War with Asia*. New York: Vintage, 1970.

CLEAVER, ELDRIDGE. *Post Prison Writings and Conversations*. New York: Vintage, 1969.

Committee of Concerned Asian Scholars. *Indochina Story*. New York: Bantam, 1970.

*COWAN, PAUL. *The Making of an Un-American*, Delta, 1970.

DEBRAY, REGIS. *Strategy for a Revolution*. Monthly Review Press, 1970.

*DEVLIN, BERNADETTE. *The Price of My Soul*. New York: Vintage, 1970.

DONOSO, JOSE, and HENKIN, WILLIAM A. *The Tri-Quarterly Anthology of Latin American Literature*. New York: E. P. Dutton & Co., 1969.

*FANON, FRANZ. *The Wretched of the Earth*. New York: Grove Press, 1961.

FRIEDMAN, EDWARD, and SELDEN, MARK. *America's Asia*. New York: Vintage, 1971.

GAY, J., and COLE, M. *New Mathematics and an Old Culture*. New York: Holt, Rinehart and Winston, 1967.

GIOVANNI, NIKKI. *Black Review No. 1*. Edited by M. Watkins. New York: William Morrow & Co., 1971.

*GREENE, GRAHAM. *The Quiet American*. New York: Viking Press, 1957.

HOROWITZ, I. L. *Rise and Fall of Project Camelot*. Boston: Massachusetts Institute of Technology, 1967.

Important Documents from the Great Proletarian Cultural Revolution. Peking: Foreign Language Press, 1970.

MAGDOFF, HARRY. *The Age of Imperialism*. Monthly Review Press, 1969.

*MALCOLM X. *Autobiography*. New York: Grove Press, 1964.

MAMNONI, O. *Prospero and Caliban*. New York: Praeger, 1964.

*MEMMI, ALBERT. *The Colonizer and the Colonized*. Boston: Beacon Press, 1965.

MPHAHLELE, EZEKIEL (ed.). *Writing Today in Africa*. Penguin, 1969.

POMEROY, WILLIAM J. *The Forest: A Personal Record of the Huk Guerilla Struggle in the Philippines*. International, 1963.

SCHURMANN, FRANZ. *Ideology and Organization in Communist China*. California: University of California, 1969.

SEGAL, RONALD. *Race War*. New York: Bantam, 1969.

Tricontinental OSPAAAAL (Organization of Solidarity of the Peoples of Africa, Asia and Latin America) , P.O. Box 4224, Havana, Cuba.

WEISS, PETER. *Notes on the Cultural Life of the DRV*. New York: Dell Publishing Co., 1970.

WINDMILLER, MARSHALL. *The Peace Corps and Pax Americana*. Public Affairs Press, 1970.

WOLF, E., and JORGENSEN, J. "Anthropology on the Warpath in Thailand," *New York Review of Books,* Vol. XV, No. 9, November 19, 1970.

The books with an asterisk before them are good places to begin. The list, with additions, was published originally in the Committee's Journal, *Two, Three, Many!*.

6. Studying in Africa

ALGERIA

COLLEGE: *University of Algiers*
ACADEMIC YEAR: *October to June*
AMERICAN STUDENTS: *None*

INSTRUCTION: *French and Arabic*
TUITION: *$120 per year*
LIVING COSTS: *$140 per month*

VISA. A tourist visa for three months can be renewed in-country, but obtain visa before leaving the United States. Four photos needed and three dollar fee. Apply Algerian Interest Section, 2118 Kalorama Road N.W., Washington, D.C. 20008. (202) 234-7246.

APPLICATION ADDRESS:
Mr. Mahiou
Dean
University of Algiers
Algiers, Algeria

Books To Read: We suggest William B. Quandt's *Revolution and Political Leadership: Algeria 1954–1968,* published by M.I.T. Press, 1969. And Marina and David Ottaway's *Algeria, the Politics of a Socialist Revolution,* published by the University of California Press, 1969. Both are excellent studies of the political nature of Algeria, but heavy reading.

THE SCHOOL. The University of Algiers started in 1909 after combining several other colleges into one school. It had the rank before independence in 1962 of a French university and the university today carries that French tradition, though attempts are being made to "Arabize" the school. There are five faculties: Letters, Science, Law and Economics, Medicine and Pharmacy, Education. The university also has some twenty institutes, rather esoteric ones, like Institute of Solar Energy. There are over seven thousand students and a faculty of seven hundred at Algiers and Constantine. A third center is under consideration.

INDEPENDENT STUDIES. Algeria, perhaps because of its own revolutionary past, strongly supports liberation movements, particularly the Palestine nationalist movement. It is also a country that believes in strict independence and non-alignment. It has attacked both the U.S.A. and the U.S.S.R. for having foreign fleets in the Mediterranean. Watching Algeria develop and maintain its autonomy would be a fascinating and challenging study.

COUNTRY NOTES. Algeria is about one-third the size of the continental United States. It has 620 miles of coastline along the Mediterranean Sea and is surrounded by Libya, Niger, Mali, Mauritania and the Spanish Sahara. Crossing the country laterally are two Atlas Mountain chains. The Tellian Atlas chain runs parallel to the coast. Between it and the sea is a fertile coastal area. To the south lies the Saharan Atlas Mountains which separates the northern areas from the Sahara Desert. Algeria's weather is irregular, but the north has summers that are hot with little rainfall and winters of rain and frost. Summers are hot and winters cold in the Sahara. Dust and sandstorms occur between February and May.

There are fourteen million people in Algeria, nearly all are Moslem of Arab, Berber or mixed Arab-Berber stock. Before independence there were over one million Europeans, now the total foreign population is about eighty thousand. Algeria is trying to interest more Americans to come to Algeria, particularly to teach. They want to introduce English in the classrooms. Arabic is the official language, but French is spoken by the intellectuals and most skilled workers.

The revolution to free Algeria from France began in 1954. It involved years of terror and counterterror. (You may have seen the film *Battle for Algeria*.) The country is now run by a strong National Revolutionary Council and the Council of Ministers, both headed by President Houari Boumediene who took over in a coup d'état in 1965 from Ben Bella.

Algeria broke off diplomatic relations with the United States at the time of the Six Day War. Both countries maintain consular relationships and all Americans in Algeria must contact the Embassy of Switzerland which maintains an Interests Section for America.

REPUBLIC OF ZAIRE

COLLEGES: *Lovanium University*   INSTRUCTION: *French*
Official University of Zaire   TUITION: *About $250 per year*
The Free University of Zaire   LIVING COSTS: *$250 per month*
ACADEMIC YEAR: *October to July*
AMERICAN STUDENTS: *No more than fifty,*
    all schools

VISA. Difficult to obtain, but if enrolled in a university in Zaire fairly simple, also easy if you have a letter from U.S. school stating you are doing independent study. One photo is needed and $26.40 for a residence visa. Apply Embassy of the Republic of Zaire, 1800 New Hampshire, Washington, D.C. 20009. (202) 234-7690.

APPLICATION ADDRESSES. Write to the Secrétaire Général of the university. Also possible to write the Secrétaire Général of the Ministry of National Education. Getting admitted takes about a year.

BOOKS TO READ. The most current piece of information is the Department of State's *Africa: This New Dialogue,* published by the U.S. Printing Office publication No. 8511, 1970. Conor Cruise O'Brien's *To Katanga and Back* tells of his time in the Congo during the United Nations assistance to the country. It was published by Simon and Schuster in 1962. Excellent book.

THE SCHOOLS. All based on the French system. A *license* is given after four or five years of study. There are about 7,000 students. (Zaire had thirteen college graduates at independence in 1960.) The largest and most sophisticated university is (Catholic) University of Lovanium. It was started in 1954 in Kinshasa. The university has 4,000 students and faculties of Theology, Law, Arts, Philosophy and Letters, Sciences, Economics, Social Sciences, Psychology and Education. Its library has over five hundred thousand volumes. Unique in black Africa. There are dormitory rooms for 2,500 male students and a large, well-equipped campus, even a swimming pool. The Free University in Kisangani has 1,100 students and started in 1963, but because of the fighting the university really has been running only since 1967. It is a private university supported by the Protestant churches with some government help. Official University in Lumumbashi has some 2,000 students and was started in 1958. It has faculties of Law, Medicine, Philosophy and Letters, Science and Applied Science. In 1969 all three of these universities were staffed by 219 Congolese and 460 foreign professors.

INDEPENDENT STUDY. This country is particularly good for study in anthropology, political science and linguistics. Students, however, need to know French to operate here. The country lends itself at the moment to graduate study, not undergraduate work. In 1970 the Peace Corps sent its first volunteers to Kinshasa, less than thirty. Black Americans are openly welcomed here. It is possible to enroll in any of these universities as auditor or special student, can be done in-country.

COUNTRY NOTES. A friend living in Zaire wrote us: "Not only do you find a lot of tribalism here, but you find deep divisions among the people because of religion. Catholics don't cooperate with the Protestants, both the Protestants and the Catholics look down on the indigenous Christian church called the Kimbanguish Church after the Congolese religious leader who was martyred by the Belgains in the 1920s, and the biggest fights, both doctrinally and developmentally, take place among the Protestants and their 34 sects in this nation." There are four thousand Catholic and one thousand Protestant missionaries in Zaire, operating seven hundred missions. That's a lot of religion.

The Republic of Zaire is about the size of the United States east of the Mississippi River. It's a huge place that lies on the equator. The whole country is hot and humid. It has a population of eighteen million, but there are less than two thousand Americans in the country, and only sixty thousand non-Africans live in Zaire. It is a country of great promise, set back from 1960–67 by economic disruptions, but beginning to develop once more. At the time of independence in 1960 the Congo had one of the most highly developed economies in sub-Sahara. The chaos following independence ended that growth.

We'll hear again from Zaire.

ETHIOPIA

COLLEGE: *Haile Selassie I University*
ACADEMIC YEAR: *October 1 to June 20*
AMERICAN STUDENTS: *Five a year*

INSTRUCTION: *English and Amharic*
TUITION: *$400 per year*
LIVING COSTS: *$160 per month*

VISA. Tourist/business visa costs four dollars and is good for sixty days. Three photos required. This visa can be renewed in-country. When applying for visa, include a dollar fifty for postage fee. Write: Embassy, 2134 Kalorama Road, N.W., Washington, D.C. (202) AD 4-2281.

APPLICATION ADDRESS.
Haile Selassie I University
Registrar
P.B. 1176
Addis Ababa, Ethiopia

BOOKS TO READ. Donald Lebine's *Wax and Gold—Studies in Amhara Culture*. The classic book on the Amharas. It has a fine section on the problems of modernization in Ethiopia. George Lipsky's *Ethiopia: Its People, Its Society, Its Culture*. A general study of the country; the book covers everything. Richard Greenfield's *Ethiopia A New Political History*. Excellent on the 1960 coup d'état.

THE SCHOOL. The main campus of the university is located on the former palace grounds of the emperor. It is situated north of the city, easily accessible by bus and taxi. The university is not difficult and American students say they are not challenged in the classroom. There are a number of excellent teachers: Dr. Taye, Economics; Ato Teferra Worg Beshad, Political Science; Dr. Taddesse and Dr. Sergew, History; Dr. Seyoum, Public Administration. There are a large number of foreign professors—Americans, British, Indian—teaching on contracts. Classes are mostly large lectures, but the university—less than a thousand students—lends itself to personal contacts.

The History and Administrative Departments are strong and oriented toward Ethiopia. Public Administration is concerned with the current problems of development in the country. Amharic language courses are also worthwhile. Naturally.

Students are radical and outspoken. They have rioted every spring since 1965, and were involved in the 1960 coup d'état. The government has shut down the university several times and in 1970 the student union president was killed. A number of students are political exiles in the Sudan. Ethiopians are polite and reserved, withdrawing. Americans have to make a special effort to make friends. Women should be careful about their relationships. Ethiopians have a strong double standard and dating is done, but limited.

INDEPENDENT STUDY. Students get special cooperation from the History Department, and there are many studies possible in sociology, economics and anthropology. Ethiopians have a penchant for secrecy, therefore, difficult for undergraduates to do research, unless arrangements are made. Easy to do a photographic essay of the country, or a study of the modern Ethiopian student in contrast with his society.

COUNTRY NOTES. Addis Ababa at 8,640 feet has ideal weather, similar to San Francisco. The rainy season is from July to September and the sun shines most days. It's a country for hitchhiking and inexpensive transportation—train, bus and lorry—taking you to all parts of the empire. Camping, hiking and horseback riding can be done almost everywhere. English gets you around and Italian or French is a good second language.

Health is not a problem if simple precautions are taken. American doctors are available.

Dormitory space is available at the university, but overcrowded and uncomfortable. Buying furniture and settling in is expensive. It's possible to live cheaply at a small hotel or off campus with other students. These arrangements can be made after you've arrived. Stay at the International Hotel, near Siddist Kilo, for the first few days.

Airlines fly daily to Addis Ababa from Europe and the rest of Africa. It is a hard country to reach overland, but can be made on a new road up from Kenya. If you go by road write and let us know how it turns out. Otherwise, by ship from the Red Sea, through the ports of Djibouti, Massawa or Assab.

GHANA

COLLEGE: *University of Ghana*
ACADEMIC YEAR: *October to June*
AMERICAN STUDENTS: *157*

INSTRUCTION: *English*
TUITION: *$700 per term*
LIVING COSTS: *$450 per term*

VISA. The tourist visa is valid up to fourteen days. It costs $2.25 and two photos are required. To stay longer, apply to the Embassy three to four months in advance. Write: Ghana Embassy, 2460 16th Street, N.W., Washington, D.C. 20009. (202) 462-0761.

APPLICATION ADDRESS.
Registrar
University of Ghana
P.O. 25
Legon, Accra, Ghana

BOOKS TO READ. Some recent good books are: *Ghana an Historical Interpretation,* J. D. Fage, University of Wisconsin Press, 1966; *Africa Must Wait,* Kwame Nkrumah, Praeger Press, 1963; *Ghana End of an Illusion,* Bob Fitch and Mary Oppenheimer, Monthly Review, 1961.

THE SCHOOL. The University of Ghana was founded in 1948 and is an autonomous institution, though it has a special relationship with the University of London and prepares students for the London Degree. It is the best university on the west coast of Africa and perhaps the best university in black Africa. It is located nine miles northeast of Accra on the Dodowa road to Legon Hill. The university has 2,530 students from all over black Africa, parts of Europe and the United States. Every year Berkeley sends students to study at the university.

The university has several very strong departments. Its Institute of African Studies is exceptional and most American students are enrolled here. Other strong departments are history (African and World) particularly because of Dr. Awdobohene and philosophy (Dr. Abraham is worthwhile in this department). Their political science department is radical for Africa. Chemistry is considered first-rate, especially because of Dr. Adjei-bakoe. Dr. Eddie Ayenso, a visiting professor, teaches biology every fall term. He is director of the botany department of the Smithsonian Institution and a renowned authority on the fruit bats of tropical Africa. If you're interested in the classics, take Dr. Kwapong. He's also vice-chancellor of the university. Eighty percent of the professors at the University of Ghana are Ghanaian and the other 20 percent are mostly British. The school has that heavy British atmosphere of large lecture halls, the tutorial system, separation of the junior and senior common rooms. But because of its size, and the tutorial system, contact between faculty and students is possible, though a bit stiff on the part of Ghanaians who have received advanced education in England.

There are five residential halls and each is self-contained with a dining hall, chapel, library, junior and senior common rooms. Women make up one-third of the student body and one of the residential halls is coed. The Ghanaians are very practical about male and female relationships. Unusual for Africa or, for that matter, the rest of the world.

The university was closed in 1969 over lack of student participation on college decisions. The strike was short lived. Students actually have it soft at the college, daily cleaning of their rooms, waited tables, etc. All they have to do is study. And Ghanaian students study. Ninety percent of every graduating class continues for additional degrees. The level of instruction at the University of Ghana is higher than most colleges in America.

INDEPENDENT STUDY. Nearly every teacher will cooperate with an American student on an independent project and serve as advisor. They are used to the system and practice it at the university. Students are asked to spend their vacations on special rural community projects for the Ghana government. American students can be involved, if interested.

COUNTRY NOTES. In February, 1966 Kwame Nkrumah was overthrown. That has altered the political course of Ghana but Kwame Nkrumah is not forgotten and may yet return to Ghana. He has been one of the great thinkers among modern Africans and has done much already to pull the continent together as a political force.

Ghana is one of those lovely tropical countries on the ocean. The Atlantic Occra can be reached by bus, taxi or hitching. Students are mobile and it is easy to get around the country, fairly adequate roads.

The Ghanaians themselves are simply charming—we haven't found nicer people in Africa. They are open, friendly and tolerate everyone, even Americans! Some trouble recently at the university, however. Students were upset in 1970 because American students were smoking dope and students complained. The vice-chancellor was reluctant to discipline the students because he did not want to offend them. The American ambassador got wind of the problem and talked to the American students.

In Africa the University of Ghana is the most receptive to American students. We hope this atmosphere doesn't deteriorate. An American student would be fortunate to be able to spend a year or more studying in Ghana.

GUINEA

COLLEGE: *École Nationale des Arts et Métiers*
ACADEMIC YEAR: *October to end of July*
AMERICAN STUDENTS: *None*

INSTRUCTION: *French*
TUITION: *Free*
LIVING COSTS: *$350 per month*

VISA. Valid for three months, needs to be renewed in-country. Apply well in advance. Three photos required. Cost five dollars. Write: Embassy of Guinea, 2112 Leroy Place, N.W., Washington, D.C. 20008. (212) HU 3-9420.

BOOKS TO READ. *The Reds and the Blacks* by William Atwood. This book by the former ambassador to Guinea and Kenya was severely criticized when it appeared in 1966, but does relate to the situation in Guinea today. Not much else available.

THE SCHOOL. E.N.A.M. is a U.S. AID project to develop mechanics and conducts two- and three-year programs. The Russians have a similar project for engineers. It is L'Institut Polytechnique and is a five-year program. The academic standard of the École Nationale des Arts et Métiers is low.

INDEPENDENT STUDY. Guinea is an intriguing country, but does not appreciate being observed. It has a socialist regime and is trying to create a new socialistic man. A non-tribal man in a united country. That transformation is worth studying but it is difficult to get into the country or out of the capital.

COUNTRY NOTES. Conakry is said to have all the charm of Moscow in the mid-thirties. Its population is the nicest in Africa, however, the economic system is falling apart. No one is starving, but there's not enough food. Conakry has regular shortages of fuel and motor oil. Besides, it's one of the most expensive cities in the world.

Many of the students leave the country after their training. It is estimated that nearly a million Guineans have left the country, causing employment problems for Liberia where one-fourth of the population of Monrovia is Guinean and for Sierra Leone, which has begun to expel Guineans. The city has a twelve midnight curfew and road blocks are set up after dark.

For the immediate future, Guinea does not lend itself to foreign students, either on independent study or at the École Nationale. For the immediate future avoid Guinea.

KENYA

COLLEGE: *College of Nairobi*
ACADEMIC YEAR: *September to July*
AMERICAN STUDENTS: *About nine*

INSTRUCTION: *English*
TUITION: *$900 per year*
LIVING COSTS: *$150 per month*

VISA. Visa valid for three months. Costs $3.15. For information on longer stay write: Embassy of Kenya, 1875 Connecticut Ave., N.W., Washington, D.C. 20009. (202) 234-4350.

APPLICATION ADDRESS.
S.W. Karania
University of Nairobi
Nairobi

BOOKS TO READ. A general book would be Joy Adamson's *The Peoples of Kenya* (New York: Harcourt, 1967). Also, *Out of Africa* by Isak Dinesen, the finest book written about East Africa. And, *Harambee! The Prime Minister of Kenya's Speeches 1963–1964,* by Jomo Kenyatta (Oxford University Press, 1964). And Kenyatta's *Facing Mount Kenya* (London: Secker and Warburg, 1953).

THE SCHOOL. The University of Nairobi began granting degrees only in 1964, but has had a longer history of higher education in East Africa. The university opened in 1954 as the Royal Technical College, a constituent college of the University of East Africa. In 1970 it became independent and has a student body of 2,212.

Because of its long period of specialization in technical subjects, the university is strongest in these fields. They offer a B.A. degree (obtainable in three years) in Architectural Studies, Design, Engineering and Science. Liberal Arts is not a strong point of the college, but we know a

Brown University student who spent a year at Nairobi studying English Literature on a tutorial arrangement with several British expatriates as teachers. He picked up his master's that way at Nairobi.

The campus is on the outskirts of downtown Nairobi, next to the YMCA on a rather small campus, sandwiched between lovely tree-lined boulevards. The buildings are new and not many. American aid has been building a number of new structures in the last few years and the university has dormitories for men and women, though we suggest you find an apartment in town, which isn't difficult to do.

INDEPENDENT STUDY. Nairobi is a *very* British college. The English have hung on in East Africa, particularly in the area of education. The vice-chancellor is, however, Kenyan, a Kikuyu, the ruling tribe in Kenya. We have known students who have been able to develop independent programs at the university and it is possible to get a student visa good for six months which can be then renewed. In case you decide not to enroll, but want to do independent study, the most interesting study in Kenya, we think, is the conflicts of tribal politics, particularly between the ruling Kikuyus and the Luos.

After the assassination of Tom Mboya, a Luo, in 1969, and the banning of the Kenya People's Union and Oginga Odinga, its leader (locally called Double O), by President Kenyatta, politics have not been easy in Kenya. Kenyatta is over eighty years old, was the leader of the Mau Maus, and brought the country into independence in 1963, but he's getting old. Violent changes should occur in Kenya within the next five years. Kenyatta cannot hold this country together forever and when he goes, it is likely everything will change with political power struggles.

Besides politics, there is the wonderful wildlife and scenic beauty of the country. Kenya is the loveliest nation in East Africa. It is also the home of Louis Leakey who has done so much work with Fossil Man, at Olduvai in Tanzania, Fort Kernan in Kenya and lately in the Omo River Valley of Ethiopia. The National Museum in Nairobi, near the university is in itself worth a trip to Kenya.

COUNTRY NOTES. Kenya's about the size of Texas and has a population of ten million. It is a country with hundreds of miles of white beaches along the Indian Ocean, located south of Ethiopia, Sudan and Somali, on the equator. The Great Rift Valley also runs through the country, from north to south, and on a clear day both snow peaks of Mount Kenya and Mount Kilimanjaro can be seen. Everywhere there is nature, wild game, a modern nation, and beauty.

No trouble moving around Kenya or into Uganda or Tanzania (though lately some problems have developed with Uganda and Kenya) by bus, train or hitching. Roads are paved and connect most sections of the country, except the northern frontier, and that is gradually coming under control.

Nairobi is called the "city in the sun," which is true. The "long rains" are only from April to June and the "short rains" from October to December. It can be quite cold during the rainy season, remember that. Nairobi is a British city, only recently becoming aware of its African consciousness. It closes early at night in the main parts of town, though the African parts are alive after midnight, but most people are off major streets by ten o'clock.

English is spoken in all major towns and Swahili can be picked up, so languages are not a problem. Everyone speaks English at the university. It is hard to find anything "wrong" with living and studying in Kenya. If we can think of anything, we'll let you know.

LESOTHO

COLLEGE: *University of Botswana, Lesotho and Swaziland*
ACADEMIC YEAR: *July to April*
AMERICAN STUDENTS: *None*

INSTRUCTION: *English*
TUITION: *$200 per year*
LIVING COSTS: *$125 per month*

VISA. Obtained from the Republic of South Africa. Get a one-year multiple entries visa. A return ticket is needed, apply Consulate General, New York, New York 10021.

APPLICATION ADDRESS.
J. M. Normand
P.O. Roma
Lesotho, South Africa

BOOK TO READ. Very little available. We suggest Robert Stevens' *Lesotho, Botswana and Swaziland: The Former High Commission Territories in Southern Africa* (New York: Praeger, 1967).

THE SCHOOL. This university began in 1945 as a small Catholic college, called Pius XII College. It is located twenty-two miles from Maseru, the capital of Lesotho. In 1964 it became a university with 188 students and thirty-one academic staff. It also has campuses in Botswana and Swaziland, both very small. There are no racial or religious barriers to admissions and the university now has students from Botswana, Lesotho, Swaziland, Malawi, South Africa, South West Africa, Rhodesia and Ireland. In 1970 there were 420 students on the Roma campus taking courses in five schools: Education, Humanities, Science, Social and Economic Studies, Agriculture. A B.A. takes four years.

The Roma campus is a small green palm of cultivation in an area of dry land and hard rocks. All students live on campus—four dorms for the men, two for women—but it is possible to live in Roma, two miles from the school. There is not much to do on campus or in Roma. Weekly film and daily games in football, cricket, netball and judo. That's about all.

INDEPENDENT STUDY. One study could be the three former territories themselves. Botswana is the largest of these three countries, about the size of Texas. Lesotho and Swaziland are two small dots surrounded by the Republic of South Africa. Students would have to be careful how and what they are studying. The geographic locations of these countries, and their natural leeriness of whites, means students should obtain permission for their work. The whole area of secondary education also would be worth studying, and not much has been done here, only a few position papers by the Peace Corps.

COUNTRY NOTES. We do not recommend this university for black students. Too much abuse and hassle with South Africa. And students have to pass through South Africa to get to Lesotho. In 1909 when the constitution of the Union of South Africa was being drawn up, following the Boer War, the African peoples of Basutoland (Lesotho), Bechuanaland (Botswana) and Swaziland asked not to be included. They have been able to remain semiindependent ever since. The country populations are small: Botswana—650,000; Lesotha—100,000; Swaziland—300,000. Travel among the countries is relatively easy, as long as visas are in order. The whole of South Africa is ideal for hitching. Remember it's a big country.

Black South Africans that we have known in exile in Africa have told us to visit South Africa, live there and learn about the country. It is the only way, they say, anyone can understand the terrible conditions of apartheid. That reason alone makes it a country worth seeing.

LIBERIA

COLLEGES: *University of Liberia*
        Cuttington College and
        Divinity School
ACADEMIC YEAR: *Late February to*
        mid-December
AMERICAN STUDENTS: *17 in special*
        program

INSTRUCTION: *English*
TUITION: *$1,300 per year (Liberia)*
LIVING COSTS: *$240 per month*

VISA. To stay longer than three months a resident visa is required and proof of some sponsor within the country. If applying to either college, they can help in obtaining visas. Two pictures are required. Apply in plenty of time: Liberian Embassy, 5201 16th Street, N.W., Washington, D.C. 20011. (202) RA 3-0437.

APPLICATION ADDRESSES.
University of Liberia
Monrovia, Liberia

Cuttington College
P.O. Box 277
Monrovia, Liberia

BOOKS TO READ. *Liberia-Evolution of Privilege,* Ernell Liebenow. Political survey and excellent. *ZinZin Road,* Fletcher Knebel. Popular novel about the Peace Corps in Liberia, entertaining, and gives some idea of the country.

THE SCHOOLS. Cuttington has two hundred students and the University of Liberia 1,200. Academic quality of the schools is limited, but there are some fine teachers and courses. At Cuttington College there is an American, John Gay, an outstanding anthropologist on Liberia. Worth studying under. Agriculture courses at University of Liberia are sound, especially tropical agriculture. The university is excellent for the study of Liberia itself and West Africa in general. The head of the School of Education at Liberia is Dr. Mary Brown, a bright, unassuming and devoted teacher. She has taught in the United States, at San Francisco University. Another good teacher is Angus Von Ballmoos. At Cuttington College Joe Knotts, head of the music department, has a fine program. Knotts has written and produced plays, among them *The Hold.*

INDEPENDENT STUDY. Liberia has sixteen or more local languages and a linguistic study would be challenging and worthwhile for the country. Also possible to do medical research at the college. It is directed by Spanish and Italian priests. Anthropology studies, particularly under the direction of Dr. John Gay, would be very valuable.

COUNTRY NOTES. Liberia is perhaps the least uptight country in the world. The people are warm, friendly and relaxed. The people know how to "take time" with each other. It is a hot and humid country. Liberia has 180 inches of rain a year, but beaches are close and swimming rough, but possible.

The University of Liberia is in downtown Monrovia, a busy place. Monrovia at night is perhaps the most "swinging" city in Africa. It is a city of eight hundred thousand and growing. Students can live in dormitories, but most find places off campus, with Liberian families, or other students. Everything in Liberia happens in Monrovia. Until recently there weren't even all-weather roads up-country to the interior. Cutting-ton College is in the interior, 150 miles from the capital and near the town of Gbainga. It is a picturesque campus with tropical trees and lawns, twenty-odd low and long white buildings, quiet and tranquil, and isolated. All students live on campus in three dormitories for the small village nearby has little to provide. Kalamazoo College has for the last few years sent some students overseas to Cuttington.

English is the official language of the country, therefore, the language problem is not a serious one, though the Liberians have developed over the years their own vernacular. The country is friendly to Americans, but has been exploited by American business and their own government. Not too much longer will Liberia remain tranquil in the sun. It's a country with people of great promise.

MALAWI

COLLEGE: *University of Malawi*
ACADEMIC YEAR: *October to July*
AMERICAN STUDENTS: *None*

INSTRUCTION: *English*
TUITION: *$750 per year*
LIVING COSTS: *$110 per month*

VISA. Visas are not required for stays up to one year. Apply to Embassy, Washington, D.C. 20008. (202) 234-9313.

APPLICATION ADDRESS.
I. C. H. Freeman
Registrar
University of Malawi
P.O. Box 5097
Limbe, Malawi

BOOKS TO READ. Most recent important book is J. G. Pike's *Malawi: A Political and Economic History,* Praeger, 1968. And Pike and G. T. Remington's *Malawi, a Geographical Study,* published by Oxford University Press, 1965.

THE SCHOOL. The University of Malawi was founded in 1965. It is based on the British system and is a small institution with limited facilities. The Colleges of Arts and Sciences (Chancellor College) is located in Blantyre as is also the Polytechnic (combination of university and pre-university level courses) and the College of Education (Soche Hill). The

College of Agriculture (Bunda) is located near Lilongwe and the College of Public Administration and Law is located at Mpemba about ten miles from Blantyre. The faculty is now about half Malawian and half expatriate, mostly British.

The students at the university are the cream of the educational system. Since the university can accommodate only a small percentage of those who pass the Cambridge exams, the university takes only the top. In 1970 there were 420 students, about sixty of them women. The students of the university and faculty of Malawi have deliberately been kept apolitical. The government has openly stated that the duties of the students and faculty are to learn and teach and to leave politics to the politicians. Consequently, there have been no demonstrations, teach-ins, etc., at the university for several years.

Because of the combination of British tradition, missionary influence and personal preference of the top leadership in Malawi, student dress and personal appearance resembles more the small, exclusive eastern prep school rather than the typical American University, *e.g.*, coats, ties, knee-length dresses, etc. (All women, for example, have to wear dresses that cover the knees. Slacks and shorts are forbidden to be worn in public except when engaged in athletics. One of the reasons the Peace Corps was kicked out of Malawi was because President Banda disliked the American "hippie" look.)

To be admitted to the University of Malawi special permission has to be obtained from President Banda. The president is the chancellor of the university and takes a great interest in it, personally following many details.

INDEPENDENT STUDY. Malawi is trying to create a non-racial society and is leading the way in advocating dialogue and contact with South Africa in an effort to change the South African views on Africans. Malawi is also conveniently located for trips to Mozambique, Tanzania, Zambia, Rhodesia and the south. Travel is easy and cheap. A study of Malawi's new relationships with South Africa and the attempts at the non-racial society are worthwhile projects.

COUNTRY NOTES. Malawi, known as Nyasaland before independence in 1964, is about the size of the peninsula of Florida. It is a land-locked country. Malawi is most famous in history because of David Livingstone who discovered Lake Malawi in 1859. Malawi likes to call itself "the Switzerland" of Africa. We're not exactly sure why, but it's mainly because they try to be friendly to everyone, covered as they are on all sides. Malawi is a poor country otherwise, but has great scenery and a reasonable climate. Also the people are friendly and Americans get along well here, if they're nicely dressed and clean shaven. It's a one-party state and President Banda has been chosen president for life. The country is also conservative, even by African standards. Not a place for lots of fun and games. Except that Paul Theroux wrote a very funny novel about the country, *Jungle Lovers*. Read it first.

MAURITIUS

COLLEGE: *University of Mauritius*
ACADEMIC YEAR: *October to July*
AMERICAN STUDENTS: *None*

INSTRUCTION: *English and French*
TUITION: *$15 per month*
LIVING COSTS: *$60 per month*

VISA. Apply to the British Embassy or nearest British consulate. Need to prove sufficient funds to get off the island. Visa costs $1.90.

APPLICATION ADDRESS.
University of Mauritius
Reduit, Mauritius, Indian Ocean

BOOKS TO READ. Really no decent book on the island. We suggest you get a copy of *Background Notes—Mauritius*, published by Office of Media Services, Department of State, Washington, D.C. It is publication No. 8023.

THE SCHOOL. Three schools in the university: Administration, Agriculture and Industrial Technology. It opened in 1965. All courses are adequate. There's a heavy emphasis on agriculture, economics and business to the exclusion of humanities. Courses are made as specific as possible on the conditions of Mauritius. The university's first priority is Mauritius and is only offering courses that have an immediate impact on the development of the country. Business courses are in French and there are at the moment no foreign students though the university would welcome American students.

INDEPENDENT STUDY. Mauritius is in many respects a forgotten corner of the academic world and plenty of opportunities for independent study. Because of the unusual flora and fauna, and the maritime climate, we suggest topics in biology and zoology. For example, there are five thousand acres of untouched indigenous forests which contain many species of plants peculiar to the Mascarene Islands. The marine fauna is extremely rich for research; the island is already famous for its seashells. Seventy-five different species of birds; twenty-five endemic.

COUNTRY NOTES. An early question might be: where is Mauritius? It's located in the Indian Ocean, inside the Tropic of Capricorn and 1,500 miles east of Africa. The island's forty miles long and thirty miles wide and rises at one plateau to 1,900 feet.

There are slightly more than eight hundred thousand people on the island, made up of three groups: Indo-Mauritians, Sino-Mauritians and a general population of people of European descent and African blood. The country became independent of England in 1968 and in past has been ruled by France, Spain, Portugal and Holland. It was uninhabited until the end of the sixteenth century, then became important in naval history. The first European to reach the island was Vasco de Gama.

Today Mauritius has a half-dozen modern cities, first-class hotels, six hundred miles of roads and miles of beaches. We think it's not a bad place to spend a year. To reach this island, travel to Mombasa then fly direct to Port Louis.

MOROCCO

COLLEGE: *University of Mohammed V*
ACADEMIC YEAR: *Mid-October to July*
AMERICAN STUDENTS: *One in 1970*

INSTRUCTION: *French and Arabic*
TUITION: *Approximately $290 per year*
LIVING COSTS: *$110 per month*

VISA. Required if staying longer than three months. Apply to local authorities: Embassy of Morocco, 1601 21st Street, N.W., Washington, D.C. 20009. (212) HO 2-7979.

APPLICATION ADDRESS.
Mohammed El Fasi, Rector
University of Mohammed V
Rabat, Morocco

BOOKS TO READ. *Honor to the Bride Like the Pigeon That Guards It's Grain Under the Clove Tree* by Jane Kramer. Yes, a strange title, but a witty and insightful account of living in Morocco; *Saints of the Atlas* by Ernest Gellner, about the central Moroccan Berbers, studies their political and religious organization; *A Life Full of Holes,* translated by Paul Bowles from the Moghrebi. An excellent study of a cross-cultural situation.

THE SCHOOL. The University of Mohammed V has three departments: (1) Letters and Humanities; (2) Sciences; (3) Law, Economics and Political Science. The Department of Letters has a branch in Fez for the study of Arabic literature. The university was inaugurated in 1959 and has expanded rapidly. About 10,500 students are enrolled. Mohammed V has a high standard for the Arab World, but not as well thought of as the American University in Beirut. The university is international, but most students come from other Arab countries. Any American student with a high school diploma would be acceptable. It's a university famous for strikes and is usually shut down by the government once or twice during the year. Dormitories accommodate only 20 percent of the students so plan on living in Rabat where small apartments are available.

INDEPENDENT STUDY. A worthwhile place for independent study, especially in archaeology. Ruins from the Phoenicians, Romans and Moors are scattered throughout the country. There's the camel market in the southern town of Goulimine. Traders come from as far as Timbuktu. A research project on this market would be fascinating. The south is noted for its pre-Saharan architecture. To live in Morocco and do anything it is necessary to know French or Arabic.

COUNTRY NOTES. Rabat is a modern city influenced heavily by the French. All government activities take place here. The great cities of Morocco, however, are Marrakesh, Fez and Casablanca, though Casablanca has seen better days. The pace is slow in Morocco and customs and traditions are strong. American women have a tough time with Moroccan men and this takes a bit to get used to. The Moslem concept of alms-giving results in a plethora of beggars and you'll need to condition yourself for this phenomenon. Middle-East problems are not an issue and Jews can live in Morocco without trouble, as long as they not mention religion. It is a relatively clean country and health hazards slight. The two largest worries are tuberculosis and venereal disease. Good French doctors are available.

A great many young Americans now live in Morocco. The style of life of these cities and the close source of drugs has attracted them to places like Marrakesh and Fez. The government has not hassled these people, but we doubt if the honeymoon will go on much longer. At the moment, however, the people are friendly and receptive. The most recent political trouble was the July, 1971, attempted coup d'état.

Travel within Morocco is easy, cheap and safe. Everything from express, air-conditioned trains to old buses. Cheapest way to reach the country from Europe is across the straits by boat to Tangier. Also you can fly to Rabat or Casablanca on Pan Am or Royal Air Maroc.

Interior Morocco is an oven in the summer and a rain forest through the winter. The coasts are comfortable, but it gets cold in winter, even in Africa. Bring an electric blanket or anyone warm.

NIGERIA

COLLEGES: *University of Ibadan*   INSTRUCTION: *English*
University of Ife   TUITION: *$200 per year*
University of Nigeria   LIVING COSTS: *$170 per month*
University of Lagos
Ahmadu Bello University
ACADEMIC YEAR: *October to June*
AMERICAN STUDENTS: *About 20 every year*
(University of Ibadan
has slightly more)

VISA. If enrolled in a university okay. Otherwise difficult. Current Nigerian Ambassador to the United States is down on young Americans, felt they supported Biafra. Three photos and two dollars needed. Apply Nigerian Embassy, 1336 16th Street, N.W., Washington, D.C. 20036. (202) 234-4800.

APPLICATION ADDRESSES. Write the Registrar of each university. Or write: The African-American Institute, P.O. Box 2382, Lagos, Nigeria.

BOOKS TO READ. Read the novels of Nigerian writer Chinua Achebe. He's extremely talented and gives an accurate picture of the country. James Coleman's *Nigeria: Background to Nationalism* (California: University of California Press, 1958). A solid study of the country. *The Lost Cities of Africa* by Basil Davidson. Should be read by anyone going to Africa.

THE SCHOOLS. The University of Ibadan is Nigeria's oldest institution of higher learning, tracing its history to 1948 when the University College was established. It is located in the city of Ibadan approximately ninety miles from Lagos, Nigeria's capital. The largest city in sub-Sahara Africa, Ibadan has an estimated population of nearly one and one-half million people. The University of Ibadan, with faculties of Arts, Science, Medicine, Agriculture, Forestry, Veterinary Science, Social Sciences and Education, is one of Africa's most prestigious institutions. The university also has the Institutes of Education, African Studies, Librarianship, Child-Health and a School of Drama. Its enrollment is over four thousand.

The drama department is the best in Africa. (Tom Hebert once taught in this department.) Ibadan gives a classic British education and the university is *very* British run. It's also a lovely campus with white buildings, tropical gardens, long winding drives. A nice place to spend time. Ibadan also has the best bookstore in Nigeria.

The University of Nigeria which has two campuses at Nsukka and Enugu was considered the second best university in the country, but was totally destroyed during the Biafran War. The university was sometimes referred to as the "Spirit of Biafra" and it is thought by many that the plans for secession were started by the intellectuals at Nsukka. Much of the "brain power" from the university contributed to Biafra's early success. The destruction of the campus at Nsukka by the federal troops was a way of expressing the resentment of Ibo superior educational achievements which was a key factor in the outbreak of the war. As examples of the destruction fifty thousand books are said to have been destroyed and the Continuing Education Center, which U.S. AID built and was the focus of the community programs, was burned.

U.S. AID had spent over ten million dollars on the University of Nigeria, wanting to make it an example of the "land grant" type of school in Africa. The University of Nigeria reopened in the fall of 1970 with most of the students and faculty back. Students and faculty came themselves to clean the rooms, and classes were held outside under trees, anywhere they could gather. There are no American students here.

Ahmadu Bello University in Zaria, northern Nigeria opened in 1962 and is in the Arab Moslem section of the country. The university has about 1,800 students. The country is as lovely as the weather: cool, crisp, dry. The University of Pittsburgh has for twelve years been running a Public Administration Institute, but the stamp of the university is Moslem, agriculture and bush. Half of the teachers are expatriate, mostly young. Father James O'Connell in Political Science is perhaps the most interesting and best teacher there. Someone worth getting to know, or just being around. Father O'Connell is a Nigerian citizen.

The University of Lagos began in 1962, closed once, in March, 1965 over the change in vice-chancellorship. It opened its permanent location in northeast Yaba in 1965. It has a campus of one thousand acres near a lagoon and out of the town. The university is beginning to grow, developing a program in computer sciences, educational psychology, mass communications. They want to attract more American students. The School of African and Asian Studies, founded in 1967, is particularly interested in students, especially black American undergraduates. There are about 2,080 students on this small campus. Standards here are lower than at the other universities. Sometimes instruction appears to be in special English. The college is American designed and rich, another one of those tropical garden settings.

The University of Ife was created in 1961 in the shadow of the University of Ibadan. It was to be the then Western Region answer to the Federal University at Ibadan. With the reduction of the Western Region —the Midwestern State was carved out of it—and with the emergence of the new twelve-state system, the position of Ife was somewhat undercut.

The university is new, in fact many buildings have not yet been used. It is located in an isolated setting and housing is limited. Distances between university buildings and residential areas are tremendous because Ife has such a sprawling campus. The university is growing. In 1962 there were 244 students, in 1970 there were 2,000. The university is trying to build a strong science and technology school. Medical students were accepted in 1971.

Leeds University in England is sending lecturers to work at the University of Ife for up to four years. The quality of instruction is high. U.S. AID has staff on campus, but they are generally resented by Nigerians and expatriates for their conspicuous use of air conditioners. Typical.

INDEPENDENT STUDY. You will be most successful if you put yourself under the direction of someone at the special institutes, agreeing to do research for him or her in lieu of what you will learn. One possibility, for example, would be to try and work with Michael Crowder at the University of Ife. He's Director of their Institute of African Studies. Or to study and research at the School of Environmental Design and Development of the University of Lagos. That program is being established by a professor from Minnesota. There are also many Nigerian scholars well worth studying under, if they'll let you. The Nigerian Universities are extremely selective and not just anyone gets in.

COUNTRY NOTES. This is a huge country, about the size of California, Nevada and Arizona combined. It is also a varied country with four major topographic areas and different weather patterns. The north is dry from October to April, and dusty because of Sahara winds. In the south the dry season is from November to April with desert winds in December and January. It rains about 150 inches on the hot, humid coastal belt, much less elsewhere.

There are over 250 tribal groups, the three major ones are the Hausa-Fulani, Yoruba and Ibo. There are only about twenty-seven thousand non-Africans living in Nigeria. Communication between all these groups usually takes place in English. Nigeria was granted independence from England in 1960 and the tribal groups had a series of conflicts finally resulting in the former Eastern Region declaring itself the "Republic of Biafra" in 1967. Fighting ended in early 1970.

The successful conclusion of the civil war against overwhelming odds has produced a certain assertiveness and determination to contain foreign influence in Nigeria. Nigerians have been outspoken in their criticism of certain Americans who have supported Biafra. Also of the Biafrans studying in America who demonstrated against the federal government. (At the moment there are about 1,800 Nigerians studying in the United States.)

Tourism and students studying in Nigeria are increasing. In 1971 the State University of New York sent twenty-five upperclassmen to the University of Ibadan for one year of studies. It is a country in which one can move around. Airplanes fly into all major cities, there is 50,000 miles of roads (9,500 paved), 2,180 miles of railways and over 5,130 navigable inland waterways. Hitching is no problem. Nigeria has two international airports and Pan American Airways flies to Nigeria daily. Living costs are high.

SENEGAL

COLLEGE: *Université De Dakar*
ACADEMIC YEAR: *October to July*
AMERICAN STUDENTS: *Twelve*

INSTRUCTION: *French*
TUITION: *Approximately $90 per month*
LIVING COSTS: *$80 per month*

VISA. Longer than three months visa necessary. Write: Senegal Embassy, 2112 Wyoming Avenue, N.W., Washington, D.C. 20009. (212) 234-0540.

APPLICATION ADDRESS.
Paul Teyssier, Lecteur
Université De Dakar
Dakar, Senegal

BOOKS TO READ. *The Mandate* by Ousmane Sembene. A novel that captures the life in Dakar. It's about the struggle betwen traditional society and the oppressive European-style bureaucracy, an outstanding book.

THE SCHOOL. The Université De Dakar was until 1957 a branch of the universities of Paris and Bordeaux. When Senegal became independent in 1957, the university still kept its French administration. As a result nearly 95 percent of the courses were concerned with the French: French history, French language, French sociology. Little at the university relates to Senegal. For example, a course in Wolof—the language of most of the Senegalese—is given by a Belgian linguist who does not speak the language. Instruction is in the French system with no discussions, only the taking of notes.

The university has had a number of strikes over the last years. Strikes have been for more scholarships, increased clothing allowances and the abolishment of mid-term examinations. However, the Senegalese students are not revolutionary or concerned about the conditions of the workers.

INDEPENDENT STUDY. Senegalese are hospitable and it's easy to travel and study in the country. Several black students have come to the country with the thought of studying at the university, found it unbearable, and spent a worthwhile year traveling and making friends. Two museums in Dakar and St. Louis make it possible for detail work on Senegal's tradition and history. It's also a country to study the French colonial influence in West Africa. A knowledge of French is absolutely necessary.

COUNTRY NOTES. Dakar is one of the more modern "European" cities of Africa, strongly influenced by the French. Located on the Atlantic, it has some of the finest beaches of West Africa. The weather is temperate in Dakar all year, with rain from July to September. Nights are cool in winter. The rest of the country is hot all year and rains are heavy in the south and southeast from June to October. During the rains the high humidity accents the heat and Senegal is unbearable. Travel is easy in the dry season, but it's often difficult to get into the interior once the rain begins. Or for that matter to get out.

SIERRA LEONE

COLLEGE: *Fourah Bay University College* INSTRUCTION: *English*
ACADEMIC YEAR: *October to June*   TUITION, ROOM AND BOARD: *$2,100*
AMERICAN STUDENTS: *Fifteen*

VISA. It will take at least three months, or longer, to get a visa. Three photos are required and two dollars. Contact Consulate General of Sierra Leone, 30 East 42nd Street, New York, New York 10017 or the Embassy, 1701 19th Street, N.W., Washington, D.C. 20009. (202) 265-7700. Make sure you get the visa before leaving the United States.

APPLICATION ADDRESS.
M.R.O. Garber
Registrar
Fourah Bay University College
Freetown, Sierra Leone

BOOKS TO READ. Christopher Fyfe is the noted authority here and anyone going to the country should read: *A History of Sierra Leone* by him and published by Oxford Press, 1961. Another valuable and recent book is Martin Kilson's *Political Change in a West African State,* Harvard Press, 1966.

THE SCHOOL. Fourah Bay University was founded first as a college in 1827 by the Church Missionary Society and is the oldest college in West Africa. In 1876 it was affiliated with the University of Durham and began allowing other students—besides school teachers and missionaries—to enroll. In 1967 it became a university and severed its special relationship with the University of Durham. The college offers degrees now in Arts, Economics, Engineering, Sciences, and graduate work in Education. (There's another university in Sierre Leone: Njala University College, which is an agricultural and elementary education institution.)

Fourah Bay has several special institutes, and their African Studies one is outstanding among them. But the college offers little more. It has a total student population of less than 1900, mostly from Sierra Leone and the neighboring countries. However, it's a well-equipped college on a beautiful campus. A very British college, lectures by rote, little discussion between professors and students, lots of examinations. American students have not found it a demanding place. The Americans coming here have mostly been enrolled through the Great Lakes Colleges Association, coming one or two a semester.

The college provides dormitories for men and women, run by wardens and matrons. Tight rules and regulations. Students can live off campus, in town. Freetown is a swinging place.

INDEPENDENT STUDIES. For Sierra Leone we suggest students take several classes, keep close to school. You'll learn a lot, especially working with some project for the Institute of African Studies. Try to learn *Krio*. That's the "lingua franca" among the tribal dialects. English is the official language, but only the educated speak it.

COUNTRY NOTES. This country of 210 miles of Atlantic coastline is about the size of South Carolina and has three million people. Freetown has a population of over 110,000 itself. The country lies in the tropics and temperatures and humidity are high. The dry season is from November to April; it rains the rest of the year. About 150 inches.

The country first saw white men in 1460. Pedro de Cinta, a Portuguese explorer gave it the name Sierra Leonean, which means "lion mountain." It was a haven for freed slaves during the eighteenth and nineteenth century, later it became the center for British West Africa. In 1961 it received its independence.

The country has a constitutional monarchy and membership in the British Commonwealth. It has had two coups since independence, in 1967 and in 1968, both simple and nearly bloodless. At the moment the country is being run by Prime Minister Stevens, and being run quietly. It is a country that has always gotten along well with the United States. It is a friendly and receptive place for Americans.

SUDAN

COLLEGE: *University of Khartoum*
ACADEMIC YEAR: *October to June*
AMERICAN STUDENTS: *None*

INSTRUCTION: *English and Arabic*
TUITION: *$750 per year*
LIVING COSTS: *$150 per month*

VISA. Is possible to stay up to one year. Visa costs about $8.33. Three photos are necessary. Sudan broke off diplomatic relations with the United States followng the outbreak of the Six Day War. Contact the Somali Embassy, Sudanese Interests Section, 3421 Massachusetts Avenue, N.W., Washington, D.C. 20009. (202) 338-8565.

APPLICATION ADDRESS.
Sayed Ahmed el Madi Gobara
Registrar
University of Khartoum
Khartoum, Sudan

BOOKS TO READ. Two fairly recent and adequate books of introduction are: Beshir, Mahamed Omer's *Southern Sudan: Background to Conflict* (London: Hurst, 1968). And, Robert O. Collins and Robert L. Tignor's *Egypt and the Sudan* (Englewood Cliffs, New Jersey: Prentice-Hall, 1967).

THE SCHOOL. This university dates back to 1898 when Lord Kitchener thought of starting a college in memory of General Gordon. It became a university in 1956 and has a minor reputation among Arab and African schools. The administrative officers of the school are all Sudanese and the student body of 2,097 are mostly from the Sudan, but the school does have a range of underclassmen from other Arab states and Africa, particularly Ethiopia. Its faculty changes rapidly, made up of expatriates from England, the United States and India. The university offers a B.A. degree in three years, but we recommend only one year of study. It has an Institute of Arabic Studies which is adequate, but nothing compared to the offerings in this area at the American University in Cairo. Its undergraduate courses for the most part demand minimal work.

INDEPENDENT STUDY. It is, of course, the place in which to study Sudan itself. The results of the July, 1971, attempted coup d'état, and the continual struggle between northern (Moslems) and southern (Christian and animist) peoples. An American student would, of course, be suspect (Sudan is a militant Arab nation) on any questions over the Arab-Israel war. Khartoum is located on the junction of the White and Blue Niles and an independent project related to the ecology of these important rivers could be undertaken. Very little about Sudan is known in America and that is unfortunate . . . for Americans.

COUNTRY NOTES. This is the largest of African countries, nearly 980,000 square miles. It stretches between the Red Sea and the Libyan and Sahara Deserts, and is a country of tremendous terrain changes, going from tropical forests and savanna to sandy hills. Most of Sudan's sixteen million people live along the Nile, and about one hundred and sixty thousand in Khartoum itself.

Sudan is run by a Revolutionary Command Council (RCC) that came to power through a military coup in 1969. It has had several attempted coups against it, and leader of the RCC Maj. Gen. Jafar Muhammad Nimeri has abolished the parliament and outlawed all political parties. In July, 1971, Nimeri purged the Communist party in Sudan for their involvement in an aborted coup d'état.

Sudan is hot and arid. The average temperature is something around ninety degrees eight months of the year, but there's not much humidity. It's a country that looks like the place where they filmed all those desert movies. As far as the eye can see, there's sand and camels.

It takes a bit more to attend the University of Khartoum, but the experiment will be worth it. There's nothing in the world quite like traveling down the Nile from Khartoum to Wadi Halfa.

TANZANIA

COLLEGE: *University of Dar-es-Salaam*
ACADEMIC YEAR: *July to March*
AMERICAN STUDENTS: *Three*

INSTRUCTION: *English*
TUITION: *$800 per year*
LIVING COSTS: *$160 per month*

VISA. When a student is admitted to the university a special visa is issued allowing him to stay longer than the normal three-month period. Tanzania also wants to see a return ticket or proof of funds to live in the country. Two photos are required and $3.15 for the visa fee. Write: Embassy of the United Republic of Tanzania, 2721 Connecticut Avenue, N.W., Washington, D.C. (202) 483-4116.

APPLICATION ADDRESS.
I. N. Kimambo
The University of Dar-es-Salaam
P.O. Box 35091
Dar-es-Salaam, Tanzania

BOOKS TO READ. The most important book to understand Tanzania's political life is Juluis Nyerere's *Ujamaa—Essays on Socialism,* published by

Oxford University Press, 1968. To get a feel for the history of Zanzibar there's John Middleton and Jane Campbell's *Zanzibar, Its Society and Its Politics*. It's a bit dry, however. Then read Andrew C. Maguire's *Toward 'Uhuru' in Tanzania: The Politics of Participation*, Cambridge University Press, 1969.

THE SCHOOL. Tanzania has only one university with campuses in Dar-es-Salaam and in Morogro 120 miles up-country. It opened in 1963 and was part of the University of East Africa, but became a separate university in 1970. It is the least developed of the three East African universities, has an enrollment of less than two thousand and a staff of about 126. It offers only limited degrees in Arts, Science and Social Science. A B.A. takes three years. Dar-es-Salaam has three special institutes, in Public Administration, Swahili and Education. Their Swahili Research program is worthwhile. Students live on campus in separate halls for men and women, but overseas students should plan to live in town. Not a problem in Dar. They accept students from all over, but usually after the B.S. Undergraduate Americans are admitted.

INDEPENDENT STUDY. Dar-es-Salaam is interesting because it gives a student an opportunity to study Zanzibar. Special visas can be arranged in Dar to travel to the island, located twenty miles off the coast of Africa. Or to study tiny Pemba. Both with long histories of Arab life in Africa. Tanzania is also the site of the Olduvai Gorge, and, of course, Mount Kilimanjaro. Both areas, and the wild game, provide unique opportunities for study in biological sciences, ecology or archaeology.

COUNTRY NOTES. In 1962 President Nyerere used a Swahili word *ujamaa* meaning familyhood, to describe the type of communal cooperation his government was trying to foster in Tanzania. In 1967 he pushed the Arusha Declaration which set out in socialistic, industrial and business terms what his government planned to do. Shortly after that he nationalized most private interests. The development of this program is the most important socialistic experiment being attempted in Africa. It is worth watching and living with.

Tanzania, which is comprised of Tanganyika and the islands of Zanzibar and Pemba, is as large as Texas and New Mexico and has somewhere around thirteen million people. It's a rich and beautiful country stretching along the Indian Ocean and contains some of the real wonders of the world. At one time it was a German territory, then British, and in 1961 became independent. Nyerere has been president since independence and is committed to socialism on the continent. His ties with China have been close and Chinese advisors have worked in Tanzania and Zanzibar since the early sixties.

Tanzania has over 3,600 miles of roads, an international airport with East African Airways, Pan American and Trans World Airlines flights. It is possible to hitchhike almost anywhere in the country on the network of roads. There is also a first-class railway out of Dar to Kigoma and Mwanza. At times the country seems to be one giant game park and tourists trek to Tanzania and Kenya by the thousands. English is spoken almost everywhere and is, along with Swahili, an official language.

The monsoons hit the country every year, in the northeast from December to March and in the south from March through May. Traveling becomes difficult in the monsoon seasons. In Dar it is hot and humid, but the beaches are within easy reach. In-country it is hot and arid until you reach the lake regions. Although the University of Dar-es-Salaam may not be outstanding, Tanzania certainly is.

UGANDA

COLLEGE: *Makerere University*
ACADEMIC YEAR: *July to March*
AMERICAN STUDENTS: *About eleven*

INSTRUCTION: *English*
TUITION: *$900 per year*
LIVING COSTS: *$190 per month*

VISA. Transit visa is valid for three months, the cost is $3.15. Obtain visa before leaving United States. One photo is required. Apply Embassy of Uganda, 1509 16th Street, N.W., Washington, D.C. 20011. (202) 726-7100. (Transit visa can be converted once in-country.)

APPLICATION ADDRESS.
B. Onyango
Registrar
Makerere University
Kampala, Uganda

BOOKS TO READ. Get *Area Handbook for Uganda* printed by the U.S. Government Printing Office, 1969. Alan Moorehead has written two books: *The White Nile* and *The Blue Nile*. Buy them both; they're in paperback.

THE SCHOOL. Makerere University began in the 1920s as the Kampala Technical School. It became part of the University of East Africa in 1963 and finally became Makerere University in 1970. It is the foremost university in East Africa.

Makerere is located on the outskirts of Kampala. A city on the shores of Lake Victoria. The university sprawls over two hills that look down on the city. It has a large campus of tropical gardens, shady walks and red brick buildings. It has, in fact, the nicest campus in black Africa.

Most of the students live in the dormitories—five of them—but foreigners should plan to find places off campus. Makerere is overcrowded. There are a few modern one- and two-bedroom apartments for married students. A place in town can be located and the university helps locate rooms.

Makerere is still a British school though it ended its special relationship with the University of London in 1963. All courses are lectures and in the British academic game, teaching at Makerere is a plus, therefore, first-rate faculty go out to Africa to teach. American professors are also present. Mostly on Fulbright and other State Department grants.

Makerere has 2,121 students from all the racial backgrounds living in Uganda—Africans, Asians and Europeans. Scholarships are also available for Africans from other countries. It is difficult to be accepted to Makerere. American students would certainly have to be upperclassmen and have strong recommendations. We expect that soon Makerere will get an exchange program developed with an American college, but nothing has developed yet.

It is possible to obtain a Diploma in African Studies in two years and a B.A. in three. Undergraduates need not be solely interested in Africa to study at Makerere. The English, History and Philosophy departments are first-rate. And we know a black American student who went to Uganda to study art.

INDEPENDENT STUDY. It is possible to live in Uganda and take courses independently, working out arrangements with individual professors, or to live up-country and teach in government schools. However, it is not a country in which to wander. In June, 1971 two Americans, a newsman and a teacher at Makerere were killed in the western region while investigating a tribal massacre.

COUNTRY NOTES. The February, 1971 coup in Uganda put General Idi Amin Dada in power and Uganda went through several months of tension. The political climate in Uganda should change again and again. Be prepared. Uganda is about the size of Oregon and astride the equator. The very tropical belt along Lake Victoria in the south merges into savanna country seventy-five miles north of the lake and into desert brush near the Sudanese border. On both the east and west boundaries are mountain ranges, with Mount Elgon, the third highest peak in East Africa touching Kenya and the Ruwenzori range forming the border with the Congo. Kampala itself is a city of approximately 330,000.

Kampala has an international airport and can also be reached by train from Kenya or up from Tanzania via the lake. Recently it has been possible to cross over from West Africa through the Congo, but that's a rough trip.

UNITED ARAB REPUBLIC (EGYPT)

COLLEGE: *The American University in Cairo*

INSTRUCTION: *English, some Arabic*

TUITION: *$1000 per semester*

ACADEMIC YEAR: *September to May*

LIVING COSTS: *$150 per month*

AMERICAN STUDENTS: *Ten (undergraduates)*
Thirty (graduates)

VISA. A tourist visa can be obtained from the Embassy of India, U.A.R. Interests Section, 2310 Decatur Place N.W., Washington, D.C. 20009. (202) AD 2-5400. Tourist visa is valid for three months, can be renewed in-country. One photo required and two dollars. AUC will assist in obtaining a student's visa when in-country.

APPLICATION ADDRESS.
The American University in Cairo
866 United Nations Plaza
New York, New York 10017
(212) 412-6320

BOOKS TO READ. An excellent book on the question of Suez is Kenneth Love's *Suez: the Twice Fought War.* (New York: McGraw-Hill, 1969). Also, Edward Wakin's *A Lonely Minority: The Modern Story of Egypt's Copts* (New York: Morrow, 1963). And Harry Hopkins' *Egypt, the Crucible: The Unfinished Revolution in the Arab* (Boston: Houghton-Mifflin, 1969).

THE SCHOOL. American University in Cairo is a former missionary school that for the last fifteen years has been pretty much on its own. It started in 1920 offering "liberal American education to students of the Middle East." It has over 1,500 full-time students from sixty-five countries, but not many from the western world. It is located in downtown Cairo, near the Hilton Hotel, Egyptian Museum and a few blocks up from the Nile. The campus is small, a cluster of old and new buildings surrounded by gardens, shaded walks, tennis courts and a football field.

AUC is most famous for its Arabic Studies Program at the master's level. Students involved with Arabic studies usually do some work here. Its other master's level degrees are not that important. But AUC is progressive enough to teach computer science.

The university has a special one-year program for American undergraduates coming from overseas. All students have to apply through the

New York office of AUC. It takes students at the college level and provides a full academic program (in English). Students have to live on campus, in dormitories—new since 1968—and women have hours. A tight campus. We do know of a Barnard woman in 1970 who managed to get permission to live off campus, but such permission is rare.

Egyptian students are cosmopolitan. They follow the fashions in the Paris and Italian magazines and dress accordingly. Women, for example, will wear longer length dresses in downtown Cairo, then change to miniskirts when on campus. American campus styles, *i.e.*, levis, patchpants, overalls, etc., are not understood or appreciated. Nor are drugs tolerated. Pushers get the death penalty.

INDEPENDENT STUDY. Not much chance here. AUC will have a full schedule of classes worked out, but possible to develop some special project with a professor while overseas. History department would be cooperative. AUC credits transfer without trouble, work out arrangements with your advisor or college dean before leaving for Egypt.

COUNTRY NOTES. Egypt is the center of the Arab World, and modern Cairo the most important city. Some sort of "peace" should be worked out during the next few years and Anwar al Sadat will shape the Arab side of the negotiations. Surprisingly little talk of the war is heard on the street. Students will naturally involve themselves in political discussions, but Cairo is a peaceful city, as is much of massive Egypt. The country is larger than the state of California and has over thirty-four million people. It is the second most populous country in Africa. Cairo alone has five million people, and Alexandria (scene of the Quartet) has two million. The U.A.R. is almost an endless desert once away from the Nile Valley. The highest point of land is 8,600-foot Mount Catherine in south Sinai. In the Qattara Depression it's four hundred feet below sea level.

About the only way to travel is along the Nile. Egypt has four thousand miles of railway and fourteen thousand miles of roads and airports in the major cities, but not much else. It is extremely hard to go "overland" though we know people who have traveled overland from Alexandria into the Sudan and Ethiopia, and beyond. A bus operates over the border to Sudan; it's rough going, however. Cairo has an international airport and ships from all over put into Alexandria. (Port Said has been closed since the Six Day War.)

Egypt has had five thousand years of history, the longest in the world. Every nation of the world has been touched one way or the other by this country. In one year you can expect to see just brief moments of this past. The Egyptian Museum will take you several weeks. Just to walk through, let alone to study. Egypt is not an easy country to live in or to study and that's what makes it so intriguing.

The following schools have programs in Nigeria, Sierra Leone, Ethiopia and Ghana:

Foreign Studies
University of Wisconsin
Oshkosh, Wisconsin 54901

Education Abroad Program
University of California
Santa Barbara, California 93106

International Education Office
SUNY
99 Washington Avenue
Albany, N.Y. 12210

International Education
The Great Lakes Colleges Association
Yellow Springs, Ohio 45387

7. Studying in South America

ARGENTINA

COLLEGE: *Catholic University Santa Maria*

ACADEMIC YEAR: *Mid-March to November*

AMERICAN STUDENTS: *About eleven*

INSTRUCTION: *Spanish*

TUITION: *$200 per year*

LIVING COSTS: *$175 per month*

VISA. You can travel to Argentina for three months just on a U.S. passport which is renewable for another three months. There is also a student's visa, but it can only be obtained if you are accepted by the university. Cost is $3.60. Apply nearest consulate or call embassy: (202) 837-0444.

APPLICATION ADDRESS.
Universidad Catolica Argentina
Rio Bamba 1227
Buenos Aires, Argentina

BOOKS TO READ. There are several fine survey books on the country, try Arthur P. Whitaker's *Argentina* published by Prentice-Hall in 1964. Also, Robert J. Alexander's *An Introduction to Argentina,* Praeger, 1969.

THE SCHOOL. The university system of Argentina includes nine national schools, four provincial universities and eleven officially recognized private universities. Of these the best for Americans to attend is the Catholic University Santa Maria of Buenos Aires.

A private, Catholic school, it costs about two hundred dollars annually and enrollment is under five thousand. Approximately one-third of the students are women and 150 come from other countries. There are excellent professors at the university. Some are refugees from the government's purge of the national universities conducted a few years ago. The school is organized into faculties—Law and Political Science, Physical Sciences, Musical Arts and Sciences, Philosophy, Letters, Theology, Mathematics and Engineering, and Economic and Social Sciences. The last two faculties are particularly recommended.

Admission standards to the universities are high for Argentinians and foreigners alike. This creates difficulties for Americans as the requirements are based upon the curriculum of Argentina's secondary schools. These have more courses than American high schools and it's nearly impossible for Americans to fulfill the Argentina entrance requirements unless they have completed two years of college.

These problems notwithstanding, the Argentina government welcomes Americans and other foreigners. As one educator explained, "The best foreign friends Argentina has are made here when they are students." The tuition is free for everyone at the national universities. This and the observation that educational opportunities are greater in Argentina than in most Latin American countries accounts for the considerable number of people from nearby countries studying in Argentina.

To make application to the Catholic University Santa Maria (or any other Argentina university) students should correspond in Spanish with the Secretary of the Faculty they want to attend. Initial inquiries should be mailed by mid-January to allow sufficient time before school opens in mid-March. (A copy of birth certificate is required, plus high school and college transcripts with course descriptions.) Most faculties require an entrance examination *or* a year preparatory course, therefore, we suggest students forgo official relationships and audit classes.

Once a student is accepted in a faculty of a university his course of study is strictly prescribed by custom and law. He has little choice in his curriculum other than to decide whether to take German or French as his second language. He takes five or six courses a year, each usually meeting two times a week. His lectures last an hour and Catholic University classes may have as few as thirty students . . . all carefully taking notes. Attendance at classes is optional though it sometimes is compulsory for laboratory or practical courses. Although it is changing, the final grade the student receives in a course is based on an oral examination administered by his professor and two outside teachers. Even so, the student rarely gets to talk with his professors, they're aloof and busy holding down other jobs. Few professors work full time at the university.

Buildings at the Catholic University are inhospitable. In winter they're cold and damp; in summer, hot and humid. Students leave them after classes and hang out in the school's cafeteria and coffee shop. With little or no central heating, men and women wear layers of sweaters in the winter, but despite the bulk, the students look stylish and neat. Most men wear ties and white shirts to school and women wear modish European styles. A friend says, "even in casual clothes, women in Argentina look neat."

The Catholic University does not provide housing. Apartments are scarce and expensive so students obtain rooms in boardinghouses or moderate hotels within walking distance of the school. Meals are not often included in these accommodations and students eat frequently at restaurants that cater to them. The cost of breakfast at one of these restaurants is fifteen cents, the cost of a filet mignon in any restaurant is about a dollar. Even if students were to eat steak every night, life can be comfortable lived on $175 to $200 a month.

INDEPENDENT STUDY. One study would be of the small group of pure-blooded Indian population, about fifty thousand, who live in the peripheral provinces of the north, northwest and south. Or a paper on the church in the country. Ninety-four percent of the Argentines are Roman Catholic.

COUNTRY NOTES. Argentina is about the size of the United States east of the Mississippi and has a population of over twenty-three million, one-third living in and around Buenos Aires. It is the second largest country on the southern continent and extends north and south for 2,300 miles. It is also a very "middle-class" country, European in nature. The literacy rate is 90 percent, one of the highest in Latin America. More than 270,000 students attend colleges.

One problem the country has is galloping inflation. Keep your money in American dollars—it should increase in value while you're there. Another advantage of Argentina is books. The country is the center of the Latin American publishing world. Books—in almost all languages and titles—are printed in Buenos Aires.

BRAZIL

COLLEGE: *Federal University of Bahia*
ACADEMIC YEAR: *March to April*
      November to December
AMERICAN STUDENTS: *Handful*

INSTRUCTION: *Portuguese*
TUITION: *Minimal*
LIVING COSTS: *$150 per month*

VISA. Visa is required for stay over 180 days. No charge, but one photo needed. For further information write the embassy at 30006 Massachusetts Ave. N.W., Washington, D.C. 20008. (202) 797-0100.

APPLICATION ADDRESS.
Universidade Federal de Bahia
Salvador, Bahia
Brazil

BOOKS TO READ. Charles Wagley's *Introduction to Brazil* is a very readable and interesting account of the country. A reference source is the *Area Handbook for Brazil* available at the Government Printing Office. A current overview of Brazil is found in "All Power to the Generals," *Foreign Affairs,* Vol. 49, No. 3 (April, 1971), pp. 464–79.

THE SCHOOL. There are a large number of universities to choose from in Brazil. And they have been expanded and updated in the last few years. Nearly every state has its own university and in some cases right next to them is a federal or Catholic university. For most of these schools a student is required to pass a stiff entrance examination. A growing practice is for students to take a year off at a school that prepares them for the exam. (A national joke is that students learn more from cramming than they do in the university. A fact that's true. Once in the university few flunk out.) Americans wanting to forgo the entrance exam should follow the Brazilian example and audit classes.

Anyone wanting to go to any university should know that higher education is under one of the strong men in Brazil's military dictatorship. Under this direction, the universities have changed from being intensely political to being non-political and the student movement has been firmly surpressed.

While in Brazil, Americans like everyone else must abide by the national legislation that makes it unlawful to speak out against the government or fail to turn in anyone who does. A feared, U.S. trained security system backs up the law and makes it effective. At the universities, discussions of current affairs are sharply curtailed and follow the approved government line. For example, a friend tells us that the issue of the Transamazonian Highway, an immensely costly undertaking of the government in the northeast, cannot be discussed in the universities save to parrot government statements.

Understandably students are suspicious of one another and Americans can expect some animosity. Although some Brazilian students will fall all over them because they are Americans, most in time will be ignored. American students should realize their friendship can be harmful to people and that they can be deported for an ant-Brazilian comment. American college students cannot expect to adjust for too long to these nerve-wracking restrictions but on the basis of student experiences in Iron Curtain countries, many can learn to live with them awhile.

The schools are watched equally so another basis for choosing a college ought to be considered. The universities in São Paulo are academically prestigious and offer the advantages of being in the country's largest city. Rio de Janeiro, the second largest city, also has fine schools. In Brasilia, the world's most modern capital city (and perhaps the world's most isolated), there's a beautiful new university for 4,500 students. It's highly recommended by some because, "It's a wonderful place for students to be. There are no distractions."

There are plenty of distractions at the Federal University of Bahia—Bahia is, we think, the most interesting state in Brazil—so go there! The university, founded in 1946 in Salvador, is housed in striking modern buildings and a wide variety of courses are taught. Some are: Architecture, Economics, Law, Medicine, Fine Arts, Library Science, Philosophy, Engineering. You name it. Because of Bahia's great cultural heritage, it's not surprising that the departments in the performing arts—ballet, theater and music—are outstanding.

The school year has two semesters and at Bahia the format for classes varies from small to massive, from lecture to seminar. For all who are enrolled, a written exam at the end of the semester is given and poor attendance may also require an additional oral examination. (As we said, it's a tight little dictatorship.)

Although the buildings are close together, campus life as American students know it does not exist. Camaraderie among the six thousand students happens, but many of the students are working during the day and attending classes at night. The majority of students also live at home, but every type of living arrangement is available for Americans. A student can easily rent a small house or rooms and cover all expenses on $150.

INDEPENDENT STUDY. A welcome contrast to the uptightness of the university is the friendliness of Bahia itself. Once the center of Portuguese slave trading in the eighteenth century, the mixture of African and Latin peoples has produced a beautiful people and culture. To a striking degree Bahia is the home for most of Brazil's leading artists, writers, movie-makers and singers. A student, therefore, interested in the effects cultures have upon one another would find a study of African and Portuguese cultural mix an exciting study.

COUNTRY NOTES. Salvador is the Bahian capital and was the old capital of Brazil. It combines colonial atmosphere and architecture and new buildings and modern living. Not bad. The city has a population of one million and is growing fast. Prices are comparatively low and the food is out of this world! Beaches are nearby, swimming year round. Cheap entertainment and the movies (uncensored) are new. For clothing, take light summer wear and one fancy outfit for Mardi Gras. In 1973, Mardi Gras is celebrated March 4, 5 and 6.

CHILE

COLLEGE: *Catholic University in Santiago*
ACADEMIC YEAR: *March to December*
AMERICAN STUDENTS: *Thirty-five*

INSTRUCTION: *Spanish*
TUITION: *$200 per year*
LIVING COSTS: *$100 per month*

VISA. Possible to stay in Chile for six months without a visa. A student visa requires a letter from the university in Chile, $25 and five pictures. For further information contact Embassy of Chile, 1736 Massachusetts Avenue N.W., Washington, D.C. (202) 667-0746.

APPLICATION ADDRESS.
Catholic University in Santiago
Alameta Bernardo O'Higgins
340
Santiago, Chile

BOOKS TO READ. An excellent book, *Student Politics in Chile* by Frank Bonilla and Myron Glazer, has been published by Basic Books, 1970. Get it! *Area Handbook for Chile,* available at the Government Printing Office. Nothing much else very good on the country.

THE SCHOOL. The Catholic University in Santiago is the best in the country. A pontifical institution, it has traditionally educated the children from the upper classes—but this is changing, like everything else in Chile. Following the pattern of most Latin American universities, Catholic University is organized into faculties. These include: Theology, Law, Political and Social Sciences, Architecture, Physical Sciences and Math, Agriculture, Economics, Biology, Philosophy and Medicine. Successful completion of work in any of these faculties leads to professional certification. In addition, there are schools at the university offering diplomas in Civil Engineering, Journalism, Psychology, Teacher Training, Social Work, Nursing, Chemistry, Physics, Astronomy and Anthropology. The faculties and schools teach over six thousand students at centers spread throughout the city. A new campus for the entire university is nearing completion in the suburbs.

Good subjects for Americans to take during a one- or two-semester period are Economics, Psychology and Sociology. The student grapevine provides information about the professors for these courses.

One of many radical experiments going on in Chilean education is taking place at the Catholic University. In some faculties, students, teachers and workers are setting up Marxian communities—one of whose characteristics is the redistribution of salaries between custodians and teachers. Overall, students are trying to participate in the revolution by changing their customary role of "alienated intellectual" to revolutionary worker. Over fifty thousand students spent their summer vacations last year building schools for farm children.

Students have a strong interest and confidence in the government of the new Marxist President, Allende. With no fear of government intervention or reprisal, political debate is vociferous and open. Every point of view is expressed from the monarchist's to the revolutionary's who is arming the peasants and workers. An American confronting a Chilean university shouldn't worry that his or her radicalism is wanting. Chilean students know that Americans have minds of their own.

INDEPENDENT STUDY. As most students of politics realize, Chile provides the only historical example of a peaceful and constitutional transfer of governmental power from democratic to Marxist leadership. Modern-day Chile presents the unprecedented situation of a socialist economy coming into existence without violent or illegal means. The burgeoning artistic life in Santiago is not nearly so well recorded as the country's political and economic revolution though a lot is going on there. Playwrights, painters and sculptors have been getting a community together and working for three or four years in Santiago. Much too little information about them and their work is available. A worthwhile independent study project.

COUNTRY NOTES. The seasons are the reverse of ours and Santiago's climate is often compared with San Francisco's. The capital is European style. Good but expensive restaurants are available and first-run American movies are shown regularly at low prices. American magazines are available at bookstores and local daily and weekly papers sell everywhere.

Students usually live in pensions that cater to them. A good bargain, they cost about one hundred dollars a month and provide room, board and laundry services. Clothes for hot and cold weather are necessary and, in general, you dress casually. Male students wear shirts and pants but not ties. Blue jeans are rarely worn; they are expensive and associated in people's minds with upper-class attire. Female students wear simple blouses and skirts—but at fashionable lengths.

Above all, Chilean people are gracious and charming. They joke about themselves and their country. It's a national talent. Chilean women are beautiful and American men can arrange dates with little effort. American women, on the other hand, have a much harder time though they may be besieged for dates. It's widely held that American women are fast and free (or is it free and fast?) .

Traveling everywhere is easy and safe except in some of the mining and border towns under guerrilla control. The train system should be avoided but the buses are better than most in the States. Hitching is easy. Chilean custom requires you offer to pay "a little something" for a ride, but don't worry about the expense. Custom also requires the driver to refuse payment and take you for nothing. A friend reports from her travels that most hitches end up at dinner in someone's home because people don't meet gringos very often.

COLOMBIA

COLLEGES: *Universidad Javeriana*
Bogotá
Universidad del Valle
Cali

ACADEMIC YEAR: *March to December*
AMERICAN STUDENTS: *Few, if any*

INSTRUCTION: *Spanish*
TUITION: *$300 per year (Jave-riana)*
Minimal (Valle)
LIVING COSTS: *$150 per month in Bogotá*
$130 per month in Cali

VISA. To obtain a student visa, present evidence to consulate proving acceptance at a Colombian university. Must show sufficient funds to study for one year—approximately one thousand dollars is needed. For further information write embassy: 2118 Leroy Place, N.W., Washington, D.C. (202) 387-5828.

APPLICATION ADDRESSES.
Universidad Pontificia Javeriana
Carrera 7a-#40-62
Bogotá, D.E. Colombia

Universidad del Valle
Apartado Aereo 2188
Cali, Colombia

BOOKS TO READ. The best reference book is the *Area Handbook on Colombia,* updated in 1970. It's on sale at the Government Printing Office for three dollars. John Martz's *Colombia: Political History* tells in detail about political events in the country since 1930.

THE SCHOOL. Approximately five thousand students attend Universidad Javeriana in Bogotá, the oldest of the country's private universities.

Run by Jesuits, its student body combines intellectuals from all economic and social classes.

Universidad del Valle is a state school modeled after U.S. universities. It's located in the Colombian lowlands in beautiful Cali, the second largest city in the country. The tropical climate is pleasant, temperature in the low eighties. Approximately two thousand students are enrolled.

Despite Colombian hostility toward America, students at both universities give U.S. students a chance to establish themselves as individuals. In general, and particularly in Cali, friends are easy and Colombian hospitality warm. Classes meet twice a week, an hour of lecture. Attendance is not compulsory and classroom time will be cut short by festivals and student strikes. The teachers are mostly Colombian and some come from neighboring Ecuador and Panama. Housing for women is available at Universidad de Javeriana, otherwise housing is easily obtained in reasonable student pensions.

INDEPENDENT STUDY. In Colombia study the Catholic Church. All pervasive, it was formerly known to be the most conservative in Latin America—but this is changing. Since 1966 and the death of guerrilla priest, Father Camilo Torres, younger priests have effectively worked to develop a socially conscious church. The political structure of the country, as well, is in the throes of change. Worth watching.

COUNTRY NOTES. Colombia is the third largest country in Latin America. Highly varied in landscape and climate, with a number of Indian cultures. Festivals and carnivals take place regularly and for the mountaineers and campers the Andes are an unlimited resource. A great variety of reading material is available. Bucholtz Libreria, one of the best bookstores in the hemisphere, is in Bogotá.

Reach Colombia by land, sea or air. To go by sea, disembark at the port of Buenaventura and taxi to Cali or fly to Bogotá. There's a bus ride from Texas to Panama City where the Inter-American Highway ends. It's 1,500 miles long. From Panama City, Avianca Airlines has a flight to Bogotá for forty-five dollars and a boat company takes passengers to Buenaventura for fifteen dollars. You can hitch, but it's a long journey we don't recommend.

COSTA RICA

COLLEGE: *University of Costa Rica*
ACADEMIC YEAR: *March to November*
AMERICAN STUDENTS: *fifty to sixty*

INSTRUCTION: *Spanish*
TUITION: *Approximately $150
per year*
LIVING COSTS: *$150 per month*

VISA. Not required if tourist card obtained prior to departure. Write Embassy of Costa Rica, 2112 S Street N.W., Washington, D.C. 20008. (202) 234-2947.

APPLICATION ADDRESS.
Universidad de Costa Rica
Ciudad Universitaria
San José, Costa Rica

BOOKS TO READ. For the best and most up-to-date information refer to the *Area Handbook for Costa Rica* at the U.S. Government Printing Office for three dollars.

THE SCHOOL. The University of Costa Rica is located in the country's central plateau, in a suburb of the capital. The country is the most advanced in Central America and its university the most modern. Seven thousand students are enrolled; three out of every ten students are women—a high proportion by Latin American standards. In addition to the usual professional curriculum of Education, Medicine, Law, etc., the university offers instruction in tropical agriculture. The finest in Central America.

The American presence is evident here (most major enterprises are owned by U.S. interests) but little anti-American sentiment exists among the students or the general population. In 1970 American and Costa Rican students demonstrated side by side against, among others, the government, the university, United Fruit and Alcoa.

INDEPENDENT STUDY. Costa Rica operates without a military establishment. She abolished it in 1948. It is also one of the few democracies still remaining in Latin America, which alone makes her an interesting country to study.

Costa Rica's Indian population is small but pre-Columbian Indian artifacts abound. The government has not intervened with professional or amateur digs and we know of one archaeologist who rented fields from farmers and discovered on her own undisturbed Indian graves.

Costa Rica is the first country in Central America to establish a national park. Opened in March, 1970, the park has a coral reef, a volcano and exotic flora and fauna.

COUNTRY NOTES. San José has all the amenities a metropolis provides. The people are gracious, so gracious it's difficult at first for Americans to feel comfortable.

To get to Costa Rica fly, boat or drive. The Inter-American Highway is adequate, but service at the borders is not. Allow time for delays. Women shouldn't travel alone. Find a friend.

DOMINICAN REPUBLIC

COLLEGES: *Universidad Autonoma*
de Santo Domingo
Universidad Nacional
Pedro Henriques Urena
ACADEMIC YEAR: *September to May*
AMERICAN STUDENTS: *Few*

INSTRUCTION: *Spanish*
TUITION: *$40 per semester*
(UASD)
$300 per semester
(UNPHU)
LIVING COSTS: *$200 per month*

VISA. Tourist card valid up to forty-five days. No charge. For specific requirements on longer stay write: Embassy of the Dominican Republic, 1715 22nd Street N.W., Washington, D.C. 20008. (202) 332-6280.

APPLICATION ADDRESSES.

Universidad Autonoma de Santo Domingo
Rectorado
Avenida Independencia
Santo Domingo, Republica Dominicana

Universidad Nacional Pedro Henriques Urena
Rectorado
Avenida de Juan Fitzgerald Kennedy
Santo Domingo, Republica Dominicana

BOOKS TO READ. Good recent books on the Dominican Republic are: Joan Bosch's *The Unfinished Experiment in Democracy in the Dominican Republic* (New York: Praegar, 1965); Tad Szulc's *Dominican Diary* (New York: Delacorte Press, 1965); and John Bartlow Martin's *One Taken by Events, The Dominican Crisis from the Fall of Trujillo to the Civil War* (New York: Doubleday, 1966).

THE SCHOOL. There are two well-established universities in the capital of the Dominican Republic. Universidad Autonoma de Santo Domingo (UASD) is the oldest university in the Western Hemisphere and is state run. The forty to fifty thousand students who attend the faculties spread throughout downtown Santo Domingo, come mainly from the poorer classes. Politics is a serious matter here and when there's student political unrest in the country, it's likely to occur at UASD.

Although old, the university has a reputation for being "new." By Latin American standards, the school's liberal and experimental. For example, within an academic field students can work out programs with professors for independent study and maintain only nominal attachment to their faculty.

Universidad Nacional Pedro Henriques Urena (UNPHU) is also a well-respected university. Less than a decade old, it's located in the suburbs, has a small enrollment and is fairly conventional. Independent studies are allowed, though infrequently. The Sociology Department is a good one. Comparatively wealthy, the students reflect the lifestyle of the country's middle and upper classes and American students seeking overseas living experiences *without* culture shock may like it here.

INDEPENDENT STUDY. In 1965, the U.S. Marines invaded and then occupied the Dominican Republic. The complicated events surrounding this period are worthy of study particularly for someone interested in U.S. and Central American relations. A word of caution: the country's political situation is grave. In the past year at least two hundred people have been assassinated for leftist, antigovernment activity. American students studying Dominican Republican affairs should proceed cautiously.

COUNTRY NOTES. Christopher Columbus first touched land in the New World on the island territory now shared by the Dominican Republic and Haiti. The Dominican Republic is only 887 miles southeast of Florida and Santo Domingo is a growing (population near six hundred thousand), reasonably clean, modern city though structures of the old Spanish colonial period remain.

The cost of living is high and we recommend students live in pensions as apartment rents are comparable to those in big U.S. cities. Clothing is also expensive, try to bring all you'll need for living in a tropical climate. We suggest wash-and-wear materials for coolness and because they resist molding.

Santo Domingo affords some entertainments, but probably fewer than U.S. students would like. Some first-run movies are shown, American movies and papers are available and a few good international restaurants and gambling casinos are open.

Beer is high, sodas are cheap. Taxis costly, buses and jitneys reasonable. Coffee lovers praise Dominican coffee and delicious tropical fruits like breadfruit, jackfruit and mangoes, are cheap and plentiful.

Beach enthusiasts will find transportation to beaches difficult to arrange. It's easier to go to Port-au-Prince, the French-speaking capital of Haiti, only an hour away by plane.

To get to the Dominican Republic, there are daily flights available from the States. The embassy reports that many people drive down. Boat travel is not so popular anymore but students might investigate passage on a freighter. They're cheap and serve good food.

MEXICO

There are twenty-four public universities in Mexico. The University of the Americas is the most famous, and most similar to U.S. schools. Eighty-five percent of the student body is from the United States, courses are in English. The other universities are patterned after the European system. A half dozen of them offer courses in language and culture, we've listed them. And there are all sorts of American college programs in Mexico.

Our recommendation is CIDOC, Center for Intercultural Documentation, in Cuernavaca. This is Ivan Illich's school. Illich is that former priest, philosopher, author, etc., who wants to de-school schools. Illich's educational ideas are the most revolutionary being voiced today. He established CIDOC in 1963. Its purpose: "CIDOC is not a university, but a meeting place for humanists whose common concern is the effect of social and ideological change on the minds and hearts of men. It is a setting for understanding the implications of social revolution, not an instrument for promoting particular theories of social action. It is an environment for learning, not a headquarters for activist planning. The main context of CIDOC is contemporary Latin America."

CIDOC is located in Rancho Tetela, a residential section of Cuernavaca. Cuernavaca is south of Mexico City, a vacation spot for Mexicans and non-Mexicans. Retired Americans flock there in winter. It is not much of a place, Cuernavaca, but the campus of CIDOC has gardens and lawns, and endless guest speakers who, in the winter months, also flock to CIDOC and warm Cuernavaca.

What to study?

There are, of course, language classes. In the first ten years of the CIDOC Language School seven thousand students have studied Spanish. The school uses the U.S. Foreign Service Institute methods and texts. Classes have only a handful of students. There are no admission requirements and the program is intense. Courses start on the first Monday of all months and run from one to four months. Teachers change groups regularly and students move from group to group, depending on their progression.

We haven't heard many good things about this language program. It depends on real motivation of the students and often young Americans, down for a semester, find it hard to spend all day studying language drills, doing lessons.

Every year CIDOC has central themes for its courses, seminars, publications. During 1971 themes were:

- small groups of dissenting lifestyles today;
- the structure of contemporary institutions and the effect their mode of production and their style of administration has on tropical countries;
- the search for fundamental alternatives to current systems in education, urbanization, transportation, medicine, design.

Some of the course titles were: Alternatives in Education; Ongoing Seminar on Alternatives in Design; Alternatives in Health Care; Journals of Travelers in Mexico; Education in Cuba—1957–1969; Violence in Guatemala; Charisma, Holy Men and Religion. Students select courses depending on interests and needs from the language school, the lecture series (El Ciclo) and the monthly offerings from the Institute for Contemporary Latin American Studies (ICLAS). The language of instruction in the ICLAS courses may be in Spanish or English depending on the instructor and students involved.

Many U.S. colleges and universities authorize independent study done at CIDOC for credit. CIDOC provides students with no certificate attesting their participation, but professors will give written evaluation. Monthly tuition for the language school is about $120 and the yearly registration fee is fifty dollars. Each course in ICLAS is thirty dollars. The lecture cycle (El Ciclo) is thirty dollars.

Mrs. Lini de Vries, who is herself something of a monument in Cuernavaca and at CIDOC (she teaches there), helps with housing. She can arrange cheap hotels or rooms with Mexican families. She has produced a useful little brochure, *General Guide for Students* and will make additional contacts for you. Lini knows everything about Mexico and Cuernavaca and will be the first to tell you. But she's a grand lady. Write her: Apdo 119, Cuernavaca, Morelos, Mexico. Or call: 2-60-39. It costs about eighty dollars a month to live in Cuernavaca. Go to CIDOC; you'll have a good time.

Besides CIDOC, American students go to the National University of Mexico. They run ten-week language courses for foreign students. National University is a huge school. The University of the Americas, which offers a B.A. degree, has English instruction, and runs about $250 a quarter. Then there's the Mexican North American Institute of Cultural Relations. Cost of tuition is about thirty-five dollars. These are intense courses of fifteen hours of classes per week for three weeks.

Some addresses:

CIDOC
Apdo 479
Cuernavaca, Mexico
Tel: 2-45-90

Admissions
University of the Americas
Kilometro 16
Carretera, Mexico-Toluca
Mexico 10, D.F.

Instituto Mexicano Norteamericano de Relaciones Culturales
Hamburgeo 115
Mexico 6, D.F.

Registrar
Special Courses for Foreigners
Universidad Nacional Autónoma de Mexico
Edificio de Filosofía y Letras
Ciudad Universitaria
Mexico 20, D.F.

PARAGUAY

COLLEGE: *Universidad Catolica Nuestra Senora de la Asuncion*
ACADEMIC YEAR: *April to December*
AMERICAN STUDENTS: *One or two*

INSTRUCTION: *Spanish*
TUITION: *$66 per year*
LIVING COSTS: *$100 per month*

VISA. Not required if staying less than ninety days. For information on longer stay write: Paraguayan Embassy, 2400 Massachusetts Avenue, N.W., Washington, D.C. 20008. (202) 483-6960.

APPLICATION ADDRESS.
Universidad Catolica Nuestra Senora de la Asuncion
Rectorado
Independencia Nacional y Comuneros
Asuncion, Paraguay

BOOKS TO READ. George Pendle's *Paraguay, A Riverside Nation* (Royal Institute of International Affairs, 1967) is the best book dealing with the historical, economic and sociological aspects of Paraguayan life. The best history of the country (in English) is Harris Gaylord Warren's *Paraguay, An Informal History* (University of Oklahoma Press, 1949) .

THE SCHOOL. The Catholic University is the best in the country. Established in the late 1800s in the capital, 3,500 men and women attend faculties dispersed throughout the city. The Faculty of Philosophy and Sciences for Education is highly respected and recommended professors are: Andres Rivarola, School of Psychology; Miquel-Angel Monpaner, Sociology; and Efraim Cardozo, the well-liked historian of Paraguay. The vice-president of the university, Father Juste, is a good contact for Americans. He enjoys foreign students and knows about everything that's happening.

On the whole, Paraguayan students are politically involved and belong to student branches of the political parties. Other quick generalizations are: They're antigovernment, anti-American, anti-Brazilian and anti-Argentinian. In fact it seems they don't like anyone, but on a one-to-one basis, the students are friendly. Young people meet in homes. *Bailes sociales* are popular. Coffee shops for congregating are non-existent.

INDEPENDENT STUDY. Independent study is newer to U.S. education than to Paraguayan. With the assistance of professors students can arrange independent study in almost any topic. The Paraguayan government wants to learn more about its own economic needs and encourages studies in this area.

A less dry subject perhaps would be the Colonos, people of Japanese, German and Korean extraction (among others), who have created communities and even cities in the remotest interiors of Paraguay. A great topic for a field study.

COUNTRY NOTES. Paraguay has one of the lowest standards of living in Latin America. This means cheap and easy living for the American student. Comfortable living arrangements in a family or a pension can be arranged.

Paraguay is run by a stable, long-standing dictatorship controlled by President Stroessner. Friendly relations exist between our government and hers.

There's a supply of reading material in English and Spanish at three international bookstores in Asuncion. The best—Libreria Niza—has everything. First-run U.S. films are shown six months late (heavily censored for sex and violence) and a film society runs foreign art films.

For in-country travel, buses are cheap and safe. One way to Paraguay is via modern houseboat on a three-and-one-half-day trip from Buenos Aires to Asuncion down the Paranai. Flota Fluvial in Argentina charges thirty dollars.

8. Studying in the Middle and Far East

INDIA

Two students, Lisa Pesce and Michael Savage, friends of ours, wrote us from India. We've included their letter in full. They went to India and Nepal in 1971 to study oriental philosophy.

Dear John & Tom,

India and Nepal are the most accessible for westerners wishing to study oriental philosophy. Most ashrams and dharmasalas are free or inexpensive. In Thubten Yeshes monastery a 20 rupee (20Rs = $1.90) by each student. Academic year is as long as you want to stay. Some teachers travel from place to place giving two week courses.

Many ashrams have courses in English, or have translators. Our teacher Thubter Yeshe speaks English and so does Zengo, a Zen monk who lives in a nearby monastery. There are a group of holy men in India called saddhus who do various things: yoga, fasting, exercises, but they speak only Hindu, are reluctant to teach, and very hard to live with.

Living on an ashram or dharmasalas is free or very cheap, maybe 1 to 4 rupees a day—10¢ to 40¢. Some provide food, some don't. Housing outside of an ashram is usually scarce due to the location of the place. In Sarnath there are several dharmasalas, a government rest house which is cheap. And large houses for rent 70–120 Rs a month.

Villagers are willing to rent rooms and in some areas you can take over their house and they'll sleep outside. In warm weather they do anyhow. For $50 a month a person can live very well.

Some places to study:
Buddha Temple (near Birla Temple)
New Delhi

Guru Maharajji
Divine Light Mission
Commercial Road
Dehra Dun, India

Nalanda University
Buddhist Temple (Bangalore)

Nalanda-Pali Institute

Thubten Yeshe Lama
Kapon, Kathmandu, Nepal

Zeno, Kapon, Kathmandu

Travel: The rail system is quite good and very inexpensive, therefore, is the best overland method of travel. It's helpful to know how the class arrangements work; first class is generally uncrowded, has padded seats and you get a reserved place. First class sleeper is very classy, providing a private compartment (with 2 berths) and, I believe, a private john. The 1st class waiting rooms have showers, and I believe there's also an air-conditioned class on some trains.

Second class (which we've never used) is virtually the same as third, except usually less crowded because no one wants to pay more for the same accommodations. It is possible to reserve seats, but it's not worth the money. Third class unreserved is not generally a good way to travel, unless you're going to some place where no one else goes; on the major runs the trains get incredibly crowded, and you may be unbearably cramped for hours. It's possible to get 3rd class reserved, which is very good and quite comfortable (all reservations must be made in advance, and if you're headed for a major center, it's wise to make the reservation a few days in advance, to insure your getting it). Just plain 3rd class reserved gives you a place on a bench which is yours. For long journeys, it's best to reserve a bunk—you're still in 3rd class but have a whole padded bunk for yourself. You're right up under the electric fans and can ride, read, and sleep in comfort.

Student concessions give you a 50 percent discount and must be obtained before you go to buy tickets or reserve seats. The concession offices are usually not in the stations, but are hidden away somewhere, so time must be allowed for that. Any kind of valid (or invalid) student I.D. usually works.

Other tips: Food on trains is available and pretty cheap, tea, candy, fruit are plentiful. Belongings really should be *carefully watched*, so many people get robbed that you should really hang onto your stuff.

Buses are available for short distances, but we don't know if they even make long runs; if they do they're not recommended. They're definitely too hot and considerably more dangerous than the trains. Student reductions *are available. Plane connections can be made to many cities around India, but as of now we don't know any prices, except for the Patna-Kathmandu flight, which is $10 ($7.50 student fare).*

Hotels are numerous. In any large city one can get fancy accommodations for probably 20 to 30 rupees a night ($2–$3). Cheap hotels are from 2 to 10 rupees a night and accommodations can vary greatly, depending on what city you're in. Screens and mosquito nets are not usually provided in the cheaper hotels. Bedbugs can be hiding in any mattress, no matter how clean it looks.

In most places, the second you step off a train, plane, or bus you will be surrounded by rickshaw drivers, taxi drivers, people getting you to come to their hotels, beggars, silk salesmen, etc., ad infinitum. For the new traveller it can get a little confusing and breathless, and one must remember to be patient and relaxed and unhurried.

Local transportation in India are: taxis, tongas (horse-drawn carriages), scooters, rickshaws, and government bus services in some places, private companies in others. Taxis are expensive—make sure you're either in a metered vehicle or have already argued about price with the driver before hand. Tongas are good only for lots of people and luggage, otherwise they're very expensive and always very slow. In major cities there are scooters with small cabs on the back; if the meter's working, it's an inexpensive, fast way to get around. Rickshaws are cheap if you know what to pay. Rickshaw drivers are some of the most hard-up people for money you'll ever run into. Bicycles can be rented or bought relatively cheaply. In Nepal motorcycles and scooters can be rented.

Travel in Nepal is limited because there's no railroad system and few roads. Taxis, rickshaws, some buses are available in Kathmandu.

Visas for India are best obtained in the U.S.

Two-three month tourist visa is easily obtainable; extensions take a long time, but as long as you apply for one, you're all right. Student visas are generally complicated and may be difficult to get.

Being in the East is in itself an incredibly educational experience. It completely changed our views of ourselves in relation to the world, the U.S., college, maybe the universe. At the same time it's both a mental and physical shock to go through in adjusting to life here. It's easy to get really unhealthy without noticing it. It can be avoided, to some extent, by knowing a great deal about nutrition. A lot of people freak out for a variety of reasons and delusions. For any kind of program/independent study, students should have a point of reference, a real interest in the country and people. There's a lot of dope and groovy things to do and it's easy to get distracted.

On the Jewel in the Lotus Hung

Lisa & Mike

A few colleges and universities direct programs in India. Friends World College of New York has a center in India, the Associated Colleges of the Mid-West have a program and the University of Wisconsin has a year program.

USEFUL ADDRESSES

Friends World College
North American Campus
Mitchell Gardens
Westbury, New York 11590

Students' Information Services
Ministry of Education & Social Welfare
Central Secretariat Library
New Delhi, India

India Studies Program
Associated Colleges of the Mid-West
60 West Walton Street
Chicago, Illinois 60610

Embassy of India
2107 Massachusetts Avenue N.W.
Washington, D.C. 20008
(202) CO 5-5050

Year In India
University of Wisconsin
Madison, Wisconsin 53706

JAPAN

We haven't been to Japan recently, but Saron Zieglas has and wrote us:

> *Many schools in Japan have foreign student programs—International Christian University, Keio, Sophia, Asia University, and Waseda University— I am going to Waseda with a program from my American school. Students can come individually and independently. At Waseda everyone who goes through a program has the unique chance of living with a Japanese family. If one goes independently he has to find a place to live or can join an apartment finding "club" for a fee and they will help find a geshuku. A geshuku is a one-room apartment in a house made up of one room geshukus and the "mother" of the house feeds everybody (room & board). Both living situations have their unique qualities about them. If you live with a family it's probably harder to find out what young people are really like.*
>
> *My program at Waseda corresponds to the American school year. Regular school terms are different from American—the year starts in April. Living expenses in Japan are much cheaper than in America if you live with the things the Japanese live with. Japanese will try to give you something special that costs more with the bullshit "you are a gigene and won't be able to live with regular lousy Japanese equipment." And anyway, if you're American*

they want your money. The geshuku *"club" is helpful, especially if you don't know Japanese. A* geshuku *costs something like 12,000 yen per month which is around thirty-five to forty dollars (including food.)*

It's important that you take language classes. I can only speak a little Japanese—but you can find out so much about the culture & society if you speak the language. Japanese who speak English (& there are thousands!) can tell you things, but it's not nearly the same as experiencing it yourself. Waseda has a division called Go-ken *which is shortened expression for* Gai Koku Go Ken *(I think) which is the foreign language division. The best for learning Japanese and the cheapest! Must apply directly to* Go-ken. *Can become "relatively" fluent within a year. Language is the most important thing to study if you come to Japan as a student. Other things can be studied independently.*

If you come should know something about the history. Japan's New Middle Class *by Vogel is very good.* Trip to Hanoi *by Susan Sontag. My "liasion secretary" (Japanese) read it and said she was going to make it compulsory reading. She says it shows a person how to be open-minded—culturally— enabling one to really learn about another country. Also, David Reisman's* Conversations in Japan, *and perhaps the Ampo Treaty between the U.S. and Japan.* Every Japanese person knows it!

Students shouldn't come with any preconceived notions about the "quiet, shy, reserved, very polite" Japanese. I came with those ideas and it only hindered my getting to really know any Japanese for what they really are. I think the best way is to come fresh and open-minded not knowing anything about what anybody says about the Japanese personality. The Japanese don't even know themselves.

The weather is relatively mild in comparison to American standards. You do need every kind of clothes for every kind of weather—but I've never heard of weather getting anything like 30 degrees below in winter or even 10 below. The Japanese food never stops being an adventure. Travel is easy. There are trains & buses absolutely everywhere—which makes it hard to find "real" country. Departure time is exactly on time, they don't wait! A Youth Hostel card is necessary. And almost everywhere there is cheap good lodging—places to meet kids. Don't come to Japan to see beautiful countryside, come to Japan to find new and interesting ways of life & thinking & meeting beautiful people.

To contact Waseda University, write:

International Division
Waseda University
647 Totsuka-machi 1-chome
Shinjuku-ku Tokyo 160, Japan

At the International Christian University in Mitaka, Tokyo, it is possible to obtain a bachelor's degree or to do one year of independent study. The university opened in 1953, has 1,221 students and ninety full-time faculty members. It offers courses in Japanese and English.

Admission to the university is similar to applying to a U.S. School, transcripts are needed, SAT scores, etc., and the deadline is May 31 of each year. The university operates on a trimester system, beginning in mid-September and closing June 30. Tuition for one term is about $255. There is limited dormitory space at about $92 per year and off-campus housing runs $20 a month. Another $100 a month covers food, books and incidentals.

Grading system is ABC and students take between twelve and thirteen units each term. It is not a difficult school and their Japanese language program is strong. Anyone who wants to receive a degree from ICU must spend the first year in intensive study of Japanese. The university will serve as guarantor for students who cannot secure a letter of guarantee. A guarantor is someone living in Japan who testifies to the applicant's character, behavior and will provide support, if needed. Absolute necessity.

For further information, write:

International Christian University
Room 1220
475 Riverside Drive
New York, New York 10027
(212) RI 9–6734

Admissions Committee
International Christian University
10-2, Osawa 3-chome
Mitaka-shi
Tokyo, Japan

We also suggest Sophia University. They now direct programs for universities like Notre Dame, Central Washington State, etc. Students can take a four-year program toward a B.A. or do one year of studies. Tuition is about $165 a trimester. Sophia University has a Graduate School in International Affairs and Far Eastern Studies and conducts six-week summer sessions. Write:

International Division
Sophia University
7 Kio-cho
Chiyoda-ku
Tokyo 102, Japan

Sophia University of America
Box 153
New York, New York 10017

Some additional addresses for special study:

LANGUAGE:
The International Students Institute
22-7 Kita-Shinjuku, 3-chome
Shinjuku-ku
Tokyo, Japan

BUDDHIST STUDIES:
Otani University
Kyoto University
Komazawa University

When first arriving in Japan stay at one of the Youth Hostels. There are over five hundred in Japan and they provide beds, showers, heating and public kitchens for rent. Also it is possible to stay initially at the International House or Asia Center in Tokyo. Obtain a multiple entry visa. This allows you to leave the country for Okinawa, Korea, Taiwan, South East Asia, Philippines and return to Japan.

One other good book to have: *A Scholar's Guide to Japan,* Dorothy E. Roberts, The Christopher Publishing House, 53 Billings Road, N. Quincy, Massachusetts 02171.

To study for any length of time in Japan a student will have to show means of support, some proof of affiliation with a university or school, and proof of a guarantor. For visa information, write:

Japanese Embassy
2520 Massachusetts Avenue N.W.
Washington, D.C. 20008
(202) 234–2266

LEBANON

COLLEGE: *American University of Beirut*
ACADEMIC YEAR: *September to June*
AMERICAN STUDENTS: *234*

INSTRUCTION: *English, some Arabic*
TUITION: *$600 per year*
LIVING COSTS: *$250 per month*

VISA. Entrance Visa is valid for six months and costs five dollars. For further information, enclose self-addressed envelope, ninety cents for handling and write Lebanon Consulate, New York, New York, 10021. (212) 744-7905.

APPLICATION ADDRESS.
Registrar
American University of Beirut
Lebanon

BOOKS TO READ. A couple of books worth reading on the history and politics of Lebanon are: Fahim I. Qubain's *Crisis in Lebanon* (Washington, D.C.: Middle East Institute, 1961) and Michael C. Hudson's *The Precarious Republic: Political Modernization in Lebanon* (New York: Random House, 1968) or, Philip K. Hitti's *Lebanon in History* (New York: St. Martin, 1957).

THE SCHOOL. The American University of Beirut was founded in 1866 as a private, non-sectarian university under a charter from the state of New York. Students from over fifty countries make up a campus population of 3,852. Twenty-five percent of the faculty come from the United States and Canada, and about 10 percent from Europe. AUB is not strong in Middle-East Studies or Arabic for Americans nor in Education, English Literature or Social Studies. But their physics and math departments are outstanding. History and Political Sciences are adequate; it depends on visiting faculty. Close contact with faculty is possible, but students need to be aggressive.

There is a quota for Americans—5 percent—and parents must live in the Middle East, but if students are older (third or fourth year of school), requirements aren't that strict and admission can be negotiated.

The campus is charming and swimming is possible most of the year, and half of the year it's possible to ski within two hours of the college. Our friend at AUB writes: "The intellectual, idealist or spiritual or naive student will be out of place. It is best suited for well-heeled hedonists out for adventure and is definitely not for the innocent nor the immature."

INDEPENDENT STUDY. We know one student who spent several months traveling with the Bedouins in southern Lebanon. It is certainly a good country in which to study the Middle-East crisis from the Arab side of the question, or to begin studies in Arabic.

COUNTRY NOTES. American students in Beirut can expect to spend a great deal of time "defending" or "explaining" U.S. actions in the Middle East. Discussions are endless and depend far more on emotions than logic. Women especially will find themselves judged by quite different mores than in the United States—as in most Third World countries double standards exist. But besides these important differences, cosmopolitan Beirut could be a city in America, except more beautiful. Beirut sits on the Mediterranean.

Lebanon is a small country, smaller than Connecticut and bounded by Syria and Israel. It stretches along the Mediterranean and moves inland to the high Lebanese Mountains and the Beqaa Valley. Lebanon is connected to Syria by railroad and by railroad and international highway running from Beirut to Damascus. Lebanon is the major gateway into the Middle East and most of the Arab World.

Lebanon has tried to play the "Switzerland" of the Arab World, operating as the money center and the neutral force. This role has not made her a favorite in the Arab World and Lebanon (like Jordan) has cracked down on Palestine guerrillas operating across their borders. Lebanon is not militant, but students, of course, are. In 1970 students took over the university for several months, not uncommon.

Besides Arabic, French and English are widely spoken in the country. The literacy rate is the highest in the Arab world, 86 percent. The population is divided between Christians and Moslems and the Moslems include members from the Sunni and Shi'ite sects.

Lebanon can most easily be reached by plane—it has a large International Airport—or by sea. Beirut, Sidon and Tripoli are the major ports. If studying the Middle East this country is the most accessible.

NEPAL

COLLEGE: *University of Tribhuvan—*
Tri Chandra College
ACADEMIC YEAR: *March to December*
AMERICAN STUDENTS: *None*

INSTRUCTION: *English*
TUITION: *$5 per month*
LIVING COSTS: *$50 per month*

VISA. Tourist visa costs two dollars and requires photo. For complete details write: Nepal Embassy, 2131 Leroy Place N.W., Washington, D.C. 20009. (202) 667-4550. NOTE: Friends in the country report: "Visas for Nepal are a problem; a two-week one is easily gotten, and after that one must play the immigration game, which has no logical rules and changes from day to day. Official looking papers and titles help, also neat Western clothes. If one wishes, bribes can be given through complicated procedures. It's a drag, and you're not assured of getting anything in return for the graft you pay out. The general situation varies with the number of tourists, hippies, etc., who are in the country at any given time."

APPLICATION ADDRESS.
Surendrasingh
Registry
University of Tribhuvan
Tri Chandra College
Kathmandu, Nepal

BOOKS TO READ. A few good books on Nepal are: Pradyumna Karan and William Jenkin's *Nepal, A Cultural and Physical Geography,* an adequate and general introduction, and Toni Hagen's *Nepal, The Kingdom in the Himalayas* that indicates for the reader the loveliness of Nepal.

THE SCHOOL. The major institution of higher education in Nepal is Tribhuvan University. In Kathmandu, Tri Chandra College—part of the university—offers degrees in Liberal Arts, Science and Business to a student body of 1,500 to 2,000 students. Classes are usually lectures and follow a prescribed syllabus that calls for written or oral examinations at the end of each semester. Although academic standards are below those American students are accustomed to, the political science and history courses are worthwhile. There are a few foreign students at Tri Chandra College, but none from the United States though they'd be welcome.

Like the Nepalese students, an American student could rent a house near the college for himself or with two or three friends. A very modest fee provides an outside bathroom, electricity and a servant to care for the household. Fifty dollars covers all expenses for a month.

The Nepalese people are friendly and foreigners are treated hospitably. American students will learn there is little "dating" as they know it. It is a new custom in the country where traditionally marriages have always been arranged.

INDEPENDENT STUDY. Beyond the formal university experience in Kathmandu, American students in Nepal have a chance to study oriental philosophy. Hinduism and Buddhism, the two major religious philosophies of Asia, are evident in Nepalese culture to a remarkable degree and monasteries devoted to their study and to meditation are open to Westerners. Our friend spent part of last year in the monastery of Thubtan Yeshe Lama—"a very nice old man." A twenty rupee monthly donation (approximately two dollars) covered tuition; one dollar a day for room and board. (Some monasteries are free.) The course of Thubtan Yeshe Lama is in English and lasted for as long as you cared to study. Other courses with other lamas lasted for two weeks, or until the teachers leave the area.

COUNTRY NOTES. A tiny mountainous kingdom, Nepal has three distinct regions. The central one, where most of the people live, contains the Kathmandu Valley—the social, political and cultural center of the country. Prior to 1947, fewer than fifty Westerners had entered Nepal. Today mountainous roads connect Kathmandu to India and Tibet and at least four different airlines fly tourists into the country. The country has over one hundred newspapers. Nepal has been discovered as an in-place to visit. The government encourages tourism although it feels Nepal has been overrun by hippies and is making efforts to keep them out. Need to cut your hair to reach Kathmandu.

Kathmandu, the capital, with a population of three hundred thousand, affords many of the conveniences of a modern city. American magazines, newspapers and a few films are available. Luxury as well as moderate hotels accommodate visitors and a variety of vehicles from bicycles to rickshaws to taxis get you around town.

Nepal is a naturalist's and trekker's dream (as well as the stalking ground for the Abominable Snowman). Lying along the southern slopes of the Himalayas, Mt. Everest, Annapurna and other famous peaks can be viewed from foot paths only one or two days out of the capital. Lodges and huts for trekkers are available for about one dollar a night. Mountain Travel Maharajguni, Kathmandu, will rent equipment and, if required, arrange for the services of English-speaking Sherpa guides. Best trekking, between April and January.

THE PHILIPPINES

COLLEGE: *The University of the Philippines Diliman Campus*
ACADEMIC YEAR: *July to April (two semesters)*
AMERICAN STUDENTS: *Approximately 500*

INSTRUCTION: *English*
TUITION: *$50 to $300 per semester (varies by schools)*
LIVING COSTS: *$100 per month*

APPLICATION ADDRESS.
Registrar
University of the Philippines
Diliman, Risal Philippines

VISA. Temporary visa valid up to fifty-nine days. No charge. For longer stay check embassy for information. Write: 1617 Massachusetts Avenue, N.W., Washington, D.C. (202) 462-1400. NOTE: It may be easier to get into the Philippines than out. Before a U.S. student may go home he has to prove he's not running from the Philippine Courts or from paying taxes or avoiding the consequences of any other illegal activity. Enormous red tape is involved; there are men you can pay to expedite process.

BOOKS TO READ. Not much recently. Try *The United States and the Philippines,* edited by Frank H. Golay, Prentice-Hall, 1966. A very readable book on the Philippines and Asia in general is *Pacific Destiny* by Richard O'Connor, Little Brown, 1969.

THE SCHOOL. The University of the Philippines is the best school in the seven thousand or so island archipelago that makes up the country. The major campus, white and modern—built after World War II—in Diliman, Quezon City, Luzon, is considered the Philippine center of academic as well as student political activity. Scholars and students from all corners of the world teach and study here and the student activists "keep the campus in continual political turmoil."

Twelve thousand students are enrolled on the Diliman Campus. Almost all the professional schools are good—the medical school may be number one in Asia. A relatively small group of Americans are receiving professional training. They are lured by the low costs, good academic standards and favorable admission policies.

The Filipinos claim in their country East meets West. Their claim rests upon geographical as well as recent historical considerations. For within the lifetime of most middle-aged people, their country has been ruled by both an Eastern power, Japan and a Western power, the United States. Today the considerable American presence is an irritant to most Philippine students. Anti-Americanism is a popular theme among students, writers and politicians. During student strikes anti-American sentiment runs high; we recommend that U.S. students take off for another island during these periods. It is not out of the ordinary or illegal for students (nor anyone else for that matter) to carry firearms and we know of a U.S. student who had close calls twice during a strike.

Housing for students includes boarding with families, living in university dormitories (they are usually filled) or renting rooms or apartments. Prices are reasonable. An American woman alone in an apartment will cause considerable comment and she will be pressured to move in with a family.

Classes usually consist of lectures and the number of students in a class will vary from twenty-five to one hundred. For the most part a final exam determines your grade although failure automatically entitles you to another chance to pass it. Students rarely buy their textbooks and prepare for exams by memorizing their carefully taken classroom notes. If an American student buys his course textbooks, he can expect to share them with the rest of the class.

The university's athletic facilities are good and open year round. One of the best golf courses in the country winds through the campus and "The Butterfly" on the golf course is the major student hangout. A swimming pool and tennis courts, kept in excellent condition—though little used—are also available.

INDEPENDENT STUDY. Due to the continuing political crisis in the Philippines, we recommend American students stay as unobtrusive as possible and not undertake independent studies that may arouse people's suspicions.

COUNTRY NOTES. The Diliman campus is approximately seven hundred miles from Hong Kong and a twenty-five cent bus ride away from the capital city of the Philippines—Manila. Like any modern city, Manila has a wide selection of U.S. magazines, books and movies available. Government censors delete scenes of sex and violence from the movies and confiscate sexy materials from the mails. *The Evergreen Review* has little chance of getting through the mail system. Four major morning and two evening papers are printed in English and a good Manila weekly is the *Free Press*.

The hurricane season comes in November and December. During this period winds are clocked at 175 miles per hour. Because you will, in all probability, be seeking the lowest and strongest part of your housing during storms you can expect to lose school time during this season. To pass the day it doesn't hurt to lay in a stock of beer and wear your motorcycle helmet if you have one.

In calmer weather, Luzon has a beautiful seashore and beach for camping. You can catch all the seafood you want—shrimp, squid, mussels, oysters, whitefish, etc.

Hippies are not popular in the Philippines although in the Diliman campus long-haired Americans are usually spared the harassment directed at squarer-looking American students. Professional Philippine men follow the hair styles popular in the United States in the 1950s and since they have no facial hair anyone sporting a beard automatically stands out.

Take loose clothing and good rain gear. Blue jeans are too tight and too hot. Men and women prefer to wear lightweight baggy slacks and shirts to school. The men wear squared-off sport shirts, the kind, if you can remember, that Harry Truman wore in Key West. Bare feet are prohibited by the student dress code.

It's easy for Americans to make friends in the Philippines. The men pursue American women enthusiastically. American men work against impossible odds to date a Philippine girl. One friend reports that the women seem afraid of American men and he has been going out on dates only since meeting women in the international student community at their house on campus.

REPUBLIC OF SOUTH VIETNAM

COLLEGE: *University of Hue*
ACADEMIC YEAR: *October to June*
AMERICAN STUDENTS: *None*

INSTRUCTION: *Vietnamese*
TUITION: *None*
LIVING COSTS: *$75 per month*

VISA. Entry visa valid fifteen days to three months and costs five dollars. For details on longer stay write: Viet-Nam Embassy, 2251 R Street N.W., Washington, D.C. 20008. (202) 234-4860.

APPLICATION ADDRESS.
Rector
University of Hue
Hue, South Vietnam

BOOKS TO READ. *Viet Nam—The Unheard Voices,* by Don Luce and John Sommer, Cornell University Press, 1969. Written by two Americans who lived many years in Vietnam, know the language and understand the people.

THE SCHOOL. University of Hue is a public university founded by presidential decree in 1957. It is the first Vietnamese university to be conceived and established by Vietnamese themselves and the second oldest university in South Vietnam. There are five faculties at the university: Letters (Arts), Law, Medicine, Pedagogy and Science. Hue has slightly more than 3,700 students and 230 professors, but only sixty-six are permanent. Most professors commute from Saigon and only stay in Hue for a few days every two months or so. Courses taught in French and English are designed to meet the special needs and abilities of students for whom French and English are second languages. Courses in Vietnamese and Chinese literature and history are offered in the Faculty of Letters, in Vietnamese.

The university has some excellent teachers. The rector has a degree from Cambridge and a Ph.D. from the University of Chicago. He teaches at the Faculty of Letters. Many of the professors have advanced degrees from French universities. A few professors are interested in helping their students better appreciate Vietnamese achievements in literature and civilization, but these are unfortunately very rare.

University of Hue is an amalgam of Vietnamese, French and American educational practices, but it more closely resembles a French university. Under the pressure of American aid and advisors, it is becoming more American and is in the process of changing over from a French certificate system to the American four-year form.

Courses consist of lectures which the students copy in their notebooks and study for exams. There is little give and take between professor and student and little independent research for lack of books in Vietnamese.

INDEPENDENT STUDY. This is not a good country for independent study. Most of the professors at the university, busy with their own students, have little time for wandering Americans. "Children of the Western World" our Vietnam contact calls them. It is possible to teach English in Vietnam. All the Vietnamese want to learn English, but as our friend says, "Vietnamese have no time for voyeuristic Westerners who want to cultivate their repertoire of life's experiences by taking their junior year in a war zone."

COUNTRY NOTES. In many ways Hue is an ideal place for a university. Because it has been the home of Vietnam's dynastic rulers, Vietnamese consider Hue to be both the source and guardian of a large part of Vietnamese history and culture. The physical as well as the intellectual atmosphere of the city of Hue is conducive to learning. Hue is a quiet, serene, beautiful town. The mountains of the Annam Cordillera chain are on the horizon and from those mountains comes the River of Perfumes which flows through the city on its way to the sea.

Our advisor on Vietnam and the University of Hue says, "Someday the University might be a place where scholars of East and West could meet as equals, but that day is a long way off. Now the best advice for students wishing to study at Hue University is to forget it, to study in some other country, or maybe to stay at home."

TAIWAN

COLLEGE: *Tunghai University*
ACADEMIC YEAR: *September to June*
AMERICAN STUDENTS: *Ten or fifteen a year*

INSTRUCTION: *Mandarin Chinese*
TUITION: *$200 per year*
LIVING COSTS: *$150 per month*

VISA. Visa valid forty-eight months. No Charge. For specific information write: Embassy of Republic of China, 2311 Massachusetts Avenue, N.W., Washington, D.C. 20036. (202) 667-9000.

APPLICATION ADDRESS.
Tunghai University
Taichung, 400, Taiwan

BOOKS TO READ. Nothing very outstanding on Taiwan. We suggest: Bernard Gallin's *Hsin Hsing: A Chinese Village in Change* (Berkeley:

University of California Press, 1966). And because of China, Barbara W. Tuchman's *Stilwell and the American Experience in China, 1911–1945* (New York: Macmillan, 1970). Also John King Fairbank's *China* (Cambridge: Harvard University Press, 1967).

THE SCHOOL. Tunghai University is a private school, financed partially by the United Board of Christian Higher Education in Asia. It is located seven miles outside the city of Taichung. It has 1,200 students, almost all Chinese residents in Taiwan. At present Tunghai is cooperating with Oberlin College in a program for college students who have already studied at least two years of Chinese. For the experimental phase of this program—1971–72—no other American students will be admitted, except rare exceptions. Students in this program take various courses especially created for the program as well as some regular university course work. Cost of the program, which includes a summer of intensive language work in Taiwan, is about $3,600. Inquiries can be made to William Speidel, Box 971, Tunghai University, Taichung 400, Taiwan or to the East Asia Studies Program, Oberlin College, Oberlin, Ohio 44074.

INDEPENDENT STUDY. We recommend that if you're interested in Taiwan you take advantage of the Oberlin College program. Other possibilities of studying in Taiwan would be at one of the three national universities: National Chengchi University, National Taiwan University and National Normal University. All are located in Taipei. Normal University offers a course in Chinese for foreigners. Two schools: Beloit and Stanford have full-year programs in Taiwan. The courses are concerned with language, culture and history.

COUNTRY NOTES. The future of Taiwan depends almost entirely on Nixon's visit to the mainland. What happens to this country should not be clear for several years. But the balance of power has shifted against Formosa. It's an island ninety miles off the southeastern coast of the Chinese mainland, not very big itself; 240 miles long and about 75 miles wide. Fifteen million people live on Taiwan.

Chinese began migration to Taiwan as early as the sixth century, but the main influx took place during the seventeenth century. Japan ruled the island for fifty years and as a result most adults speak Japanese, as well as several dialects. Mandarin Chinese is the official language of the country and is taught in all schools. There are about four hundred thousand Christians on the island, but the predominant religion is a Chinese combination of Buddhism and Taoism. There are also a small number of Chinese Moslems.

The Tropic of Cancer cuts across the island and the climate is semitropical. September to June are the hot months, June to August the wet ones. The island is also in the earthquake and typhoon belts and violent rains, floods, winds and tremors are common. The highest point on the island is Yu Shan, 13,100 feet above sea level. Most of the country is flat, however.

Taiwan is an "easy" foreign country to live in. Their internal transportation system is one of the best in Asia, the country is productive and the majority of the people—84 percent—are literate. During this "period of adjustment" to the mainland it will be a country to watch, and well worth living in.

TURKEY

COLLEGES: *Middle East Technical University*
University of Ankara
Robert College
ACADEMIC YEAR: *October to June*
AMERICAN STUDENTS: *Very few*

INSTRUCTION: *Turkish*
TUITION: *Varies, about $1,000 at Robert, less at other colleges*
LIVING COSTS: *$200 per month*

VISA. Cost of visa for stay of over three months; multiple entries, $10.50. For more information write: Turkish Embassy, 1606 23rd Street N.W., Washington, D.C. (202) 667-6400.

APPLICATION ADDRESSES.
Kayit, Kabun Burosu
Siyasal Bilgiler Fak
Ankara University
Ankara, Turkey

Kayit, Kabun Burosu
Robert College
Bebek Istanbul, Turkey

Kayit Kabun Burosu
METU
Ankara, Turkey

BOOKS TO READ: There are many good books on Turkey. A select few: *Ataturk* by Lord Kinross; *The Development of Secularism in Turkey* by N. Berkes; *Turkish Nationalism and Western Civilization* by Ziya Gokalt; *Politics and Government in Turkey* by C. H. Dodd; and *The Emergence of Modern Turkey* by Bernard Lewis.

THE SCHOOL. We recommend the Middle East Technical University (METU) in Ankara. It is known for its Business Administration courses and is also the most leftist university in the country. On a beautiful campus built in the 1950s, the school is patterned after American universities. There are segmented class schedules, seminar courses and classes with as few as twenty-five students. Course work frequently requires written papers. Although 3,500 students attend, the university is a friendly place and students and faculty know each other.

The school of Political Science of the University of Ankara used to educate the country's royalty. Today it still retains a reputation for relatively high academic standards and its best courses are in Economics, Finance and Political Science. Getting in can be difficult. Strict entrance examinations must be passed and a quota system exists for foreign students. There are students from Japan, Germany, Africa and a few from the United States.

Many foreign faculty members teach here, sometimes by means of an interpreter. Classes are large, 100 to 150 per section. But as the course level increases the number of students per class declines until in the highest level only twenty or so students will be enrolled. Classes begin at 8:30 A.M. and continue straight through until 12:30 P.M. The afternoon is devoted to sessions in language labs and course workshops. Traditionally the political leaders of the country are educated here or at Robert College.

Robert College was a missionary school of high academic quality and in 1971 it became part of the Turkish Higher Education System. Like METU, Robert College has been modeled after U.S. schools. The best departments are Economics, English and Business. The number of students is small, not more than one thousand.

For the past two years several student strikes have closed most Turkish colleges and brought a change in the government. The new government has written laws forbidding campus demonstrations. We doubt if this will stop the Turkish students.

INDEPENDENT STUDY. The Ottoman Empire spans thousands of years and a good portion of the earth's surface. Modern historical times might also be particularly interesting to Americans, especially the period of Kemal Ataturk, who organized men, women and children in the early 1920s to eject the occupying powers from Turkey—the only remaining portion of the once vast empire.

COUNTRY NOTES. Ankara and Istanbul are modern, cosmopolitan cities. Flying time between the two is one hour. Istanbul forms a geographical gateway between Europe and Asia. The air route to mainland China includes a stop at Istanbul; trains leave regularly for Europe and the Middle East. Reading material from America and Europe arrives daily by air and movie houses show current American, European and Turkish films.

Istanbul, formerly Constantinople as the song goes, was the capital of the Byzantine Empire, and has extant architectural wonders. It's a city of mosques, palaces and bazaars, some from the Middle Ages when Constantinople was the world's largest city. It is still large and crowded.

Living arrangements vary, and expect to pay more if staying in Istanbul. Turkish students live in dormitories or with families. A few rent apartments together. Students in Turkey are entitled to discounts, some of the best include 50 percent off on movie and theater tickets and public transportation.

Americans should expect Turkish students to be reserved. Developing friendship takes time and it helps to show genuine interest in Turkish history and culture. One way of getting to know Turkish young people is through professors. Often they invite students to their home for family gatherings. Dating customs are conservative. For example, American men cannot expect Turkish women to kiss them until they are engaged. Single women do not go out in the evening and so men and women meet in the afternoon, in groups.

Many Turkish people have the impression from American movies and U.S. soldiers in Turkey that Americans only think about two things: drinking and sex. Turkish women, therefore, are afraid of American men and it will be difficult to get to know them. American women have fewer problems, especially since Moslem law allows Moslem men (but not women) to marry non-Moslems.

About the Authors

TOM HEBERT has studied at Linfield College in Oregon, University of Washington, University of Guanajuato, Mexico, Dallas Theater Center, Baylor University, and UCLA. He taught at Prairie View A & M in Texas and the University of Ibadan, Nigeria, while with the Peace Corps. From 1966 to 1968, he lived and worked in Vietnam. In 1968, he joined UNICEF as a Refugee Relief Officer on the Biafran War. A management consultant, he has worked for the Peace Corps, Old Westbury College, and Antioch College. He lives in Washington, D.C.

JOHN COYNE holds degrees in English from Saint Louis University and Western Michigan University. He has also studied at Georgetown University, George Washington University, and Haile Selassie University. For five years he was with the Peace Corps, working in Ethiopia and Washington, D.C. He was Director of Student Services and International Education at the experimental college Old Westbury from 1969 to 1971. Mr. Coyne lives in Washington, D.C., where he works as an educational consultant.

The authors welcome further information and suggestions. Correspondence can be sent to 1503 Q Street N.W., Washington, D.C. 20009.